For The Carmel Valley
Public Library —
I hope readers enjoy this jazz trek
through music in and from Japan...
best, always,

Bill Minor

JAZZ JOURNEYS
TO JAPAN

May 25, 2004

Jazz Perspectives
Lewis Porter, Series General Editor

Open the Door: The Life and Music of Betty Carter
By William R. Bauer

Jazz Journeys to Japan: The Heart Within
By William Minor

Four Jazz Lives
By A. B. Spellman

Other Books of Interest

Before Motown: A History of Jazz in Detroit 1920–1960
By Lars Bjorn with Jim Gallert

John Coltrane: His Life and Music
By Lewis Porter

Charlie Parker: His Music and Life
By Carl Woideck

*The Song of the Hawk:
The Life and Recordings of Coleman Hawkins*
By John Chilton

Rhythm Man: Fifty Years in Jazz
By Steve Jordan with Tom Scanlan

*Let the Good Times Roll:
The Story of Louis Jordan and His Music*
By John Chilton

Twenty Years on Wheels
By Andy Kirk as Told to Amy Lee

JAZZ JOURNEYS TO JAPAN

THE HEART WITHIN

WILLIAM MINOR

THE UNIVERSITY OF MICHIGAN PRESS

ANN ARBOR

2007   2006   2005   2004   4   3   2   1

A CIP catalog record for this book is available from the British Library.

Library of Congress Cataloging-in-Publication Data

Minor, William, 1936–

    Jazz journeys to Japan : the heart within / William Minor.

      p. cm. — (Jazz perspectives)

    Includes bibliographical references (p.   ) and index.

    ISBN 0-472-11345-3 (alk. paper)

    1. Jazz—Japan—History and criticism.   I. Title.   II. Jazz

perspectives (Ann Arbor, Mich.)

    ML3509 .J3 M46 2003

    781.65'0952—dc21   2003012774

Jazz Journeys to Japan: The Heart Within is dedicated to

watashi no sensei to tomodachi (my mentor and friend) Akira Tana

and *watashi no subarashii yome* (my wonderful daughter-in-law)

Yoko Takitani Minor.

ACKNOWLEDGMENTS

This project took six years to complete, to fulfill, and the book itself would never have come to pass without the assistance of many people. First, I would like to thank all of the fine jazz musicians, fans, producers, promoters, and writers I interviewed whose names will become familiar to you (if they are not already so) in the pages that follow. I also want to thank those "lesser-sung" or unsung (for lack of space) heroes in both the United States and Japan who generously granted to me their time, solid assistance, and often friendship. They are: Rob Hayes, Chika Okamoto, Sumiko Inoue, Chris Wenner, Megumi Asaoka, Yoshihiro Nakagawa, Shu Naruse, Tomoyuki Shoji, Paul Contos, Jan Deneau; Akira Nonomura, Kohei Morishita, and Hisataka "Mac" Machida (of the Global Jazz Orchestra); Justin Fink, Vic Kobayashi, Bunky Green, Jim Shon, Scotty Wright, Hiroshi "Bamboo" Takeuchi, Takeshi "Sticks" Inomata, Robert Schneider, Herb Wong, Milt Fletcher, Eddie Mendenhall, Keiko Matsui, Hiroko Kokubu, Jim Costello, Tim Jackson, David Murray, Sadahiko Oda, Alex Hulanicki, Suzue Tomi, Hiroaki Yoshida, Yoshiko Uchida, Gregory Levine, Milo McFarland, Sami Kaneda, Andrew Simons, Akihero Minami (the surgeon who restored our son's facial features after his accident!), and the lady with the great noodle shop in Nikko.

I have acknowledged, in the bibliography, profile pieces of value, but I would like here to acknowledge writers who contributed reviews or bios that helped me complete my knowledge of jazz artists in and from Japan: Chuck Berg, Jeff Kaliss, Deni Kasrel, Ken Micallef, and Doug

Ramsey (*JazzTimes*); Stuart Broomer, Chris Kelsey, Shirley Klett, and Scott Yanow (*Cadence*); John Corbett and Howard Mandel (*Down Beat*); Lynnea T. Stephen (*Ms.*); Don Heckman (*Los Angeles Times*); Esme M. Infanta (*Honolulu Advertiser*); Seth Markow (*Honolulu Weekly*); Phil Elwood and Annie Nakao (*San Francisco Examiner*); Wayne Saroyan (*Oakland Tribune*); Evantheia Schibsted (*San Francisco*); and—nearly most invaluable of all—Shigeyo Hyodo. Check the Internet Magazine Jazz Page—<http://www.impr.com/index_e.html>—for information on everything that's happenin' in Japan, and everybody!

I am grateful to the editors who published or posted on-line my own profile pieces on Japanese and Japanese American artists, pieces that were converted into chapters of this book: Bill Smith at *Coda*, Howard Mandel at <http://www.jazzhouse.org>, Wayne Saroyan at <http://www.jazzwest.com>, and Paul Baker at <http://www.jazzinstituteofchicago.org>.

I want to thank the following photographers, whose work is also credited within the gallery section of the book, for granting permission to use their work: Gildas Boclé, Stuart Brinin, Vera Hørven, Yozo Iwanami, Steve Minor, Ryo Natsuki, and Ebet Roberts. Every possible effort has been made to locate the holders of copyright material, and I also want to thank David Murray (photos courtesy of the Monterey Jazz Festival Archives) and Masahiko Satoh for photographs they provided.

I want to thank Chris Hebert, my editor at the University of Michigan Press, who proved to be the best, most insightful, sensible, and understanding editor any writer could ask for on a project of this scope and size; Lewis Porter; and the exceptional copyediting and production team of Marcia LaBrenz, Carol Sickman-Garner, and John Grucelski.

And last, but by no means least, I would like to thank my "support" group (friends and relatives): Stu Brinin; Rick Carroll; Bink and Trixie Ichinose; Yuri Kochiyama; Kitty Margolis (and Monty); Bruce Forman; Dottie Dodgion; Bryan McConnell; Andy Weis; Elliot Roberts; Jim Hinton; George Lober; Ron Peet; Richard Mayer; Nancy Raven; Karl Dobbratz; Susana Wessling; Maribeth Anderson Payne; Shigehumi and Sumako Takitani; Kazuko and Katsuyuki Kawagishi (and family); Minako and Noriyoshi Nakamura (and family); Katsunori, Kyoko, and Emi Matsumoto; Hisayo Oshima; and as always, with gratitude and love, my mom, Dorothy, my sister Emily (who reads everything I write), my wife, Betty, and Tim, Emily, Blake, Steve, and Yoko. *Dōmo arigatō.*

CONTENTS

CONTENTS

Introduction

RECENTLY RETURNED FROM A SECOND trip to Japan, I was sitting at the
kitchen table late at night, sipping sake, leafing through photos of
Kiyomizudera and Kinkakuji temples in Kyoto, the bright orange buildings of the Heian Jingu Shrine, the Daibutsu (Great Buddha) and sacred
shika (deer) in Nara—and photos taken at two Tokyo jazz spots: J Club
and Pit Inn. A feeling of serenity came over me, sudden and unsought,
the way the Zen masters say it's supposed to come. Don't worry. No
overlarge claim of satori or enlightenment here. Just a nice sense, as I listened to Masao Yagi play "'Round Midnight," of general well-being. Yagi
recorded an album of tunes by Thelonious Monk in 1960. The Japanese
liked them so much they brought over the real thing, and Monk in
return recorded a popular Japanese song, "Kōjō No Tsuki" (Moon Over
the Desolate Castle). The Gene Krupa Trio had also recorded this tune
in Japan in 1952, along with "Sho, Sho, Shojoji" (Badger's Party), a children's song. A contemporary San Francisco artist named Miya Masaoka
has recently recorded "Moon Over the Desolate Castle" and "'Round
Midnight" on the koto, a traditional Japanese instrument made from two
pieces of paulownia wood shaped like a crouching dragon.

Small world? Indeed.

The Japanese word *kokoro* covers a lot of ground. A dictionary
offers three meanings: spirit, heart, mind. I like "the heart within" and
have chosen that as the subtitle for this book. I'm carrying on an inner
(*honne:* underlying reality, true feelings) rather than just an external
(*tatemae:* appearance, based on convention) love affair with Japan, a

country not my own. I have carried on a lifelong love affair with the cultures of three countries not my own: Greece, Russia, and Japan. I set out to study each and did so for years, attempting to learn their respective languages, read their literature, acquaint myself with their history—long before I set foot on their actual soil. It took me twenty-three years in the case of Greece, thirty-five to get to Russia, and forty-one for my first trip to Japan. The wait was well worth it. I have written about each place: some travel pieces and a slender book of poems called *Goat Pan* on the first; *Unzipped Souls: A Jazz Journey through the Soviet Union* on the second; and now—this book on jazz in and from Japan.

Jazz music became a passion for me about seventeen years ago, when I started to write seriously about what had been another lifelong interest and also began to attempt to play it (I was once a totally undeserving house pianist at a place called the 456 Club in Brooklyn) with more purpose than I'd had before. The first book I wrote about international jazz and this one were completed under quite different circumstances. My wife and I traveled nine thousand kilometers in the former Soviet Union, which at the time—the tail end of the Cold War in 1990—was still a somewhat mysterious and even forbidding place (Lithuania, where we'd booked a hotel in Vilnius, was literally removed, by Liquid Paper correction fluid, from our visas). Japan, on the other hand, was from start to finish of two visits an accessible and fully engaging nation. The *people* we met in both places were wonderful (warm, open, willing to tell their stories), the Russians generous to a fault, but it was Japan that captured my heart. I didn't want to leave. Why did I feel so totally at ease there? I suppose one purpose of writing this book was to find out.

Because of a history of seclusion and political risk, there were just a few top jazz artists in the Soviet Union at the time we visited, and they were spread out. Trumpeter Germann Lukianov and bassist Tamaz Kurashvili rehearsed for festivals over the phone, Lukianov in Moscow, Kurashvili in Tbilisi, Georgia—more than fifteen hundred kilometers, or eleven hundred miles, apart. Yet before we left on our first trip to Japan, I had listened to hundreds of Japanese jazz artists on recordings and knew many more by name. I had a long list of potential contacts, more than I could ever accommodate in the length of time set aside. Rob Hayes and Chika Okamoto of Berklee College of Music in Boston sent me a list of 333 Japanese alumni! When I started research on jazz in the former Soviet Union, friends and acquaintances were surprised that such a thing even existed. When I started the present project, the same

2

people said, "The Japanese *love* jazz, don't they?" How they knew this, I didn't know. It seemed to be common knowledge. My own interest was related to *why* the Japanese loved jazz so much and just *how* they went about playing it—the shape that interest or love had taken over the years.

I encountered a single type of jazz musician in the former Soviet Union: fine isolated performers with an immense hunger to perform, at last, with world-class artists, to go out into the world at large and prove how well they could play. But I discovered there were *three* basic types of Japanese performers: (1) those who had been free to do just that, to go out into the world, ordinarily taking up residence in the States (some for so long that they were no longer known in Japan); (2) those strictly Japanese performers tucked away in Tokyo, Osaka, Nagoya, Kyoto, and elsewhere, whose work was generally not known outside of Japan (such as the fine pianist Hisayuki Terai who, with his wife, Tamae, runs—and performs at—the Over Seas Club in Osaka); and (3) those who had managed to straddle both worlds, truly international artists who were known in both countries and frequently traveled back and forth between the States and Japan.

I discovered that jazz life in Japan, ironically, was infinitely more complex than in "Russia." Because of ethnic and cultural diversity, tracing roots or influences in the former Soviet Union was relatively easy (pianist Aziza Mustafa-Zadeh, from Azerbaijan, for example, merging traditional folk modes, or *mugam,* with jazz), but the effects of assimilation and influence in Japan are much more subtle, even evasive. I had joked with friends that, given the geographical demands—the spatial dimensions of the former Soviet Union and the tendency there for people to think on a grand *War and Peace* scale—I should, by contrast, reduce my findings on Japan to a haiku. But the subject of jazz in Japan (and Japanese jazz *outside* of Japan) proved far too expansive for a 5–7–5 syllable format.

The title of this book, *Jazz Journeys to Japan,* is used in a special, comprehensive, metaphorical sense, the word "journeys" redefined. My Japanese jazz journey began at inception, in the States, and included a great deal of history (although jazz in the former Soviet Union, surfacing and going underground in accord with the political climate, also had an interesting, if more limited, history). In a *New York Times* article Blue Note Records producer Michael Cuscuna said that, when the popularity of our only indigenous art form, what has been called "America's classical music," went through a serious slump in the States, "Japan almost single-handedly kept the jazz record business going during the late 1970s." Japan had already made *major* contributions to the world of jazz—and in *many* ways. Reviewing a CD release by drummer Masahiko Togashi, John Corbett wrote, "Precious little has been written in English about the history of jazz in Japan. In the eyes of many Americans, the land of the rising sun is recognized as a major *consumer* of the music, but a fascinating tradition of Japanese jazz musicians exists, extending far beyond the smattering of recognized names like Toshiko Akiyoshi and Sadao Watanabe." There was much for me to learn, and understand, *before* I set out on the actual geographical journey.

I had trouble finding out about jazz and just getting into Russia in 1990. When I wrote about that ordeal, my editors said, "Can't you get us to Moscow *faster?*" My reply was, "This journey started long before I set foot in the Soviet Union; it started *here.*" I had my first live exposure to two Russian musicians—Sergey Kuryokhin and Igor Bril—in the States. Previous exposure was even more the case with Japan. Before we arrived in Tokyo on July 22, 1996, I had acquired a substantial collection of Japanese CDs; had met, heard live, and interviewed a number of Japanese musicians from Eiji Kitamura to Makoto Ozone; had discovered a highly active Japanese American jazz community (many of whom were experimenting with traditional Japanese instruments); had been lent and had read drummer Akira Tana's insightful ethnomusicology thesis, written at Harvard, on jazz in Japan; and had found myself at an international jazz festival held in Hawaii, where I talked to Toshiko Akiyoshi and Tiger Okoshi. Unlike the situation in the former Soviet Union, much of the jazz in Japan had *come to me*—as part of my "journey"—before I even boarded a plane to cross the ocean.

A critic whose judgment I esteem wrote that *Unzipped Souls* was "part travelogue, part narrative about the state of Russian jazz, and partly about life in the Soviet Union during that transition period; it reads almost like a novel." He also said I had gone out of my way "to talk to every top Russian jazz musician [I] could locate." I hope all of that is true also of what I offer now in this book on the jazz of Japan. Both books were written in the belief that we truly *are* what surrounds us; that "influences" in music extend beyond this or that particular player or even era; that influence is far wider, more comprehensive than we have been led to believe. Just as children are shaped by, beholden to *all* that their parents say and do, so is jazz music the product of the total culture from which it emerges, whether such influence is intentional, acknowledged, or unconscious.

A fascination, a passion, began for me as a young student of the visual arts at Pratt Institute in the mid-1950s, when my introduction to Ukiyo-e prints (by way of Toulouse-Lautrec's silkscreen posters, the "Divan Japonais," with their deliberate violations of Western perspective) compelled me to light out from Brooklyn up to the Metropolitan Museum of Art one day and return with a collection I still treasure: *Japanese Color Prints,* which contains Hokusai's *Great Wave Off Kanagawa,* Utamaro's *A Beauty and Her Likeness in a Mirror,* and work by Hiroshige, Harunobu, Shunsho, Sharaku. I also discovered the wondrous woodcuts of Shiko Munakata. I was hooked, and an acquaintance with the rich legacy of literature, Zen Buddhism, and Japanese music— *gagaku* (court music), other forms of traditional music, and Japanese jazz—still lay ahead.

So, forty-three years later, recently returned from my second trip to Japan, I sat at the kitchen table 'round midnight, listening to pianist Masao Yagi, thinking of what a long, fine, strange trip it *all* had been, the entire journey. My friends still made jokes about my respective "periods," my Greek and Russian and now Japanese. But sipping sake (*tsumetai,* cold), I smiled, thinking, "This is the best. *This* is the real thing." In Greece, I was still young, full of fitful animal high spirits; in Russia, the ghosts of Osip Mandelstam and Dostoevsky dogged me, with deep troubled delight, all the way. Now, I thought of the Zen master Dogen's tanka on *mujo* (impermanence):

> The world may be
> compared to what?
> The moon, reflected
> in dewdrops:
> a crane's bill shakes them free.

Why and how, in such a vast, unstable, fugitive world, had I been allowed—by way of the visual arts, literature, religion, and especially jazz music of Japan—to know so many moments of probably undeserved peace, joy, pleasure, and appreciation? I realized it *was* the purpose of this book to find out.

First Trip to Japan,
Stopover Hawaii:
A History Lesson, in Flight

Flight 187, coach class to Hawaii, left San Francisco Airport just about noon, guaranteed lunch and movie. I don't remember the lunch. I don't remember the movie—which I might have stolen glances at but would not have succumbed to in full anyway. Much to the chagrin of our fellow passengers, perhaps, once we'd been commanded to drop our window shades and the plane's interior—although it was still daylight outside—went movie dark, my wife Betty and I left our overhead lights ablaze for reading. I was actually studying, contemplating, what I knew of the history of jazz in Japan, going over notes I had assembled before we left the States.

My wife, Betty, was sitting next to me. She had agreed to accompany me on a jazz journey to Japan I had first proposed nearly a year ago, but had agreed a tad more reluctantly than she had to a similar trek we made in the summer of 1990 through the former Soviet Union. Betty wanted to go to Paris.

"*Everybody's* written about jazz in France," I'd said at the time. "They've even made movies about it."

"I still want to go to Paris."

So here we were, on our way to jazz in Japan, our first stopover Hawaii. Fortunately, Betty loves Hawaii (we were married there forty years ago, and she enjoys returning to the scene of the crime). I had discovered that two Japanese musicians I wanted very much to interview (and who would prove of immense significance to me and the rest of the journey)—Tiger Okoshi and Toshiko Akiyoshi—would be performing at the Hawaii International Jazz Festival, held, conveniently, just at the time we'd settled on for starting out for Japan.

I had, over the past year of preparation, also assembled not just notes on the history of jazz in Japan but a substantial collection of recordings made by Japanese musicians, and I had even managed to hear them, live, and meet a number of them. I was still somewhat overwhelmed by the *extent,* in Japan, of this art form I love, especially compared to the relatively fragmented or scattered presence of jazz in the former Soviet Union, and I knew that, in flight now, I had lots of information (names, dates, etc.) to sort out.

Jazz had been a part of the Japanese cultural scene for nearly a quarter of a century before the postwar inundation of GI musicians and fans that produced indigenous counterparts such as pianist Toshiko Akiyoshi, alto saxophonist Sadao Watanabe, clarinetist Eiji Kitamura, and saxophonist Hidehiko "Sleepy" Matsumoto. The latter, when he performed at the Monterey Jazz Festival in 1963, the first Japanese artist to appear there (playing baritone sax alongside Gerry Mulligan no less), prompted an ordinarily enlightened critic, Ralph Gleason (who should have known better), to regard him as a novelty, "interesting only as a curiosity." But jazz was no longer just a curiosity, a novelty, to the Japanese. Purportedly, jazz arrived in Japan as early as 1921, when a young man named Shigeya Kikuchi, serving as secretary to his father on a U.S. business trip, returned to his native country with a load of Dixieland 78s. Japan's own "Roaring Twenties" were inaugurated by the Great Earthquake of 1923—which devastated Tokyo, the city burning for forty hours but, as Edward Seidensticker has written, reconstruction, in typical Japanese fashion, having begun "before the last embers were out."

Musical resuscitation took place in halls frequented by dancers gyrating to steps imported from America. Violinist/bassist Ichiro Ida, from Kobe, created the first professional Dixieland orchestra, called the Hilarious Stars—this instinct for curious monikers later providing a succession of "Herds" that make Woody Herman's differentiations look bland: Cats Herd, the Counter Herd, New Blue Herd, etc. Japanese jazz bands have, since that day (and long before rock groups) adorned themselves with interesting names: the Tokyo Cuban Boys, the Sharps and Flats, Rhythm Aces, Six Lemons, Six Brothers, Six Joes, Six Joys, Laughing Stars, Luck and Sun Jazz Band, the Cozy Quartet Plus One, Albatross, Swing Ace Big Band, the Gay Stars, the Gay Septet, and Field Holler Jazz Orchestra, to cite just a few.

Before leaving the States, I had made the acquaintance of American drummer Akira Tana who, as it turned out, had written his undergraduate thesis in musicology at Harvard on jazz in Japan, and he had sent me *A History of King Jazz Recordings,* an excellent compilation, a ten-disc collection that contains music recorded from 1937 to 1942 by groups with such names as the Fraternity Syncopators and the King Novelty Orchestra, music much in the vein of early recordings by Duke Ellington, Chick Webb, and Jimmie Lunceford—albeit, I'll admit, with less verve, swing, or sprightliness. Listening, it was interesting to hear the prewar repertoire switch from "St. Louis Blues," "Pagan Love Song," "Goody Goody," and "When It's Lamplighting Time," to songs whose titles all ended with the word *bushi* (a somewhat antiquated word for "song" in Japanese). Japan, with its new *hakkō ichū* policy (literally, bringing the eight corners of the world under one roof), had undertaken the task of "rescuing" China from Western imperialism. Thus the jazz tune "Kiso Bushi," based on a folk song sung at a festival along the Kiso River, although labeled "scherzando" (playful) in the original version, had become by the late 1930s a solemn, almost dirgelike military march replete with tenor saxophone and clarinet jazz riffs.

In 1939, two years after the "Rape of Nanking" (where, during Japan's "undeclared war" with China, at least one report lists 20,000 women assaulted and 300,000 people massacred—a Japanese estimate placing the figure at a mere 150,000), Chinese folk songs presented as jazz tunes (this "American" musical idiom still allowed) were popular. In 1940, the popular tune "Kōjō No Tsuki" (Moon Over the Desolate Castle) tolerated a sax solo that tipped its hat to Coleman Hawkins, and the same year's "Kanton No Hanauri-Musume" (The Girl Selling Flowers in Canton) is unabashedly two-beat sweet, sporting a muted trumpet solo and thumping section work spiced with loud cymbal splashes. As late as 1942, martial vocal choruses, heard on "Kusatsu Bushi," were still seasoned with drum riffs reminiscent of Gene Krupa, but after that jazz-based music disappears—as do words such as *bēsubōru* (baseball)—for the duration of the war. When jazz music reemerged after the war, the repertoire was made up of Stephen Foster songs such as "Oh! Susanna" and "Old Folks at Home"—as performed by a combo led by Hiroshi Masuo, formerly a pianist with the wartime King Novelty Orchestra.

Later, critic Masahisa Segawa, who was introduced to me as the "Leonard Feather of Japan" (there would appear to be two of everything in Nihon or Nippon—two Japanese words for the nation itself; another equally esteemed Japanese critic, Yozo Iwanami, was also introduced to me with that appellation; two clarinetists, incidentally, Eiji Kitamura and Shoji Suzuki, are called the "Benny Goodman of Japan"), would tell me that Shigeya Kikuchi was probably not the *only* person to return from the States in 1921 with jazz in hand. "Around that time," Segawa said, "*several* persons took jazz recordings, sheet music, or any information about jazz and brought them back to Japan; so these along with many dance records were already available." Kikuchi was a young pianist, and he wanted to play and develop a jazz style for himself. A student at Keiō University when he returned, he called his classmates and organized a small band. Also at this time some Nisei—Japanese American—musicians came to Japan from the United States. One, Takaji Domoto, met with Kikuchi and other students and taught them how to play jazz.

Segawa also felt that there had been considerable jazz activity *before* the 1923 earthquake: "Already in Tokyo and Osaka—particularly in Osaka—there were many dance halls. I mean *ballrooms.* So already there were many Japanese bands playing dance music—very primitive dance music. Many Japanese were dancing at that time. Many music sheets [Segawa used this phrase, and I liked it!] had been introduced, so they were playing these tunes." By 1935, Nisei singers had come to Japan, along with many Filipino musicians, among whom the Conde brothers were best known. Masahisa Segawa told me that clarinetist Raymond Conde is still playing actively. "There were four Conde brothers," he said, "and two—Raymond and Billy—stayed in Japan. They married Japanese ladies and they have families, and they have Japanese nationality." Two Filipino musicians, Francis Kokiko and clarinetist Conde, became the core of the most popular combo after the war: the Gay Septet. And out of the Gay Septet came such current players as drummer George Kawaguchi and tenor saxophonist Hidehiko "Sleepy" Matsumoto. "Those Filipino musicians taught *them*," Segawa said.

When I mentioned Micky Matsuyama and the King Jazz Orchestra, on the *History of King Jazz Recordings* that Segawa himself had compiled, the critic replied, "That too was about 1935, I think, a little later than the Osaka bands. Whether we can call this *jazz* or not, I don't know. But already, in 1923 or 1924, American dance music or American popular songs had been recorded by Japanese, and these songs were sung in Japanese." In 1928, two major American recording companies—Victor and Columbia—established subsidiary companies: Japan Columbia

Records and Japan Victor Records. The year 1928 also saw the beginning of electronic recording in Japan, so the sound quality on recordings was better. Both Victor and Columbia issued the same songs, "My Blue Heaven" and "Song of Araby," sung by the same person, Tamara Teiichi, with the Amazon Trio. "The bands were a bit different," Segawa said. "One was a student band, the other professional. But they both used exactly the same sheet music. Therefore they both sound very similar." "Watashi no Azura" (My Blue Heaven) was one of the most widely sung American songs. "And 'Arabian Uta' [Song of Araby]," Segawa said, "was *never* recorded in the States. Only the sheet music was issued there—so that's a very strange thing." The composer Carl Fischer wrote "Dardanella" and many other early popular songs in the United States, but someone bought "Song of Araby" and brought it to Japan, where Keizo Horiuchi, a very famous music composer, translated it into Japanese and recorded it. "So this song was recorded *only* in Japan, and very widely sung," Segawa said.

When I asked Masahisa Segawa about the *quality* of bands at this time, whether groups such as the Fraternity Syncopators were actually good, he replied, "There were two kinds of musicians in the main development or model in Japan: professional musicians and college students." The sources of professional musicians were military bands or children's bands (or boys' bands). Many department stores had their own boys' bands or children's bands, for advertising purposes. They taught them how to play, and they eventually became professionals, so these musicians made up one stream. The college students were mostly the sons of well-to-do families. They had money and could import records and sheet music. The most advance-minded college-student players listened to Duke Ellington or Jimmy Lunceford, and they wanted to play the most advanced jazz in their bands. Those student bands did not have to worry about money, so they could play whatever they liked to play. But the professional bands worked in dance halls, so they had to play only songs that appealed to the dancers.

In 1941, Segawa told me, the government prohibited anyone from playing American songs, so the first Japanese bands tried to play non-American songs in a jazz style or manner—tunes like "Song of India," which was composed by Rimsky-Korsakov, a Russian composer. This was classical music, but Japanese bands also played Tommy Dorsey's version of "Song of India." Gradually the police caught on, so in 1943, the government issued a very detailed order to prohibit jazz. "No band could have more than two saxophones," Segawa said. "No band could use a mute or cup with a trumpet. No drummer could play four beats— restrictions like that. So they were trying to *kill* jazz. The military bands still had to use *some* woodwind instruments, but they could only be used in these bands, and for military music."

The second "Leonard Feather of Japan," Yozo Iwanami, whose contributions to the *New Grove Dictionary of Jazz* I had found invaluable in the States, would tell me that, although big band "swing," or dance music, was quite popular before World War II, the postwar Occupation provided Japanese their initial heavy firsthand exposure to the music. That was when Japanese jazz had its biggest evolution: "New jazz— bebop from the United States—could be heard because of recordings and radio shows. The soldiers brought this music. There were many army clubs, air force bases, other camps, and Japanese musicians played only jazz at such places. And there were many nightclubs in the cities for dancing: in Tokyo, Nagoya, Osaka. But jazz clubs? In the mid-1950s, maybe two or three. The American soldiers' clubs were the jazz clubs. From 1945 to maybe 1955, it was the military bases that let Japanese jazz grow up. Hidehiko 'Sleepy' Matsumoto played at the American soldiers' clubs. And Toshiko Akiyoshi. Many jazz players started there. Sadao Watanabe . . ."

In 1947, a group called the Gramercy Six recorded for Victor Hot Club (a record company established after the war). "They were one of the first combos to play bebop and cool jazz," Masahisa Segawa told me. "It was a fad for Japanese musicians to try and play bebop. Hiroshi Masuo's 'Oh! Susanna' is just one example of that, but there were very few tunes recorded in that vein that still remain, so there was no alter- native: I took Masuo-san's version for the *History of King Jazz Record- ings*. But Masuo-san was not really like Coleman Hawkins or those pre- war jazz musicians in the States who tried to adopt the bebop idiom and make it their own. He was one of those who couldn't completely absorb the bebop style, so he gave up and went back to swing."

A mix of 1930s and 1940s American styles, and "cool jazz" by way of Gil Evans, Gerry Mulligan, and Lee Konitz, exerted its influence in the early 1950s. Kiyoshi Koyama, editor of *Swing Journal*, produced a recording of nine native musicians in this idiom. Drummer George Kawaguchi's 1953 trio recording of Gene Krupa's "Drum Boogie" inau- gurated major interest in jazz. By 1954, over 170 radio broadcasts were disseminating the music throughout the country, broadcasting live jazz

11

performances from nightclubs and dance halls. When television began, there were attempts to show jazz programs. In 1956, the first long-playing recordings appeared in Japan.

"Benny Goodman's *Carnegie Hall Jazz Concert* LP was one of the most popular jazz LPs in Japan," Segawa said. "It sold out." When I mentioned the similarity of Gene Krupa's style of drumming on "Sing, Sing, Sing" to *taiko,* Segawa said, "That's why Mr. Suniko Ichi has used jazz drumming in his arrangements of Japanese folk songs. Actually, Suni-san used Japanese *taiko* and koto too." When I asked Yozo Iwanami who the first American musicians he'd heard live were, he replied, "Probably the Gene Krupa Trio. With Charlie Ventura and Teddy Napolean. Then Jazz at the Philharmonic in 1953. J. C. Heard was the drummer, and he stayed in Japan for maybe one or two years. And I heard Louis Armstrong, with his All Stars. Cozy Cole, Barney Bigard, Arvil Shaw. Trummy Young was on trombone."

Yozo Iwanami was the first person to tell me about Shotoro Moriyasu, who committed suicide in 1955 and whom the critic considers "the most talented modern jazz pianist in Japan." I mentioned that I had asked pianist Kotaro Tsukahara to list the most important postwar pianists in Japan, those who, he felt, had exerted the greatest influence, and Shotoro Moriyasu had been first on his list, followed by Toshiko Akiyoshi, Kazuo Yashiro, and Yoshitaka Akimitsu. Iwanami said that, after Moriyasu, Akiyoshi was "the next most talented pianist," but he considered Yashiro a great pianist too. Yoshitaka Akimitsu was mostly a swing player, in the Teddy Wilson mode, whereas Shotoro Moriyasu "was like Bud Powell; the conception came from Charlie Parker."

Modern recording techniques were well in place by 1957, when clarinetist Peanuts Hucko, a member of Benny Goodman's band, supervised a recording by Shoji Suzuki and the Rhythm Aces. This record—"Suzukakino Michi" (its melody by Haida Harushko, a Nisei guitar player who wrote many Westernized Japanese popular songs)—became a best-seller in Japan, and the group undertook a concert tour throughout the country. At the time, audiences included young Japanese women so moved by the music that they "swooned," just as American girls had once over Frank Sinatra. An all-female theater genre called *takurazuka* was extremely popular during this period, but the rise of jazz contributed to a shift toward interest in male performers. Coffeehouses, clubs, and cabarets fostered the rapid popularization of jazz, providing employment and hands-on "schooling" for Japanese musicians.

12

At the close of the 1950s, both recording opportunities and radio presentations of the music flourished. *Swing Journal* conducted a critics poll modeled on the American equivalent, highlighting the achievements of Japanese artists. Masahisa Segawa spoke of 1960 as "the year of the real development of modern jazz in Japan," everything from hard bop to the avant-garde. The major influences were John Coltrane, Miles Davis, Lenny Tristano, and, somewhat later, Ornette Coleman and Archie Shepp. "*Many* types of modern jazz were being developed," Segawa said. "The New Century Recording Institute was a group of jazzmen, but not a band. It was a group of young men who got together to study and play advanced jazz. They did hold concerts from time to time." The Shiraki Hideo Quintet was part of a rather early period of modern jazz, so they stayed in the mainstream mode, not playing avant-garde or free jazz. But in the hard bop vein, the Shiraki Hideo Quintet was one of the most advanced. The producer of the 1965 Berlin Jazz Festival invited the quintet to play not only American jazz but some Japanese-style jazz also—so they took a koto player. "I think the combination worked successfully," Segawa said. MPS Records—a German label—recorded that performance. Shiraki Hideo, unfortunately, died very early, and the quintet broke up right after its Berlin appearance.

In the 1960s, a controversial issue first raised its head: the negative response to an attempt on the part of local musicians to use national materials in their work, rather than relying on standards or blind imitation of American models. Some native musicians were suspicious of Shiraki's motives for using indigenous elements, seeing this as a ploy to gain international favor. Should the use of traditional materials constitute "Japanese jazz," or should the overall personal expressiveness of the musicians themselves?

The late 1960s to early 1970s was the period when avant-garde and free-style jazz were most active. "Yosuke Yamashita's trio was one of them," Segawa said, "but there were so many others!" Japanese performers organized Shinseki Ongaku Kenkyu Jyu (the New Century Music Recording Institute), focused on ways to offer jazz of a uniquely Japanese character, but when Masao Yagi released a recording of Thelonious Monk tunes, promoters turned directly to the American pianist's work itself, bypassing Yagi. Appearances in Japan of musicians such as Monk and saxophonist Charlie Mariano, who recorded directly with Japanese musicians, paved the way for the American emergence of one of the most gifted local musicians (and Mariano's wife for a while),

Toshiko Akiyoshi. She left Japan to attend Berklee College in the States in 1957 and then returned to record a trio date hailed by critics and audiences alike. At the turn of the decade, jazz was a fully accepted art form—an integral part of modern Japanese society.

By way of my reading before I left for Japan, I had become acquainted with a number of both older and contemporary Japanese jazz musicians and heard them on recordings: Akira Miyazawa, who had played in Sadao Watanabe's Cozy Quartet and whom Yozo Iwanami described as "among the most creative tenor saxophonists in Japan"; trumpeter Terumasa Hino, whom I hoped to hear and meet later in the trip (at the Mt. Fuji Jazz Festival in Yokohama); a fine young pianist, Junko Onishi, who'd been making a name for herself at the Village Vanguard in New York. And there was drummer Takeshi "Sticks" Inomata, whom Akira Tana had befriended. Born in Osaka, Inomata moved to Tokyo in the 1950s. He played in a group, the West Liners, led by tenor saxophonist Konosuke Saijoh. "Inomata is a drummer who has taught many other musicians," Iwanami would say. "And there's George Kawaguchi, another drummer. He's a very big star in Japan. He uses two bass drums, like Louie Bellson. He likes drum solos." (I had a recording of "Killer Joe" on which Kawaguchi appears to hold his own with Art Blakey, no less!)

I also had acquired recordings by drummer Masahiko Togashi, whom Iwanami would call "a genius, very good percussionist, who also lives in Tokyo." "*Imano Kako Nogaku* [We Now Create] was, I think, the title of an LP recorded by Togashi," Masahisa Segawa would tell me later. "He was one of the most advanced, or mature, jazz drummers. This was before he was injured, before he was paralyzed. So at that earlier time he made many adventurous recordings."

I had learned of tenor saxophonist Kosuke Mine, who performs with pianist Masahiko Satoh's group Randooga; bassists Yoshio "Chin" Suzuki (who'd played in New York with Art Blakey's Jazz Messengers) and Teruo Nakamura; and tenor saxophonist Satolu Oda, who's recorded with American pianist Hank Jones. A few of these performers were, at the time of our flight to Hawaii, merely names to me, jotted down in my notes as having made a contribution to the history of jazz in Japan, but fortunately, during our first trip to Japan (in 1996) and one that followed two years later, I would have a chance to hear them, live, and to meet and interview many of them.

Nearly as interesting as the evolution of jazz in Japan was the

14

American response to it. As I implied by citing Ralph Gleason's commentary on Sleepy Matsumoto, that reception has not always been favorable. Early American (post–World War II) critical commentary on the Japanese attempt to play "our music"—"America's classical music," an indigenous art form—was frequently condescending, the tone mocking, belittling, if not laced with outright bigotry. I assembled the following collage from articles ranging from a 1959 *Saturday Review* piece to one in a 1990 issue of *GQ*. In the earliest, informed that "there's jazz all over Tokyo," an out-on-the-town American jazz writer ends up making fun of everything from (an admittedly still young) Toshiko Akiyoshi— "who played as though she had grown up on player-piano rolls cut by Bud Powell. I . . . felt about her as I feel about acrobats who play trombones while doing half-gainers and back-flips. Once the experience has been absorbed, one need not have it again"—to after-hours joints—"We visited two of those and found no jazz to speak of, let alone write about." Nightclub renditions of "Body and Soul" and "Satin Doll" are dismissed as "all poor imitations . . . female vocalists who turn out to be men, usually after you pay the cover." A trumpeter is described as "milky," having "learned more from Ralph Lauren than from Harry James." A seventeen-piece band hosted three girl singers in satin and rhinestones "wrapping their Asian tongues around such red flags as Aretha Franklin's '(Wait Till) The Midnight Hour.'" Musicians under twenty offered lunchtime jazz, but "it wasn't that the sum of the rhythms, tempos and notes per second approached the cost per acre of land in downtown Tokyo. It wasn't even that the bass player and the guitarist were playing in different keys. . . . It was the lack of technique, the lack of style, the lack of history, the utter absence of any proof that these guys had learned how to play their instruments before they tried to imitate James 'Blood' Ulmer or Elvin Jones."

Witty stuff, perhaps (and perhaps—under some of the circumstances—deserved; I wasn't there; I don't know), but what intrigues me when I read it is the tone, the underlying preconception, the *attitude*. These quotes reside within the perimeter of 1959–90, yet they all convey the same note of condescension ("the lack of technique, the lack of style, the lack of history") and a somewhat mean-spirited stance. It's as if—in our eyes—the Japanese are *not supposed* to be capable of playing this music, so we simply hear what they come up with as incorrect or ludicrous imitation. A 1960 *Time* article, entitled "Shinu, Shinu, Shinu," comments on the three thousand union-registered jazz musicians "noodling away at the out sounds of such current favorites as Sonny Rollins, Art Blakey and Miles Davis. They have even picked up the lingo and added soy sauce"—the article citing such expressions as cool (*koo-roo*), beat (*beato*), and *shinu* (literally, "I die") for being overwhelmed by the music. Not very polite responses to a people who specialize in politeness.

I will confess to being intrigued and appalled by American ethnocentrism, perhaps because I've spent so much of my own life attempting to work my way out of it. We certainly have a right to feel proud of jazz, our indigenous art form. (I won't continue to call it "America's classical music," because I think of Charles Ives, Samuel Barber, Howard Hanson, Virgil Thomson, Aaron Copland, Donald Ashwander, Morton Gould, Percy Grainger, Ned Rorem, John Adams, Terry Riley, Jake Heggie, etc., in that context.) But shouldn't we be a bit more aware by now that this music is no longer exclusively *ours* (if the form of "fusion" called "jass," a genuine assimilation of European classical music, African polyrhythms, field holler, brass band, hymnal, blues, pop dance, minstrel songs, and ragtime strains ever was)? The response one encounters— even on the part of critics who should know better—seems the result of a form of unconscious (or conscious?) resistance, a refusal on our part to give up the mantle of origin and originality (which was false to begin with?) in the face of what is now a truly international art form.

In his book *The Japanese,* Edwin O. Reischauer admits that "Western history shows no parallel to the conscious Japanese effort at massive cultural borrowing" (with the "possible exception" of Peter the Great), yet he also acknowledges "the broad area for self-expression" found in the visual arts, music, dance, and literature (for example, the *watakushi shōsetsu,* or "I novel," with its "introspective, almost embarrassingly frank examination of the writer's personal feelings"). Even a not-so-sympathetic observer such as Arthur Koestler, in *The Lotus and the Robot,* states that the Japanese "eagerness to copy was not due to any inherent tendency . . . but to the hunger for knowledge of a people just emerging from two hundred and fifty years of solitary confinement." In his *Short Cultural History,* George Sansom addresses "those who are inclined to think that the Japanese have excelled only as copyists of foreign institutions," saying, "That they had the courage and wisdom to copy in the first place is greatly to their credit, and their later history shows that they have never rested content with an uncritical acceptance of imported models." Edwin M. Reingold, in *Chrysanthemums and Thorns: The Untold Story of Modern Japan,* says the charge that the Japanese are at best imitators is "too casual an admission, though a revealing one," since the Japanese "have often denigrated themselves in this regard." Reingold, however, goes on to say that, in light of innovations and experimental inventions in a host of areas (automobiles and electronics, anyone?), the Japanese no longer "like the lingering charge" that they lack originality. Yet the implication, or accusation, seems to remain, in the minds of music critics, that as far as jazz goes, Japanese artists are just clones. As far as I know there is yet to emerge a "Benny Goodman of Russia" (although Goodman's family was *from* Russia). It seemed to me that a few too many of the American critics I'd read, commenting on this music, had taken the easy way out, adopting a condescending approach that allowed them to write off the Japanese contribution to this universal language as second-rate imitation. Based on what I'd already heard on recordings at home, I wasn't buying that attitude, and I was off to Japan to find out if I was right.

THE HAWAII INTERNATIONAL
JAZZ FESTIVAL

I N 1957, MY WIFE BETTY and I spent a honeymoon summer on the island
of Kauai, prestatehood, living in a small cabin, really a shack (though
fortunately not a "little grass shack," as in the song), on the only open
spot on the Wailua River. At the time, the island boasted just one hotel,
the Coco Palms, which we could not afford, but which Mitzi Gaynor
occupied with her entourage throughout the filming of *South Pacific*. At
the time, Kauai seemed lost in some nineteenth-century plantation
dream or haze. It hosted endless beaches, a narrow-gauge train that took
sugarcane to a mill, a ramshackle general store, and a single movie theater specializing in samurai films with no subtitles. We went to the theater often and have been ardent Japanese-film fans ever since. (Actor
Toshiro Mifune, not John Wayne, is my all-time warrior hero, and director Hiroshi Inagaki's trilogy on Musashi Miyamoto, the most famed of all
Japanese swordsmen, is still one of my favorite sets of films.) I quickly
mastered the stark guttural cries of *bushido* warriors as they impaled
their opponents or were impaled by them—cries similar to the *kakegoe*,
or the vocal ejaculations of *taiko* drummers.

For that honeymoon summer, I'd brought along a stash of my
favorite ten-inch jazz records—the Gerry Mulligan Quartet, Chet
Baker's "I Married an Angel" (with its fine solo by Zoot Sims), Art
Tatum, Teddy Wilson, Erroll Garner, Lennie Tristano, Woody Herman,
Frank Sinatra (*Songs for Young Lovers, Songs for Swingin' Lovers!, In the
Wee Small Hours*)—but we discovered that our shack on the only open
spot on the Wailua River lacked electricity.

Now, forty years later, we checked into our favorite Waikiki hideaway, and I felt as though we were already in Japan, for the ABC stores and streets were packed with Nihonjin, tourists eagerly making purchases at the many shops that traded in yen, the magazine racks loaded with publications in Japanese, the sounds of the language I had been attempting to learn for a year parading through my head at a frenzied pace.

Betty and I had lunch with friends we'd met when I was a student in the University of Hawaii art department in 1956: Bink and Trixie Ichinose. As we feasted on roast duck, shrimp in paper-thin pasta, spinach and scallops pastry, fried daikon, and bean-curd rolls, we talked about jazz and our trip to Japan. Trixie, the most outspoken "submissive Japanese female" (she's Japanese American and not submissive at all) I've ever met, said, grinning derisively, "Have you become a Jap lover?"

"Mochi wa mochiya," I wanted to reply, but I couldn't think fast enough in Japanese to say it. "For rice cakes, go to the rice-cake maker." If you do a thing, do it right: go to the source, 100 percent. After lunch, when we visited a bookstore that housed more fine handmade rice papers and delicate art supplies than books, I realized I *had* fallen in love with things Japanese; and the amazing fact was—as in the case of jazz music—I hadn't yet had to leave the States to find things Japanese!

I thought about a jazz artist such as the one I hoped to interview in Hawaii, Toshiko Akiyoshi, who had in her music successfully fused the use of traditional Japanese instruments, such as *tsuzumi* drums and the *shakuhachi*-flavored intonation of Lew Tabackin's flute, with big band writing—especially on a piece such as "Kogun," an homage to a Japanese soldier living in a Philippine jungle for almost thirty years, not knowing the war has ended. The title means "forlorn forces," or "alone." The piece itself begins with a giant cry, "Yooohhhh," accompanied by *kotsuzume* and *ohtsuzumi* drum accents and rattling *suzu* (a small tree of bells used in Shintō ceremonies) and featuring Tabackin's flute, its subtle overtones floating above full-band section work stretched, strained, "bent" like the intonation of *gagaku* (traditional Japanese court) music itself. It's a powerful document.

Yet other Japanese musicians I'd talked to in the States, such as pianists Kotaro Tsukahara and Makoto Ozone (when the latter appeared with vibraphonist Gary Burton at a place called the Bach Dancing and Dynamite Society in Half Moon Bay, California), were simply not interested—or at least not yet—in incorporating native elements in their

19

work, feeling that "jazz" was just jazz, not necessarily Japanese or even American, finding inspiration in a host of sources from Bud Powell to tango, in Makoto's case. I'd found it interesting that Makoto Ozone told me that, should an interest in making use of indigenous Japanese elements take hold, he would need to "study" them, even though one might assume that, for him, they'd come with the territory, so to speak; they were a part of his background. I'd decided that I too—for such elements were decidedly *not* a part of my cultural inheritance—had better spend time arming myself with at least a rudimentary knowledge of what set Japan apart from other cultures in its approach to art.

The Hawaii International Jazz Festival was in its third year. Unlike the Monterey Jazz Festival (for which I had recently been commissioned to write a book celebrating its fortieth anniversary—just like our marriage!), Hawaii's event was still in its infancy. That is, it was a loose, somewhat casual affair (aside from a giant blowout at the Royal Hawaiian Hotel that would feature both Toshiko Akiyoshi and Tiger Okoshi the next night), but an affair befitting the "laid-back" islands. The festival lasted four days. The first night's concert featured the Four Freshmen (reconstituted) and Ann Patterson, saxophonist and leader of the seventeen-piece Maiden Voyage big band. A blues and Latin night offered John Hammond, Poncho Sanchez, and Willie K (short for William Kahaialii, a local proponent of something called "Lava Rock"). Daily clinics were held in the Lanai Room of the Waikiki Sheraton. They had been organized by Bunky Green, director of jazz studies at the University of North Florida, educational director of the Hawaii festival, and an excellent alto saxophonist himself. Among the workshops offered were Toshiko Akiyoshi's "Experiences as a Successful Woman in the Jazz World" and Tiger Okoshi's "How, When, and What to Practice."

I headed for the festival's temporary "office," a chaos-charged room once I found it, where a local wit serving as an official (who, when he later gave me his *meishi,* or business card, turned out to be Jim Shon, chair of the Energy and Environmental Protection Committee in the State of Hawaii House of Representatives) asked, when I requested phone numbers for Toshiko and Tiger, "You're not a stalker are you?"

"No," I replied, "I'm just a journalist."

"Same thing," he said.

I arranged to interview Toshiko Akiyoshi at noon the next day in room 426, the suite assigned her at the Waikiki-Sheraton. When I phoned for Tiger Okoshi, a desk clerk said, "Is he a guest or an employee?" When I finally got to the trumpeter, we agreed to meet the next day also, after his Royal Hawaiian Hotel sound check.

3

THE TIGER . . .

WHEN I MET TIGER OKOSHI at his sound check, the Royal Hawaiian Hotel—where that evening's performances would be held—was being lavishly decorated. A pink Waikiki prominence when I first arrived in the Islands, the hotel now seems buried among younger, more recently erected contenders. A circuitous path among them opens onto a swatch of lawn where, that morning, tables were being adorned with crisp pink cloth. Japanese lanterns, also pink, danced in a genial tropical breeze. The hotel's own Laura Ashley pink and green facade found resonance in tall palms and a green and pink canopied stage. A large ancient banyan tree seemed to regard this current face-lift with total indifference.

Trumpeter Tiger Okoshi was already on stage, dressed in a sleeveless green T-shirt and shades, looking very much like Miles Davis, tamed. He was trying out a wide range of effects—from growls to full shakes—on his trumpet, pushing the sound system to its limits but pleased, apparently, with the response. The tune was "St. Louis Blues." While the group that would accompany him, the Outtakes, did their thing, Tiger danced back and forth between mike and mixing board or else stood stock still, strumming his trumpet as if it were a guitar.

The sound check over, he immediately came down to where I was sitting and introduced himself. We started to talk, seated at one of the pink tables, but the Outtakes, now assisting vocalist Jimmy Borges, drove us inside the hotel to find some privacy. Seated beside the large window of a boutique selling the most current, and expensive, island fashions, Okoshi began by praising the Hawaii International Jazz Festival.

"Just getting back to Hawaii is a wonderful thing," he said, "no matter what the reason is. We have to keep this happening. The festival is only three years old. Three years old . . . you just start to walk!"

I explained that I was working on two projects simultaneously: my Japan jazz journey and a book celebrating the Monterey Jazz Festival's fortieth anniversary.

"See, see," he said, "you have to keep it *happening!*"

I could sense, right away, just how he'd earned the name "Tiger," for Tiger Okoshi is a man born to make and keep things "happening." I told him I'd read an article in *Zasshi* magazine in which he talked about his work with autistic kids in Boston. His face grew serious, intense.

"Do you remember the earthquake we had in Japan? The big one!"

"Yes," I replied. "Kobe."

"I had been living in the States since 1972, for twenty-four years, but I just happened to be back there *that day*. I was sleeping near my mom. Eighty years of Mom! And I saved her, and I saved all my brothers and their families, who were upstairs. *This* trumpet was buried. We also dug out some dead bodies—all that stuff."

Because of his Kobe experience, Tiger Okoshi has, for the last two years, been involved with about 120 students (ranging from age six to twenty) who are autistic and attend a school called Boston Higashi School (*higashi* means "east").

"But Japan is a country that is very tough on those minorities," Tiger said. "The Japanese have a tendency to push them away, a lot more so than in the U.S. So I thought, 'Let me take those kids in Japan by the hand and lead them *outside*.'"

In Japan, he facilitated nine classes with children from age seven to seventeen. He conducted a four-week session that included vibraphonist Gary Burton, pianist Makoto Ozone, and his friend Aydin Esen, "a genius pianist from Turkey." Tiger didn't just play jazz for the kids; he worked directly with them. "I'm jumping around a lot; sometimes I even got *kicked*. What I do is pull out a little yellow handkerchief and I say, 'This is a doll.' Then I put it on a table and I say, 'This is *me*.' Then everybody *sings*. I'm like a kindergarten teacher. Folk singers or rock musicians or jazz musicians may play concerts for those kids, but I wanted to be right in there! Those kids want to shake hands! They want *skinship!* They want to play my trumpet! I just want them not to be afraid to try to *come out* and try new things."

I apologized for having missed his workshop the previous morning, saying that one of the festival's officials (Jim Shon) had told me, "You've got to talk with Tiger about his approach." I said this man claimed the way Okoshi worked with kids was "absolutely magnificent."

"Well, I produced a recording called *Echoes of a Note* about two or three years ago," Tiger said now, "and I feel that we are the echoes of those jazz giants, of those big fat notes. Like Miles Davis, Dizzy, and Fats Navarro. Lee Morgan. You name it. Trane and Parker, Lester Young. All those people. Bix Beiderbecke. Those were *fat notes* they played for us, strong enough so that we can become the echo of them."

Echoes of a Note does not contain the standard homage of imitating or attempting to play like Louis Armstrong. You can't out-Armstrong Louis Armstrong, so, wisely, Tiger Okoshi decided to truly *transform* the music. He turned his respect into something truly original, totally his own. And the instrumentation is unusual: Bela Fleck on banjo and Gil Goldstein on accordion.

"I knew Bela and I'd always wanted to play with him. I thought he was very unique. I knew the accordion player too. I saw him with Pat Metheny's band and it sounded great. I thought, 'Man, the way you play the accordion!' So I asked him. My record company wanted me to do straight-ahead jazz, and I said, 'I want to use a banjo.' They said, 'Oh come on, Tiger. We don't need a banjo.' So I said, 'Check this guy out. Check him out.' So they did."

"They must have died when you mentioned the accordion."

"Once again, *I'm* the one who can hear what it sounds like. A Harmon mute and an accordion? A Harmon mute's *teeiiiiinnnn* sound to an accordion's *wha-wha-wha.* And you know the banjo's *tine-tine-tine,* all together." He began to orchestrate with his arms, reproducing the full ensemble sound. "It worked beautifully."

When I'd talked to Jim Shon the previous day, he'd said that Tiger was doing "great things with rhythm" in his workshop; that his instructional approach made effective use of *images,* so that kids could associate what they were playing with something else they knew.

"When we rehearse with new bands," Tiger Okoshi said now, "we have to have the written music. You have to put that music down on paper for students so they can see certain notes. But the *rhythm . . .* once you start to play . . . let's say I have a one-beat rest and the rhythm is one-two, one-two-three-four *kah! Kah!* That means one-*two*-three-four, one-*two*-three-four, but actually I want them to do *this.*" I won't attempt to repeat this phonetically, but here he went off on some wild scat flight.

"People say two and four means puh-*pah*-puh-*pah*-puh-*pah*-puh-*pah,*
but in between *puh* and *pah* there are tons of little things going on,
important rhythms, and *those* are the things I want to teach! If you are a
boxer, you cannot just go *boom-boom-boom-boom* all the time, because
the next time you'll get hit. So I tell them four/four is like eight/eight.
Same thing: eight eighth notes instead of four quarter notes. So I'm going
to divide one-two-three-four, one-two-three-four into one-two-three,
one-two, one-two-three, like three plus two plus two, or three plus three
plus two, or two plus three plus three . . ."

I wondered if the students could actually follow such higher mathematics. I barely could.

"Of course they can! I wrote out all the rhythms"—he was off
again on another fine elaborate scat sequence—"and I made everybody
sing it. So now on *two* it's not going to be like *um-pah;* it's like *chick-a-
chick-a-PAH.* That's the kind of thing I do. Rhythm things. And the harmony thing. There's rhythm and harmony and *feeling.* I cannot teach
anybody the feeling. I could talk about it. All about what a fool they are
because they are in love—that sort of thing."

"I was talking with Bunky Green yesterday," I said, "and he told
me, 'When I'm playing "'Round Midnight," I think about my wife, how
long we've been together, how much I care for her. I'm playing emotionally, but I always know when to come back in on the *changes.*'"

"Right, sure! But the truth is he's not really thinking about his *wife*
at all. Musicians just don't have that much *time.* We *say* it that way, that
we are thinking of someone else, but we are very busy just hearing a lot
of sounds. We don't have enough time, or space, to think about different
things. A lot of notes are going by besides your own sound. I come up
with a, well let's say a C-minor chord, something with C, E-flat and the
G and the B-flat. Those are the basic things. That is your *house,* and C is
the bed, and E-flat is the toilet, and the refrigerator and—what else do
you need? TV. All right. Those are the laws, and you can go back and
forth and do lots of things with that, but it's not enough. So we add some
tension, a few more fancy things maybe. A telephone. A mirror, or something like that. And along comes something a little more comfortable;
it's called a *scale.* And I show them some stuff just using the scale notes,
up and down. It's comfortable, but you can't go too far with it. You still
have to stay in your house. So gradually you think, 'Okay, those are the
basic chord notes, and I've added little *luxury* things that are called
scales.' And I say, 'Okay, there are some other notes between those scale

notes. They're called *approach* notes.' These are *pah-rah-TOR-ah, pah-rah-TOR-ah.*" Ascending, he illustrated the transitions for several measures, with fine pitch, a pleasing voice. "You are putting a few more things around your bed, around the TV, whatever . . ."

"To personalize it all?" I said. "The way people actually do their own rooms—so that what surrounds them is an extension of what they are as people?"

"Right, right, right! Now you've got this room with everything you want in it. All you need now is a girlfriend. I shall teach you how to go outside of the house, you know? That sort of thing."

During the sound check, I noticed him not just *telling* the drummer about something he wanted him to do but *acting it out* for him, as if Tiger were playing drums himself.

"I've played with the drummer, but not with the guitar and bass player before. It's the first time we've met, and that first meeting is always important. I can't bring my ego out and say, 'No, don't play *that.*' You can't do that; they don't want to hear a speech. It has to be a conversation, a dialogue, *our* conversation, the four of us. I cannot say, '*I* want to talk about *this,*' and have them reply, 'I don't want to talk about that.' But you know, some people try to do just that."

The drummer was Noel Okimoto, whom Tiger had played with at the same festival last year. The Outtakes had sent him their CD, so he knew how they played and "wasn't worried about a thing."

I mentioned a statement of his, again in the *Zasshi* magazine article, about Japanese musicians, how they are "very curious to begin with; they want to learn; they want to do their research. That they get really close to what is *supposed* to be done, yet you feel they should be looking for something different—their own jazz, their own message." He said he still felt that way, so I asked him if that last phrase referred to the actual use of native elements (and instruments) or just finding their own *voice,* their own style.

"I don't remember what came before and what came after when I said that, but learning the jazz language, people ask, 'How do I get into jazz? How can I improvise?' The answer is simple. 'Learn the language.' They reply, 'How?' 'People are talking all over the place,' I say, 'Pick up those CDs, whatever. Go out and listen and learn how they are talking to each other.' That's the main thing. And then there's that larger *echo*—all those big fat notes from the past that tell us, 'Go and do what *you* want to do.' I try to find another message from them than just playing the old notes or the *feeling* of topics we're talking about. God or whatever in a particular era, black or white—whatever the topic was. I'm no longer associated with that. My topics are more up to date, I hope. But I know those other vocabularies, and when to use them. I'm saving them for the right time. 'Whoo ho, he used *that* one. He *knows!* He knows what jazz is!' That's the whole thing. I've spent a lot of time thinking about jazz and playing jazz and talking about jazz. And hearing jazz. But some people in Japan are not that way at all. Because of the culture. It's a different culture. You just don't hear jazz all the time as you can in the States."

I mentioned something else he'd said in the *Zasshi* interview: "Jazz musicians in Japan have been close to the level of American musicians much more than Japanese baseball. . . . I play with the major leagues all the time." Did he still feel that way?

"Japanese musicians really learn how to *talk,* but they still cannot . . . well, I'm reluctant to say this, but it's a matter of conversation again, dialogue, not just giving a *speech.* If you practice with a music-minus-one tape, or a metronome, you're just *soloing.* It's not communicating. For small, stupid topics, that could be fine. For ten minutes we just talk about small things. But if all the heads want to explode with full knowledge, then you have to put down very tough words, hard words, and that's *not* just carrying on a small conversation. That's communication. That's the first time you truly understand what a simple word can mean. People say, 'How do you do?' But that should mean, 'I love you!'"

We were back to Louis Armstrong again. (What a wonderful world!) I asked him who his favorite Japanese players were.

"Makoto Ozone. We do a lot of duets now. I think today or next week he is going to be playing a Mozart piece, with Chick Corea and a symphony. He was practicing that during the autistic children's program in Asahikawa. After practicing he said, 'Tiger, you know what? Every time I play this piece, I can hear *you* playing all these melodies.' And I said, 'All right, why don't we do it?' So starting next year we may do a concert that is half just classical pieces, legit classical, and the second half jazz duets. You know you just keep looking for something different to do."

When I had talked to Makoto Ozone in California, he'd said that, although he admired Toshiko Akiyoshi's use of indigenous Japanese elements in *her* work, he was not really (yet) interested in working with traditional Japanese elements, or instruments, himself, but he was interested in "the tango." How did Tiger feel about mixing cultural elements?

"A long time ago, when I first heard some big band do that—maybe it was Toshiko, *shakuhachi* mixed with jazz—I hated the idea. You shouldn't mix up the cultures for business purposes. 'Oh, this is fun.' 'That's a typical Japanese way,' I said, 'a *mismatch*.' A mismatch of this musician and that musician. If you wanted to go to Japan for a gig, they'd say, 'Okay, but use this guy on drums, or use that . . .' 'Wait a minute,' I said, 'I have my own band.' And they said, 'Sorry.' You have to be very careful with those authentic instruments, I think. Once, McCoy Tyner was playing the koto. When I saw that, I just *left*." Here Tiger imitated, perfectly, the atrocious sound of thick strings imperfectly plucked. "It's okay, I guess, but it's just not my cup of tea. I don't want to mix those things up. Beauty is beauty *as is*. And the *shakuhachi*. I really respect the *shakuhachi* as is. It's one of the strongest sounds, I think."

So, no immediate plans for pulling *gagaku* music into his own recordings . . .

"I *might* do something like that some day, but I think I would try it in a different way. I would not ask *them* to play jazz music at all. Because of the different scale, the different intonation. Especially with a big band that goes"—here he imitated—again perfectly—the overwhelming collective sound of big band section work—"and then . . . there's the *shakuhachi*. I don't think people could even hear that really nice acoustic bamboo sound. And to use the *shakuhachi* sound on a synthesizer! I'm old-fashioned in that sense. If musicians like it so much, they should play together for the next twenty years. But I've never heard anyone do that. They just get together for business purposes. 'Oh, what a combination! Oh, that was successful! Nobody has done *that* before!' You know the Japanese. The highest, the fastest. Nobody has been *there* before. That's the thing. 'Oh, nobody has ever heard *that* combination. That was good. Good-bye!' But if you like that so much, why don't you stick with it until something really good comes out?"

We talked about his performance that night on the Royal Hawaiian stage, and he said that, should the group get a chance to do an encore, "I'm going to do a ridiculous thing—a really ridiculous thing. And if I don't get a chance, nobody will ever hear this . . ."

"Something *atarashii* [new]?"

"Yeah, yeah! We didn't rehearse this one. The encore. We didn't rehearse. But if you are there, you will see something really ridiculous."

That night, when Betty and I found our seats reserved at table fifty-seven on the Royal Hawaiian lawn, all of the tables were adorned with luau-abundant settings. An elaborate sound system provided music that seemed more rock than the fusion it was attempting to be, prompting Betty, who'd had an afternoon of gentle, sinuous swimming, to say, "This seems like odd music for a jazz festival."

When the live music started, the Outtakes came on first (had that been *their* CD playing before?) on a tune called "Devil's Foot." The Outtakes were followed by vocalist Jimmy Borges, a former Royal Hawaiian regular, his subsequent credentials ranging from Vegas to Rio. Decked out in a flaming white suit, he pointed to one of the members of the Outtakes and said, "He was almost my son-in-law," then broke into Hoagy Carmichael's "Skylark," one of Betty's favorite songs. Borges had the mannerisms, if not the chops, of Tony Bennett, but a good voice with which he offered "Happy Birthday" to a member of the audience recently turned twenty-one. ("To me that's just a game in Las Vegas," he said.) He closed with a Latin-tinged "Our Love Is Here to Stay."

Then the Tiger came on. And come on he did. He was dressed in a loose, flowing Gandhi shirt with mandarin collar and full sleeves, his handsome face framed by a full pitch-black head of hair that looked freshly tailored. He played "St. Louis Blues" much as he had at the sound check that afternoon, yet also *not* as he had that afternoon. He had a well-fed (dinner over) and strictly musically hungry audience in front of him now, and he did not let them down. The first few notes resembled "Summertime," but he slid into the familiar frame, that in turn replaced by his own solid invention. Tiger Okoshi's tone was "fat," rich, commanding, whether sweetly fluttering or going full force, and he has a stealthy way of ascending and descending, making full use of "anticipation notes." Okoshi is also quite a showman (as I expected), horn held aloft at dramatic angles, turning to coax more fill from his sidemen and smiling broadly when he got it.

After "St. Louis Blues," he joked, "That was a song I wrote . . . a long time ago," and I thought of what he'd said that afternoon about echoes.

"St. Louis Blues" is on his CD homage to Armstrong, *Echoes of a Note,* which also includes a playful, nearly teasing, muted, up-tempo "Hello Dolly" (as much a tip to Miles Davis as it is to "Pops"); a rock-out Mike Stern–supported (Stern is Tiger's friend from Berklee) "Saints Go Marching In"; Bela Fleck's handsomely banjo-inflected "St. James Infirmary" (Okoshi with the Harmon mute again, brooding with a twinkle in his eye); a wonderfully deliberately creaky "Old Rockin' Chair"; a soulful "Sleepy Time Down South" (with a lanquidly joyous banjo solo); and a respectful, lullaby-lovely "What a Wonderful World."

At the Royal Hawaiian Hotel, Tiger Okoshi offered a "song of mine" (as he said) called "Finders, Keepers." It's from another fine CD, *Two Sides to Every Story*—a riff tune in high register that starts out with a prodding, almost marchlike, Spanish-flavored beat. At home in any register, Okoshi seems to have "total field" vision, seeing where he wants to go in an instant and going there. Dizzying heights get combined with soft inflection, pinched tones with full blare. The CD version of this tune features a Jack DeJohnette drum solo described in the liner notes as "heroic," but Noel Okimoto wisely did not attempt to fill *those* shoes. The Outtakes worked well with Okoshi at the Royal Hawaiian concert, as the trumpeter acknowledged. "We just talked about the most important things," he told the audience, "and you heard that," adding that he'd just met the guitarist and bass player that afternoon.

The next tune was another original, "Fisherman's Song," one with a story attached—a story Tiger told. A boat returns to shore at five in the morning; seagulls are just waking up to check their wings out. The musical mood matched perfectly: "a really *quiet* story," as Okoshi had promised in his introduction, its melody offset by orange and vermilion lights dancing over the pink canopy beneath which the artists played, the audience humming the instantly memorable theme while Tiger let the silences between his spare, muted excursions speak. After a guitar solo, Okoshi's reentry was so soft he seemed to be playing offstage, even though he was standing directly in front of the mike. Again, on "Monday Blues," he showed his versatility, his range of tone, mood, and time, full pyrotechnics unleashed, the rhythm section providing a more than just adequate kick behind him.

Tiger Okoshi got the encore he craved, and the promised "ridiculous thing" turned out to be a new tune called "Easy for You to Say," one announced as "very very hard for me to play." Okoshi's excited performance was exacted at a breakneck tempo that threatened to leave the Outtakes in its wake, his own solo excursion impressive, full of daring and flare, its impossibly fleet ascents befitting the expansiveness of his unique personality. After, he thanked the crowd, saying, "Now we're going to bring up my hero from Japan, Toshiko Akiyoshi"—another great artist I was eager to hear, and meet.

. . . AND THE LADY

I felt as if I had been trying to track Toshiko Akiyoshi down for ages. Back in the States, I had phoned New York and, learning that she was coming to the West Coast, had tried to arrange a meeting with her when she performed in Carmel, California, a concert Betty and I attended— but we could not find a suitable time for an interview. Now, I had arranged to talk with Toshiko the afternoon before the concert at the Royal Hawaiian Hotel, and the setting in which I met her (one of my long-time musical heroes) was nearly comically exquisite after the long chase. We met on the fourth floor of the Waikiki Sheraton, in the suite of rooms she'd been assigned there, overlooking a dream view of the surfer-studded green gin ocean and stately, if too often photographed, Diamond Head. A half-empty bottle of Merlot sat perched on a dining-room table, along with a bowl of fruit. Toshiko Akiyoshi greeted me wearing a loose beige leisure outfit that resembled Baghdad pajamas— there was a pewter shine or glow to them. We sat down on a long couch, I cranked up the tape recorder, and for the next hour or more she was straightforward, serious, witty, maybe slightly sleepy still (it was noon, musician's noon), and gracious.

Back in California, I had listened to much of her recorded music. Toshiko Akiyoshi is well represented on the *History of King Jazz Recordings* Akira Tana had sent me before I left, first with her trio in 1961 (which featured San Francisco drummer Eddie Marshall), playing tunes like "Long Yellow Road," an original whose initial deliberately trudging, halting persistence is converted to fleet and feisty, almost grandstanding bop; "Hakone Twilight"; "Kisarazu Jinku" (a traditional Japanese song with Latinized rhythms); and "Deep River." She also performed with a quintet that featured alto saxophonist (and fellow Berklee grad) Sadao Watanabe and three fine Japanese drummers taking turns: Masahiko Togashi, Hideo Shiraki, and Takeshi "Sticks" Inomata. This quintet offered jazz standards such as Miles Davis's "So What," Charlie Parker's "Donna Lee," and a much lesser-known tune by Charlie Mariano (to whom Toshiko was once married), "Watashi no Bēthoben" ("My Beethoven"). But mostly I'd been listening to pieces by the Toshiko Akiyoshi Jazz Orchestra, featuring her long-term husband Lew Tabackin, pieces in which she had deliberately striven for "Japanese" effects.

At a 1991 Carnegie Hall concert, Toshiko presented "Children of the Universe," a work commissioned by Yokohama City for a world peace conference, a work she prefaced by saying, "Basically I wanted to say that we are all connected, but that sounds like a New York telephone commercial." Tabackin's flute and the sudden Noh cry "Yoohhhh!" merge—the latter stretched like silk to a breaking point, registering surprise, a full orchestra drone picking up on the intonation perfectly, the whole a powerful cry of celebration, a paean for peace, Hiromitsu Nishikawa's *tsuzumi* drum accents increasing in rapidity and volume.

Akiyoshi's *Kourakan Suite* was commissioned by the city of Fukuoka, in Kyushu, and celebrates the 1980s excavation of an ancient guest house containing a "wondrous variety" of centuries-old artifacts that some say belonged to a group of people who had migrated from Iran, along the silk roads, "one thousand years ago." According to Toshiko, they were "looking and hoping for happiness and prosperity." This "multicultured suite" is presented in two parts. The first, "Kourakan," celebrates the discovery by way of Walt Weiskopf's soprano sax and Toshiko's piano solo, both seeming to reenact the journey itself with all its high risk and precarious hope, and a final, nearly languid (fatigued) arrival. The second portion, called "Prayer," features the voice of Nnenna Freelon (Toshiko's daughter, actress/singer Monday Michiru, sang this part at the initial performance in Fukuoka), a sustained, melismatic call to prayer offset by gongs and bleating horns, very Ellingtonian (the Duke is one of Toshiko's heroes).

Other pieces with a strong Japanese flavor are "Desert Lady-Fantasy," composed by Lew Tabackin, based on *Suna No Onna* (Woman in the Dunes), a novel by Kobo Abe, the musical rendering so vivid and faithful to its source you can feel the grit of sand on your body and in your teeth: a Bolero-like progression, a light slightly kinky vamp mounting to screeching escape and pursuit and ending with a resigned drone and mournful flute and bass clarinet work that matches the fate of the novel's hapless dune-trapped "hero" or protagonist. The piece also reminded Toshiko of Northern Africa, and she wove the otherworldly singing of "Somalian ladies" into the whole. "Children in the Temple Ground" begins with traditional Japanese chant, a simple pentatonic piano theme, Toshiko's delicate touch offset by not so delicate percussion, then a near reverent mood sustained throughout. Such pieces led Lew Tabackin to comment on just how much Toshiko draws on "her own culture, not fighting it like so many foreign jazz musicians who try to prove themselves by being ultra-American. She achieves a special kind of oneness."

Seated overlooking a glittering blue-green Pacific Ocean, I started our interview by mentioning a friend of mine who, having joined the army in 1954 and serving in the Honor Guard in Tokyo, met Toshiko and wrote to me saying, "She's one of the best I've ever heard; I wish you could hear her someday." I showed her the *omiyage* (souvenir) my friend had sent me from the Blue Chateau Tea Jazz Salon forty-one years ago, the same card I had shown Eiji Kitamura, much to his surprise.

"My goodness, the Blue Chateau!" Toshiko exclaimed.

At my request, she began to recreate that postwar jazz scene, when in the summer of 1946, she returned to Japan from Manchuria, where her family had been living. Shortly after that she started to play professionally.

"My father could no longer provide a piano, so I took a job in a dance hall so I could play the piano there. That was in Fukuoka, quite far from Tokyo. I don't know what was going on in Tokyo at the time. I didn't get there until maybe a year and a half later. I spent ten months in Fukuoka. They needed dance halls for American troops, and they had classifications"—she laughed—"like NCO clubs, officer's clubs, sergeant's clubs—what have you. Of course the Japanese wanted dance halls too, so there was a shortage of musicians. Consequently, there were some very strange combinations in groups. For example, in the group that I got my first job with, the leader was an ex-navy bandleader who played violin, so we had that, alto saxophone, accordion, drums, and piano. No bass. That *was* a very odd combination! But you could *pass*

33

with an odd group like that, because they didn't have enough musicians."

The music the group played was based on "Hit Kits" published by an American service club. These Hit Kits came out twice a month and were basically lead sheets for individual songs, although not really a fake book, because there might be just a four-bar introduction for "Shoo Fly Pie" or "Five Minutes More," or, with luck, the melody and lyrics and simple piano accompaniment.

"That's what our leader had and I don't know where he got them, but basically we would just play from that. I didn't know anything about chord changes, so I had to learn very quickly. I'd never seen those changes before. I think that most groups were like that then."

"Was there any *context* for those songs? Had you heard them before?"

"No, I had never heard them. Any of them. But you know those songs have a very simple form and I have a pretty good ear, so I sort of got by, just like everybody else. No one was playing *great* in those days. An interesting thing: at the time they had a *fee,* and there was a kind of exam. What would you call it? Not really a contest. But there was a Japanese—quote unquote—*authority* in the jazz field. Every group had to go and play for a committee, and *they* would assign you a special classification. A, B, C, something like that. The reason they had that was probably because most of the jobs were really for Americans."

These ratings seemed to exist in order to "just set fees." You were paid according to your special classification. The first group Toshiko played with worked in Japanese dance halls. "I think I got a thousand yen a month, which was quite a lot of money in those days. Musicians then, because there was not enough housing, were also given a place to live."

Some big bands existed, what Toshiko calls "the Glenn Miller type." Five saxophones, usually three trombones, and three trumpets, sometimes four. The American clubs featured stock arrangements, "*really* stock": a four-bar intro, then some modulation, the middle part saved for a singer.

"I didn't know what a stock chart was, so the first time I heard that I thought, 'Oh wow, how great! Someone *arranged* that!' When I started I was in a small town, but they already had a couple of clubs for Americans. And there were about two or three clubs for the Japanese. I played

34

in that first band, then I got a job in a better band, and then a few months later I left Fukuoka and went to Tokyo."

In a video about Toshiko Akiyoshi called *Jazz is My Native Language*, she says that her parents—especially her father—were not at all happy about her playing jazz.

"No, they weren't! Traditionally, in the middle-class Japanese family, the father is the provider and the mother, well, her job is usually that of the 'architect' of the household. She handles financial allocations and what have you. If you have a daughter, she is not supposed to go to work. Until the time you get married, you stay home. So here was a problem. Not only was I going out and playing in dance halls, which was something unthinkable in my family's mind, but after World War II, in which my father lost all of his assets, the degree of order in the family structure collapsed, so to speak. I was sixteen at that time, and my parents had lost a certain amount of authority. Maybe that's why my mother was much more understanding. She tried to talk to my father for me, for he was terribly upset—although he really couldn't prevent me. It wasn't the music so much, I think, as the kind of *places* you played in, where you worked. A dance hall was like a *bar*, and my God, that was something unthinkable to my father—that his daughter would be playing in a bar!"

When Toshiko arrived in Tokyo in 1948, people like Sleepy Matsumoto were already playing. Drummer George Kawaguchi was already something of a star.

"I saw him playing in a dance hall one afternoon, and I was really impressed. You know, WOW!" She laughed. "Needless to say, there was much more jazz activity in Tokyo. Well, maybe I shouldn't say 'jazz.' It was mostly dance music. There weren't any *jazz clubs* per se. In Japan, what we call a 'live house' today didn't actually appear until 1952."

I had heard that people like Hampton Hawes and Cannonball Adderley were stationed in Japan around this time.

"Cannonball—not that I know of. But Hampton Hawes was. He came in the same year that JATP [Jazz at the Philharmonic] came, so that's got to be '52, I think. An interesting thing was each military band knew who was going to be stationed in Japan, and each tried to get those people in its band, if they liked them. Yokohama had the 289th Army Band. And Tokyo had an air force band called the 293rd, I think. But the Yokohama band wanted Hamp, so I guess they pulled strings, and he ended up in Yokohama instead of going to Korea or someplace like that. And there were a few other jazz players before Hamp came."

Toshiko listened mostly to available "V discs," which, according to her, contained many different kinds of music, big band and otherwise. The first time she had access to those records was when she got a job in an officer's club band, in Fukuoka. In the afternoon, when there was no one in the club, she could practice.

"They had a large record player and a lot of V discs. I heard Duke Ellington's 'Diminuendo in Blue' and 'Crescendo in Blue,' and also Harry James's 'It's Been a Long Long Time.' With its vocal. And I think Willie Smith played about a four-bar solo. No, it was an eight-bar solo in the middle part."

"Was Bud Powell on any of those records?"

"No, I heard Bud Powell much later. Much later. There wasn't really much *jazz* on those records, I think. Duke Ellington's band just happened to be there, in a big band collection. But none of those small jazz groups were on there. The closest thing was the Gene Krupa Trio, with Charlie Ventura, on 'Dark Eyes.' They actually came to Japan, sometime like '51 or '52? I'm not quite sure, but I know they came. Maybe it was later. There was a USO tour. Oscar Pettiford came too. They went to different camps on the USO tour, but they didn't bring a pianist because most of the places they came to, the army or navy clubs, didn't have a piano. And Les Brown's band came to Japan, for the American troops. The first performance strictly for Japanese was Jazz at the Philharmonic, in 1952. They were in Tokyo. Charlie Shavers, Roy Eldridge, Bill Harris, Flip Phillips, and Benny Carter. And one more saxophonist. Willie Smith I think it was. And of course the Oscar Peterson Trio. And Ella Fitzgerald too."

"Is that when Oscar Peterson first heard you?"

"That's the first time, yes. That was the first time I heard him . . . and he heard me. I was pretty much a copycat of Bud Powell in those days. I had a quartet and we played in the evening. I also had a kind of all-star quintet that played in a jazz club in the afternoon. That club opened on October 15, 1952. If it wasn't for that club, Oscar probably would not have had a chance to hear me. JATP came at the very beginning of November, so the timing was quite right."

In 1956, Toshiko left Japan for Berklee College of Music, in Boston.

"I think it was on the strength of a record I put out. The school needed publicity. It was a very small school then. Just 340 students or so. So that worked out very well for both of us."

An amazing film clip exists of Toshiko Akiyoshi's appearance on the popular TV show "What's My Line." She enters the studio in a kimono and writes her name in kanji on a blackboard and then, as her profession, writes "jazz pianist" beneath it. In *Jazz Is My Native Language,* Toshiko says, "I really have no part in jazz music. I come from a different musical culture, and that's always considered a handicap."

That was *her* conception in Japan at the time. "It was *felt,*" she said. "If you think about it, jazz is basically a fusion of Europe and Africa. If you want to be really technical, we were at one time—maybe a thousand or a million years ago—all the same, but basically the *oriental* element is not really *in* jazz. The jazz fusion was born in America. In the days I was talking about, people thought music from the Philippines had better jazz *feeling* than Japanese. It was natural, logical—and we're talking now about forty-five or fifty years ago—because the Philippines was under American colonization. Therefore they had been exposed to jazz for a much longer period of time than the Japanese. When I began to play, people had an expression. They said, 'Her playing has the smell of *butter [batākusai].*' Which meant it wasn't Japanese. So at that time being Japanese was considered a handicap. That's the way it was. And I'm sure that if you have that quote from the video, you must also have what I said about twenty years ago, when the Duke died. I had decided by then that my Japanese heritage was a positive thing. I decided to look at it positively rather than negatively. *That* was my turning point."

"When did you first *consciously* incorporate Japanese traditional elements into your music? Was 'Kogun' the first piece?"

"I think it was 'Kogun.' No, actually, if I were to say the very first one, it's got to be 'Sumiya,' which I wrote in 1967. I had a Town Hall concert and I decided to try to show just about everything I could do, and hopefully somebody would *notice.* So I produced 'Sumiya' for that concert. But no one noticed. That piece utilized certain sounds from *gagaku* music. I had a trumpet player doing them, against the theme. On 'Kogun' I first utilized Japanese instruments. I'd always wanted to use them. I always liked the *tsuzumi,* but no one had used those drums before. I think it was one of those 'try to see if it's worthwhile,' or worth it, things."

"Was it difficult?"

"Of course it was difficult! The point is: if you're just going to use it for the sake of using it, then that's not hard. And it will come out that way: very superficial. But if you turn it into a *blend,* if you bind it all into one music . . . for example, one thing I like to say is, if you put sand inside a clam shell, you get a *pearl.* You just *bother* the shell a little, so it tries to integrate the sand *being there.* That's the same kind of thing. It shouldn't sound like . . . well, when you eat food and one little seed or pit or whatever gets in there and it's unpleasant; it shouldn't be like that. It has to be integrated to the point that it *all* sounds together. And *that's* hard. The first time is really hard. The second time is hard too, but the first time is always hard. I think the tendency for most Japanese players is to stay away from it. I've heard a few people try, most fusion not strictly jazz groups, because they offered me their cassettes, but they were not quite . . . they didn't sound very Japanese. There's nothing wrong with that, but if you are infusing something into the music, a different element, it should become *richer*—that's the important part. If you infuse an element and it just remains something else, that's not what I'm trying to do."

I asked her about some specific pieces, such as "Children in the Temple Ground."

"That's a Japanese folk song. I just orchestrated that one. The Japanese music is basically *gagaku* music. It didn't have any harmony, so we gave it some. This is the only song I can think of that is pure instrumental music, using the *biwa* [Japanese lute] and *okedō* [offstage drum used in Kabuki]. This song was written around the time of Haydn and Mozart. But most of them, as you know, were meant to accompany lyrics, the story, in Bunraku [puppet theater] or Kabuki. And as you know, there was no harmony. But if you look at it in a slightly different way, it's quite open to inventing harmony, so . . . I did."

Other pieces in which she incorporated Japanese elements?

"There's the *minamoto* [origin, source] piece, the one we played at Carnegie Hall. It's called "Children of the Universe." And *Kourakan Suite,* which employed Buddhist chants. Different types of chants. A brand-new piece I just recorded—we have to mix that next week—also employs some Japanese music. So I have a few."

Toshiko has made several appearances at the Monterey Jazz Festival—the first with a 1973 Piano Playhouse featuring her, Ellis Larkins, Billy Taylor, and John Lewis; the last with Tabackin, bassist Ray Drummond, and drummer Eddie Marshall in 1987. Because I was working on that festival's official history, I asked her about those appearances, most of which were memorable to her—especially the Piano Playhouse and a first 1974 appearance of her big band. At the time, she was thinking of quitting jazz because she didn't believe she'd done "anything to change the pianistic world"; her career needed a boost—the band a critical success—and, according to Lew Tabackin, "people got the idea of the potential of this band, and the greatness of Toshiko's music—thus launching *its* career."

Toshiko Akiyoshi told me that this year marked her fiftieth anniversary in jazz and the fortieth of her arrival in this country.

"Many things are happening in Japan. First of all, in June, Yamaha has an annual jazz festival that's basically for Japanese jazz musicians, and this year, because of my fiftieth year as a career, I was there. On July 31, I have to go back to Japan for a concert that is not jazz but in the classical field. They want me to do something *different*. And I will have a fiftieth-anniversary concert tour in October. So there are a few things happening. And a book that I promised to write seventeen years ago, an autobiographical book, is coming out this year."

"One last question? In the video, you made a comment on Lew's flute playing, that you want that *shakuhachi* sound . . ."

"Yes, yes. It's not just a scale, as in the West, or making a phrase or melody. In Japanese Zen Buddhism there are what are called 'night shadows.' It's a different *side* of a note, that sound. It's *bending* notes, and there's a special French flute that accommodates this. But Lew first just *did* it; then he began to listen to *shakuhachi* masters. On 'Kogun,' he just *did it.*"

That night, at the Royal Hawaiian, Toshiko took her seat at the piano and frowned.

"I asked someone to have a telephone directory here," she said, with mock peevishness, or maybe the real thing. "And I find a *pillow*. A pillow is not adjustable, but a telephone directory is."

While festival officials frantically rushed off in search of a telephone book to replace the pillow, the trio launched into "Long Yellow Road," a tune that was written—she later said—"after I came to the United States and took the very long road to being a jazz musician." In the middle of the piece, someone rushed on stage with *two* telephone directories, and the audience applauded. The tune came to a concert-lavish close, and Toshiko seemed content: with the opener and with the now perfectly adjusted piano bench. She played "Remembering Bud,"

39

followed by Powell's own "Un Poco Loco"—the former tune's haunting slow elegiac stride offset by the latter's steady left-hand configurations and fierce rhythm. Toshiko has a habit of kicking her left leg straight out when pleased with an accent or particular effect, and she also scat sings or hums to herself as she plays, sounding like a subdued version of the truth-disclosing medium who appears in the movie *Rashomon,* creating an eerie disclosive effect, but I like it.

At both concerts she played "a fairly new song," an original written for "the small village of Morita, five thousand population, babies and everyone," a piece commissioned for the town's new amphitheater, which was capable of holding the entire population. "Most places just have *pachinko* [Japanese pinball] parlors," she added, "so I thought this town was great. Apples and rice. In wintertime they have nothing to do but wait for spring." This tune was followed by the sea changes of "Haru No Umi" (The Sea in Springtime), a song she said was "famous in Japan," written by Michio Miyagi, a blind koto player whose family, after Toshiko recorded the piece, phoned to tell her "they didn't want it played that way . . . but if Mr. Miyagi were alive," Toshiko added now, "I think he'd probably get a kick out of it."

At the Royal Hawaiian concert, Akiyoshi brought on Gabe Balthazar, introducing him as "my very old friend and your hero," and the two played "Polka Dots and Moonbeams," the alto saxophonist exploiting his full range from basement soul notes to high squeal over the pianist's tasteful comping. They closed with "Bop Suey," sixteen jazz standards that included everything from "Confirmation," "Salt Peanuts," "Donna Lee," and "Now's the Time," to "How High the Moon" ("Birdology 101," as Balthazar dubbed it), and they were rewarded with a standing ovation.

On the last night of the Hawaii International Jazz Festival, Betty and I attended a concert celebrating the event's educational program. "We're giving away more money tonight than any other jazz festival in existence," director Abe Weinstein proudly announced. The evening's program, called Scholarship Night, featured the Punaho (a local private high school) Shades of Blue Jazz Band and an aggregate made up of students selected by band directors from all over the island of Oahu. They were joined by Tiger Okoshi, who came on stage to tear up the place with "I Remember Clifford." This was followed by stellar horn work on

Count Basie's "Shiny Stockings" and a rocking, steady homage to the "fat notes" of Louis Armstrong on "Summertime."

When we left Hawaii, we flew over Kauai, that island I still regard as our lost paradise, in spite of whatever startling changes may have been inflicted upon it. Flying over Kauai, high in the sky, we convinced ourselves we could see the Wailua River and the "only open spot," which once served as our Garden of Eden for a single summer, converted now—we've been told—to a tract of single-story houses. But I didn't care. I had too much good recent jazz music still singing in my head and much more to come, I knew, in Japan. From this point on in our flight we saw, as Betty wrote in her diary, "nothing but ocean."

TOKYO: MASAHIKO SATOH

WHAT ARE YOU STUDYING NOW?" Betty asked on the flight from Oahu to Tokyo.

"Some Japanese aesthetic principles," I said. "Want to hear about them?"

"I'd like to go to Paris," she replied, staring out the window at an ocean of clouds.

Actually I knew she was in a fairly good mood, even having settled for second-best, this first leg of the trip, landing in Hawaii—which we'd obviously enjoyed richly and which, thanks to Tiger Okoshi and Toshiko Akiyoshi, had added to my slowly accumulated store of knowledge about jazz in and from Japan.

"*Yūgen,*" I said.

"Sounds like a person's name. Or maybe some kind of dog food. What is it?"

"An aesthetic concept implying the conveyance of an emotion without explicitly stating it. A level of beauty that transcends the surface of materials, yet remains in harmony with them. It radiates mystery, a sort of spiritual essence."

"That's nice," she said. "Being subtle."

"Right! Want to learn about *sabi* and *wabi*?"

"Are they twins?"

"No. Separate concepts. *Sabi* is austere simplicity tinged with melancholy. Appreciating loneliness, poverty, or even desolation. A desirable quality found in everything from Japanese poetry to music to the tea ceremony. It literally means 'rust,' the rust of age, that greenish-blue patina formed by surface oxidation, the 'feel' of antiquity, a special kind of beauty that's the result of aging."

"Like us," she said.

"Well, sure, if you want to think of it that way. Whereas *wabi* is more like a mood: tranquility, especially of a rustic nature. It literally means 'quiet' and carries the connotation of refined, harmonious simplicity. It's related to *shibui,* which is restrained beauty, a holistic approach, highly restrained classic beauty."

"Like me."

"Right again—exactly! And the last concept, and in some ways the most important, the one that governs them all, is *aware,* or *mono no aware:* sensitivity to things, all those moving, touching aspects of human existence that inspire poignancy, sorrow, sensibility. You know who dug this stuff? Van Gogh. He said he envied the Japanese and the great clarity that all things have for them. He said their art is as simple as breathing and that they could make a figure with just a few sure strokes, as if it were as easy an act as buttoning one's waistcoat."

"*He* went to Paris."

"For a while, yes. But when he moved from there to Arles, he left all of his Japanese prints behind, saying he no longer needed them because all he had to do was keep his eyes open. 'Your perception changes,' he said, 'and you look more as the Japanese do; you experience color differently.'"

"So what's any of this have to do with Japanese jazz?"

My wife, with her fundamental practicality, has a way of stopping me in my tracks. "Hmmm," I wondered, "just what does it all have to do with jazz from Japan?" I turned back to her. "That's what I hope to find out," I said, smiling.

Mist, mist, and more mist. Rectangular fields of rice, wide, green, growing within the mist. Slivers of rivers beneath the landscape's skin. That was my first impression of Japan. Then an occasional freeway and clusters of tile-roofed homes. Closer to Tokyo, you begin to notice the customary city stuff, although most of it is labeled by or couched in the still—for all my linguistic efforts—mostly indecipherable kanji. What's customary are shipping derricks, construction cranes, a river rendered dismal by heavy industry, commercial canals, loading and unloading zones, high-rise apartments (with futons hung out to air), a fully lit baseball field, and, not at all customary in the States (we have space!), transparent green-tented driving ranges—many of them. Then a single sign in *eigo* (English): BMW.

We found ourselves lodged in a giant snarl of traffic and just sat there, somewhere along the forty-kilometer trek from Narita Airport to Tokyo. Moving once more, the closer we got to the city, the more we found it shut out, each set of freeway lanes enclosed within, not subtle, tasteful *shōji*, but giant ugly screens made of wire mesh.

I made my first significant sociological discovery about Japan in the restroom at Narita Airport. Japanese men, attending to bodily necessities, are *very* vocal, very social, even at the urinal, natural relief accompanied by grunts and groans and sighs of pleasure that rival the spontaneous effusions of *taiko* drummers. In his brilliant, very loose treatise on the Japanese sense of beauty, *In Praise of Shadows,* Junichiro Tanizaki shocked Western critics (one called the account "eloquent, though sometimes perverse") by bestowing lavish praise on the native toilet, calling it "truly a place of spiritual repose," listing a host of delights: listening to softly falling rain, the chirping of insects, the songs of birds, etc. "Here, I suspect, is where haiku poets over the ages have come by a great many of their ideas"—that could only be experienced while indulging in an activity we in the West are not inclined to celebrate much in polite conversation. The great novelist makes much of the ability of the Japanese to make poetry "of everything in their lives," transforming what "by rights should be the most unsanitary room in the house into a place of unsurpassed elegance." I'm not sure just what he would have made of being stuck on the freeway. We could only entertain ourselves, once we started to move again and actually entered the city of 8.5 million souls, by scanning the giant billboards that grace buildings with the poetry of our own language: Virginia Slims, Coca-Cola, Kent, Fuji Futures. Office employees were hard at work beneath them. Hordes of them, it seemed, were clustered in brightly lit rooms that all looked alike.

Once safely ensconced at the Asia Center, we realized the place would prove perfect for our needs. Our room was snug, a tree poised just outside the window, with a view of a garden and patio below. We also had the deep tub we'd dreamed of, and mostly *silence*. Betty commented on the fact that in a city of 8.5 million people, "we have no traffic noise at night." No noise aside from that of a very conspicuous crow in the neighborhood, who would start cawing around five in the morning and was, on occasion, still at it at noon. From the size of his voice, I took him to be about as big as a sumo wrestler.

My quest to find the consummate Japanese jazz musician took far less time than I anticipated. If I'd hoped eventually to meet someone in Japan who had absorbed the best that the American tradition could offer, mastered its vocabulary, and could play on a level equal to that of the finest international performers (yet also retained the best from his roots, remaining true to his own cultural imperatives, having made maximum progress toward a legitimate synthesis of jazz and traditional Japanese music)—well, I did so within my first three days in Tokyo.

Masahiko Satoh was not the first musician I saw after we arrived in Japan. I called pianist Kotaro Tsukahara and critic Yozo Iwanami, both of whom I'd met in California at concerts given by clarinetist Eiji Kitamura (Kotaro playing piano with Eiji's quintet). However, Satoh was a significant central figure, a genuine *find,* who would become a sort of touchstone when I talked to subsequent musicians. It would prove impossible *not* to compare their range of contributions to his, which were considerable, whether they leaned toward the "left" (free, avant-garde, or fully improvised music) or "right" (ardently attached to the mainstream). Masahiko Satoh also seemed the legitimate heir to aesthetic principles set forth by Toru Takemitsu, a composer I would learn he much admired.

I had heard Masahiko Satoh described as a "genius" before I met him, and after talking with him, I can support the appellation, but he had none of the airs of genius. And photographs I've seen don't do him justice. In them he appears slightly haughty, distant, stern, proud. Or in other photos, he resembles someone who might have emerged from a high-tech garage experimental phase and gone instantly from nerdhood to success in the mold of Bill Gates. In real life, Masahiko Satoh is a handsome man with fine "samurai" features, a relaxed, articulate, engaging man, even slightly hip. Satoh was quite laid-back when he chose to be and prone to humor. We met in the lounge of the Asia Center.

He discussed his brief Americanization at the hands of the Berklee College of Music. Satoh was the fourth Japanese to attend, preceded by Toshiko Akiyoshi, Sadao Watanabe, and bassist Yasuo Arakawa, with whom he would team up while a student. He discovered that much of the school's core curriculum was, as he told *Cadence* magazine in an interview, "a review of what I already got in my musician's life."

Masahiko Satoh started to play jazz piano at seventeen and already had nine years experience when he arrived in Boston at twenty-six, although this time around, the lessons came "logically." He told me he had made abundant use of the college library. "I only stayed at Berklee for two years, but every day I went to the library to read as many books as I could." He read *Perspectives of New Music* and Norbert Wiener's *Cybernetics*. He got interested in serial and dodecaphonic music. At that time there were no synthesizers. Both Columbia and Princeton Universities had IBM 7020s, "a computer big as a room. I also read about world music, about ethnic music as a source, and those were the major things I learned."

Such studies were offset by other lessons acquired firsthand "at jazz clubs." He heard Chick Corea ("playing upright piano at a suburban jazz club in Boston"), Miles Davis (in his Herbie Hancock, Eddie Gomez, Tony Williams, Wayne Shorter incarnation), plus John Coltrane, Bill Evans, and Sarah Vaughan. Satoh felt he was finally getting a chance to see jazz actually being "created," and it was "the most impressive thing in my life in Boston." Art Blakey heard him play just once and asked him to join a Jazz Messengers tour, but Satoh remained in school and settled for a job in a Japanese food shop, working for $1.50 an hour, earning thirty to forty dollars each month. "I also played piano at a dining room in a hotel on one corner of Boston Common Park for seventy dollars a week."

When he returned to Japan, he called agents and asked for a job as a studio musician. He had studied composition and arranging at Berklee (and has susequently arranged for Nancy Wilson, Helen Merrill, Art Farmer, and Toots Thielmans). He needed money to support his mother (an East Asian concession many Americans might not make) and also pay his own rent. "Of course I like jazz," he told *Cadence,* "but it was necessary to be a musician for money." He also made the decision to further steep himself in Japanese culture, a decision he'd made *before* Berklee (thinking he would be away from Japan for at least four years), visiting temples, listening to traditional music such as Shōmyō (Buddhist chant) and contemporary works written for *shakuhachi, biwa,* and full orchestra by Toru Takemitsu.

In 1971, Satoh also performed at the Berlin Jazz Festival with bassist Yasuo Arakawa (his companion from Berklee days) and drummer Masahiko Ozu. This event was described as "a turning point in [Satoh's] career," and his "unrestricted piano improvisation" employing a ring modulator ("a device practically unknown in Europe at the time") was highly praised. One piece he played, "Poise," makes ample use of silence and handsomely distorted (slightly "alien," sound-modulated) chords, dynamics that keep you on your toes, the textures running from nibbling to rippling to crackling to a distinct growl. Yet Satoh somehow manages to retain the flavor of a silent, spacious landscape. Another piece, "Route 29 E," gets off to a charged start—sound transformed into another element, color: something you *see* as well as hear, the variety suggesting the risk and surprise of an open road with few familiar landmarks—followed by a kamikaze- (divine wind) driven, drum-saturated storm greeted, at the close, by much applause. The Germans dug it.

In his *Cadence* interview, Satoh talked a bit about an active Tokyo free jazz scene in 1969, and I asked if he would reflect on those days now.

"Nineteen sixty-nine, wow! There was a place called New Jazz Hall. It was a floor above the Pit Inn, used for storage of instruments, drum sets. It was a big space, by Japanese standards. They had an old grand piano up there. Some musicians said, 'This would be a good place for doing something of our own,' so they borrowed it, actually for *nothing* as far as cost. It was managed by musicians and not the owner of the Pit Inn. And they started to play whatever they liked. The members were trumpeter Itaru Oki, who lives now in France. Mototeru Takagi, tenor saxophone and bass clarinet. Sometimes—he's quite popular now— trumpeter Toshinori Kondo. They were mostly young musicians. Yet at the same time there was another big group of free musicians, like Yosuke Yamashita and drummer Masahiko Togashi. They did not appear in the New Jazz Hall because they were already quite popular on the jazz scene, so they played downstairs, in the Pit Inn itself."

"Just the youngsters upstairs . . ."

"Yes! I played downstairs, but sometimes upstairs too, by myself or conducting some sort of big 'composer's orchestra,' maybe five to ten horn players. There was a large free jazz movement at that time."

In the interview I'd read, Satoh said he didn't know about groups like the Art Ensemble of Chicago or other free jazz movements elsewhere at that time, just as contemporary avant-garde artists in Russia had told me they didn't know about movements in the 1920s similar to their own but felt that compatible cultural conditions had produced the same kind of music, years later.

"That was partly correct in Japan too," Masahiko Satoh said now, "because I really didn't know about the many movements abroad. Several years before this time I had decided to establish *myself,* my own style, *not* listening to orthodox foreign jazz, or any other type, because I started my career copying Oscar Peterson . . ."

"Weren't you playing one night somewhere and turned around and Oscar was *there?*"

"Right, right! So I decided that no matter who came along, this was going to be *my* music. In 1969, I hadn't been listening to many records, so I didn't know about the Art Ensemble or groups like that. But many young players did know about them at that time."

I mentioned the issue of imitation that kept coming up with regard to jazz in Japan and said that Toshiko Akiyoshi had told me that when she started to play, people said her style had "the smell of *butter,*" meaning it wasn't Japanese.

"The older critics were very conservative. They were always very eager to decide someone's *position.* Was he in the school of this or that guy. But one thing I don't understand today is, among the musicians who are in their early twenties, we have so many good bebop musicians in Japan. They *love* that 1950s acoustic style . . ."

"The Wynton Marsalis disease?"

"Exactly, right!" Satoh said, laughing. "I studied bebop at that time, of course, but then, bebop was *contemporary* music. It was *the* live music, but today bebop is like . . ."

"*Gagaku?*"

"*Gagaku,* yeah! That's right. Maybe it's easy to take something out of that bebop style, because it's established; it's solid. There are many theory books and schools and classes, so it's relatively easy to acquire the technical side of that type of music."

Masahiko Satoh never became disenchanted with free jazz per se and has successfully incorporated much of its uninhibited energy into his subsequent work, but in his *Cadence* interview, speaking of pianist Yosuke Yamashita, he did somewhat equate the power of its creativity with its power "to destroy." What is the difference?

"I was thinking of the year you mentioned, around 1969, or 1970–71. There was a very radical student movement in this country. Young student power ruled, so in all the arts—not only music—a tendency to destroy the existing theories existed. In everything! In music, everybody wanted to destroy orthodox harmony, orthodox music. Even in 'serious music,' we had 'chance operation,' an interest in new systems of notation, graphic squares and things like that. This tendency was everywhere. So in jazz there was a movement called 'new jazz.' And Yosuke Yamashita was not the only guy who wanted to *destroy*. I myself played that way in the New Jazz Hall. It was like taking a hammer."

"Not literally smashing up pianos, I hope . . ."

"No, but we played like that. *Very* percussive. But I realized that destruction brings nothing. We started out in free jazz as if there should not be *any* rules, but that's very tough—playing without rules." He laughed. "It comes down to nothing. Just *energy* comes out. I found out there had to be some positive approach, a way of thinking, in order to create music freely. So maybe that was the starting point of finding my own way. I don't know if it could be called a theory, but I think I almost established some vague mental rule that would control the music."

Masahiko Satoh gave me two CDs—*Double Exposure* (a trio recording of 1988, with Eddie Gomez and Steve Gadd) and *Randooga* (the work of a large group formed in 1990 that fuses many forms of music, its roots in world folk melodies). These CDs illustrate the evolution of his thinking and match with two I already had (*Amorphism* [1985], again with Gomez and Gadd; and *Explosions: Live at Pit Inn Shinjuku* [1994], under the leadership of drummer Masahiko Togashi). One can trace the path both composition and performance have taken for him. On *Amorphism,* the earliest recording, Satoh exploits all the resources a piano contains. The pieces are all originals. On one, "Ken Sen," he investigates every rhythmic possibility from breakneck speed to disrupted dissonant figures that dissipate into a repeated riff. A host of moods (everything from intimations of Mozart to Cecil Taylor) run by, this the most explosively "free" piece on the CD. "Sai Kau," by contrast, is richly melodic, a slow waltz that displays relaxed, straightforward swing. "Ut Pala" is laced with steady, persistent chimes that suggest Buddhist impermanence.

With Satoh working with Steve Gadd and Eddie Gomez again, in a more acoustic context, *Double Exposure* affords his customary offering of variety and surprise: a mix of original tunes—"Bamboo Shoots," "Evening Snow," "Fumon," and "Nouvelle Cuisine"—and jazz standards such as "All Blues," Sonny Rollins's "Saint Thomas," and "Alice in Wonderland." "Bamboo Shoots" is built on a sort of crazy fugue with figures attempting to march in place but inadvertently smashing into each other, like dodge-em cars at a carnival. "Evening Snow" takes us to another world, delicate, contemplative, even pretty, laced with the sonorous "breathing" that Satoh admires so much in the work of Toru Takemitsu. I asked him about this, whether the influence of Takemitsu was strong, and his reply was "yes, yes, yes, yes."

When Toru Takemitsu, a classical and film composer who died in February 1996, was asked about his own jazz links, he acknowledged his debt to Duke Ellington and George Russell, adding that the two greatest influences on his writing were Japanese music and jazz. His father had been a jazz fan who owned many 78 records (Jack Teagarden, Jimmy Noone, Ellington, and others), and when Takemitsu first discovered a draft copy of Russell's *Lydian Chromatic Concept of Tonal Organization*, he struggled through it with the aid of a dictionary. He described this work as being "so beautiful and full of poetry" that it exerted a strong influence on his own music. When Takemitsu finally came to the United States on a grant he was asked what he wanted to study. The administrators laughed at him when he said, "The music of Duke Ellington," and he was not allowed to use the money for that purpose.

It was ironical, and appropriate, that Masahiko Satoh should mention Takemitsu, because just before Betty and I had left for Japan (and not long after the composer died) I saw an excellent PBS documentary on him. Much of it was made up of testimony from various directors he had worked with, most of whom agreed that the shy, slight Takemitsu (director Seiji Ozawa said Takemitsu resembled "John Louis Berrault with diarrhea") was "one of the best film composers of the last thirty years." Hiroshi Tishigahara, who directed *Face of Another* (1966), claimed that "the placement of music gives life to things that weren't expressed in the images . . . the film evolves to a higher realism." Tishigahara also commented that in *Woman in the Dunes* (1987; adapted from the excellent novel by Kobo Abe), Takemitsu used sound "not as landscape, but character," frantic *taiko* drumming (plus the sound of ripped clothing and distorted instruments) "enhancing" a public rape scene. Takemitsu himself said that his score for a film about Ukiyo-e artist Toshusai Sharaku, in which he employed a large ensemble, shows the influence of jazz on his music.

Before Takemitsu, Japanese films were so full of music it became monotonous. He introduced another aesthetic principle: *ma,* or emptiness, saying, "A sheet of paper is not empty until you make the first mark." Takemitsu said he didn't much like trumpets and kettle drums. He was not fond of the tympani "bottom" in Western music. "My music is bottomless. I have only the top. That's because I'm Japanese. But

50

Japanese instruments had never been used in Japanese films. I desperately wanted to use Japanese instruments." When he did, people were shocked. His use of the *biwa* caused a sensation. "Isn't that a strange response?" Takemitsu asked afterward. Yet Takemitsu's major source remained typically Japanese. "My music is deeply influenced by nature and by Japanese gardens. Each element is precious. Every rock. Every tree. The entire universe is reflected in all of them." The PBS documentary—simply entitled *Takemitsu*—closes with the composer standing in just such a garden with its mix of sunlight and shadow, light and dark, whiffs of mist, flittering reflections, gold koi in clear blue water, delicate ferns and solid rock, snow falling gently and timelessly on the slender branches of trees. The Japanese garden, Takemitsu reflected, "is not a linear experience at all. It is circular. One always comes back, like the cyclical rings of karma. I write music by placing objects in my musical garden. This is a distinct Japanese sensibility, I think. The sound of a breeze through the pines, the wind in a bamboo grove. To capture these sounds would be perfection. This way of thinking and feeling influences everything, including the music I write for others."

"Takemitsu's manner of *breathing* in his music," Masahiko Satoh acknowledged at the Asia Center, "has influenced me very much. But it's not just his own thing. It's the universal Japanese spirit. Yet he's the only guy who can make that spirit take shape in a score. There are still many great composers like Takemitsu-san in Japan, and I know many of them, and they are all doing something a little bit *different*. They have done something just a bit different from the Western type of thinking in some way, but Takemitsu is the most straightforward in expressing the Japanese spirit in a score. No hesitation. And he's always *thinking*."

I asked him about the Japanese aesthetic principles I had been trying to understand on the flight from Oahu to Tokyo: *yūgen, sabi, mono no aware*. Was there truly a Japanese aesthetic that ran through all the arts, visual, literary, even jazz?

"It still exists, but we have been losing much of it recently. If you are aware of those principles, that Japanese aesthetic, you are likely to find them *somewhere*. But generally we are losing that sense."

Masahiko Satoh gave me the *Randooga* CD as a gift, and that led to a discussion of the role of jazz education in Japan. Randooga was formed in 1990, a large ensemble group with a single requirement: that each member improvise with an inherent knowledge of folk melodies from around the world, themes handed down from generation to generation but approached in this context without Western preconceptions about traditional ensemble performance and harmony. The group's first efforts featured Western artists such as Wayne Shorter, Nana Vasconcellos, and Ray Anderson, but it was re-formed with Japanese musicians who represented a wide range of genres: jazz fusion, *gagaku,* post-avant-garde, contemporary. This group issued a CD called *Kannabi* in 1992, and in 1993 Satoh opened Randooga Dojo, a school for "kids" from eleven to fifty years of age, professional musicians mixed in among them, dedicated to collective improvisation. It's been a long wide road from Satoh's early post-Berklee teaching days to Randooga Dojo, and I was curious as to how he'd managed it. I mentioned that people had been telling me there's no school in Japan comparable to Berklee. Nor university programs on the scale of places like North Texas State. But universities did have jazz bands, didn't they? The High Society Orchestra at Waseda University?

"Ah, that's a *club.* A jazz club, but its band *was* voted best college band. The High Society Orchestra is just a group that many students play in. Waseda is an ordinary university. It does not have a music department, so maybe these students are studying economics, and after class they get together and play some swing."

Satoh himself teaches once a week: arranging and theory and piano. He's also written a book on music theory for a small private school. A small part of it focuses on his positive approach to playing freely.

"How to handle a given element," he said. "The existing music is a complex of elements. Once you have a single element, you can analyze the rest fairly easily, and when you can handle them all easily you can easily find the next step. That kind of thinking."

He offers an analogy: *shogi,* or Japanese chess.

"Anticipating, or reading, the other player's next move." Free jazz players have three different responses: "yes," "no," "ignore," with variations on each. The best artists have "many variations," lots of experience or background to draw on, and intuition based on experience. "I'm always *neutral,*" he told *Cadence.* "I am always open. I can't imagine a good musician coming to a dead end in free jazz play," Satoh told me. "When you listen to it, just open up and enjoy it. There is no need to listen to free jazz logically. I move one thing and the opponent moves another. According to his move, the next possibility is like ten. Against ten, I have ten possibilities, so that makes one hundred moves. Against one hundred you have ten more possibilities, so that makes one thousand. So playing free jazz *is* like chess. It comes down to, how many possibilities can I read? If I find more, the level gets even higher."

At the Asia Center in Tokyo, when he handed me his recent Randooga recording, *Mahoroba,* he said, " I took melodies from all over the world as a source and remade them. It's a different approach. This is a free improvised concert based on simple melodies, folk melodies that had simple words. I like many different types of music."

And indeed, many different types of music are represented on the Randooga recording, complex elements approached with intuition and a sense of freedom, or *ease,* that makes it all look easy, when it's not. But these were not "kids" on the CD. Some of Japan's top musicians are featured, such as tenor saxophonist Kosuke Mine (one of the best) and Kazutoki Umezu (another of the best) on soprano, alto sax, and bass clarinet. Liner notes by Hisayuki Ikegami recount a conversation with American pianist Cecil Taylor at the Montreux Jazz Festival. Taylor asked Ikegami why Japan had not developed its own unique form of jazz, and the latter responded by saying that Masahiko Satoh, a musician of international stature, *had.* Ikegami told Taylor he could introduce him to Satoh and, jokingly, added that Satoh just *might* let him join Randooga, but he wasn't sure. In his liner notes, Hisayuki Ikegami mentions an album (*Yamataifu,* music based on *tendai-shu,* the rhythms of Buddhist chants) Satoh recorded upon his return from Berklee, music so different it was considered shocking at the time—just as that of Cecil Taylor once was. The music reflected not some flight of fancy but "real life" understood so well that it upset people. This was music without borders, distinct from all predecessors, neither "sophisticated" nor "urbane" nor "Americanized" but, as David Sanborn acknowledged (when he first heard Randooga and asked them to appear on his TV show), "unusual yet universal."

The mixture of sounds on Randooga's CD *Mahoroba* is rare and effective. "Bushuu-Karigoe-Bushi" (a samurai hunting song) combines Bon dance vigor with the Celtic roots of bluegrass, a stately full ensemble theme crackling with step-dance rhythms and the wit of Sun Ra. "Honjo-Lak" is *very* Japanese, with its *gagaku* roots (steady bowl-and-stick *taiko* backing). "Tagin" (which may be a play on *shigin,* a poem or story chanted in distinct rhythms) is a *taiko*-based piece; and "Midare-Haidai" contains *midare* (which means "chaos" in Japanese) but ends with snappy Central Asian percussion.

Hisayuki Ikegami provided lyrics for "Uzuki-Bayashi" (Song of April), using an older word for that month, *bayashi,* meaning "song" (or more exactly a form of accompaniment that induces hand-clapping). This piece, the longest in the set, has a hypnotic African groove suggesting a bare plain where sound—rippling conga drums, squeeze drum, distant squealing sax, accumulated "small sounds"—carries far, ominous, infectious, danceable, the culmination a ritualistic orgy that everyone gets in on, resolved by a six-note repeated chant and a joyous *whoop* at the end.

If Masahiko Satoh has made use of the full range of international folk melodies in his work with Randooga, he has also focused on Japanese elements exclusively in collaborations with a thousand-voice (well, nearly: 998) Buddhist choir and exceptional native instrumentalists, such as *shakuhachi* master Hozan Yamamoto. Critic Yozo Iwanami would tell me that Satoh was one of few artists—Toshiko Akiyoshi among them—who had made "exceptional use of traditional Japanese instruments."

"I've done compositions for *biwa* and *shakuhachi.* I'm deeply interested in Japanese culture and its way of thinking. Its concept of time, its concept of *breathing,* as I said before. I find it very stimulating to play with the *shakuhachi* and *biwa,* or koto, that special *moment* they can provide. So when I work with Western instruments—like the bass or drums—I still try to use that concept, I try *not* to use ordinary [Western] time. The Japanese concept of breathing, of time, is, I believe, a strong trend in me. My own *tampopo* [dandelion] growing in my own soil? Maybe I go to an extreme trying to be *local,* but maybe that way, someday, you find that you are very universal. If you dig far enough, if you go far enough into your own soil, you may go to the opposite side of the earth."

I asked him about the concert he gave with one thousand monks.

"A thousand monks, yes, wearing the *kisa,* or Buddhist formal wear, chanting. Well, actually 998 monks, for two of them couldn't show up. We gave a performance. These monks have a special way of reading, what will I call it—their Bibles? 'Bibles' is probably a funny way to put it. Maybe the Buddhist bible. They *chant.* The practice comes from India originally. The first Japanese performance was in 700 or so. In Nara. The ritual is called Shōmyō, and the particular school I worked with is called Shingon-shū. Even within Shingon-shū there are also many schools, and one school called the Buzan-ha, the Buzan school, chants.

So I took the notes and made a score. I copied down even the small ornamentation or inflections, and I composed music behind that, something for flute, saxophones, percussion, synthesizer."

The performance took place in 1993, in Budōkan, a large stadium in Tokyo.

"It was like a typhoon . . . a *great* experience. I would like to do it again, if I have a chance. It was impressive because these monks come from all over the country. And we had to pay for all that. But there is a performance in which thirty to forty monks chant, one that is often held in the National Theater here."

I mentioned the objection some Japanese musicians I'd spoken to had about using traditional instruments, some feeling the attempt was "phony," even "claptrap." Satoh thought for a moment, as if he found such criticism irrelevant; then he said, "The *shakuhachi* player I worked with is very versatile. He's great. He is one of the top players in this one school, the Tozan school, one of two biggest in Japan. The other is the Kinko school. But Hozan Yamamoto is maybe the fourth or fifth great master of the Tozan school. He has played with a big band called the Sharps and Flats. He played at the Newport Jazz Festival in 1967. Hozan Yamamoto is great, a master."

I would discover this for myself when I returned home and American bassist David Friesen sent me a cassette he'd made with Satoh and Yamamoto—*Hozan, Friesen + 1.* I would also discover another side of Satoh on CDs I found or received: recordings that show his classical inclinations: *Touch of Spring* (1988) with flutist Masami Nakagawa (including works by Tchaikovsky, Mozart, Faure, Beethoven, Scriabin, and Ibert); and *Prelude to a Kiss* (1997) with violinist Junko Ohtsu. "There was no improvisation on the violin parts," Satoh would write, "all the notes she played were written out. I have tried to give jazz tunes a classical aspect." Clearly, Satoh keeps a wide range of very good company. And sources.

Masahiko Satoh and I concluded our conversation by discussing the future of jazz, and jazz musicians, in Japan—one that, as it turns out, does not seem all that different from the future of jazz musicians anywhere, including the United States. I mentioned that I had read somewhere that, given the 333 Japanese graduates of Berklee College, musicians were now returning to Japan rather than remaining in the States and that, doing so, they were likely to create a uniquely "Japanese" jazz.

"I cannot say that, because I have seen no signs of a new movement

55

among them. There are many good players here, but maybe the person who suggested that meant "jazz" by a very narrow definition. Stereotypes. There *are* many good musicians, but they are not creating a new type of music, a new school of jazz."

In his *Cadence* interview, Satoh said that in the United States, there are *some* men of genius, but not much depth, whereas in Japan, musicians are good to average, but geniuses like Seiji Ozawa are very few. Did he still feel that way?

"It's the nature of Japanese people to reach a certain level of competence. Maybe that comes from the educational system. Japanese education tends to make clone-type human beings, but not unique. It's like mathematics: they fall between this level and that level. You have to remain on a certain level in *all* subjects. In European countries and the United States, you could get an F in mathematics, but you might get an A+ in music. And we have big problems with *teasing* in our classrooms. Children won't recognize anything *foreign* to them. Everybody wears a white shirt, but if someone wears a pink shirt, they're *out*. This is the system in Japan. Even in music, teachers present the theories, the methods, and students want to learn those theories, those methods. But that's all. So they never step out of that or go beyond that."

"What prompted you to do so?"

"For them, I'm probably a strange person," he said, laughing.

I asked if it was possible for someone—strange or otherwise—to make a good living in Japan as a jazz musician.

"I think the situation is quite similar to that in New York. Someone's working driving a truck or that kind of thing. I am *writing* about 70 percent of the time. And I will keep writing. Piano pieces, orchestra pieces, instrumental pieces. And I'll keep playing, in clubs, but not much. A couple times a month. Most musicians cannot make enough money just playing in clubs. It's very hard. In Japan's system, they are all one-night stands, only. You make about ten thousand or eight thousand yen for one night. So what's that: one hundred dollars or eighty dollars. And the average musician works at most three nights a week, if he's lucky. So playing music professionally, especially jazz, is difficult. And King Records and Toshiba are the only two companies that publish jazz. Avant-garde musicians have to record with small independent labels, or privately. It's very difficult. Even for my generation, recording is rare. Or is becoming very rare. Many people are trying to establish a new method of distribution, using the Internet, or direct mail, catalog sales. So maybe in a couple of years the market will change—drastically I guess. I think the big companies cannot afford to release jazz now. It never breaks even."

Local. Universal. The paradox fits Satoh, whose unique accomplishment, firmly rooted in Japan, reaches out to embrace the entire world. I seemed to hear his music everywhere, the perfect accompaniment, as we toured Tokyo (the city itself a massive paradox) over the next few days.

Many writers have commented on the coexistence in Japan of the old and the new, of long-instilled tradition set side-by-side with habits picked up from the West, but the situation seems far more complex, and dynamic, than that to me. What I felt throughout Tokyo resembled what occurs when, in the world of nuclear physics, matter is bombarded by a 6.2-Bev proton beam, producing desired mesons plus a whole crop of new "strange" particles, some with masses greater than protons but short-lived. These decay into other particles. It's an intricate, ongoing process in which old and new are bedfellows, yes, but in constant flux, abiding in essence but altering, deforming one another—no one thing returning to its source, for that source can never be the same again, nor can the future as a result of these interactions.

The streets of Tokyo are composed of just such a swirl of rapidly arriving and decaying particles, colliding, caroming, feeding off one another, constantly changing into something else: the fleeting image of surfers amid tsunami-large waves on the vibrant electrical billboard in Roppongi; the sensuous Caucasian faces of fashion models pouting on Ginza subway walls; video screens in shops in Akasaka, alive with a dance of consumer delights but occasionally fading, for just a second, to a screen as blank as a rockless Zen garden, immaculately white; the sudden appearance, in Marunouchi, of a horde of *sararīman* coming at you, armed with slick suits and attaché cases, as threatening as the bulls of Pamplona (but *ahead* of you, not behind), as you emerge from a subway well and flatten yourself against a cold tired wall for protection. And the thick honeycomb clusters of navy blue schoolboys and schoolgirls at the JR Station in Shinjuku, their jackets, caps, and jumpers, their white blouses as mandatory as the forthcoming long evening of homework under the watchful eyes of *kyōiku mama* (education moms), even more tyrannizing than their teachers. Or the looks of shopwomen in Aoyama's New Otani Hotel basement-arcade minisupermarket, kerchiefs knotted about their foreheads like the prying cloth lanterns of coal miners, these women who supervise displays of food and booze: every shape and style of sake bottle imaginable, endless counters loaded with daikon, ginger, *tsukemono* (pickles), slabs of sashimi staring up at you (raw squid, tuna, octopus, eel, shrimp, orange roe), and tempura-encrusted sweet potatoes and zuccinni.

And through all of this material flux, the delicious and dangerous "suchness" (*kono-mama* or *sono-mama:* this or that "as-it-is-ness") of Tokyo, as rich and varied as Masahiko Satoh's music, runs the inalterable silence of Zen, its wordless solemnity. Steven Heine, paradoxically writing of Zen master/poet Dogen's grudging facility with language, called his gift "a direct means of achieving a polyphonic plentitude of meanings, images, ideas." The *kotoba tarazu* (sparse words, or "words that are too few") employed to convey *yojō* (overflowing feeling) that Heine attributes to Dogen might well apply to the economy of means, the strain of good sense, the absence of ego, the silence from which a multitude of implications springs in Satoh's art.

Writing on Japanese court poetry, Robert H. Brower and Earl Miner comment that Zen Buddhism, advocating contemplation, "confirmed [the poets'] intense preoccupation with the *details* of experience. . . . By prizing the moment and its detail, the poets invested both with an importance that transcends both. . . . The poets esteemed the real; but by the real they meant not so much the thing or state in itself as the thing or state infused with the observer's apprehension of it." And at the heart of what is *real* lies impermanence. In Dogen's words, "The first and foremost thing to be concerned with is detachment from the ego through the contemplation of impermanence," but this does not produce fatalism or passivity but discipline and action: the action/motion and discipline of Satoh's music. In such "free jazz," and in life, transiency (as the very structure of reality) is embraced, renewal and awakening are celebrated, false attachment is discarded, and the observer—poet/musical artist—is no longer a mere spectator but is now fully immersed in the unfolding of impermanence—or *music.*

Did I really *hear* all of this in the jazz art of Masahiko Satoh, his game of *shogi,* or Japanese chess, with its one-hundred-times-ten and even more (endless!) possibilities, the music I found reflected in nearly every step I took in Tokyo? You bet I did.

6

YOZO IWANAMI AND AMI'S BAR: SCOTCH AND JAZZ

M USEUMS AND TEMPLES BY DAY; jazz clubs at night.
This became our Tokyo pattern, along with finding a means to evade the August heat we'd been warned about. "Why did you decide to come *now?*" people inquired, but we'd had little choice about the season. Betty is an elementary-school teacher's aid, and August was the only month she had free; it was also the month when the Monterey Jazz Festival in Noto was held—a festival I wanted very much to attend because of its off-the-beaten-path location, hoping to prove one of the contentions in Akira Tana's Harvard thesis, that jazz pervaded "every sector of Japanese society."

Fortunately, much of Tokyo occurs underground. Giant shopping malls seem to stretch from subway station to subway station, and they are more than adequately air-conditioned. We've long prided ourselves on being incessant walkers, throughout London and Leningrad and Athens, but you won't last long aboveground in Tokyo in August—as we found out on the first day. Five minutes on the street and I was drenched, my clothing reduced to a dishrag. Yet most Japanese, apparently, even the *sararīman* in their smart suits—dressed to the nines, neat as pins—don't sweat a lot. Maybe it's diet. Whatever, faint with the heat, we headed underground.

For our third day in Tokyo, I scheduled an afternoon meeting with critic Yozo Iwanami, whom I'd first met in Monterey, which he'd visited as part of a concert tour by Eiji Kitamura. I hadn't had a chance to interview him then, so I looked forward to the opportunity now. He was a highly respected critic. He'd given me an article he'd written about his West Coast trip, and he'd even reviewed my book on jazz in the former USSR for *Swing Journal* in Japan.

But before I talked with him at the Asia Center in Tokyo, Betty and I had a day of temples and museums to attend to. We headed for Shibuya, where we discovered a cool quiet street lined with gingko trees and brick buildings ("This could be a college town in the Midwest," Betty sagely observed), plus pricey shops, such as Paul Stewart Men's Clothes, in whose windows three hip headless mannequins held, in turn, a slick gold alto saxophone, drumsticks, and a muted trumpet. These mannequins sat astride a bar stool (Jack Daniels in plain view) or lounged on a white wrought-iron park bench. Other high-fashion vendors bore names like Octopus Army and Rap City, and record store street racks offered "Jazz Best-Seller" CDs (one thousand yen, slightly less than ten dollars) by Stan Getz, Art Tatum and Charlie Parker.

We visited the Meiji Jingu Shrine, advertised as "a welcome contrast of serene solemnity" to the rampant consumerism of Shibuya's Omotesando Avenue, which it was. We stood beneath one of two immense but nonthreatening torii gates made from seventeen-hundred-year-old cypress trees, forty feet high—the largest but not the tallest gates in Japan, we would learn. The shrine's main building has a stark interior protected by a graciously curved, pale green copper roof that seemed to melt into the sky. We checked out a wide array of talismans, charms for everything from passing exams to safe driving, and we clapped our hands together twice in prayer for a friend back home who was dying of cancer. Would the music move me as much as that moment did?

We also had time to take in the Ota Museum, not far from the grounds of the Meiji Jingu Shrine. This turned out to be our favorite gallery because of a display entitled "The Moon Depicted in Ukiyo-e," nearly all of my woodcut heroes responding to that theme. Hiroshige's moon, in *Yodo-gawa River,* smiled on the solemn efforts of near-naked men towing a barge. Hokusai's *Snow, Moon and Flowers* was a winter scene, and Yoshitoshi planted his moons in a thick mist and within varied settings, one moon in *The Ghost of Yugao* (from the novel *The Tale of Genji*), another a Bon festival moon with—God forbid—"commoners dancing" beneath it. Moon drunk and happy, I staggered out of the Ota Museum. Museum visits would prove to be a vivid and meaningful counterpart to jazz. The visual arts of Japan set high aesthetic standards, establish benchmarks I couldn't help but wonder if contemporary music would meet. In Japan, you can't escape the proximity of the old with the new. It seemed a small step from Yoshitoshi's jolly peasants to the hordes of impossibly well-behaved students in Shinjuku, milling about after school, compacting a depot that processes two million commuters at rush hour twice a day, nine trains and subway lines converging.

Back at the Asia Center, I met Yozo Iwanami in the lobby, and we went upstairs to the relative serenity of the lounge, where he had lots of photos of Japanese jazz musicians to show me—many of which he later bestowed as gifts. I commented on his invaluable contributions to the *New Grove Dictionary of Jazz,* which I had read at home: biographies of artists that had helped shape my sense of the history of jazz in Japan. Yozo Iwanami had brought along the book he had written on jazz in Japan, and he showed me a photo of Shotoro Moriyasu, the musician who committed suicide at "maybe thirty" and the one—as I said previously—Iwanami considered "the most talented modern jazz pianist in Japan." Iwanami himself began writing about jazz in 1958. His book was published in 1983. It contained many more photos of musicians, and he showed me these, describing each artist in a very succinct manner (his English, he apologized, was limited). I was seeing and hearing about the lives of musicians I'd had stateside acquaintance with only through CDs. Once I'd completed my photo tour (as interesting, and important to this study, as what I'd seen in the museums that morning), Iwanami and I talked about the club scene in Japan.

"There are maybe twenty to twenty-five clubs in Tokyo," he said. "Out of the city, in Yokohama and Hachioji, in the suburbs, maybe five or six clubs. So twenty in Tokyo. Kobe, Kyoto, and Fukuoka in Kyushu have clubs, but not so many. Many musicians work here in Tokyo and in the suburbs."

"And festivals?"

"Maybe twenty to twenty-five, in the summer. All over Japan."

I mentioned Tiger Okoshi's view that Japanese jazz artists had now reached a level of major league play. True?

"Japanese players perform on a year-round basis now, and many work with American musicians in both Tokyo and the United States. Toshiko said, 'Japanese jazz musicians have very good *feeling,* but a little less *energy* than American players.' However, if you are born with guts, or energy [*yūki,* courage; *genki,* health or pervasive energy], a Japanese player can measure up. Alto saxophonist Akira Sakata is a very aggressive player. He used to play with pianist Yosuke Yamashita, who now plays George Gershwin—sometimes 'Rhapsody in Blue'—and Japanese folk songs."

I mentioned the large number of Berklee grads returning to Japan. Would they create a unique brand or style of "Japanese" jazz?

"You must know Toru Takemitsu, the classical composer? He has a very unique *oriental* feeling, a Japanese conception, in his music. And Toshiko Akiyoshi is writing very unique Japanese-flavored compositions for her own orchestra. Masahiko Satoh and Masahiko Togashi have a unique Japanese feeling. Junko Onishi has played popular Japanese songs. Sleepy Matsumoto sometimes plays both folk and pop songs. He has very unique interpretations of these originals. And Satoh and Togashi have both used traditional Japanese instruments. But in Japan, most of the musicians are studying *bebop*. The very young musicians understand this music well, but they do not play with so much energy. These young musicians play with other young musicians, and they make many records. If you hear those recordings, it sounds as if they have a large tone, but *live* it's not so strong. Do you know Tomonao Hara, the trumpeter? And Eijiro Nakagawa; he is a very good trombone player. And Masahiko Osaka, the drummer. The Osaka/Hara group is very good."

I would later identify these artists, who record for King Records, as part of what that company calls the "jazz restoration in Japan." Iwanami also mentioned three other young musicians he could "recommend very highly": Nao Takeuchi (tenor sax), Joh Yamada (alto sax), and Yutaka Shiina (piano). We then discussed the university system, as I had with Masahiko Satoh. Iwanami mentioned two big bands with solid reputations: the Keio Light Music Society (which has appeared at the Monterey Jazz Festival) and the Waseda High Society Orchestra. He said that last year Heineken had sponsored a competition for young pianists and would do so again this year for saxophonists. And Yamaha-gakki (both an instruction and a record store) sponsors a college student orchestra contest.

When we finished the interview, we met Betty, and the three of us walked up to the Aoyama-Itchome subway station, which has its own *chika-gai* (underground shopping mall) hosting many restaurants. We checked out a number of window displays: the shelves on which sit plastic mock-ups of food, created with such verisimilitude that they occasionally threaten to prove more appetizing than the real thing once you get inside. Fortunately, that was not the case this night. After dinner, we hopped the Ginza line to Ami's Bar: Scotch and Jazz, owned and operated by a woman Iwanami described as "the only major female vibraphonist in Japan"—a woman who would also turn out to be his former wife.

Three flights up, the club consists of a small room, intimate of necessity, which somehow manages to house a Yamaha grand piano (they must have dismantled it piece by piece to bring it in), a vibraharp, a short bar set in front of a wall of scotch whiskey (the drink of un-choice; there is no other), and space left over for about fifteen customers. Jean Dubuffet graces the only wall space (a clown with a flowerpot on his head). Kiyoko Ami herself was a short pretty woman in a bright red dress tattooed with dancing Juan Miro–ish arabesques, a thick white belt highlighting her admirable figure, her hair sporting a boyish cut frazzed in front, giant earrings that resembled Christmas tree ornaments adorning her ears. If the ingredients sound at odds with one another, the total effect was harmonious. She was a vibrant, no-nonsense, accomplished woman for whom the club is the culmination of a dream.

She fell in love with jazz when she first heard Frank Wess play flute, telling herself, "This is beautiful; this will become my life." Her mother wasn't thrilled at the prospect (just as Toshiko Akiyoshi's otōsan—father—had frowned on her playing in clubs or bars) and said, "You are not my girl; go away." Ami replied, "Dōmo arigatō gozaimasu" (thank you very much), and departed. She studied classical piano and then switched to vibraharp, finding the instrument difficult at first.

"I still can't handle the four-mallet technique that Gary Burton started," Kiyoko said. "I don't have the strength between my middle finger and forefinger. It *burns* when I try."

Her idol, Milt Jackson, has performed at Ami's, and she has mementos of his visit—one of which is a handsome, personally autographed photo of "Bags" at work, or play, hunched over Ami's vibraharp. But her most precious memento is the memory of how her heart thumped when he played. "I had tears in my eyes," she says, "and in my *gut*."

She's been on tour—Vancouver, Seattle, Indianapolis, Toronto, Frankfurt (Germany), and Italy—with former Lionel Hampton pianist Eric Gill, with whom she has recorded. Ami has fond memories of "Le piubelle canzoni jazz festival" and a spaghetti factory she visited in Italy.

An interesting occurrence this night, something I don't think would happen in the States (I benefited from the policy myself in Japan), was that Ami, a definite pro, invited a gifted amateur to come up and play with her. The amateur, in this case, was a Mr. Satoh, an obvious *sararīman* in a neatly tailored suit who even, much to the amusement of the friends with whom he'd been sitting, carried his attaché case up to the very small bandstand. Once there, Satoh-san was cool and confident and fit Ami's repertoire—"Stardust," "Softly as in a Morning Sunset," and "C Jam Blues"—easily, compatibly. The guy was *good*. I found out later that he'd been studying for ten years and that, as we could hear when he performed, playing vibes had become more than an avocation. It was a rich complement to his active business life.

I even got *my* turn. A tall attractive woman in a black sheath dress had been plunking ice cubes in our drinks (scotch, of course) throughout the evening. She also proffered small attendant dishes of noodles, pickles, peanuts, and rice crackers to line our *hara* (stomachs—as in hara-kiri, or ritual suicide by cutting, *kiru*, one's gut). Her name was Kishiko Aizawa, and she turned out to be an aspiring vocalist. She sings at Ami's on Monday and Wednesday nights: tunes such as "All of Me," "Bye Bye Blackbird," "Slow Boat to China," Jobim's "How Insensitive," Cole Porter's "You'd Be So Nice to Come Home To." Kishiko complained about the difficulty of singing in *eigo* (English), of attaining correct intonation and enunciation. But encouraged by the others, she and I sang "Everything Happens to Me" ("What is," she asked after, "*mortgage* all my castles in the air?") and then both lost our way—at least it was simultaneously!—somewhere in the middle of the lyrics to "Summertime." I tried my favorite Cole Porter song, "Everytime We Say Goodbye," alone, on the Yamaha grand piano, then Fats Waller's "Ain't Misbehavin'."

"*That's* it; that's what I want!" Kishiko said, "that throaty, that *sexy* quality . . ."

I'll confess, knowing my patched, squeaky, nasal voice all too well, I was perplexed by whatever must have come across as *sexy* to her, but I smiled in gratitude. Thinking of "Summertime," we all discussed the significance, in spirituals, of phrases like "spread your wings and take to the sky"—the portion of the tune we'd both forgotten. Amateurs didn't dominate the evening, fortunately, for the sets were made up of tunes performed by Ami on vibes and her pianist, Ryoko Iwasaki. Classically trained like so many Japanese pianists are, Ryoko is an alumnus of the

Waseda High Society Orchestra that Iwanami had praised before. She was also part of a piano/bass/drums combo within that unit and—as it turned out—had been a student of Masahiko Satoh's for two years. She and Ami provided a handsome rendering of my favorite Johnny Mandel tune, "Emily," and then a frisky "Days of Wine and Roses," followed by a slow, tender "Moonlight in Vermont." The pianist and Ami together managed to make a woman sitting close to the vibes weep throughout "When You Wish Upon a Star" (who says the "inscrutable" Japanese don't show their feelings?). They added a jazz twist to the haunting melody and sad words of "Hamabe no Uta" (Song of the Seaside: "Waves come and go, the color of the moon, the shadows of stars, all those who have died before us"). The evening closed out with, appropriately, "Bag's Groove," Mr. Satoh emoting side-by-side with Ami, for whom this tune has a special significance—and it showed.

Kiyoko Ami's musical style is smooth, nimble, easy to listen to—which by no means reduces it to "soft jazz" or "easy listening." As she proved on "C Jam Blues" and "Bag's Groove," she can swing, she can jump, performing with gracious power, with *chikara* (strength). Although she did not play her own pieces the night we were at her club, she is also a fine composer—as I would discover on two CDs she gave me as *omiyage* (souvenirs) of that evening. One CD, *Rhapsody in New York*, features Ami with American drummer Carl Allen. The title tune, "Rhapsody in New York," an original by Ami, opens in a sprightly manner, with tight unison work and bright vibes. "Moon Flower," another original, suggests an exotic, languid, tropical setting. On "Manteca," Carl Allen provides polyrhythmic interplay with fellow percussionist Rudy Bird that turns the piece into a drummer's delight, and a finely burnished version of Dizzy Gillespie's warhorse rouser.

The other CD, *Rhapsody in Manhattan* (this one recorded in Japan with a different, all-Japanese group, the Joyful Four), contains two more originals: "Dream More Dreams" and "Blues for Audi Park." Again, the standards are appealing: a skipping Latin "Melancholy Baby," each syllable of the instrumental refrain carefully enunciated ("mel-an-chol-y," etc.), creating a quaint rhythmic effect; "Django" offering a fitting homage to her idol, Milt Jackson, the effect as subtle as those *uguisu-bari* (nightingale floors) Betty and I would experience firsthand in Kyoto: palace floors deliberately made to squeak by way of a complex mechanism placed beneath them—a clever device to discourage intruders from attempting to enter the Shogun's private quarters.

On the night of our visit to Ami's Bar, Betty and I were made to feel like anything but intruders. Yozo Iwanami, who seems very reserved by nature, was obviously having a grand time serving as genial host, and Kiyoko Ami and Kishiko-san were embarrassingly attentive as hostesses. In the States, you would never find a frontline musician such as Ami, especially in a club she *owns,* serving drinks and ice, but I didn't sense any resentment on her part. I felt as if we had been privileged to attend, and be absorbed in, an intimate, informal, cozy family gathering, the tight quarters of the club contributing to this effect, as spatial limitations in Japan can.

When we left, Kishiko Aizawa of the black sheath dress blew me a kiss I could feel ricochet off my cheek, and I "kept" that kiss as another *omiyage* of Ami's Bar and the friends we'd made there. Once I'd squirmed my dead (sleeping) legs out from beneath a small tight table and managed to revive them somewhat, we were back on the street. I bowed my thanks to Yozo Iwanami for a fine evening. Betty and I said *oyasuminasai* (good night, sleep well) and then hopped our subway back to Akasaka.

7

HOTOTOGISU

IN JAPAN, THE *HOTOTOGISU* CORRESPONDS to the English cuckoo. From early summer on, it sings day and night and ceases in autumn. Like a few too many jazz singers perhaps, it is said to cough up blood and die after it has sung 8,008 times. Nobel-prize winner Yasunari Kawabata claimed that a single poem by the Zen master Dogen, stringing together conventional words and images, transmitted the essence of Japan. Two of the poem's juxtaposed words are *natsu* (summer) and *hototogisu*. "In summer the cuckoo sings" might serve as a somewhat bland translation of the line, but the *hototogisu is* "Summertime"—in A-minor no less.

During the summer after I graduated from high school, I was surrounded by *hototogisu*. I worked for my uncle Max Gail, who ran a large and successful orchestra agency in Detroit. About to go off to the University of Michigan in the fall to study art, I designed and "executed" some fliers for the bands my uncle booked. Aside from practicing a trade I then thought I would enter someday (advertising), what attracted me most about working at my uncle's were the secretaries. They were all singers in the various bands, pert and pretty as vocalists were required to be in those days, and not much older than myself. Exacting their secretarial chores, they strolled about the office singing tunes like "Nevertheless," "Dream a Little Dream of Me," "Guilty," and "You Belong to Me." Not one of those girls would ever belong to me, yet nevertheless (ho ho), I dreamed overlarge dreams of them at night, guilt free.

Although my pubescent stage arrived some time after the big band 1940s heyday of "girl singers," the tunes and standards of physical beauty for vocalists (Helen O'Connell, Doris Day, Jo Stafford, Rosemary Clooney, Boyd Raeburn's vocalist/wife Ginny Powell) were embedded in my mind. I was not oblivious to "art" singers, the real thing, more musically oriented vocalists such as Ella Fitzgerald, whom I saw with JATP in Detroit. I can still see Ray Brown setting his bass aside and coming down front to tell an overly appreciative fan of his—then—wife's charms to "shut up." I heard lots of Dinah Washington (who was considered "Queen" in Detroit), and I heard Sarah Vaughan and Carmen McRae live. But, as was the case with too many people (both male and female) at the time, it was the *image* of the "girl singer," not her musicality (if she had any), that attracted me. There's a classic photo in George T. Simon's book *The Big Bands* of a love-stunned teenage male, arms akimbo, standing in front of a smiling June Christy while his girlfriend, at his side, looks up at him with distinct disapproval. The kid is *gone,* converted to Dream City, never to return. Perhaps "falling in love" is not such a bad criterion after all, if the singer proves *that* convincing in her song, giving the impression that she is singing *just for me* (which is okay, as long as every other spectator in the room feels that way too). Evaluation still tends to get tied up in the entire musical package the "girl singer" projects, the persona as well as the art.

The situation gets even more complex when I attempt to evaluate Japanese vocalists, who tend to embrace the conventional "girl singer" image with a vengeance (the Meiji-period wholesale conversion to the West still in effect) and also run up against the problem of language. How do you sing convincingly, how do you make your fans *honestly* fall in love with you and your song, in a medium that's secondhand (sometimes to the point of your having to sing phonetically, lacking full understanding of the words)? Even my favorite Japanese singer, Shoko Amano, after extensive training at the capable hands of pianist Norman Simmons, slips and sings "*fry* me to the moon" on "You Belong to Me." Can't be helped. It comes with the territory, but to many American ears such unique inflection probably doesn't have the exotic charm of a French or Russian accent. Our own cultural bias is at work here, admittedly, and—while in Tokyo—we deliberately sought out a vocalist I'd met in the States to see, and hear, what the life of an *hototogisu* was like in Japan.

We'd spent another scorching day trying to stay off the streets in Tokyo, tracking down museums. We'd gone to the Tokyo National Museum in

Ueno Park, to the zoo there as well (penguins in their formal wear, like musicians off to some country-club gig), and had our first exposure to the tent sites of the most clean and tidy street people I've ever seen, their "homes" shored up with plywood, bicycles parked nearby, laundry draped over bushes and a formal fountain in the park. After, we got lost trying to find the J Club, although, fortunately, it was night, and the day's heat had abated. Getting lost in Tokyo—not at all a difficult thing to do—can be interesting and even entertaining, if you have time for it, but I wasn't sure we did. Jazz shows start early, because the subways stop running around midnight. I once heard a New York musician standing outside the Tokyo Blue Note exclaim, "Man, I've never had to start playin' at no *6:30* before!"

The J Club was another walkdown, a red carpet flecked with a snowflake design leading us to a door that, opened, disclosed a some-what dark, cozy (small) interior: a short bar and about sixteen very low tables, most of which lined the wall. Candles sputtered as they floated in glass enclosures along with lemon rinds. Small spotlights were sus-pended from black rods attached to the ceiling. Cards on each table rec-ommended Guinness Stout as the beverage of choice, and large photos of jazz performers Bobby Watson, Marcus Miller, Miles Davis, Wynton Marsalis, Sonny Rollins, Dizzy Gillespie, Ray Brown, Laurinda Almeda, Herbie Hancock, Oscar Peterson, Hank Jones, and Sadao Watanabe (with B. B. King, Frank Sinatra, and Sammy Davis Jr. thrown in for good measure) gazed down from the walls.

A black Yamaha grand piano, a wooden bass on its side, and a set of yellow drums occupied the front of the room, the whole reminding me of the small intimate clubs I used to love in New York City—the majority of which did not survive the 1970s rock wars and are now extinct. We talked briefly with vocalist Yoko Sikes, whom I'd met in Monterey months before. She then excused herself to change into the striking red dress she would perform in. I had first met Yoko at an IDEA (International Disabled Exchange Adventures: a group providing exchange programs for persons with disabilities in Japan and the United States) potluck given before an International Jazz Jam in Monterey, and she had told me she sang professionally in Japan and later sent a letter that included a schedule of upcoming Tokyo appearances, including the J Club date in Shinjuku. In her letter, Yoko Sikes added that jazz clubs in Tokyo had a "music charge" that ran from fifteen to twenty-five hun-dred yen (fourteen to twenty-three dollars at the time) and that "it seems expensive, just like other things in Japan." Actually, the cost is comparable to that of clubs in the States—aside from Japan's Blue Note clubs, which, as I would later find out to my shock in Osaka, cost an arm and a leg and perhaps some other appendages thrown in as well.

Yoko Sikes was born in Yokohama and grew up in Tokyo. According to an indefatigable informant, Shigeyo Hyodo (before leaving the States, I had discovered "Shigeyo's Jazz Page" on the Web), Yoko "received a guide from Toshio Oida, who is the most famous Japanese male jazz singer, during the Tokyo Music College high part enrollment" (?), married an American in 1970, "immigrated to Washington, D.C. in the task place with the husband in the same year," and remained in the States for four years—enough time for her to learn to sing at ease in smooth idiomatic American English, with conviction and emotion that seem quite natural—before returning to Japan with her husband. In 1985, she received a Newcomer of the Year award for jazz vocalist; she recorded her first album—*More Than You Know*—in 1989 and began to appear on NHK English program radio broadcasts.

After Hiromu Aoki's trio warmed up with "Love Walked In," Yoko Sikes opened with "The Song Is You," a tune that fit her range well. "These Foolish Things," with its sultry intonations, also worked nicely. Yoko-san did a fine job of exploring the possibilities of the bridge: extending the "you-u-u" on "You came, you saw," eliciting three syllables, a melismatic effect, from the word "had" in "this ha-a-ad to be." "The Island," a dramatic piece, was sexy ("not a soul can see us . . . taste me with your kisses, find the secret places"), but the suggestiveness was offset by a subdued, unexploitative (although earthy) delivery: "teach me how to please you . . . lose yourself inside me . . . make it last forever." Yoko Sikes has just the right "torch-singer" touch, no overkill, and she phrased the words handsomely. Next, on "It's All Right with Me," rendered up-tempo, she seemed comfortable with the rapid format. "Stranger in Paradise" was supported by Aoki's solid block chords, and perhaps a few too many trills, but the pianist generally offered spare, tasty voicings and "fill."

Some mike problems plagued the first set, but, the situation remedied, a fine, slightly cracking Chris Connor quality came through in Yoko's voice throughout the second. She sang "With a Song in My Heart" and "Once Upon a Summertime" and scatted her way smoothly into "I Could Have Danced All Night," in her element now, voice and gestures relaxed yet buoyant. "I've Grown Accustomed to His Face" and

"On the Street Where You Live" completed the "My Fair Lady Medley," just bass and drums on the latter tune, so that when the piano came back in, the whole group truly *swung*. "No More Blues," "Georgia," "Angel Eyes," and one of my all-time favorites, "Blame It on My Youth" rounded out the evening—a good selection of songs, a solid, engaging performance.

Between sets Betty and I were introduced to Hiroshi "Bamboo" Takeuchi, who had attended one of the International Jazz Party performances in Monterey. He told us he'd been a jazz DJ at age twenty-two in Nagoya, thirty years ago, having first heard the music on radio, then in clubs, during the Occupation. He spoke of the "culture shock" of that time, the "total transformation" of Japanese society after the war. He'd met his wife, who was present, in Nagoya. She too had been a jazz DJ. We all discussed some points Akira Tana brought up in his thesis on jazz in Japan. Takeuchi felt there *was* a big gap in the ability of American and Japanese jazz artists, that the latter lack exposure to "the black experience that found the blues," that they lack "the soul" of black music, that jazz in Japan is still largely "imitation." I was surprised by what seemed a rather uncharitable estimate of his fellow citizens' efforts, but I didn't try to argue in the other direction; I just listened.

During a break, pianist Hiromu Aoki illustrated another of his talents: origami. He folded colored paper (produced magically) into an elephant for me and a small intricate penguin for Betty. It had been a good night: a full, fitting introduction to live Tokyo jazz life. Jazz clubs are called "live houses" in Japan, a phrase I liked.

I don't recall ever hearing an actual *hototogisu,* the bird itself, on either of my trips to Japan—probably because I was there in August both times, and the early-summer bird may well have reached its fabled fate by then, having sung its 8,008 times and passed on. But I did manage to hear a few vocalists live and did collect recordings by as many vocalists as I could. On the cover of her CD *Dreamin',* Miyuki Koga appears dressed in some sort of cast-off Cinderella red crepe netting that defends a pink gown, the abundant crepe also tangled in her pitch-black and slightly tousled hair (decidedly *not* a Japanese ideal; poet Akiko Yosano shocked readers with her book *Midaregami* [Tangled Hair]). But neither this getup (including ostentatious gold gloves) nor even her *voice* is what, for our purposes, is most interesting about Koga. It's her approach to her career. In the liner notes to *Dreamin',* producer George Otaki

71

bemoans song selection on the part of recent jazz vocalists, finding it "quite limited" both in the U.S. and Japan. He concedes that Ellington, Gershwin, Cole Porter, and Richard Rogers are great composers but feels that vocalists should choose from the entire "wide variety of beautiful songs" written by *many* different songwriters between 1910 and 1950— what he calls "the golden time of the American popular song." Singers today, Otaki feels, focus too much on improvisation, having forgotten their role as *interpreters* of great songs. He goes on to explain his concept of "training a Japanese jazz singer, Miyuki Koga"—the *sensei*/student (or disciple) principle at work here again. "I do not allow Miyuki Koga to improvise or distort," Otaki states, because he feels vocalists ruin songs by "making too many changes in the originals." He does *allow* Koga the right to "sing the beautiful songs as straight as possible, following the original melody." This concept, he continues, has been the basis for all of Miyuki's recordings

So what, working strictly (and I mean strictly) within what Otaki calls "the great, immortal, cultural phenomenon, American Popular Song," does Miyuki Koga *sound* like? Koga's "My Buddy" makes you want to be her "buddy" for a time, is a credible opener, but not surprisingly, the vocalist has a slightly irritating, breathless, bedroom urgency to her voice, a very *manufactured* sound. "I Surrender Dear" suffers from overkill, a little too much "surrender," sounding breathlessly insincere—a near parody of Marilyn Monroe. A blues medley—"A Blues Serenade" and "Serenade in Blue"—resurrects two fine tunes from the American Popular Song book, but they don't seem to match Koga's placid, innuendo-laced style. She moves nicely from the verse intro to the main body of "Put the Blame on Me" (her throaty vamp playfully teasing, sultry, and it works), and the CD's final song, "Let Me Sing and I'm Happy," a good lounge closer, allows Koga to open up a bit. However, overall, I couldn't help but wish she'd followed her producer's aspirations less and remained true to her own.

In contrast, Kimiko Itoh is a veteran singer with a fairly extensive international track record. On the cover of a CD called *Follow Me,* she is displayed as very much the "girl singer": gazing off into a haze of gold light, sporting what is either an overlarge, heavily bejeweled bracelet or a highly unusual tennis sweatband. On the title tune, she displays intonation that is more professional than Koga's (seasoned control) and, as is often true of the recordings of these vocalists, excellent company by way of Steve Gadd on drums, Eddie Gomez on bass, and Warren Bernhardt on piano. She handles the twists and turns of the lyrics with agility; even with the expert rhythm section, Itoh, a pro, doesn't seem to need much steering. Yet nearly every song, including John Lennon's "Love" (with its pretentious verbality: "Love is touch, touch is love . . . Love is reaching, reaching love . . . Love is living, living love"), is taken at the same tempo, and the effect grows monotonous. Itoh sings well, but once again, she seems a singer in need of material more in tune with *her own* nature. "If I Loved You," the CD's closer, may provide that—the direct, fond, even cozy, conversational tone just right.

When Itoh appeared with pianist Makoto Ozone at the Montreux Jazz Festival in Japan, in August 1998, a *JazzTimes* reviewer, acknowledging the fact that she's an "accomplished vocalist," praised her rousing opener "On a Clear Day" (in the style of "her idol, Carmen McRae") but felt that, as the set progressed, she seemed to lack "warmth or emotion, or connection with the lyrics." A less charitable critic wrote that Ozone simply outclassed her.

Another vocalist, fortunately not the standard pretty "girl singer," is Yoshiko Goto. The cover of her CD *Day Dream* reveals a finely etched Marlene Dietrich profile, one hand extended, holding a long red-tipped cigarette. The musical mood is that of the "slum glamour romanticism" James Agee admired in Marcel Carne's film *Children of Paradise* mixed with the New Wave Godard of *Breathless*. Born in Tokyo in 1933, Yoshiko Goto started singing in 1952 with Eiji Kitamura and Kiyoshi Yamaya. She visited the States in 1967 and returned for a longer stay from 1970 to 1972, at which time she recorded *Yoshiko Meets Ray Brown* for Nippon Columbia. She has worked with a number of fine musicians in Japanese clubs, Masahiko Satoh among them.

On the title tune, the lovely Ellington/Strayhorn "Day Dream," Goto handles the verse portion well, and when she finally enters the song, she seems at one with the material, *herself* alone (no superficial external standards here), and heartfelt (*makoto*, sincerity of purpose, is a prized Japanese virtue). Goto's major problem seems to be pitch, her reentry after alto saxophonist Yoshio Otomo's solo wavering, uncertain. A fine natural quality is present, a lack of artificial phrasing, on "I Wish I Knew," but so is the iffy pitch. Goto attempts to slur notes, to be instrumental, but the effort doesn't always match up with the lyrics, and the effect seems lax, somewhat inattentive. The series of slow ballads seems monotonous. Are Japanese jazz vocalists somehow locked into this sort of "dreamy" tradition? Or is it a fear of fitting the words into faster tempos? A tune she does full justice to is Janis Ian's "Jesse." With bowed bass backing, she's serene, sexy, lonely (a "hole in the bed where we slept"), at one with the folk narrative feeling. I got goosebumps, and I may be a sucker for this sort of song, but Yoshiko Goto's phrasing on the final "come home" makes you want to do just that. Listening to this song, and to another vocalist's, Akiko Yano's (not known as a jazz singer), version of "Hard Times, Come Again No More," the handsome Stephen Foster song she sings in English (with Charlie Haden on bass and John Clark on French horn), I couldn't help but wonder if jazz is, perhaps, not really *the* natural genre for some of these *hototogisu,* given how well they do on tunes with folk flavor.

Two of my favorite genuine Japanese *jazz* vocalists are Ayako Hosokawa, who has recorded for Three Blind Mice in Japan, and Shoko Amano, who works with pianist Norman Simmons in New York.

On one Hosokawa CD, *Call Me,* she sings with the highly respected Toshiyuki Miyama and the New Herd. The liner notes claim that, because of her "good sound and gentle expression," many professional musicians have hailed Hosokawa as "the best singer" in Japan. In 1977, when she made her debut album on the Japanese jazz scene, she was living in San Francisco (where her mother and daughter still live) but returned to Japan for an extensive tour. In 1984, she made up her mind to serve her musical career there and remained in her hometown, Tokyo. *Call Me* is a fine performance. In the company of a strong, spirited big band, Ayako Hosokawa provides solid interpretations of "Scotch and Soda," "Call Me," "Love Is Here to Stay" (with a Nelson Riddle, behind-and-around, Sinatra punch to the arrangement), and Billy Joel's "Just the Way You Are." Up-tempo, there's a swinging, smooth, sensual, straight-forward quality, and a measure of bemused detachment, to her voice.

Another CD, *A Whisper of Love,* recorded fourteen years after *Call Me* (surgery on throat polyps having intervened), also offers its share of rich selections: a brittle, highly individual "Dream a Little Dream of Me" ("kiss" pronounced "keys") and "Tea for Two" taken at a (surprisingly) slow ballad pace, intimate and ironic, the emotion plausible (I actually believed she *could* bake a sugar cake "for all the boys to see"). A final tune, Eric Clapton's "Tears in Heaven," with its gospel voicings, is quite moving ("I must be strong . . . and carry *on,*" presented with tasteful, not fake, quavering).

For me, the most resilient, individual, engaging vocalist from Japan, the *ichiban* (number-one) singer, is Shoko Amano. Jazz writer

Leslie Gourse finds her voice "soft and malleable—ideally suited for jazz," her improvisations "surprising and fresh," a *slight* foreign accent adding "charm to her interesting harmonic ideas." Gourse also praises Amano's "carefree adventurousness," and I agree, on all counts. Shoko Amano was born in Tokyo. Her father worked as a cook on a U.S. army base, and the singer states that she did not become familiar with the wide range of Japanese cuisine until she moved to the U.S. "I was more accustomed to bacon and eggs for breakfast." Perhaps her diet and her subsequent odyssey in this country—one that took her from L.A. to Chicago to a twenty-fourth-floor New York City apartment—are responsible for her apparent ease with idiomatic English.

Amano's father listened to jazz, but she was originally drawn to pop and R&B. At age twenty-six, she was encouraged by members of an eight-piece band she worked with in L.A. to try jazz songs. She started listening to Ella Fitzgerald and Betty Carter. She says, "My career, my life, and my hopes reached a new high point when I introduced [producer] Hiroko Hashiguchi to [pianist] Norman Simmons." Hashiguchi himself says Amano first began listening to jazz "passionately" in 1956, starting out with Sonny Rollins's *Saxophone Colossus*, realizing that "*any* song can have freshness depending upon each performer's interpretation." Simmons was playing at Bradley's in New York, and Hashiguchi was immediately taken with his playing, so Amano's "dream started to come true when she offered to record us together." When Simmons first met Amano he found her "typically shy and polite" and admired her "tremendous enthusiasm and dedication to the music." At the recording session, she recalls the *basuman* standing right in front of her. He "looked like Buddha and I felt protected and relieved." That bass man was Rufus Reid, who has appeared on two of Amano's CDs, *Shoko Celebrates in New York City* and *500 Miles High*.

The first tune on the former CD, "Where or When," projects fresh, engaging, appropriate phrasing, plaintive longing on that key question "where or when" (she convinces you she really *is* trying to remember). Amano's flexibility—a voice that can shift easily from admonishing to coy to straightforward to nonchalant—is impressive. On Cole Porter's classic "You'd Be So Nice to Come Home To," taken at a truly upbeat tempo, her voice is so inviting, hospitable, you want to be sure to be there at the door to say, if and when she comes to visit, "Yoku irassyaimashita. Dōzo oagari-kudasai!" (It was good of you to come. Please come in!) Amano expresses just the right shade of self-implication, even self-pity, on "I'm a Fool to Want You," and on "The Island," with its sexy lyrics ("teach me how to please you . . . lose yourself inside me")—after a curiously overlong synthesizer Hollywood-movie avalanche—she provides the erotic treatment the song deserves, turning her dream island into an inviting, if perhaps somewhat sandy, love nest. This tune seems popular with Japanese vocalists. (Yoko Sikes sang it at the J Club.)

Shoko Amano's 1990 CD *500 Miles High* is just as engaging. Song selection is a positive factor—two Gershwin tunes, two by Jobim, two by the Beatles—but a vocalist still has to be able to *sing* whatever's being offered. Norman Simmons's tasty bop comping and the vocalist's excellent rhythmic sense turn the Beatles' "Something" into a genuine jazz piece. Shoko Amano really shines on "Body and Soul" and "The Man I Love." On the first song, she commits *both* body and soul, and the latter is as loose and conversational as a singer dare get—Amano, again, well in control of the effect.

Each of the six singers I've commented on has sung her songs (not 8,008 yet, I hope) and paid her dues. If I seem to be more critical of vocalists than of instrumentalists, it's with their challenge of making peak emotional sense in a language not their own in mind. But each of these Japanese vocalists will reward your time—as I feel they did mine.

8

SWING TIME IN GINZA: KOTARO TSUKAHARA AND EIJI KITAMURA

PIANIST KOTARO TSUKAHARA WAS ACTUALLY the first person I phoned when Betty and I arrived in Tokyo. I'd met him when, back in Monterey, I was working for IDEA (International Disabled Exchange Adventures). To raise funds, the organization had put on a benefit jazz concert that featured clarinetist Eiji Kitamura and his quintet, of which Kotaro was a part. I interviewed him when he returned for another benefit concert, and we had since become friends, corresponding by mail. I now looked forward to seeing him again.

When I interviewed Kotaro Tsukahara in Monterey, he told me that, born in Tokyo in 1952, he had, "about ten years ago, visited Eiji Kitamura's music hall" and liked Eiji's music very much. "At first we played together about once a year, then twice, and it went on. All the other members of the current group had known Eiji beforehand. When all five of us got together we realized we were playing good music." Kotaro's own first influence was Oscar Peterson. Then a friend said, "Don't listen to Oscar Peterson anymore. You have to listen to Bud Powell." Kotaro claims he didn't understand Powell the first time he heard him, but "I began to." He also loved Phineas Newborn Jr. and Hank Jones, but "not just pianists. I liked Ella Fitzgerald, Charlie Parker, and, most important for me, recording with Milt Jackson three years ago—a very important step for me." Yet Kotaro says the most important event in his jazz life was meeting Eiji and playing in the United States.

When he performed at the Mt. Hood Jazz Festival in 1991, Kotaro Tsukahara received a standing ovation. Leonard Feather, hearing the pianist at an international jazz party in L.A., which featured many top performers, gave "top honors . . . to Kotaro Tsukahara, a superb neobop pianist who backed [Bob] Cooper." Kotaro studied classical music from the age of three until high school. Smiling, he told me he always wondered why, between the first and second movements of a symphony, no one claps; "they just clear their throats." Classical music consists of adhering to the text, but jazz, from the beginning of his acquaintance with it, "was always up to me. I had to develop an ability to express *myself* within the music." Kotaro says he now has a hard time playing with classical musicians, but he certainly finds no obstacles working with his own trio: bassist Mitsuru Okuda and drummer Yuki Haraguchi. Kotaro had sent me a CD, *Spring Blues,* recorded live at La Maison de Musique in the "Jazz Republic of Tokamachi" in Japan.

Kotaro Tsukahara is much at home with a variety of styles and tempos. On the CD, "My Heart Stood Still" opens with block chords, then employs solid agile runs reminiscent of Bud Powell. "John's Abby" is taken at a breakneck pace (the pianist's classical background an asset here by way of the brilliant use of parallel hands in octaves); on "But Not for Me," Kotaro provides both spare, tasteful improvisation and open stride, with intricate counterpoint at the close. He is decidedly a two-handed pianist. He'd also sent me a video, *The Kotaro Trio: Live in Yume Studio,* with tunes ranging from jazz classics such as "Moten Swing," "Oleo," and Tad Dameron's "Our Delight," to standards such as "Sweet Georgia Brown" and "Little Girl Blue," a tastefully unrestrained funky version of "Night Train" thrown in for good measure. Kotaro can also play the blues, as demonstrated amply by "Black Coffee," and his talent for original composition is displayed by way of "K.T., My Dear" (a fine, richly developed ballad in D-flat) and the rapid-fire "Saphine," with its playful altered tempos. In one of his letters, he promised—should I come to Japan—a visit to the Jazz Republic of Tokamachi, in Niigata prefecture. The pianist has a five-year stipend there for composition, at a retreat-estate established for artists working in various disciplines.

In Monterey, Kotaro Tsukahara and I had discussed the unbridled ego of a trumpet player in an American group performing at the Monterey Jazz Festival: the disruptive effect created. Thinking of consensus as a cultural ideal in Japan, and thinking of the tight sound Eiji Kitamura's group possessed, I asked the pianist and Eiji about this, saying, "Your group is *close,* almost familial. You play handsomely *together,* no one person attempting to steal the sound from the others." Kotaro responded, "We have that type of musician [ego-centered] also in Japan, and when I play a solo, of course I want everyone to know I'm playing. I want to make sure everyone is listening, but I also believe in *orchestration*. Musicians have to listen to each other's sound. You have to strike a balance." At the time, Eiji himself added, "I believe the best musicians are *always* thinking of balance. If just one person has got it in his head, that's not music. I like John Lewis and the Modern Jazz Quartet's 'Django,' because they are all together. I learned much from them."

In Tokyo, Kotaro and I agreed to meet at the Asia Center that night, and when he arrived he brought a delightful young *hototogisu* in tow, a singer he'd discovered named Shiho Sukoi. Kotaro was his customary charming ("really quite charming," Betty wrote in her diary) self, buoyantly bright, his prankish smile wide beneath his full Clark Gable mustache. He had been windsurfing that day, and his hair looked it, his face flushed, glowing. He seemed pleased with himself in a manner that extended beyond whatever prowess he might have displayed atop water. Having the twenty-year-old vocalist Shiho Sukoi (Kotaro is forty-four) by his side probably didn't hurt. Although Kotaro can be shy, which contradicts his dress (he sports bright orange or gold suits at the jazz party concerts), he reminds me of the hero of Natsume Soseki's novel *Botchan* (the word somewhat akin to the archaic English "young master"), a work Donald Keene calls "probably the most widely read novel in modern Japan." Botchan is Huck Finn, Lucky Jim, and Holden Caulfield rolled up into one, a naif, a righteous rascal, never tamed. Kotaro had just returned from Paris, where he had performed with Eiji Kitamura's quintet, and he had been studying French—at the expense of his English, he said, apologizing to us.

Shiho—influenced by Ella Fitzgerald, Sarah Vaughan, and Dianne Reeves, along with Louis Armstrong (which didn't surprise me) and Dinah Shore (which did)—began to sing in earnest about five years ago. As a student, she played clarinet and sang pop, soul (à la Aretha Franklin), and hip-hop music. Her favorite pianist—aside from her mentor, Kotaro, of course—is Phineas Newborn Jr. (also, not so coincidentally, a great favorite of Kotaro's), but she has listened to lots of Bud Powell, Erroll Garner, and Bill Evans. Kotaro first heard her sing at the Rose Room in Shibuya about two years ago. As a vocalist, Shiho's priorities are: (1) to *swing* ("To *feel* the music, to sing only *me*"); (2) to sing in good company (as an integral part of a group, say a trio); and (3) to communicate well in English, so that an audience can catch the message of the song, emphasizing continuity ("Don't stop, word by word") and maintaining an overall texture or tone. She would like to work with only the very best musicians (such as Kotaro) but says that it's "difficult to find them now."

Shiho said she knows hundreds of songs by heart, but very few jazz songs. Betty asked if she knew one of her own favorite tunes, "Skylark," and Kotaro said Shiho wasn't "quite ready for 'Skylark' yet." In order to expand her repertoire, the vocalist is listening, diligently, to CDs. There are, she said, too few radio stations playing jazz in Japan, and none doing so exclusively. Her performances, so far, have been confined to Tokyo and Chiba, but she said, smiling, that she has her sights set on New York and . . . Monterey.

The four of us chatted until almost midnight in the Asia Center lounge. Kotaro said he had a full date book, playing in Fukuoka in Kyushu, in Kobe, Osaka, with intermittent gigs in Tokyo. While Betty and I were in the city, he would be performing at the Swing City Club in Ginza, and he invited us to be his guests for both dinner and "show" there, an invitation we readily accepted.

I'd written the liner notes for Kotaro's most recent CD, *Right On*. I would now—having listened to many Japanese jazz pianists (both live and on disc)—stand by all that I said there. Kotaro is, in a world that offers such a wide range of jazz piano styles, one of the musicians I most enjoy listening to. On *Right On,* Kotaro once again displays his flexibility, his solid taste and skill in a trio setting, but he also proves to be, on three numbers, a sensitive and inspirational accompanist behind Shiho. And on two tracks, "Saphine" (the title a spelling of "Phineas" slightly rearranged) and "Right On" (the words inscribed for Kotaro by vibraphonist Milt Jackson when the two recorded together in 1990), the pianist shows, once again, that he is also a fine composer.

A smooth boogie-woogie vamp introduces Shiho Sukoi singing "Lullaby of Broadway." Her intonation is both swinging and sultry. On other tunes, Kotaro and the trio pay homage to Hampton Hawes by way of his funky "The Sermon," with its gospel-blues vamp and more parallel-hands-in-octaves finesse—a technique Kotaro shares with Benny Green, and with much skill. "Chelsea Bridge" displays Kotaro's heartfelt, mature, "ballad" style: it is a beautifully rendered version of this beautiful tune. A vertigo-inducing "Dizzy Atmosphere" turns into a repeated bop riff and sharp runs reminiscent of Bud Powell—an encyclopedic display of piano effects concluded by a subtle fade-out. Kotaro's other original, "Right On," concludes the CD.

Betty and I planned an all-day excursion that would permit us to see a host of Tokyo sights, ending at the Swing City Club in Ginza on the night that Kotaro had invited us to dinner. First we thought we would get up at the crack of dawn and visit Tsukiji, the city's infamous early-morning fish market where members of the wholesalers' association bid on the day's catch, 90 percent of the fish to be consumed in Tokyo that day having arrived—via truck, not ship—from ports all over Japan. Bidding is over by 6:30 A.M., and we weren't even out of bed by then, but we did manage to visit the area around 9:00, the sushi bars and fishmonger stalls that line the street fully active. We crossed an overpass into the relative seclusion and wooded ease of Hamarikyu Garden, a tranquil spot with misty remnants of Tokyo buildings hovering—a dreamy afterthought—above the trees but not allowed in. We strolled to the spot where we caught the water bus that takes you up the Sumida River to Asakusa and the Sensoji Temple.

The Sumida has been celebrated in a series of *edo byobu* (folding screens) by Hokusai and in the novel *Sumidagawa,* by Nagai Kafu. The latter, elegiac in tone, describes an end-of-the-century Tokyo as it succumbs to the imposition of Western "civilization." Yet aside from what Kafu describes as the "incessant shilling of the cicadas" and "weather turned oppressively humid, a greasy claminess clinging to the skin," our river trip was more in the vein of the joyous pictorial sprawl of Hokusai's *Panoramic View of the Sumidagawa:* musicians and a dog-faced dancer performing Kagura (Shintō music) in the Yoshiwara Pleasure District and sake-happy *sakura-* (cherry blossom) seeking pilgrims crossing a bridge. The bridges *we* passed beneath were ultrasleek, modern, and strung like harps. Long slender excursion boats sat laced together in harbor. The balconies of cold, concrete, high-rise apartment complexes sported walls of laundry or futons set out to air in the sun. As our boat chugged up the river, creating a breeze that assuaged the heat, I imagined that I was listening to music provided by Kotaro Tsukahara and Eiji Kitamura on a duet recording called *Dream Dancing*—the two on board for a perfect excursion gig that mingled with the stories the guide told about the various bridges we passed under.

Back in Monterey, after the first benefit concert he'd played, curious as to how he'd come to be dubbed the "Benny Goodman of Japan,"

I'd also talked with Eiji about his life in jazz. "I first heard Benny Good-man," he told me, "when I was sixteen years old. I didn't know jazz then. Only I heard Beethoven, Bach, Mozart. But I found a recording by Benny Goodman and I was very surprised. When I closed my eyes, I saw many many big buildings and streets just like in America. 'What kind of music *is* this?' I asked myself. I was so excited I listened every day to [the] record 'Don't Be That Way.' Just three minutes! I wanted to play some-thing jazz myself. That's when I found the clarinet." He joined an ama-teur student band while attending Keio University and went on to play with Saburo Nambu's quintet in 1951, forming his own group in 1954: the Cat's Herd, consisting of vibraharp, piano, bass, drums, and clarinet, the name chosen in homage to Woody Herman. Kitamura first won *Swing Journal*'s readers' poll as number-one clarinetist in 1959 (he's won every year since), fronting a group that performed regularly on NET-TV's "Morning Echoes" program; he was the first Japanese artist invited to participate at the Seattle International Clarinet Society Conference in 1986. He toured Japan with Buddy DeFranco in 1989, without rehearsal. "We made head arrangements and, every time, it fit: same time our breaths! He likes my quintet because we can do *any* style."

Kitamura actually performed with Benny Goodman in 1959, at a jam session organized by the American Embassy in Tokyo. He began to copy Goodman's style, then, hearing Lee Konitz and Artie Shaw, theirs. He wondered if his own approach to jazz was "true or imitation, and I have doubt every time I play." Performing with another pro, Hank Jones, he thought, "I'm okay," yet when he finally got to play with Teddy Wil-son, in 1969, the pianist, concerned about imitation, actually advised Kitamura to take up another instrument. "I tried tenor saxophone," said Eiji. Yet he stuck with the clarinet, adhering to Wilson's advice to "keep your own idea," to develop his own approach and style—which he has: a style characterized by clarity, purity, a rich lovely "wood" tone (a legacy from Artie Shaw perhaps, or even traditional *shakuhachi* music), and a knack for speed and embellishment reminiscent of DeFranco. Having learned "many many things" (substitute chords, progressions) from Wilson, he also received encouragement and sound advice from Earl "Father" Hines.

When I asked Kitamura about formal training, his background, he flashed his very genial smile, nodding, and said, "Only myself. Every time I listened to records—Benny Goodman, Artie Shaw, Buddy DeFranco, Edmond Hall—I wondered, how to play improvisation? I could make a phrase maybe, but when I went to the army forces club, the soldiers taught me many things. Do you know Hampton Hawes? I didn't know his name at this time, but he played with me and showed me modern style."

"You had the best teachers in the world!" I couldn't help but interjecting, conducting this interview.

"Yes," Kitamura replied, with his polite nod, almost a bow. "Jazz greats were very gentle and very kind for me."

Cruising up the Sumida River now, in Tokyo, I heard (imagining Eiji and Kotaro's performance on the *Dream Dancing* CD) the title tune, by Cole Porter, taken at an open, airy bounce, Kotaro's modified, slightly staccato stride offset by Eiji's frictionless sailing through the phrases, his spacious dance, as much at ease as we felt on the boat, taking in the city. "I'll Be Seeing You" has a frisky lilt to it, lacy piano figures, Eiji's handsome counterpoint, the whole turned into a swinging romp. Such uptempo tunes are offset by a slow, brooding, proper degree of dignified self-pity on "Everything Happens to Me," Eiji's stately, no-frills remorse transformed into pride of place as we sailed up the Sumida.

Once docked, Betty and I walked up to Asakusa's Kaminarimon (Thunder God Gate) with its huge red paper lantern marking the entrance to Sensoji Temple, which you don't actually reach until you've traversed a long walkway laced with stalls selling every trite or gaudy tourist trinket imaginable: tea sets, bad paintings, umbrellas, toys for children. For me, the temple's main attraction was a large pot, a huge bronze incense burner over which you bathe your hands, thrusting your face into the smoke to ward off illness. Thus purified, you climb the steps of the main hall and offer a prayer to Kannon, goddess of mercy.

After paying such homage, we took the Ginza line from Asakusa station and transferred to Tokyo Station, where we had business to conduct: obtaining *shinkansen,* or bullet-train tickets, for our forthcoming trip to Wakura Hot Springs. Betty discovered a retrospective show of the work of the great woodcut artist Shiko Munakata on display on the top floor of the Dainaru Department Store—an establishment that also houses a fifth-floor putting green, so that avid golfers, awaiting a train, can kill time *that* way. The myopic Munakata carved his woodblocks at fever pitch, his chin nearly resting on the board, the unrelenting manner in which he worked suggesting, to museum director Masayoshi Honma, "the insistent strokes of the plectrum used by the player of the thick-necked *shamisen* as he beats out, allowing not a moment of respite, the dynamic, incessant rhythm." Trusting wood blocks the way a jazzman would his instrument (he believed the blocks possessed *hitogari,* or energy, produced when the soul of the artist meets the soul of the wood), Munakata called the birth of a print "a happy, teasing expectation," a phrase that could easily be applied to jazz improvisation. "A print springs out by itself," Munakata said, "just as joy, wonder or sorrow does." Once again I'd found an aesthetic, derived from another art, that fit jazz practice perfectly in Japan. Soetsu Yanagi, Munakata's mentor and patron, said, "Essentially, it is not really a question of old or new, but of the beauty of the elemental."

Swing City was what I would call a posh club, although a signboard outside the door simply announced "live jazz" ("Kotaro Tsukahara: Solo Piano"). An avocado green entryway stands adjacent to a curved window, panels sporting a black bass drum jutting from the wall, the club's logo inscribed on its round surface, a larger bass drum with the same logo suspended above a glossy silver art-deco awning that runs the length of the building. Once we entered we were struck by black baby grand pianos that served as tables, patrons perched on bar stools, and— the feature attraction—a large grand piano that sat before a wall-sized slanted mirror that reflected its keyboard. This is where Kotaro—who greeted us wearing a flamboyant black and gray striped tuxedo (Kotaro is just about the only person I know who can make a tux look flamboyant), his pants held up by keyboard-bearing suspenders, and a snappy bow tie—would perform. A wide ledge flanked the stage piano, and we were directed to seats there facing the mirror—recipients then of an exceptional meal: octopus and lobster for Betty, salmon pasta topped with roe for me, all decidedly "uptown" (including the service), a gift from Kotaro, who hovered in the background, awaiting his term at the keyboard. I was afraid to look at the prices on the menu but did: Betty's dish twenty-four hundred yen, mine fourteen hundred—not really all that expensive, compared to a similar meal in the States.

Shiho was there also, looking absolutely stunning in a form-fitting crimson dress, and we were introduced to the pianist's mother, a distinguished woman dressed in white who, we learned, gives cello lessons. Kotaro's father, deceased, was a classical composer of stature (we also learned), so my friend comes by his talents naturally, although his mother, when I told her of my fondness for her son Kotaro's work, emphasizing his extraordinary technique, just smiled and said, "He's getting better." Whatever, he was an obvious crowd pleaser at the Swing City Club, a personable and passionate entertainer, offering a mix of sprightly jazz standards (Chick Corea's "Spain," Bill Evan's "Waltz for Debby") and ballads ("I Cover the Waterfront," "Smoke Gets in Your Eyes," "I've Got a Crush on You"). The diners loved it all, a man next to Betty attempting to impress his date, who was wearing a kimono, by snapping his fingers in time to each and every tune, but unfortunately on beats one and three, rather than the proscribed two and four. The house lights were extinguished for "You Don't Know What Love Is" and trimmed suitably blue for an extended Gershwin medley that commenced with portions of "Rhapsody in Blue." Shiho was introduced and sang, "How Long Has This Been Going On?"—handsomely. It was a full evening of music for which the pianist was sufficiently rewarded by wild rounds of applause.

I'd had a ball playing my own fairly limited brand of piano in the cozy, hospitable parlor of Ami's, but I waxed nervous when Kotaro asked me to come up at the Swing City Club and play "Ain't Misbehavin'" with him—although I went. I got the treble part, Kotaro providing rich lower register chords and runs that filled up all the empty spots, and the crowd seemed to dig it—one man borrowing Betty's camera and snapping a quick sequence of photos that, once developed, documented the fact that we were having one hell of a good time. After, I would even kick myself for not having worked up the nerve to *sing!* The pianist asked me to tell the audience about my trip, which I did (in English, fortunately), and then his mother too made a speech, pointing out in Japanese the importance, to her (and the audience, she felt), of something I'd said about jazz as a genuinely *international* language.

Betty and I found ourselves feeling very much at home in a setting we'd been, initially, a bit wary of (scanning its elegance when we walked in). Japanese jazz lovers seem to have a knack for converting nearly any setting into a comfortable and compatible *hōjō* (ten-foot-square hut, as in the classic book *Hōjōki,* by Chomei), one that keeps expanding with graciousness. We were especially pleased to meet Kotaro's Mum, a charming, sophisticated woman who asked Betty to "take care of my son when he is in Monterey." When we left, Kotaro and I gave each other a big hug, which made his Japanese male friends crack up with laughter. They asked us to do it again and laughed raucously again, as if this were the most hilarious and absurd custom in the world—aside from relentlessly bowing, I suppose.

On our return to the Asia Center, the subway was packed, happily intox-icated young couples engaged in another custom you don't see too much of in Japan: "making out" in the open, in public no less. But none of the *sararīman* on board, more than slightly intoxicated themselves, nor the sober old ladies returning from God knows where, saw fit to censure the couples. Leaving the Nogizaka subway station, we took what had become a favorite shortcut home, through General Nogi's shrine. Known to the West as "the hero of Port Arthur," General Nogi's destiny was more complex than this simple encomium would suggest. On Sep-tember 13, 1912, on the night of Emperor Meiji's funeral, the general and his wife each committed seppuku (ritual suicide), or in this case *jun-shi* (vassal's death). At the time of Nogi's suicide, an editorial called "The Soul of a Samurai" asserted that Nogi's last act was a warning that the members of the military class were growing to be "lovers of money and Western luxuries."

I thought of the Western luxury, jazz, we had just spent an evening listening to and of the juxtaposition of these two sides of Japan: Kotaro's overt joy in the music he has dedicated his life to and General Nogi's act of loyalty that deprived him of life. I didn't try to make immediate sense of it all but just stared at the plain (very "Western") wooden residence and the irregularly shaped white stone that contains Nogi's stern and purposeful visage set in green metal relief, the kanji for "gift" or memo-rial inscribed in black beneath it.

Having already gathered evidence in Tokyo—from Masahiko Satoh to Kiyoko Ami to Yoko Sikes to Kotaro Tsukahara—of the popu-larity, pervasiveness, and persistence of jazz in a nation that, on the sur-face (aside from the superficialities of Westernization), appears to have so little in common with the United States, I still had to ask, Why *jazz?* Then I realized that—aside from seppuku—Japanese traditional culture provides a readymade template for jazz. Howard Hibbett's description of the *ukiyo* (floating world) of the Genroku period (1680–1740) could well serve as a description or even definition of jazz, with its blues coun-terpart and "Storyville" mythology. The essence of *ukiyo* was "an unre-flective enjoyment of the moment—a moment valued for whatever was newest in the arts, as well as for the casual virtuoso who could improvise beautifully." Yet, according to Hibbett, Genroku artists were also thor-oughgoing professionals: actors, dancers, and musicians trained from childhood. The purpose of such long training was "to combine spon-taneity and skill, through a mastery of traditional techniques. The painter had a repertoire of effects, and worked very swiftly; poets, as well as storytellers, were ready to improvise on any suitable theme." Popular songs, the kind sung by courtesans, were called "*ukiyo*-tunes." Yet, like the blues, *ukiyo* retained the overtones of its earlier Buddhist use to suggest the sad impermanence of earthly things, "the transience of life."

Ukiyo, like jazz, even had its puritan counterpart, its detractors forewarning that "a woman . . . ought not to become addicted to tea or sake. Enjoying amorous songs or music is a special peril; she must avoid all improper amusements." The name of the Genroku period's popular form of theater, Kabuki (eventually written to mean "song and dance art"), retained its original sense of "lewdness" or "abandon" (troupes of women "allured men by singing, dancing, and performing humorous skits"), just as the word "jazz" (jass) does. Is it any wonder jazz took hold in Japan? The nation was set up for it in the seventeenth century, long *long* before F. Scott Fitzgerald concocted "The Jazz Age"!

KING RECORDS, THE JAZZ RESTORATION IN JAPAN, AND *SWING JOURNAL*

Bᴀᴄᴋ ɪɴ ᴛʜᴇ Sᴛᴀᴛᴇs, ᴅʀᴜᴍᴍᴇʀ Akira Tana had given me the name of Yoichi Nakao, the man in charge of the "International Repertoire" at King Records in Japan and the producer of a number of fine jazz recordings I already possessed. In Tokyo, I phoned him and we arranged a time to meet. The address seemed simple enough—1-2-3 Otowa, Bunkyo-ku—and the directions were fairly basic, for Tokyo: a city of 8.5 million souls in which street numbers (when they exist) are not consecutive or sequential and mail gets delivered God (or *kami*, gods) only knows how. I was told to take the Yurakucho line to Edogawabashi exit A1, to cross a bridge, and that the twelve-story King Building would then be on the right side of the street. "You can't miss it," Nakao said, and, miraculously, I didn't. I ordinarily, by now, gave myself ample time to get lost finding any destination in Tokyo, but on this outing the grace period wasn't necessary. Arriving early, I found a modicum of shelter from the substantial August heat on the grounds of a small temple near the building in which King Records is housed.

I hadn't exactly expected a silver-haired, six-foot-four CEO, but if I had, Yoichi Nakao would have been even more of a shock than he was when he came out to greet me. Wearing large, slightly tinted shades, his black hair parted in the middle with shocks falling to each side, he had a green short-sleeved shirt buttoned at the collar and sported the fresh bright face of a schoolboy. He looked so young it was impossible to tell just how old this executive really was, and he possessed a zeal, a busy, constantly on-the-go, upbeat nature, that enhanced his youthful appearance.

The actual office area looked afflicted with the typical Japanese problem of lack of space. Employees seemed herded into an area of desks set off by an old-fashioned wooden rail, boxes (of recordings, I assumed) stacked everywhere. I was directed to a narrow room adjacent to the office area, wall-to-wall shelves lined with CDs, television sets (why this?), and a guitar in a dark brown cloth bag. Plus more cardboard boxes, not labeled King Records, but "Fruit of the Loom (Premium Quality Active Wear)"—and again, why this? Yoichi Nakao disappeared and reappeared and disappeared. While I waited for another magical return, piped-in music offered the Beach Boys' "I Wish They All Could Be California Girls," and I had to smile, hearing this tune so far from home.

When he settled in to a seat across from me, Nakao let his youthful enthusiasm shine through as he described a current King Records project. He was recording Delfeayo Marsalis with a Japanese rhythm section, young musicians who'd already recorded with the trombonist's celebrated brother Wynton. The musicians who made up the rhythm section were members of what Nakao called the "jazz restoration in Japan," a movement described (in liner notes of CDs that Yoichi Nakao would give me) by critic Masahisa Segawa—one of the "Leonard Feathers"—as "a long-awaited younger generation of jazzmen finally emerging in Japan." Segawa compared their "dramatic appearance" to that of the Wynton Marsalis Quintet in 1982 (which featured both the trumpeter and older brother Branford), heralded in the States as an onslaught of "young lions" (players still in their teens or twenties) who helped, according to Segawa, "instill unprecedented vigor into the world of jazz." They combined tradition (a "straight-ahead four-beat acoustic sound") with innovation, experimenting with fresh harmonies and instrumental techniques.

The critic traced the Japanese branch of this youthful revolution to drummer Yoichi Kobayashi, who, born in 1953, arrived in the States in 1982 and survived as a street musician in New York, founding a group called "Good Fellas" that featured then-unknown saxophonist Vincent Herring; drummer Masahiko Osaka (a student at Berklee College); and pianist Makoto Kuriya, who while in the U.S. developed a musical theory known as "X-Bar," which he would later use as the name of his own group. Returning to their native land in 1992, all three Japanese musicians "actively recruited new players," such as trumpeter Tomonao Hara, trombonist Eijiro Nakagawa, and guitarist Yoshiaki Okayasu.

Thus the "jazz restoration in Japan" was born. Kobayashi, hailed as "one of the greatest bop drummers" (he celebrated the twentieth anniversary of his musical career with a national tour in 1996), called himself the "Art Blakey of Japan" and organized a second all-rookie "Good Fellas" aggregate made up exclusively of Japanese performers. Masahisa Segawa ends his assessment of the movement's potential by stating that "today's jazz restoration in Japan, led by the young lions born after 1960, is about to enter a new phase: a full-fledged war."

Ironically, the word "restoration" in Japan implies revolution, an inheritance from the Meiji Restoration, named after Emperor Meiji, who ascended the throne in 1867 at the age of fifteen and whose *fukko* (return to antiquity) would actually turn Japan on its head, introducing an oligarchy whose slogan was *bummei-kaika* (civilization and enlightenment) and thus unleashing a wild tide of Westernization. Yoichi Nakao's eyes shone with just such high hopes for the jazz restoration movement; what was more, as I would soon find out, he had a suitable—flashy and fully modernized—battleground on which the contest for the future of jazz could unfold. Leaving the cramped office quarters behind, we stepped out into the heat of day and strolled up the street to a place where, if war was to be waged, it would happen on grounds second to none: a bright, beautiful new recording studio that, aside from its obvious technological advantages, would prove to be something of an architectural wonder in its own right.

On the way there, Nakao regaled me with information that illustrated the high seriousness and art of the young musicians who make up the jazz restoration in Japan. His primary example was an alto saxophonist, Kyoto-born Joh Yamada, age twenty-seven, who "wants to *study* more" before making an album of his own. "Most musicians would be very happy to make a recording right away," Nakao added, "but Joh Yamada wants to wait." A former student at Hitotubashi University, Yamada enrolled at Berklee in Boston in 1989, drummer Masahiko Osaka and pianist Junko Onishi his classmates. Blessed with striking good looks, Yamada has acquired a host of female jazz fans in spite of his *gaman* (patience), his willingness to wait for a recording debut. Yoichi Nakao also emphasized the point that this generation of musicians had proceeded directly to acoustic jazz, bypassing the temptations of a "fusion phase" completely. He used the word *ishi* (will, or willpower), emphasizing the intentionality or *tenki* (turning point) nature of the youthful jazz movement—another similarity to the Meiji era.

90

Indeed. Entering King Records Sekiguchidai Studio is like entering another era, or perhaps your own future dream house. Nakao himself seemed to adopt a sort of pride-induced samurai strut. Brightly burnished blond hardwood floors are offset by the black rims of glass doors. A splendid Yamaha grand piano sits poised like some oversized but fully graceful three-legged ballerina upon the floor. A speaker system lodged on the walls is so spiffy, so clean, you'd be tempted to eat off of it, as inviting as lacquer bowls. The acoustics of the room approach perfection, I'm sure. Everywhere, I saw Japanese design in its most natural, simple, efficient state: combining strict order with the teasing asymmetry the Japanese love.

I was taken to a smaller, more intimate "teahouse" enclosure that served as a room for mixing and mastering recordings. There, I was introduced to the *sensei* (master) mixer and his two assistants and shown to a seat that faced an imposing desk replete with all the computerized tools of the trade, along with two large consoles for playing tapes and two monumental speakers set on a stagelike area at the room's end. Yoichi Nakao excused himself and set off on producer's chores elsewhere, and I sat and watched and listened to the intricate proceedings before me. The verbal exchange that accompanied the "mix" was too rapid for me to comprehend, although I did understand when an assistant said, "Kakimasu" (I will write it down), seizing a clipboard and scrawling something on it in haste. The group was working on "Some Day My Prince Will Come," as recorded by Dusko Goykovich, a Yugoslavian trumpeter Nakao described for me (the producer would appear and disappear with the alacrity, the high nervous energy, of a firefly) as the "Miles Davis of Europe." The rhythm section on the recording was made up of Japanese "young lions": Yutaka Shiina on piano, Masahiko Osaka on drums, and Shin Kamimura on bass. When the team of technicians had mixed "Prince" to their satisfaction, they went to work on a piece called "Tokyo Shuffle Blues." After one of the assistants nodded what seemed to be final approval, the master said, "Kiite, kudasai!" (Let's listen again, if you please!) They listened to the same take over and over and over again, until (fine as the music was) I was nearly sick of it. Their perception seemed to grow more precise, more critical, as mine declined.

Although I found the process interesting, I was nearly grateful when Yoichi Nakao returned and took me back to a studio where— beyond a glass window and the largest mixing board I have ever seen (it ran the full length of the wall), its tidy display of levers and dials as intricate as the controls of a giant jetliner—a symphony orchestra was recording with a *shakuhachi* master.

Before I left, I was loaded up with King Records Co., Ltd., literature, an English-language version of its compact disc catalog—one provoking outright lust on my part when I glanced at its wide selection of Japanese traditional music (*gagaku,* Noh, *biwa,* koto, *shakuhachi*); work, festival, and regional music; Kabuki and Bunraku pieces; an extraordinary range of world music (Iraqi, Azerbaijani, Pakistani, Hindustani, Vietnamese, Mongolian, Gamelan from Bali, Nigerian—you name it!); classical music; marches; Buddhist chant; "relaxation" music; jazz; pop; Japanese rock; and a "Let's Dance" collection that featured waltz, tango, fox trot, samba, rumba, jive, and quick step.

Yoichi Nakao assuaged my lust, slightly, when he gave me a generous sampling of CDs from the "jazz restoration in Japan" series. When I thanked him profusely in Japanese, he complimented me on my command of the language, a command I then—thrown off guard by this unexpected commendation perhaps—proved I didn't have. Nervous, I used, by mistake, the word *itadakimasu* (a blessing uttered before meals) instead of the appropriate *dōitashimashite* (Oh no, you are much too kind). It was a stupid elementary error on my part that prompted a quick lesson in the use of the all-purpose *dōmo,* a word that covers every occasion from regret over a faux pas to answering the phone and even established greetings such as hello and good-bye.

Gripping my stash of CDs, I bowed in gratitude for all forms of Yoichi Nakao's generosity, including the language lesson.

Unfortunately, at the time of the jazz restoration in Japan, the United States jazz scene was touting its own crop (or pride) of young lions: Joshua Redman, Benny Green, Roy Hargrove, Kenny Garrett, Maria Schneider, James Carter, Christian McBride, Nicolas Payton, Geri Allen, Charlie Hunter, etc. I say "unfortunately" because, before I left for Japan, I'd only heard of three members of that nation's own jazz restoration, and I'd come across them mostly by accident. Young trombonist Eijiro Nakagawa showed up with his father, trumpeter Yoshihiro Nakagawa, leader of a group called the Dixie Team (the *meishi,* or business card, he gave me said "Y. Nakagawa & Dixie Dix") that performed at the International Jazz Party (then in its sixth year) concert in Monterey. I chatted with Yoshihiro Nakagawa at a Friday-night potluck dinner sponsored by

IDEA, and the next night, at the concert, his son caused a sensation. Eijiro Nakagawa, a musically "gifted" child at the tender age of three, joined his father's group at six and received a special audition at Berklee College when he was sixteen (when he also began to record in New York). The second "accident" happened when I was reading a review of a CD called *Favorites*, a recording that featured a group led by drummer Masahiko Osaka and trumpeter Tomonao Hara. I went out to find the recording immediately and was witness to some very fine, and exciting, music.

Favorites includes a number of my own personal favorite tunes— "Everything Happens to Me," "All the Things You Are," "I Remember Clifford," "Just Friends," and "I Can't Get Started"—so it wasn't at all difficult to be well disposed toward the selections. But it was the performances that stood out, the interpretations. Osaka and Hara were assisted by Tetsuro Kawashima on tenor and soprano saxophones, Shuhei Mizuno on piano, and Shin Kamimura on bass. It's a tight group, alert and astutely listening to one another. The first tune offered is a laid-back "Night in Tunisia," which, after its slashing drum start, subsides to a vamp and light trumpet topping. Hara has a handsome tone, mostly midrange but capable of piercing high notes he doesn't abuse, and Kawashima's solos contain a fine steady *genki* (energy or health). The group isn't "electrifying" in the manner of Roy Hargrove's group (with the exceptional Willie Jones III on drums), but it exudes pride, precision, poise, and what Hart Crane called "the logic of poetry," a sort of formal passion, an asymmetrical "attack."

My two favorite pieces on *Favorites* are originals: Tomonao Hara's "Getting Out of the City," with its bright disarray (a sense of traffic lights changing at random, on whim), a city's raw spirit under just partial control, fine interplay between Kawashima and Mizuno (the latter's frisky, nimble-witted rejoinders); and Masahiko Osaka's "Chal's Tap," which allows him to come front and center, showing his range from cymbal-charged carnival-flavored Latin rhythms to full-kit solo exploits behind Kawashima's tenor solo. Osaka, born in Akita, thirty years old, shows why he was recently voted *ichiban* (number-one) drummer in Japan. Influenced by his father, a guitarist, he started to learn drums (he likes Elvin Jones and Tony Williams) in elementary school. He came to the States in 1986, graduated from Berklee in 1989, toured with classmate Delfeayo Marsalis, and returned to Japan in 1990, where he established the quintet with Hara in 1992.

Tomonao Hara was born in Kanagawa, took up trumpet in elementary school, cultivated jazz as a college student (by way of Clifford Brown), and, regarded by some as the core of the contemporary Japanese jazz scene, was voted *ichiban* trumpeter in Japan. Hara and trombonist Eijiro Nakagawa have put together an excellent CD called *For Musicians Only*. Two top "restoration" pianists lend their services to the rhythm sections: Yutaka Shiina and Makoto Kuriya (the latter works with two other groups, Baltimore Syndicate and his own X-Bar Trio). Nakagawa, Hara, and Osaka all appear on one of the more interesting CDs given to me by Yoichi Nakao, an evening of "duels" recorded live at Jazz Court "TUC," in Tokyo, in 1995. The recording is called *Twin Heroes: Jazz Battle Royal* and presents a number of jazz restoration "young lions" competing among themselves. Alto saxophonists Seiji Tada and Joh Yamada square off on "If I Should Lose You," Tada's clear, unembellished Willie Smith sweet float mixed with quickening runs, Yamada angular, occasionally even harsh, his sense of rhythm pleasantly erratic, supplying variety and surprise. The best, most lively trumpet exchange engages Tomonao Hara and Yoshiro Okazaki on "Just Friends." Veteran tenor saxophonist Sleepy Matsumoto takes on Tetsuro Kawashima in a fun, funky, decadent duel on "Moritat," Matsumoto cutting loose with a wild spate of notes, Kawashima meeting him on his own ground, a back and forth chase turning into a genuine battle royal, dissonant and wild.

I was also given two *Jazz Restoration in Japan* CDs, volumes three and four, featuring the work of the foregoing artists but also fine pianists and drummers I was not familiar with. The pianists were Keichi Yoshida and Yuichi Inoue; the drummers were Yoichi Kobayashi, Shuichi "Ponta" Murakami (whom I would hear later in Yokohama), and Shingo Okudaira. Keichi Yoshida is featured with Tomonao Hara on another Hara original called "Plain." Yuichi Inoue is an impressive pianist whose trio work on an original, "Whenever I Miss You," and the standard "I Want to Be Happy" shows a deft, intelligent touch, enticingly understated on the first tune, dazzling on the second, with his fleet as hell (seemingly impossible) extended bop runs. On volume three of *The Jazz Restoration in Japan*, alto saxophonist Atsushi Ikeda's group Inside Out is represented by "Free and Strong," a piece containing multiple rhythms, crisp chirping alto sax cries, and a fine spare solo by guitarist Satoshi Inoue.

All in all, exposure to the jazz restoration in Japan left me acquainted with a host of excellent young performers, and I could see why Yoichi Nakao and his colleagues at King Records were so excited about the "event."

When I arrived at the offices of *Swing Journal* for my appointment with Bunichi Murata, the magazine's chief editor, I was pleased to discover that the man who would serve as translator was Jake Mori, a journalist I had met in Monterey at an Eiji Kitamura concert. Mori is a large man, by Japanese standards, with a stocky body and the wide stoic face of a sumo wrestler. Bunichi Murata wore a striped short-sleeved shirt and an active abstract expressionist tie. He was a slender, serious, distinguished-looking man.

I'd read somewhere that *Swing Journal* had the largest circulation of any jazz magazine in the world. "Numbā one?" said Mori.

"Yes," Murata replied. "Next year, we are going to celebrate our fiftieth anniversary."

"Omedetō gozaimasu" (congratulations), I said.

"I have been the chief editor of *Swing Journal* for about four years now, but I'd been a reader of the magazine for more than twenty years before that."

I suggested that editors in the United States might very well envy— even be jealous of—the magazine's success. What did he attribute it to? Did that success reflect the influence or importance of jazz in Japan?

"Nan deshō-ka?" Mori said.

"Hmmmm. The circumstance was right, because for forty years we were the *only* jazz magazine in Japan, but the jazz scene itself is changing. From the time that I was just a reader, a subscriber, until now, as chief editor of *Swing Journal,* I have seen radical changes . . . the greatest change took place in the 1970s. I think perhaps because, just as with the coming of rock music to America, the social status of jazz changed. Just as society changed, so did jazz. Looking back at the articles of that time, I can see that jazz had become part of the 'rock society.' We don't see those kind of articles here at *Swing Journal* anymore. People understand the music on its *own* terms now. Our readers' interests have changed, just as social values have changed."

I mentioned having heard Yoko Sikes at the J Club and Kotaro Tsukahara at Swing City, saying that there seemed to be quite a bit of jazz activity. How many clubs were there, altogether, in Tokyo?

"Hyaku go-jū," he replied to Jake Mori, but I understood that without translation (150) and was surprised. "Possibly 150. Clubs where jazz is played. But *exclusively* jazz, we really don't know the number of those clubs. But so-called jazz spots, yes, more than a hundred."

I said that I'd been surprised to discover that both of the clubs I'd been to had full schedules of jazz each night. Murata presented me with a sheet that included a list.

"Perhaps you can see here." He pointed. "From here to here, these are jazz clubs, live spots that include jazz music."

"That's amazing," I said. "Where I live, jazz clubs are being converted into *sports* bars."

Murata smiled and laughed softly, sympathetically, when this last phrase was translated. I said that, in comparison, the scene appeared to be quite healthy in Japan, at least in Tokyo. I mentioned the two opinions I'd received on the quality of the jazz: Tiger Okoshi's feeling that Japanese performers were now major league, playing on the same level as Americans; and the DJ from Nagoya's view that a "gap" still existed, as far as the level of ability went. Which was true?

"Hmmmmm. In my opinion, there isn't a big gap. I have not seen, recently, *any differences* in levels of performance. Of course, I'm not talking about late, great players. Maybe before the seventies there was no comparison, but these days, Japanese players are showing considerable improvement in their abilities."

I mentioned the young musicians associated with the jazz restoration in Japan, and Murata nodded. I also mentioned players known in the United States—such as pianist Aki Takase and guitarist Akio Sashijima—who were not well known in Japan, or not any longer.

"I think, talking about Aki Takase, it really depends on *who* is evaluating her ability. I think Aki Takase herself felt this way: 'Perhaps I should play in Europe rather than Japan, because European people will evaluate my abilities differently, will be more responsive to the type of music I play.'"

"Do two groups exist: performers known only in Japan and Japanese players known mostly in the U.S.?"

"Hmmmm. *Big* question."

"Makoto Ozone goes back and forth. Tiger Okoshi has a home in Boston. Toshiko goes, well, everywhere it seems!"

"I don't think it's a *trend* or anything like that. It's a personal matter, and up to the ability of the performer to play jazz. And I'm thinking that this relates to the audience for *Swing Journal*. We publish the magazine not just for the jazz *maniac* but also for ordinary jazz fans. Favoritism extends not just to straight-ahead jazz, but free jazz and fusion as well. So it really depends on what kind of jazz a person is playing. Maybe Takase is playing in the free jazz style, whereas on the other hand, Makoto and Tiger Okoshi perhaps play more straight-ahead or mainstream jazz. It's a *no boundaries* sort of music, and there is an audience for each kind."

I asked about the sort of educational programs one found at Berklee College of Music in the States. Anything similar in Japan?

"We don't have that kind of conservatory, no. But a number of music schools do have a brother or sister relationship to Berklee College, or other music conservatories in the United States."

When I mentioned universities such as North Texas State, jazz programs within a conventional music curriculum, Murata said, "It's not like that here. A significant trend is to find a name player in Japan who has his *own* school, his own type of training, and study with that person. That's happening now here in Japan. And because of this practice, a university such as Kunitachi, a music university, which doesn't have an authentic jazz program, has students studying music who go out and find a teacher who will help build their own jazz musical foundation. But there is not yet formal training in jazz education."

I mentioned the 333 Japanese graduates of Berklee College. Would they return, or had they returned, to their native country to conceive and establish a uniquely "Japanese" form of jazz? I mentioned pieces such as Toshiko Akiyoshi's "Kogun."

"I am sorry to say that, as far as a piece like 'Kogun' goes, we do not have it just now. We really don't know exactly what Japanese tastes are just now in jazz, so in terms of a unique national form, we regret that we don't have a significantly Japanese taste—or form. Jazz music is becoming more and more *international,* and there are no boundaries now. So we don't really know what a Japanese taste or form of jazz would be. It's really up to each player. Jazz has become a very personal music. My personal feeling is that we have not really educated people in Japanese traditional folk taste so much. I think it makes up a very special case on the international jazz scene. But traditional Japanese music history seems to be studied only in certain times. I regret the circumstances surrounding the *traditional* Japanese jazz scene, but one thing I really have bright hope for is the youngsters in Japan, including groups like the Osaka/Hara Quintet. They are so talented, and so thoroughly trained in the American manner of jazz education. They are really improving day by day, so suddenly we have hope that they are going to build a new kind of jazz tradition in Japan. This new generation has had a very positive effect on the more mature generation, such as the pianist Mr. Yosuke Yamashita—and perhaps Makoto Ozone and Tiger Okoshi as well. These more mature musicians are becoming aware that we need to bring more of our kind of music to the world, our unique offering. At *Swing Journal*, we are supporting both that younger generation and the more mature generation as well. I think that if these two generations can get together more often, our situation is just going to get better and better."

10

SIMA

BEFORE WE WERE TAKEN TO the office of Yasuhiko "Sima" Shimazaki for an appointment, Betty and I visited the Imperial Palace and grounds, an appropriate side tour for the day, because Shimazaki is perhaps the most imperial of the jazz-affiliated producers I would meet, although he doesn't look it.

I first met Shimazaki, described to me as a "mogul" (he owns a large media conglomerate in Japan), in Monterey, where he was producing a film on local drummer/vocalist Dottie Dodgion for his television program *Music Dolphin*. Shimazaki owns a million-dollar condo at Spanish Bay, a site separated from the modest home Betty and I own by (among other things, such as a security pavilion and guards, a golf course, etc.) a ten-minute walk. "We're neighbors," Shimazaki's wife said to Betty when they met, and I thought, "Well, sort of." The Japanese media "mogul" was doing fine things for local musicians (he'd also featured pianist Jan Deneau on his TV show in Japan), and I chatted with him during the filming of the Dottie Dodgion special. He told me to look him up when I came to Japan—and now I was.

In Tokyo, Shimazaki's chambers would prove to resemble a slightly scaled-down version of Hearst Castle in California, so a visit to the Imperial Palace beforehand turned out to be appropriate. The first thing we encountered on the palace grounds was a complex of fountains, ranging from old-fashioned Versailles to contemporary, hip "sheets of sound" (a waterfall cascading over concrete in this case). The innermost portions of the Imperial Palace, Hon Maru, remain inaccessible, but our favorite area was the exquisite East Garden, securely tucked away in the monstrosity that is Tokyo, a niche that harbors innumerable niches: shrubbery as handsomely shaped as breasts; sinuous winding paths accompanied by green streams that reflect trees that look as if they'd just been recently designed, manufactured, installed, and then freshly manicured.

The Japanese are thought of as possessing a great love of nature, and they do, but strictly on their own terms, and those terms are *small,* nearly miniature. They don't love nature in the raw, the wilderness with its merciless disregard of all other forms of life. The Japanese love nature trimmed, tamed, truncated (defamed and deposed from its high disorder), tended and taught how she should behave. The Japanese work very hard, unnaturally hard, to transform things into some ideal natural state. And I must like my nature that way too, because I could have strolled within the timeless placidity of the East Garden forever, had I not been reminded that we had an afternoon meeting with Yasuhiko Shimazaki on his own (gardenless) palace grounds.

Sima's "boy" (that's exactly what he called him over the phone, in English, when we arranged a meeting) picked us up at the Asia Center. I'm still not sure just what section of Tokyo Shimazaki's office is located in (he also has one in Paris, on Rue St. Dominique, but I don't think we drove that far), but when we arrived we walked through a foyer being converted—the furniture covered with transparent plastic—into an art gallery. Upstairs, we were taken to a room furnished with an assortment of objects—souvenirs of Shimazaki's travels, more than likely—truly worthy of Hearst Castle: elaborate figurines, ornate silver goblets, saucers, cups, assorted statues (a four-foot-tall metal Don Quixote among them), an active aquarium, and paintings (very Victorian, pre-pre-Raphaelite) on the wall.

I recalled that, while in Monterey, Sima had told me that he had decorated the living room of his million-dollar condo with original works by Vargas, purchased in Carmel. When visitors asked if his wife disapproved of this display, he responded with one word, "Nostalgia," explaining that American GIs had brought copies of *Esquire* magazine to Japan during the occupation and that's how Yasuhiko Shimazaki had acquired a taste for Vargas girls.

A second room to which we retired was more state-of-the-art. We took seats at a long table that faced an elaborate "home entertainment center," obviously business oriented, set for display. A long-legged girl, a Japanese version of Vargas's work, took a seat next to Shimazaki, and I was introduced to a tall, lean, elderly gentleman who possessed a face animated even in its reserve, masklike, the features seemingly hand-carved, like those of an exquisite Bunraku puppet with somewhat hollow cheeks. This man was Yasuyuki Ishihara, a record producer. In contrast, Sima's appearance suggested the rugged insouciance of a *daimyo* (feudal lords who controlled Japan's provinces for more than seven hundred years and were patrons of the arts), his face fleshy and proud.

Shimazaki presented me with several generous *omiyage:* scripted outlines for his radio show; a cassette tape of the same; posters advertising jazz events such as a concert in Japan by Toshiko Akiyoshi, Joshua Redman, and Gene Harris; a "One Hundred Gold Fingers Piano Playhouse" that featured Marianne McPartland, John Lewis, Hank Jones, Tommy Flanagan, and other stellar keyboard artists.

"When I was twenty-three years old, almost forty years ago," Yasuhiko Shimazaki began of his own accord, "I joined the TBS Broadcasting System Company as a fresh boy. Mr. Ishihara was the *big boss,* the boss of all the American jazz divisions. We have, since that time, become very close friends. I love both popular jazz music and *girls* . . ."

Both Mr. Ishihara and the young woman seated next to Shimazaki laughed. So did Betty and I, although we were far less certain than they, perhaps, of why and of the direction this soliloquy might take.

"As a young TV and radio boy, I needed beautiful young girls, all the time," Shimazaki continued. "I needed to appreciate, to applaud them, through dance. I wanted to dance with them all. I wanted them to dance with me to jazz music."

Shimazaki now introduced Betty and me to his radio program.

"I will play just five minutes for you, because it's in Japanese and will be difficult for you to understand."

"Nakanaka muzukashii des ne—nihongo wa" (Japanese is a *very* difficult language), I said.

"Yes!" he replied, laughing. Then he turned to the young woman at his side. "Even for *her.* The Japanese language is a very complicated language. There are very many ways in which a thought can be expressed. There are different ways for women and young people and adults, for rich and poor, to express their thoughts."

The young woman nodded and hummed in agreement.

"The young are newcomers to our Japanese language. They have an *American* style of expression. Very loose, easy, very flat. So when we talk about jazz or America or Americans, Mr. Ishihara and I have the older, traditional way of speaking, but *she* is only nineteen years old. I become very confused when I listen to her Japanese, because it's a very fresh *American* style."

I asked him about the audience for jazz in Japan.

"It's a pitiful story. Frankly speaking, our Japanese adult people are very rich. Statistically, they have—if we compare the situation with the average in America—five or six times more *big money* in their bank accounts or at the post office, but they have no activities outside the house. If you take a look in New York, Paris, Milan, Los Angeles, Hawaii, or here in Roppongi or Shibuya, you will see *kids,* many members of the younger generation. These young boys and girls are out spending money they get from their parents. If you watch television here, those shows belong to people of the younger generation only. There are no programs for adults. Nothing. But if you attend a jazz concert, such as the piano playhouse in Tokyo, it's very hard to find that younger generation, those kids, in the hall. Do you understand? So it's very hard to produce a *jazz* program on radio or a jazz program on TV. As an entertainment producer, it's very hard to find sponsors or clients for jazz music programs. I am now fighting that trend, struggling to change the direction. Fortunately, we have found Fujitsu [sponsor of the "One Hundred Gold Fingers Piano Playhouse"], so we can do some promotional activity for jazz music in the very near future."

I mentioned the jazz restoration in Japan, focusing on the exciting music I'd heard performed by the Osaka/Hara group on their *Favorites* CD.

"Yes," Shimazaki replied, "but it's very hard, very hard, for them to find opportunities to play. I have been holding jazz concerts at my yacht club here since last year. Not bad, not bad. But we need to do something to promote American jazz in Japan. We need efforts to try to promote someone like Dottie Dodgion. Perhaps some fans have read a few lines in *Swing Journal,* but basically, no Japanese really knows her name. *Swing Journal* is special, exclusively a jazz magazine, the only jazz magazine. The readers of that magazine belong to a minority, like Mr. Ishihara. He has written articles for *Swing Journal,* but most people never even pick up the magazine. Every time I am in Monterey now, I get jazz musicians together from that area and San Francisco, and I tape their music for my TV program. Soon people will know Dottie Dodgion's name, and that she is a world-class drummer and vocalist."

I asked about his own first exposure to the music, and that of Mr. Ishihara.

"Talking for myself," Yasuhiko Shimazaki said, "when I became fifty-five years old, seven years ago, a friendly competitor, another producer, came to see me, and she said, 'You should be a disc jockey, a music promoter, because your voice is very *sweet*.'" Sima does have a deep, rich voice, perfect for a DJ. "Generally speaking, fifty-five means retirement age for most Japanese working people, but I needed a *new* direction, a new era for myself, a new *age*. The girls I chose were about the same age as my granddaughter." He laughed a rich, throaty laugh. "My wife always says, 'Ah, you are *funny*, you know? Why do you choose nineteen-year-old girls?' I say, 'Because I am listening to the *love music* of America.' I must become a *boy* again. It's a kind of imitation love."

Betty and I laughed, although frankly I didn't fully understand what he was talking about. I hoped it was the radio program: the customary dialogue that's carried on for many entertainment events between a *bijin* (a pretty girl or a hostess) and an older male "expert." But I wasn't quite sure. Fortunately, as it turned out, this was the case—mostly. Shimazaki had been a jazz fan for some time.

"People now sixty to seventy were once the jazz lovers in Japan," Shimazaki said. "They *were*, but not now. They are strangely connected to the Japanese philosophy of life. When they were young, they loved to listen to jazz and pop music. American pop. But now that they've become a bit old, they no longer want to listen to jazz. It's funny."

"They've gone back to *gagaku*?"

"Naw, naw . . . *no* music at all. I always say to them, 'Why don't you listen to jazz—that music we loved when we were young?' But you know, in Japanese society, it's very hard to keep our minds young until we die. Do you understand? If you listen carefully to their Japanese language, almost all of their excuses will include the word *toshi*. *Toshi* means 'age.' Bill, how old are you?"

"Sixty."

"Sixty? Sixty means *old*," Shimazaki said. "As a person, I intend to keep on loving jazz music. And I will keep on loving young girls. I will keep loving sports cars. I will continue to love yachting. And I will remain hardworking. Do you understand? It's my personal philosophy. People say, 'Mr. Shimazaki, you are sixty-two years old. Why did you go to England and enter motor car races?' Last year I *did* go to England. I wanted to get into the Royal Competition sports car races, and I *did it!*"

He thumped the table for emphasis, hard. "I ran and ran and ran, 170 times, on that circuit. I was the driver! Mr. Hirata!" [This was the name of Sima's "boy."] Show him the license! It's true. See, here are the magazines. Here is the evidence. This is one of the leading motor car magazines in the world! It includes my records. Mine is a very unusual Japanese way of life. Stupid sixty-two-year-old *adult!* I always tell ordinary Japanese people, '*You* could do this!' I am a member of the Rotary Club. Very rich, high status, elite people. When I tried to cross the United States, they said to me, 'Mr. Shimazaki, you must take care of your health, your life.' I said, 'Okay. I don't really care too much about my life, but I will try.' Now, many Rotary Club members are trying to follow *my way*—not just putting their money in the bank and saving it—but becoming my type of funny Japanese person!"

I asked Sima if I might ask Yasuyuki Ishihara a few questions. The older producer spoke in Japanese, and Yasuhiko Shimazaki translated for me. I learned that Ishihara was born in 1925.

"Mr. Ishihara's father loved dances. Both he and his son liked jazz and expressed this interest by listening to dance music from the States. Mr. Ishihara was a ten-year-old boy when he first listened to jazz. He remembers hearing the Benny Goodman Trio, with Teddy Wilson and Gene Krupa. The song was 'Moonglow.' Just like me with 'The Tennessee Waltz.' When I started my radio program, Mr. Ishihara was still senior executive of a recording company, Universal Songs. I realized that I needed the help of powerful professional people like Mr. Ishihara, so I made a phone call to him. I said, 'You must come *here* now; you must leave your management office and join my staff.' One or two years later, he did become one of my music directors. He selects the songs, one by one."

As a sample of his taste, Mr. Ishihara showed me—and then, in typical Japanese manner, gave me—a CD he had produced in Los Angeles for Tokuma Japan Communications, *Groovin' High: Sonny Stitt and His West Coast Friends*. It featured Stitt, Art Pepper, and Lou Levy. I was dying to ask Mr. Ishihara about his experiences during the war (a young producer of jazz records, he had been drafted in 1943, becoming a Zero pilot who listened to Benny Goodman Trio recordings before he took off on missions), but observing the inherent dignity that seemed to stamp his character, I knew I never could. I did mention discovering—while working on my book about jazz in the former USSR—that Stalin had forced all saxophonists to turn their instruments in to the local *militsia* (police) in 1949 and then asked about the ban on American music throughout the war years in Japan.

"We were forbidden to *speak* English," Shimazaki translated. "We were forbidden to write in English. Baseball is an American sport, but it was very popular in Japan. We called it *bēsubōru*, but during the Second World War, we were forbidden to use this word in English in either writing or speech. So we would say *yakyū*." This word contains the kanji for "field" and "ball."

"Did Japanese people continue to play *yakyū*?"

"Yeah, yeah," Shimazaki said. "For instance, 'radio' is an American expression. Until World War II, we Japanese said *rajio*. But our military government said, 'Do not use American *rajio*.' So we would say *denki* [electricity] or *denki gomki*. It's very funny. Of course Mr. Ishihara knew, throughout the war, that American jazz was forbidden by the military government, but he kept listening to it . . . how would you say it?"

"On the sly? In the closet?"

"Yeah, in the closet! It was a crazy situation."

Mr. Ishihara said he was *asked* to join the Japanese Air Force and served from 1943 to 1945. He was eighteen years old when he went in. "We lost the Second World War," was all he said now. Later, I wished I had asked if his previous vocation as a jazz producer made him suspect in any way, but obviously his loyalty had been put to the test, and I feel now that I *know* the answer, without having been so rude as to ask the question. We did discuss musical activity just after the war. Again, Sima jumped in with his customary alacrity.

"'Sentimental Journey.' Glenn Miller! I was an eleven-year-old school boy, so that was the beginning of my listening to jazz. But Mr. Ishihara joined the Columbia Record Company of Japan. CBS Columbia Records. He was an assistant producer. Then he joined the TBS Broadcasting System when he was twenty-three years old."

"I met Flip Phillips, Ben Webster, Oscar Peterson," Mr. Ishihara himself said, his eyes aglow, the names thickly accented. "Roy Eldridge, Charlie Shavers, producer Norman Granz. Jazz at the Philharmonic."

He didn't meet Thelonious Monk—whom Sima described as Mr. Ishihara's "loved one"—until much later, on the great pianist/composer's first visit in the mid-1960s. He also met Art Pepper. He now showed me other recordings he'd produced, reissued CDs featuring Bobby Shew, Bill Watrous, Bud Shank, Shelly Manne, and Lee Konitz.

"Mr. Ishihara must be the oldest of the jazz critics and producers in Japan," Shimazaki said. Then, conferring with him: "He has produced forty jazz CDs. I sometimes read his Japanese liner notes over the air. They are like a textbook for a DJ."

"I have many young American friends," Sima said, our meeting winding down. "Sometimes, when I ask them about American jazz history, it's very hard to get an answer. They say, 'Are you really Japanese? How do you know so much about jazz?'"

I mentioned a young bass player I'd met who knew all the changes to "As Time Goes By," played the tune with appropriate feeling, but had never seen *Casablanca*.

Shimazaki roared with laughter, turning toward the young woman at his side. "Ah ha! *She* loves *Casablanca!*"

"Sō desu ka?" (Is that so?) I said.

Later, walking through our own district, Akasaka, we discovered what seemed an interminable set of stairs, flanked by red vertical banners splashed with white kanji (more than likely the names of patrons, as at the Inari Temple complex we'd visited). We climbed these stairs and discovered a temple complex lodged high in the hills. We'd also stumbled upon rehearsal for a five-day *matsuri* (festival): a wondrous parade that featured children in colorful kimonos, marching, and a vocal chorus accompanied by violins, trumpets, accordions(!), and *taiko* drums. We learned that, unfortunately, we were too late for the Takigi-Noh and Kyōgen (musical) performances that had already occurred, as well as for a *taiko* drum troupe, but we did return that night for "Chinese Acrobaticism"—a colorful, skillful display of gravity-defying athleticism. We got stiffed for thirty dollars apiece, but it was worth it. Food booths served teriyaki chicken on a stick and delicious noodles, and a friendly woman who'd arrived at the same time we did gave Betty not only a cup of sake, saying, "Kanpai!" (To your health!), but her handsome fan as well.

I don't think we've ever been anyplace (aside from the year Betty and I spent in Greece) where we were more likely to run into some sort of festival or celebration at nearly every turn—and always with a rich musical component—as in Japan. We found glassed-in karaoke booths on the streets—one with a girl in a blue baseball cap perched in front of a music rack and monitor, singing, emoting for friends who squatted in front of her or sat on the sidewalk.

On our last night in Tokyo, we went to Body and Soul in Aoyama, run by Kyoko Seki; the place advertised itself as a "low-end venue," recently relocated in the basement of a brand-new building just around the corner from its decidedly "high-end" competitor, the Blue Note, a club we couldn't afford. Mama-san Kyoko Seki had a reputation for being vigilant as a Ginza hostess in administering to her regular customers, and hearing that she was something of a fixture in the jazz scene, I expected a tough-nut Bricktop seated on a barstool with a cigarette slung from her scowl. I should have known better in Japan.

The interior is dark, refined (one scuffed panel, a remnant from Kyoko Seki's previous site, had been signed by prestigious performers), separated into a long bar, tables and chairs set around drums and piano, and a low balcony section in the back, where Betty and I took seats for a good overview of the band. The bassist in the trio performing that night turned out to be the much-lauded Benisuke Sakai—and he was as good as everyone had told me he was. I don't recall the name of the pianist, not because I wasn't impressed but because he was preceded by a guest musician who sat in for the first few tunes—none other than Masahiko Satoh himself. As usual, Satoh was superb. He came over and talked to us after, telling me that he had just arranged to record a CD in February with a twenty-year-old classical violinist named Junko Ohtsu. She was in New York just now, Satoh said, giving a concert.

When the regular trio went to work they did so on a free piece that, unfortunately, featured the drummer: a handsome man with salt-and-pepper hair, wearing a plain white T-shirt, but prone to overlong solos, one of which occasioned a one-man standing ovation on the part of an elderly drunk seated at a table next to the band. Benisuke Sakai created a soulful lyric groove that the pianist, resorting to tricks and trills, didn't take advantage of. The bassist—unlike the somewhat ham-fisted drummer—seemed reluctant to solo until the pianist pointed directly at him, but Sakai came through nicely with speed-demon triplets and high-register evocations. The crowd seemed to love it all, regardless of merit, applauding vigorously, getting their money's worth (there's a thirty-five-dollar cover charge).

Kyoko Seki had been paying lavish attention to a sumo wrestler and his sizeable entourage throughout the evening, but she came over to our table just as we were leaving.

"You must go?" she asked.

I explained that we had to catch the subway before it shut down at midnight. Asked how long we would be in Tokyo, I replied that we were leaving the next morning, and she said that was a shame. Gracious, she walked us to the door, and we stood outside in the still warm night. When I said the bass player had been superb (I'd made it a point to tell Sakai I felt his playing was *subarashii*—wonderful), she was even more gracious. We had a full round of mutual bows and thanks and good-byes. When we got off the subway near the Asia Center, we stopped at an AM/PM store to get juice and Danish for the morning, thus capping off our ten-day jazz honeymoon in Tokyo.

FLASHBACK: MORE ON WHAT PROMPTED ME TO GO TO JAPAN

J UST SHY OF A YEAR BEFORE Betty and I flew to Hawaii on the first leg of our jazz journey to Japan, I stood looking down over a railing into the lobby of the Marriott Hotel in Monterey, California. Finding just a trickle of fans arriving, I was nervous and worried. I had never been responsible for publicity for a benefit jazz concert before. At the time, I was working for the organization I've already mentioned, IDEA: International Disabled Exchange Adventures. This was *their* first benefit concert too. The ticket table was topped with baseball caps and T-shirts bearing a pink or green IDEA logo, designed in Japan by some of the musicians who would be performing that night. The entire group, led by clarinetist Eiji Kitamura, was seated not far from the ticket table, in large deep lounge chairs: pianist Kotaro Tsukahara, guitarist Yoshiaki "Miya" Miyanoue, bassist Yoshinari "Sammy" Asami, and drummer Takeshi "Sadao" Watanabe. Kitamura—a short, handsome, distinguished man with snow white hair—was talking to his manager, Kazuko Suzuki, better known as "Miss Lazy River" because of the unique way she has of pronouncing that song's title.

Events in any life may seem fortuitous. So much so that we are taken completely by surprise when, and if, they actually shape themselves into some central story. Killing time to kill my nerves at the Marriott, I thought back on the events that had led up to this moment and would eventually—and inevitably—lead to the jazz trek to Japan itself.

When I was eighteen I set out on my own for New York City, a fledgling visual artist with a host of dreams (love, fame, talent, beauty), attending Pratt Institute in Brooklyn and living too much by myself in an old brownstone until a fellow student, Tetsuo Yamashita, took pity and introduced me to a remarkable family up in "Hell's Kitchen," the projects along Amsterdam Avenue. Bill and Mary Kochiyama (who shared very cramped quarters with their six wonderful children) ran the Nisei Service Organization and handled about a million other charitable functions that put large demands on their selfless time.

I began to play for benefit dances (I was also a fledgling musician and had, such as it was at the time, an "orchestra"), apparently playing often enough to earn honorary membership in the 442nd Association (I still carry my card in my wallet with pride), a group of veterans of the most highly decorated unit in American military history, Japanese Americans all. I was also introduced to the Hiroshima Maidens, twenty-five women who, after the bombing, were so badly disfigured they were brought to New York to undergo extensive plastic surgery, just to restore their facial features. I recall, at a Coney Island picnic we all attended, conversing with one of these brave women. Her face was that of a person with a silk stocking stretched over it, the dime-sized "O" that was her mouth registering neither laughter nor sorrow. We all played softball that day, the Maidens spirited but not very good at this game because their burned hands made it difficult for them to hold the bat. Needless to say, this was a heavy dose of reality (truth, not beauty) for a nineteen-year-old boy—which is what I was at the time.

That's fortuitous event Number One. Number Two: thirty years later, living in California, teaching at Monterey Peninsula College, I rode my bike to school each morning for nearly twenty years until one day, turning my head rapidly from left to right to gauge traffic, I fell over. A previous case of "killer flu" had left me with loud ringing in both of my ears and vertigo seizures that became more frequent. I was diagnosed as having Ménière's disease, a disorder of the inner ear. A doctor at the Stanford Medical Center wished to operate immediately (an invitation I wisely declined, since his hands shook badly and I might have lost my stereophonic hearing even if they didn't, that hearing something I prize—along with my 442nd Association card—to this day). After a three-year quest (so desperate at times I became infatuated with alternative "medical" practices bordering on voodoo), I finally found a doctor who made sense, one who felt that my former case of flu, a viral infection, was responsible for my condition and that the disorder could be controlled by strict diet (no salt), vestibular exercise, and Meclizine. He was right. Out of necessity, I started riding the bus to work and discovered I had much excellent company there among the disabled, another "organization" to which I now belonged.

Story Number Three: our youngest son, Stephen, spent a year in Kyoto, Japan—teaching English. He survived an extremely serious motorbike accident, hit head-on by a garbage truck going sixty miles an hour and thrown twenty feet, a *jiko* (accident) that would have left him with severe facial scars had it not been for the skill of a twenty-seven-year-old Japanese plastic surgeon (events not quite so fortuitous anymore!). Steve's spirit, his return to life, was assisted by a young woman named Yoko Takitani, one of his language pupils who did not desert her temporarily no longer handsome gaijin (foreigner) boyfriend but, like Ruth in the Bible, took up residence at the foot of his hospital bed each night and saw him through the ordeal. The two have been happily married now for ten years and are living in San Francisco.

These small separate scenarios, spaced out in time, might have remained that way—isolated fragments of a life—if it were not for the appearance, on a spring day in 1991, of a charming, purposeful, and very persistent woman named Sumiko Inoue, who stood in the doorway of my office at Monterey Peninsula College. She had been given my name as someone connected to jazz life on the peninsula. She said she was interested in putting on a benefit jazz concert for an organization (IDEA) she was starting. Born in Kurashiki, Japan, in 1950, Sumiko, fond of music at an early age, had been given permission as a schoolgirl to practice on a grand piano right next to a classroom devoted to children with, as she described it, "special need." As she went about her own musical studies, she became increasingly preoccupied with the fact that these children had been set apart, were not allowed to learn alongside everyone else. From that point on she dedicated her life to them: visiting, at twelve years of age, a home in Yokohama for the "mentally disabled"; working in a Red Cross program while in high school; learning Japanese Braille; and continuing to question the practice, in her country, of isolating the handicapped. When she came to the Monterey Bay area in 1977, she worked with mentally disabled clients at Pacific Grove's Gateway Center and began to have a dream, a vision, of people with disabilities "singing and dancing together."

Not one to let dreams lie idle, and attending the Monterey Jazz Festival for the first time, Sumiko discovered her countryman, clarinetist Eiji Kitamura—something of a festival mainstay—sitting close by, eating his lunch. "I knew what I had to do," Sumiko says today. She introduced herself with an apology ("Moshi wake arimasen" [I am terribly sorry to interrupt you]) and told him, "I would like, if you ever have a free hour, or even half an hour, for you to share your music with my clients." Kitamura, a generous man in his own right, agreed to play a benefit concert, and from that first contact on, Sumiko's vision acquired what she calls "some clear voices." So—to make this story short(er)—I too became involved. At the Marriott, while Kitamura's sidemen chatted among themselves and he took serene puffs on a pipe, "Miss Lazy River"— wearing a bright red spandex jacket that was too big for her, a tote bag slung over her shoulder, an attaché case in her hand—also glanced over the railing at the mere trickle of jazz fans entering the lobby below. She too had a vision, a dream, but one that really meant *business*.

Fortunately, jazz fans did arrive, and a dozen or so Japanese businessmen attending an electronics convention defected from *their* event and came to hear the music. A contingent of clients from Gateway Center clapped with glee and danced (in their chairs), and the music was great. All my fears were in vain: first, that no one would show up; and second, that as an organization, compared to the larger world of genuine musical entrepreneurs, we were a sorry band of amateurs groping our way in the dark. After what turned out to be a highly successful benefit concert, Kazuko Suzuki told Sumiko she'd been worried herself, "because you had never done anything like this before." "Now she tells me!" Sumiko said.

At the concert, the brilliant American guitarist Bruce Forman and cornetist Bill Berry joined Kitamura's group on "In a Mellow Tone." Forman, bobbing and weaving like a boxer, a full body as well as heart, 100 percent performer, exuded fierce, fast, "breathless," seemingly endless lines accented by full chord slashes. When Yoshiaki "Miya" Miyanoue followed he declined, wisely, to follow in Forman's frenetic footsteps, providing equally proficient but different effects, cultivating his own subdued, spare, genial tonalities and kind percussion: a finely raked Zen garden set alongside Forman's manic Versailles. It was a cordial duel, a handsome exchange between two masters, each in his own right, reflecting different cultures and distinct personalities, the two shaking hands and laughing once the chase or "cutting contest" was over.

A reception—a full meal—was held for the musicians and IDEA staff members at the Jugem restaurant ("The Largest Sushi Bar in Monterey"). The restaurant was closed to the public, and a long line of home-cooked potluck treats had been laid out: teriyaki chicken, *tako* (octopus), *ebi* (prawns), *sake* (smoked salmon), *unagi* (eel), *ika* (squid), *maguro* (tuna), even grapes and potato salad prepared for those with Western tastes. Kitamura's quintet deported themselves as the most truly gentlemanly jazzmen I'd ever met: still wearing sport coats and ties, gregarious, joining in on several toasts celebrating the success of this first joint venture, saying both "Cheers!" and "Kanpai!" (To your health!) even though pianist Tsukahara raised a glass of milk—his post-gig beverage of choice.

After the concert, I couldn't help but go home and compare Eiji Kitamura's "Avalon" (Kitamura known as the "Benny Goodman of Japan"), the second tune the quintet played on the night of the IDEA benefit concert, with Goodman's version as performed at his 1938 Carnegie Hall jazz concert. The latter's version is four/four, straight-ahead, pulsing, the clarinetist content to remain somewhat light, even airy (liquid, his lines laced with chromatic descents), above the steady eruption of Lionel Hampton's vibes and Gene Krupa's drums. Kitamura, by comparison, playing with his mentor Teddy Wilson on a Concord recording called *Seven Stars,* commences with a riff, has more body, more "wood" in his tone, and is not at all spare with notes. The tempo is more relaxed, not as driven, Kitamura's solo more attuned to arpeggios than paraphrase, more ornate, embellished—his fleet yet floating innovation, ironically, less understated or "Japanese" than Goodman's.

Listening to this music, I thought about the "homage" Japanese performers pay to their "masters." Such homage, I feel, is individual, original, yet full of obvious respect, much in accord with well-ingrained cultural traditions. One such is the *iemoto seido* (*iemoto* system), discussed by Donald Keene in the context of Noh and Kyōgen theater, in the study of which the first question asked is, "Nani ryu desu ka?" (Which school?) Keene claims this question can be asked of *any* traditional Japanese art, and he could just as well be talking about jazz. The *iemoto* system has functioned in poetry (*waka, renga, haikai*) and music (the making and playing of instruments such as the *shō, hichiriki, biwa,* and *wagon*); there was even a *shijo* (*hōchō no ie; ie* is the Japanese word for "house" or "family"), or house of the Slicing Knife, in the culinary arts, whose practice was preparing living fish to be served as sashimi. The current *iemoto seido* family head is a thirty-eight-year-old ex-rock-band drummer who performed with a group called Izumi Yoji and

Spanky! He is the forty-first-generation head of a house established in 886 A.D.

The mentor in such *shitei/kankei* (master/pupil, or better yet, master/disciple) relationships might even serve as a surrogate parent. In his book *The Enduring Art of Japan,* Langdon Warner presents a chapter called "Shinto, Nurse of the Arts," explaining that a knowledge of natural processes (the "all-pervasive animism that bound together the spiritual and material life") was the basis of all arts that transformed "raw materials into artifacts," thus turning the artist into a sort of priest: "to be right has always, until lately, been to be religious." Mastery required an apprentice to reach a certain level of skill before he was finally initiated into the "charms and procedures necessary to insure success."

These traditions have survived into the modern world, carried over into business organizations and military units, "a congenial way for Japanese to consider a group." Do they apply to a musical group—a jazz ensemble? The answer, I believe, is *hai* (yes). One's model or master, in such cases, is not a person to be *supplanted* but *revered.* To exceed or "cut" one's master is an act of disrespect—which is certainly an attitude diametrically opposed to that fostered by way of the jam session "cutting contests" that became a means by which younger American artists came of age or gained recognition during the early days of jazz, often at the expense of their "masters."

Even before I set foot in Tokyo, I saw this attitude, whether acutely conscious or just culturally ingrained, at work among the Japanese jazz musicians I met. When I interviewed jazz artists from the former Soviet Union, each was fiercely competitive in that each, chock full of elaborate theories, offered a manifesto as to why his or her approach to the music was the "true" one, why this or that was "the only way" to play jazz or even *live.* Japanese artists, on the other hand, are exceedingly more humble, modest. Guitarist Yoshiaki "Miya" Miyanoue told me that he liked Wes Montgomery's "warm effect" and practiced his thumb method—"up and down, up and down"—for ten years, adding, "Most people cannot wait ten years for anything." When I asked Miyanoue about his "duels" with Bruce Forman, he shook his head and, bowing profusely, said, "Oh no!" No such thing. He admired Mr. Forman very much. "I respect Mr. Forman *sooo* much. No contest, no duel!" Most Russians, by contrast, would gloat over their assumed victory—one both ideological and actual in their minds. But not the Japanese.

Later, after I became good friends with pianist Kotaro Tsukahara, I made the mistake of asking *just one* member of the Kitamura quintet, Tsukahara, over to my house for dinner. He apologized and said he must refuse. I quickly learned that the group customarily dines together after a concert at a Chinese restaurant (!) selected by its leader, Eiji, a man some years senior to his sidemen and obviously revered by them as both *sensei* (roughly translated, "teacher") and *shujin* (master), or even *kobutsu* (old master), as the great Zen master and poet Dogen, founder of the Soto sect in Kamakura-era Japan, affectionately referred to Juching, the man who guided his way to enlightenment in China.

Physicist Makoto Kikuchi has pointed out that the original form of the Japanese verb "to learn" (*manabu*) came from the word *maneru*, which means "to imitate." Kikuchi explains a different cultural approach to originality in terms very similar to the Shintō principles cited earlier. Speaking of the teamwork built into the Japanese system of education, Kikuchi sees it as a "cultural advantage." Consensus and loyalty must certainly prove to be assets for jazz musicians who, in spite of abundant room for solo improvisation, must constantly truly *listen to* and key off one another and frequently perform as a tight ensemble or "family."

I learned a great deal about not only the history of jazz in Japan and Japanese aesthetic principles before Betty and I left on our trip but also cultural traditions or habits that were unique and seemed ingrained, no matter what stark or crude "Western" changes had taken place. And I was fortunate to form lasting friendships with musical artists. I had Sumiko Inoue and IDEA to thank for much of this, and I knew or could sense—a year before I actually went—that there was far more to learn and an important "jazz journey" that Betty and I must undertake.

SUMI TONOOKA AND KENNY ENDO

O N ONE LEVEL, I FELT the IDEA benefit concert had restored a portion of my humanity to me, but meeting musicians such as Eiji Kitamura, Yoshiaki "Miya" Miyanoue, and Kotaro Tsukahara had also obviously awakened a dormant love affair with Japan. I recalled my then-fashionable 1950s flirtation with "Zen" (prompted in my case, as in many others, not by the real thing but by J. D. Salinger) and my discovery of haiku by way of a suitably small Peter Pauper Press edition a girlfriend gave me. Now, nearly forty years later, advanced publicity for the thirty-sixth annual Monterey Jazz Festival announced the appearance of a "brilliant" young pianist from Japan I was not familiar with: Sumi Tonooka.

When I started doing my homework, however, I discovered that Sumi Tonooka, although she *is* brilliant—as both pianist and composer—and relatively young (thirty-seven), was born in Philadelphia, the City of Brotherly Love, Pennsylvania, U.S.A.: child of an African American father and Japanese American mother, as homegrown as the proverbial apple pie, sushi, and Delta blues. Personable, purposeful, and very pretty, sporting a warm maternal edge (one of her finest compositions, "Here Comes Kai," was written for her son), yet full of youthful zest and intentionality, Sumi made her first Monterey Jazz Festival appearance at a clinic held on composition.

"It's funny," she told me after. "I'm starting to get some national and international attention now, and people are referring to me as this 'bright light,' you know, a young new face, but I've been playing professionally since I was eighteen, so that's over nineteen years now."

Indeed, at the clinic, Sumi Tonooka conducted herself as a seasoned pro. She began by saying that composition was "a very mysterious process," one that, for her, commences with "something very personal," something *felt:* "a picture of someone I know, or a very vivid picture in my mind." She then played a tune she'd written called "Phantom Carousel," one inspired by a vision of a carousel turning round and round on a mountain shrouded in mist, the voices of children "in the air" but no children present. The piece had also commenced as an exercise given her by a teacher who requested she use the six notes of an Egyptian scale: C, C-sharp, E, F, G-sharp, A.

That night, I heard Sumi, performing with her trio on the festival's main stage, play a portion of a piece called *Susumu,* a suite she would later tell me was "one of the biggest things I've ever attempted to do, about fifty-five minutes long" (I would also receive a videotape of its live performance, which I will describe shortly). The excerpt was both lyrical and abrasive, always dramatic, with its own unique piano accents over cello-mournful, bowed, ostinato bass. Following what I felt was an excellent performance, Sumi proved she was merely human by inadvertently thanking the "San Diego" crowd for the warm reception. That's where she'd been the previous night.

Sumi Tonooka is a well-trained musician, getting out of high school early (at fifteen), setting out on her own to study in Boston, Philadelphia, and Detroit. She went to the first city to check out the music scene ("Berklee, the New England Conservatory, but I didn't like the atmosphere; I didn't feel that that was where I was going to learn jazz") and then found Marcus Belgrave in Detroit, always a good town for the music. One of her more influential teachers was Madame Margaret Chaloff. "She taught me a very special technique or system," Sumi says, "where one of the main ideas is that you use your energy in such a way that it's a very relaxed means of playing, yet very powerful. It's as if air is coming out of the bottom of your fingers, as if you had holes on the tips of your fingers and were *blowing* on the keys. It took time for the points to sink in, to internalize my lessons with her, but they were very valuable."

Sumi Tonooka mentioned "breath-length phrases," avoiding a pianist's inclination to sound "cluttered"—a concept I would discover as important to nearly all of the musicians I would eventually talk to, both Japanese American and those in Japan.

"When you play the piano," Sumi said, "it's easy to just run on

117

because your hands aren't necessarily connected to your breathing. Yet we have to breathe to live, right? You need to pause before you move on to the next thing. This gives you time and space to develop. It's more natural, so I definitely try to think about that when I'm playing."

Sumi also studied with the great pianist Mary Lou Williams.

"I like to talk about Mary Lou," she replied, when I asked her about that experience. "I was about eighteen, before I went to college, after I'd come back from Boston and Detroit. I just called her up one day and asked her if she taught and she said, 'Sure.' My mother went with me to my first lesson. Mary Lou was living in Harlem in a flat she'd occupied for some time. Thelonious Monk and Bud Powell had hung out at her place and used to play her piano. I played the same piano they'd played! She said to me, 'You don't need to study. All you need to do is get out there and play.' And all she did was *play* for me. I watched and I learned a lot, just by that. She didn't work on technical aspects at all. It was all *feeling*. A lot about the blues, 'cause that's really what her playing stems from, even though she'd always had this incredibly modern, fresh approach to everything she did. She was very warm, beautiful, very spiritual. The whole thing is about a *lifetime,* a lifelong pursuit, trying to get it and keeping on."

Although Sumi Tonooka proved *not* to be a musical artist from Japan, I discovered a link that turned out to be more immediate and meaningful. I told her about my experiences in New York, "falling in love" with Japanese art and literature, meeting the Kochiyama family, playing for benefit dances, the Hiroshima Maidens, my honorary 442nd Association card—the works. Again, the *central story*—"karma," if you will—that was binding up seemingly disparate, or fortuitous, events was at work.

"Bill and Mary are good friends of mine," Sumi said. "They're notorious in New York. A very famous family, politically. They still live in the same project; I don't understand that, but they do."

The last time I'd seen Mary Kochiyama had been in her appearance on TV, addressing the congressional hearings on reparations. This led us back to Sumi's major work, the *Susumu* suite.

"The problem when I wrote this piece was I had never experienced the camps myself," she said. "Usually when I write I base a composition on stuff I've been through, but this was a bit different. It happened to my *mom*." Sumi had her own feelings and emotions and decided to deal with them by way of research on poetry and prose written by people who'd been interned: an Issei tanka called "The Arrest"; her mother's account of the Nisei experience; and the work of Russell Endo, a Japanese American of Sumi's own, Sansei, generation. She wanted to address each generation's experience of what had happened for them and show this musically. "The first piece, which is Issei, is most traditionally Japanese in its feeling."

"Do you play *shakuhachi*?"

"No. What I did was: I had long sessions with a guy who does, excellently, in New York. He performed on the 'Out from the Silence' piece, along with Fusako Yoshida, who plays koto. I had sessions with her also, not so much to learn how to play the instrument but to learn *about* it, how it works, how it functions, what the notation is, the aesthetics. When I learned that koto had a different notation system than *shakuhachi,* I was like, 'What am I going to do here?' I had to work out a compatible system of how we were going to communicate, and it worked out very well, very closely, right from the beginning. I had no idea how much work was going to get involved. But you just have to dive right in there."

"Ganbatte!" (Go for it! Never say die!) I said.

"That's it," Sumi concurred.

Not long after my conversation with Sumi Tonooka, she sent me two videos: one of the suite called *Susumu,* the second a premiere performance of her *Taiko Jazz Project.*

The first work, subtitled *A Tone Poem in Three Movements,* began with meditative piano figures, somewhat bluesy, and a handsome shot of Sumi—in a brilliant purple (*murasaki*) *happi* coat—seated at the piano. Sumi then explains the impetus for the piece. "My mother grew up on a farm on Bambridge Island, near Seattle. She was fifteen when the gates of Manzanar closed behind her. Even now it makes me angry to think that my mother was a prisoner in the country she was born in, taken from her home and isolated behind barbed wire. The music is a means of coming to terms with what happened."

That music—Rufus Reid on bass, Sumi's brother Stephen Hideko "T" Morris on vibraharp and percussion, Ronnie Nyogetsu Seldon on *shakuhachi,* and Akira Tana behind a full drum kit—serves as an effective counterpart to what Sumi says, shifting back and forth between strictly jazz rhythms and respectful silence. Then we hear the voice of Sumi's mother, Emiko: "A national emergency has been declared by President Roosevelt. . . . *Jap* fliers bombed and have destructed Pearl

Harbor in Hawaii. . . . All I felt was that our family life, my life, was somehow affected because we were members of the *enemy race*. . . . There was some kind of danger for us, and what it was I didn't know."

Sumi Tonooka begins each movement of *Susumu* with a poem written by someone from that generation, "to use *their* voice to get into the music." Part 1, called "The Arrest," begins with Fusako Yoshida seated at the koto, making full use of that instrument's haunting, pentatonic, percussive quavering, and singing—after a *shakuhachi* intro—the words to a poem by Sojin Takei:

> The time has come
> for my arrest
> this dark rainy night;
> I calm myself and listen
> to the sound of the shoes.

Sumi's mother describes her own mother standing before a "big bonfire," flinging books, photographs (of relatives back in Japan), anything written in Japanese—diaries, journals, account books—into the flames. Part 2, "Out from the Silence," opens with Sumi's mother reciting her own prose, "trying to make sense of this thing" (at the time the war broke out she was sixteen). Emiko Tonooka then says, "If I was a Buddhist, like my parents, this upheaval could be faced with calm. But the only belief that might possibly have sustained us was a dream of a mystical democracy . . . a lifelong yearning for the reconciliation of my two worlds." This theme is reinforced by popular swing music from that time in history, Sumi setting the tempo at the piano, the tone somewhat (and appropriately) dissonant within the context of "big band" familiarity—projecting the incongruity, the *insanity,* of the internment experience.

At one point in the narrative, Sumi's mother begins to cry. Her daughter reaches out to comfort her, and the music grows cacophonous. Rufus Reid grittily bows his bass; Sumi's hands flash up and down the keyboard in a nightmare flourish. Part 3, "Susumu," based on a poem by Russell Endo, begins with Sumi explaining, "I like this poem because it incorporated the kind of spirit and energy I was looking for as far as how *I* felt. I wanted to bring it all out. A driving piece, forceful; I wanted it to be jazzy and upbeat; I wanted it to be strong."

Sumi herself recites Endo's work:

You are entitled to overhear. . . . *Susumu,* my name, means "progress" in Japanese. The dust that seeped through the makeshift barracks in Arizona wet my parents' taste for the American Dream. My luck will have to be different. I want my wheels to skim the blaze of the wind over all the ruts. I want my wheels to spin so fast that we stand still. Are you with me? Then we may say in the summer breeze, "Susumu."

Sumi explains, "I chose an up-beat rhythmic pattern. The line is a very fluid, quick line, with another theme built on top of that. It's like layers of these different things happening all at once."

This intricate design *works.* Sumi's soulful, forceful bop lines are laced with spare "Japanese" (minimalist) effects, her chin dipping and rising in time to right-hand runs and trills, a full drum-kit flurry by Akira Tana, and Sumi up from the piano bench to lead the ensemble's fluid lines *out.* Speaking again, she concludes, "There's been a lot of good that's happened as a result of people *coming out* and talking about the camp experience, but I don't think that it is something that can ever really be put behind us." Then, echoing philosopher George Santayana's famous words on those unfamiliar with the past running the risk of repeating it, "It happened and I think it should always be remembered that it happened and that it should never happen again."

The second video I received from Sumi, the premiere performance of her *Taiko Jazz Project,* introduced me to Hawaii *taiko* master Kenny Endo, poised before a large *ō-daiko* drum. He is joined by Yukio Sachi, who performs on both *shakuhachi* and smaller *taiko* drums throughout the performance, and Akira Tana again, on a standard jazz drum kit. The piece contains marvelous interplay among all three drummers: that sense of synchronicity mixed with subtle displacement, of overt athleticism combined with passive nuance, all that makes *taiko* drumming so exciting. *Taiko* drumming may well go back to Japan's mythological foundations, when Amaterasu, the Sun Goddess, harassed and insulted by her brother Susanoo's obnoxious behavior, retired into a cave and left the world in darkness. The world was *danced* back to light when the sensuous Ame no Uzume coaxed Amaterasu from hiding by way of a lewd and humorous performance before the other gods assembled at the cave's mouth. Their laughter aroused the curiosity of the Sun Goddess, and out she came. The myth does not specify the use of drums to achieve this end, but I like to think that some form of percussion must have contributed to the result.

Kenny Endo grew up in Los Angeles and played drums in his high school band. Attending his first *taiko* performance, he claims you could feel the music "with your whole body." He knew immediately he wanted to play *taiko*. His father was Japanese, his mother Nisei, and in 1980 Endo went to Japan to study both the language and *kumidaiko* (ensemble drumming). He joined a professional Japanese group and then moved to Hawaii with his wife, Chizuko, and their two sons. He opened his own school of *taiko* drumming in 1995. Chizuko is an instructor there, and their sons are students. Endo also offers a full curriculum of courses at Kapi'olani Community College that ranges from Children's Beginning I Taiko (ages five to twelve) to Advanced—which includes everything from *matsuri-bayashi* (festival music) to *hōgaku hayashi* (classical drumming) to *kakegoe* (vocal exclamation).

Forty-four years of age, Endo has a severe regimen for staying in shape for the exertions required by *taiko* drumming. Five to six days a week he does fifty push-ups, seventy-five sit-ups, two sets of ten pull-ups, thirty side waist bends, two sets of thirty arm curls lifting a chair in each hand, and grueling "rocking-horse" exercises, topped with a three- to four-mile run. Endo told journalist Bill Harby, "You should never let your technique show. You shouldn't *look* like you're about to die. What should come out is not the impression that you're fast, or that you're having a hard time. What should come out is the pure music, the pure spirit. That's part of the reason why doing this type of physical exercise is important."

And pure music and pure spirit are exactly what come out in his performance in Sumi Tonooka's *Taiko Jazz Project.* Some of the music remains very much in the Japanese tradition; much of it is played off against, and within, the context of jazz. A host of colors are provided by Robin Eubanks's trombone and John Blake Jr.'s violin. Throughout, within, and behind all this (blending with Sumi's craggy Monk-like rhythms), Endo contributes effects ranging from choriamb (beat-slack-slack-beat) to double antibacchius (beat-beat-slack-beat-beat-slack) "feet." He and Akira Tana are solidly in sync and offsetting one another handsomely.

At the concert's end, a very pleased Sumi Tonooka introduces the entire group, along with her mother and brother, saying, "It's been a family affair up here tonight." Once again, in connection with Japanese-based jazz, that word "family" (*kazoku*) turns up. Indeed, my own Japanese jazz "family" had grown tight at home in the States. Sumi Tonooka's friendship with Bill and Mary Kochiyama, my New York "family" of thirty years ago, was one more link in that central story I found shaping up. I wrote Mary Kochiyama, whose first name was now Yuri, and she wrote back, commenting on my meeting Sumi ("Yes, it's a small world"); sending me a wonderful article written about Bill, who died of cancer at age seventy-two ("a man who never let anybody take away his belief in humanity"); and asking if I had met Akira Tana, the drummer on two of Sumi Tonooka's CDs and on both *Susumu* and the *Taiko Jazz Project*. She gave me his New York address and phone number.

I wrote Tana and learned that while an undergraduate student at Harvard, he had written his East Asian studies ethnomusicological thesis on "Jazz in Japan," a sixty-four-page document he too modestly described as containing "no big conclusions." He graciously offered to send it to me. We also arranged to meet in Half Moon Bay, California, where he'd be playing soon.

AKIRA TANA

I sat in a hot outer reception room at Douglas Beach House in Half Moon Bay, California, a jazz venue otherwise known as the Bach Dancing and Dynamite Society. I was waiting for Akira Tana, scheduled to give a concert that afternoon with the group he shares with bassist Rufus Reid. Passing the time, I was studying Japanese. *Easy Kanji* was my text. What a joke! There is no such thing as easy kanji. I had been through two "easy" hiragana and katakana books, the two systems of phonograms, each containing forty-six characters, used to supplement the 1,945 kanji ("for daily use"), or characters inherited from the Chinese. I'd learned about 100 kanji so far, which meant I only had 1,845 more to go—a task I wasn't sure I could complete that Sunday afternoon, waiting for Akira Tana, even though he was late.

"Shiyo ga nai" (It can't be helped), I muttered to myself.

When the group finally arrived, considerably late, Pete Douglas stood before an audience that looked very much like a family (more than likely Akira's, who was born in nearby San Jose) and introduced "a Bay Area boy who made good and is back." Tana was perched behind his drums, wearing a flamboyant Hawaiian "Aloha" shirt. The mood was just right: a serious cultural event combined with the ease of an outing. The group, which, along with Akira and Reid, consisted of John Stetch on piano, Craig Bailey on alto, and Mark Turner on tenor, launched into a tune called "Billy" that is one of my favorites on their CD *Looking Forward*. It's a kick-start—quick snare triplet followed by a fast tom-tom riff—up-tempo tune with smooth unison work and Craig Bailey's spirited alto solo. Akira, supplying fast fill and crisp bass drum accents, propelled the group handsomely. "Billy" was followed by Dizzy Gillespie's "Con Alma." Throughout this tune, and all the rest in the set, Akira Tana's son stood beside him, his father turning to smile reassuringly after a quick cymbal slash startled the boy. This was indeed a family affair, but not casual or lax. High musical standards were set. The last tune was Akira's modal composition "Elvinesque," his tribute to another fine drummer, a piece that commenced and ended with some fierce percussion worthy of its namesake.

After, I introduced myself to Akira Tana, and we agreed it would be best to conduct an interview after the second set. He had friends and family present he hadn't seen in some time and felt he should circulate among them now. He did have time to tell me a few of his impressions of a recent trip to Japan.

"I think, given the way education about this music has proliferated, universally," he said, "you can go anywhere in the world now and hear guys that are really *playing* the music, because they have absorbed it. I think knowledge of the cultural context still may be foreign, although I think there is recognition now that this music comes from a certain cultural and political context, even though the depth of what they know about—and feel about it—may be limited. The music is institutionalized now. You've got all these big bands in high schools and colleges—*school* stuff. Kids are learning much faster and playing great, but they sound like they've been studying from books, and the music has actually *changed*. It's not something of the streets anymore, or of the culture as much. It's become more than that. Consequently, players sound that way also. That's why you hear a lot of young players who dazzle you with their technique and sound, but the *feeling* is not the same as it was maybe twenty years ago. In Japan—and also in other parts of the world—I think it's the same."

Akira Tana excused himself to go mingle with fans, relatives, and friends before the second set—which turned out to be every bit as good as the first, if not better. They played another tune from *Looking Forward:* Akira's own "Skyline," and his drum solo, coming on the heels of a "fake" ending, allowed him to display his comfortable yet impassioned familiarity with every portion of a drum kit—agile bass drum footwork, then straight rolls behind a tenor sax coda. The final piece, "Elegy," dedicated to bassist Sam Jones, was a rouser: a supple, high-spirited, street-dance, carnival event that allowed all of the musicians to join in the general joy, which inspired hand clapping on the part of the crowd.

I conducted the interview while Akira dismantled his drums, ably assisted in the process by his son Ryan, who had stood faithfully, and proudly, by his father's side throughout both sets. I attempted to follow Akira and Ryan around with my tape recorder while they folded cymbal stands and loaded the snare and toms into their cases. I asked Akira about using a rhythm section—he, Rufus, and a pianist—as a core unit on which various combinations could be built. The CD *Looking Forward* was the work of Tana Reid Productions, with trumpeter Tom Harrell joining Turner and Bailey—rather than just a horn front line backed up by a largely "pickup" rhythm section, as is more often the case when musicians come to town.

"Right," Tana responded. "You can't escape rhythm sections. Think of the major groups we talk about in jazz. John Coltrane's group with Elvin Jones, Jimmy Garrison, and McCoy Tyner. Miles's group with Tony Williams and Ron Carter. Or Red Garland or Wynton Kelly with Paul Chambers. Not to say that the unit Rufus and I have established measures up to the impact of those rhythm sections, but it's the whole idea of sound. The *sound* those groups created was based on the concept of drums and bass. We consciously wanted to put something together to create a sound with what we do, and so a lot of the time—as in those other groups—the rhythm section really dictates the sound of the group as a whole: the sound of the group and the direction the music would go in. We want to be in a position to actually dictate the sound as far as the group goes. So that's basically the concept we're coming from: putting the back line in the front. Playing with different groups and different leaders, we have experienced so much; that's why I think we like the *variety* we get now, because we've known a lot of variety in terms of backing up various artists."

On their recent three-week tour in Japan, the group shared the bill with vocalist Carmen Lundy. "In Japan, they didn't think that we could really draw without a singer, for they love vocalists there, so we had her come make the trip with us. We were all over the place. Five cities in Hokkaido: Kushiro, Rumoi, Urakawa, Sapporo, Hokodate. We were in Tokyo at the very end and did an NHK radio broadcast from Yokuri Hall. We were also in Okayama, Hiroshima, and Kumamoto."

Following him about as he finished packing his drums, I asked Akira about the work he'd done with Sumi Tonooka and Kenny Endo. "I've known Sumi for quite a long time," he replied. "Actually, Rufus and

I did a trio recording with her that came out on her own label." (He was referring to *Taking Time,* which also features saxophonist Craig Handy.)

I mentioned the video I had, and the fact that in the second portion of the *Susumu* suite, he seems to be *conducting.*

"Conducting, yeah!" he said, smiling.

"How much of the *taiko* piece was scored?" I asked.

"A lot of it was left up to the individual soloists, but there was also quite a bit of structure within the piece as a whole. There was a lot of room for improvisation. The stuff that Sumi had written down for the *taiko* on some pieces for *taiko and* drum set was a little too long, in terms of what she intended, and I don't know if she was very happy about it, but we actually had more input in terms of what Kenny would be doing, because Kenny was the *taiko* artist and he knew *how.* So she kind of left that area up to us."

I asked Akira about a CD he'd made with a fine pianist from Japan, Kai Akagi. It was called *Sound Circle* and featured what was billed as the Asian American Jazz Trio, which included Rufus Reid. How did that come about?

"Mark Izu called me to play at the Asian-American Jazz Festival in San Francisco. The tenth one. He suggested that we use a trio. I'd known Kai when he was playing with Miles Davis, and I used to see him on video when he was playing with Airto Moreira years ago. We'd never played with each other. I met him in Europe when he was with Miles and I was over there with Jimmy Heath. But this opportunity came along and we played the festival. I had been doing some producing for King Records in Japan, so I went to them with this project and said, 'This is kind of interesting.' Kai was playing with Miles at the time, so they wanted to have him recorded because his name was *out there.* So that's how it came about. We also did a short tour of Japan with the trio."

"I've forgotten the name of the tune the trio does that you wrote for your mom. It's on *Sound Circle* and another recording."

"'Hope for Now,'" Akira said. "Tana-Reid also recorded that on *Passing Through.*"

"I was listening last night to the two versions of it."

The trio version, featuring Kai Akagi, starts off with a quick piano flourish, then settles into steady midtempo: Akagi impressionistic and bop-oriented by turns, the piece providing fine invention on the part of all three players. The full-group version—Tana, Reid, Rob Scheiderman on piano, Craig Bailey on alto sax, Dan Faulk on tenor, and Guilherme Franco on percussion—has a more explosive beginning. The unison work provides some haunting tonalities, juggles or shuffles the mood just as the trio version does, but the tempo is more rapid, allowing Reid's nimble bass to shine through, along with fine horn solos by Bailey and Faulk, offset by Tana's cymbal splashes.

I mentioned Akira's mother, a remarkable woman who got her master's degree at seventy-one and then began winning poetry contests.

"She got her degree from San Jose State," Akira said. "She has published two books of poetry." Then, "Are her books available?" He called to his brother, who said they were available in several libraries: Palo Alto, Santa Cruz, etc. Akira Tana's father was a Buddhist minister, and his mother came from a very religious family—her father a minister in Hokkaido, in northern Japan. His father's parents had come to the United States, and Akira was born in San Jose, California. His mother's family had been large: eight girls and one boy, who himself became a minister, as did three of the sisters. Akira's mother played the koto and piano and wrote tanka poetry. In 1949, in Japan, she was one of the winners of the Emperor's Prize for poetry, a contest that receives entries from all over the world. In an interview in *Cadence* magazine, Akira Tana refers to her as "an inspiring woman." Both of his parents were interned during the war.

The drums were all packed, and family members were waiting for Akira. We did have time, but not much, to talk about something I'd found interesting: the musicians I'd met from Japan (such as Eiji Kitamura and Kotaro Tsukahara) were attracted to mainstream American jazz, whereas the Japanese Americans (such as Sumi Tonooka and Kenny Endo)—more than likely because of the important discovery, or recovery, of their roots—were engaged in employing traditional Japanese music, and traditional Japanese instruments, in their work.

"Takeshi Inomata mentioned something to me," he said. "He said I should do something with my impressions of Japan while I was on tour there. I thought about it. Over the years, interviewers and reviewers—probably because visually they see me as being Japanese—actually *hear* Japanese influences."

"In the *Cadence* interview," I said, "you said the Heath Brothers, when you took a solo, said they heard some *taiko* influences in it, although you weren't sure if that was because of the music or because they were seeing a Japanese face. Although you did say there may have been a subconscious influence through your mother."

"That's right."

"Some of the cymbal work maybe? The splashes? The washes?"

"And some of the tom-tom work, sure. I wish I had more time to compose. I'm starting to get into so much more of the business aspect and all of those other areas. The educational aspect too. But I'd like to get into doing something like that: incorporating maybe not so much traditional Japanese instruments but just *impressions*—musical impressions of Japan."

Akira Tana's ethnomusicology thesis, "Jazz in Japan," written at Harvard in 1974, begins with a discussion of the nation's pre–Meiji Restoration (prior to 1868) status as an "insular country" with a "unique capacity for cultural borrowing and assimilation," starting with primarily Asian influences, such as the music Prince Shotoku (572–662 A.D.) imported from Korea and used in ceremonies to dedicate Buddhist statues. A larger body of indigenous music, folk music, "floated unnoticed" and unmentioned in chronicles, according to Tana, until after the Heian period (794–1185). Aristocratic decay and "internecine struggles for power" forced Japan, during the subsequent Kamakura (1185–1333) and Tokugawa (1600 on) periods, to "look inward for her strength." Comic dances known as *dengaku* became so popular that officials neglected their duties in favor of attending them on a daily basis. The Japanese ability to adapt foreign influences and then convert these forms to something all her own became clear later, during the Meiji period (Japan finally open to the West after more than two hundred years of self-imposed, or Shogun-imposed, isolation). Sources were no longer located just over the waters to the west but far to the east. Author Natsume Soseki, although heavily influenced by European literature at the start of his career, spoke of a "cultural identity crisis" in music. Western music was "loud" and burdened with "heavy theory." Tonic and dominant chords overpowered the subtle melodic effects of Japan's traditional pentatonic tones. The martial appeal of Western music might help Japan win wars (as it did at Port Arthur against Russia in 1905), but its unique qualities, its very strangeness, did not invade Japan at an "early or primitive stage in its national development," as Asian music had. It arrived at "a highly developed stage," and the process of acceptance and assimilation was now more complex—perhaps even "forced and premature."

Much of what Tana says in his thesis is based on the premise that jazz—at least in *its* own "primitive" or developmental stages—was (1) American (America's only—as is so often claimed—indigenous art form); (2) an art form still regarded by many Americans as "alien," a form of "esoteric expression only a select few can appreciate"; (3) associated with "segments of society" diametrically opposed to "the majority's outlook on life"; yet also (4) to some "a way of life," a form of musical expression of "immense artistic value"; and finally (5) black. Although Americans of "divergent backgrounds" enjoy it, the music, Tana claims, is "at its roots, a musical expression stemming from one cultural tradition," that of black Americans.

Tana regards "the continuum of Black music" as not only "conspicuous within, but crucial to Black culture . . . the basis upon which it is built." Borrowing (which he sees as whites borrowing from blacks) is analogous to plagiarism, reaching the status of a "criminal act" on the part of the media in its preference for white artists over black ("Just as the Black man has been exploited in America, so has his music"). This claim may have been felt more urgently, and been easier to substantiate, in 1974 than it is today, for recent scholarship tends to call *anyone's* exclusive right to jazz into question, right down to place of origin (the hegemony of New Orleans). Consummate Harlem stride pianist James P. Johnson, who was African American, claimed he played jazz "long before any of the early Crescent City bands traveled north." Johnson heard the music in Kansas City, St. Louis, and Baltimore before he ever heard of Jelly Roll Morton and attested to the influence of musical styles from not only Charleston and Memphis, as far back as 1912, but—at the hands of "great ragtime pianists"—the Midwest as well. The word "jazz" (or "jass") itself originated in San Francisco at the turn of the century.

A major problem remains: just when and *where* did this music known under so many different names become "jazz"? But aside from the immediate effect of Tana's premise, this topic of debate lies outside our range here. In 1974, Akira Tana felt the struggle for the recognition and respectability of jazz—as a "valid art form"—had its political counterpart in the "increasingly more militant" movements of the time. He saw jazz as a "highly sophisticated form of protest music," and he felt that the Japanese were not sufficiently acquainted with this social and political context and that a lack of a sense of history impaired their full understanding of the music.

In spite of this reservation, Tana goes on to praise what he felt was a "salubrious" climate for the acceptance and appreciation of jazz in Japan, because (1) like Europe, it had longstanding artistic traditions and (2) artists were treated with "fairness and respect." Much in its favor is Japan's interest in promoting as "wide a dissemination of the art form as possible," and through as many channels as possible. American musicians enjoy well-organized, extended tours in Japan and recognition that, Tana believes, has been "lacking for so long in their own country." Jazz musicians are received in the same manner that dignitaries and celebrities are. If publications indicate the "measure of popularity of an art form," jazz has also done well in Japan on that score. *Swing Journal,* modeled on *Downbeat,* presents—Tana feels—a much broader base of "extensiveness and thoroughness of coverage," a more complete overview, than its American predecessor, and can boast of a wider circulation. *Swing Journal* once had, in fact, the widest circulation of any jazz magazine in the world.

In the introduction, I mentioned Michael Cuscuna's contention that, during the late 1970s, Japan "almost single-handedly kept the jazz record business going." Akira Tana feels that the Japanese, in their effort to absorb the music in every possible way, "have provided fresh territory for American and European record companies." Jazz is distributed on a wide scale in Japan, and recordings that have lost their market appeal in America, and are out of print, are frequently reissued in Japan. As far as an audience for the music is concerned, Tana asserts that "appreciation and respect for jazz as a musical art form of America" pervades every section of Japanese society. In large urban areas, live jazz—whether presented in concert halls, clubs, or small coffeehouses—is readily available, and knowledge of the music's "existence and expressive value is recognized even in quite remote areas." Tana provides the example of his uncle and aunt in Iwamizawa, a small town in Hokkaido (one hour west of Sapporo by train), who, along with cassette recordings of Louis Armstrong, Miles Davis, Duke Ellington, owned recordings by Charles Tolliver's progressive big band Music Incorporated. The couple "expressed high regard and admiration for jazz as an art form," although they said (with customary Japanese modesty?) that their knowledge was "not very thorough." Tana also talked to a relative, a rice farmer, who expressed "respect for jazz."

He cites four categories that make up the urban audience for the music: (1) students, who may show a "faddish interest"—or genuine—in jazz, fashion, politics, and social lifestyles of the West; (2) recent college graduates, in their early to mid-twenties, who work for firms or in offices, for whom "jazz is a leisure activity extended from their college days," one for which they provide "patronage"; (3) upper- and middle-class business executives, *sararīman*, members of society who are patrons of the arts in general; and (4) the community of artists in Japan who, "aware of the artistic merit of the music," are interested in forms of artistic expression besides their own. Tana cites the example of a recent college graduate in a comfortable position with a company, a man who follows jazz with "astounding fervor," committing improvised solos to memory, frequenting clubs and attending concerts "at every opportunity, fanatically clinging to the art form as a symbol of non-conformity."

As an "American product," jazz is given "equal footing" with other Western contributions: governmental, social, and artistic. Yet, paradoxically, Tana finds the Japanese jazz environment "a more positive one than that of America." He begins his discussion of the "unique position of the Japanese jazz musician" with the premise: "Unlike Western classical music where it is assumed that the *audience* is at fault if it cannot appreciate musical subtleties, jazz is still fighting to gain an audience that can satisfy the simple need of appreciating the music and the jazz musician." The Japanese artist is unique because he or she is a "specialized listener of the music, firstly as a student, and secondly as a member of the audience," yet he or she must seek "acceptance and recognition for his own musical expression in Japan," as opposed to "mere imitation of American jazz." In order to do this, he or she must contend with the popularity of "the models upon which his own creations are based."

Although Japanese jazz performers participate in entertainment activities, in clubs and coffeehouses located in the Ginza and Shinjuku areas of Tokyo, the majority of them come from "another class in the social hierarchy." They come from fairly stable social and economic backgrounds that are characteristic of the middle and upper classes. For one thing, they have to be able to afford the expense of serious study. The fathers of three musicians Tana interviewed were a doctor, a high school teacher, or employed by an import company. Most come from merchant, business, or professional families. And there are dynasties, such as the case of Yoshiaki Masuo and Yoshio Suzuki. The first is the son of a jazz pianist who gained "reputable stature in the Fifties in

Japan"; the second is the son of the owner of the internationally renowned Suzuki violin company (the father invented the "Suzuki Method"). Makoto Ozone's father is a pianist in Kobe, and the Watanabe family has produced Sadao and Humio, the Hino family trumpeter Terumasa and drummer Motohiko.

Because of the general homogeneity in race and color in Japan, "there is not much emphasis or apparent conflict among jazz musicians themselves and the audience over the ethnicity of participants, as there is in America . . . so Japanese jazz performers can vie for work solely on the basis of their competence as musicians." The serious pursuit of studying jazz in Japan is "a leisure activity that becomes a professional occupation for those who succeed." Japanese differ from Americans in the fact that they must begin their musical education "by learning concepts foreign to their culture and mode of thought."

Jazz education programs were not introduced in Japan until the mid-1960s. Before that time, musicians copied compositions, melodic configurations, and improvised solos from records, *note for note*. In this way they were similar to pop and motion picture stars prior to World War II, who sang the lyrics of American songs without understanding their meaning. Although there are many schools of music in Japan that offer jazz curriculum (A.N. Contemporary School of Music and the Yamaha School of Music are two of the largest), they are very few in comparison to the schools that teach Western classical music. The methods are imported wholesale from Berklee College of Music in Boston. Japanese schools, according to Tana, teach the technique "as an end in itself." He goes so far as to say that "jazz education in Japan has failed." The institution is separated from "the environment in which jazz has been traditionally created."

Employment opportunities, however, are abundant in Japan. Because of the art form's popularity, the expanding motion picture and recording industry, and the demand for musical entertainment in various clubs, discotheques, and cabarets, "there are numerous areas and establishments in the field of musical entertainment where Japanese jazz musicians can seek employment." Many top musicians can be heard on motion picture sound-track recordings, on late-night TV programs, and in the "many hundreds of jazz clubs and coffee houses that are located in almost every metropolitan area in Japan." Tana adds that "the act of compromise in America is one of economic necessity. Because the majority of Japanese musicians come from financially well-off economic and social backgrounds, the act of compromising one's own musical convictions is predominantly a matter of aesthetic choice."

On the other hand, "the search for self-expression continues. The Japanese jazz musician is first and foremost a *listener* of American jazz. His model for musical expression has been American jazz. What has set him apart from the average Japanese listener is his own desire to acculturate the music for the purpose of creating his own." Akira Tana talked to musicians who felt that Japanese audiences were "meaningless," that their technical understanding was "considerably less that that of the performer"; these musicians felt they were performing "for a wall of blank faces." One musician felt that jazz was "50 percent a faddish element of Japanese society" and said he played "for himself and other fellow musicians, not the audience." Another musician's self-image as an artist reflected uncertainty and lack of optimism. He considered Japanese jazz a reflection of his society. Along with all too rapid Westernization, he felt that Japanese performers may have absorbed technical skill but have not absorbed, or understood, the emotional content of the music: "As the West's influence in Japan may seem superficially acculturated, vacuous and sterile, so is jazz played by Japanese." This musician has since left Japan for New York, where he is seeking work with American musicians.

Yet Tana does quote American pianist Bill Evans on the importance of improvisation as a part of Japanese cultural tradition. In the visual arts, "the artist is forced to be spontaneous . . . he must paint in such a way that an unnatural or interrupted stroke will destroy the line. Erasures or changes are impossible. Deliberation cannot interfere." Evans compares this to the challenge of "group improvisation," where, aside from "the weighty technical problem of collective coherent thinking, there is the very human, even social, need for sympathy from all members to blend for the common result." A Japanese musician quoted this passage for Tana, adding, "Just as Bill Evans implies . . . improvisation has been an integral part of certain aspects of Japanese art." He feels that, in the highly Westernized phase that Japan is presently in, jazz will "catch on and flourish." This musician also felt that "the Japanese jazz performer is at a stage in his development where his own musical statements and expressions have found uniqueness and validity; that the time of idolatry of American performers and their music is coming to an end, as a natural course of development."

Akira Tana's Harvard ethnomusicology thesis would prove invaluable to me later on when I was in Japan, acting as a sort of checklist, a means of comparing his views (from 1974) with what I myself was discovering twenty-two years later. Tana ends on an up note, saying that the gradual growth of "self-confidence as an artist and the impression he is making with this music, indicate a *promising future* for the Japanese jazz musician." Given the fact that "music is a universal language," he looks forward to a time when—given the Japanese gift of acceptance, adaptation, and acculturation, and through "self-recognition of their own cultural background which can contribute to their own creations"—an expression of a "unique Japanese character" will be possible, without sacrificing "her own identity."

I was ready for Japan, but before Betty and I left, I had one more stroke of "fortuitous" good fortune, an encounter with one more portion of the jigsaw puzzle of jazz in Japan that would prove to fit perfectly and be of invaluable aid. I was able to meet and talk with the remarkable pianist/composer Makoto Ozone.

MAKOTO OZONE

WHEN I DISCOVERED THAT MAKOTO Ozone would be appearing with vibraphonist Gary Burton at Pete Douglas's Bach Dancing and Dynamite Society in Half Moon Bay (where I'd heard and met Akira Tana), I contacted the ever-reliable Rob Hayes at Berklee College (which Makoto, like so many other Japanese jazz musicians, had attended). He sent me the pianist's fax number in Japan, so I was able to arrange a meeting with this, by that time, more than "promising" young pianist.

Makoto Ozone appeared with the Gary Burton Quintet on a 1986 CD called *Whiz Kids*. He also appeared duo with Burton on the recently released *Face to Face* and had his first recording, simply called *Makoto Ozone*, produced by Burton in 1984. The pianist was twenty-three at the time and looked about ten years younger. Thin as a rail, a haunted, nearly hungry look on his face on the LP cover, he peered over the top of an ebony piano and played like a monster, a full-fledged pro. The album consisted of original compositions, one of which, "Crystal Love," had changes that ran from D9sus, to Gmaj7, to A♭, F♯dim7, G♭13, B7, E♭maj7, and D7♯5, and resolved by way of Gmin7, F, E♭min, or E♭maj7—whichever you chose. I tried to play the piece and gave up. I sat back and dug Makoto's stellar performance, listening as he moved effortlessly through the changes he had himself conceived, amazed by his skill and sensibility.

Ozone and Gary Burton have a rich musical compatibility, and I looked forward to seeing them live at the Bach Dancing and Dynamite Society. When February arrived, and the Half Moon Bay date with it, they didn't disappoint—playing a number of tunes featured on *Face to Face*. One of them was an Ozone triumph called "Opus Half," originally recorded by Benny Goodman, Teddy Wilson, Lionel Hampton, and Gene Krupa. Makoto Ozone learned the tune from his father, who lives in Kobe and whom Burton has described as "one of Japan's best jazz pianists," adding, "Makoto's knowledge of historical jazz piano style is at least one valuable family inheritance." "Opus Half" is Ozone's piece de resistance, a joyous raglike romp. In Half Moon Bay, the pianist controlled its wild stride with samurai precision and panache, the pace furious, but Makoto, a master of genuine two-handed jazz piano, was cool as cool can be throughout the intricate exertions.

Another tune from *Face to Face*, "Bento Box" (a *bento* is a Japanese box lunch), an Ozone original, was also a delight, the pianist loosening up, joking about Burton's pronunciation of the title, saying, "He finally got it, after all these years!" The tune itself was subtle, playful, sassy, Makoto's assertive accents propelling Burton's wide-open solo, the pianist's own solo then made up of elegant, swinging, extended lines. The piece concluded with a buoyant link-up that left both performers smiling broadly.

I talked with Makoto Ozone between sets. Dressed in a snappy black and white jersey with long sleeves and slick black loafers with small honest-to-God bows, Makoto Ozone lit a cigarette ("I live in a country where people still do that") and sipped a Pepsi. On the stage, in the company of Gary Burton, he'd been very self-effacing, nearly deferential, very "Japanese" in the respect he showed his former *sensei*. On his own, he's quite hip. He was laid-back, casual, relaxed, open—"American," if you will.

I asked him about a statement he'd once made in an interview about trying to improvise with "consonance," employing the regular major-7 chord to relieve the "tension" and "dissonance" found in more extravagant jazz outings.

"I've freed myself a little more from that feeling. That was a period of time when I was sounding too much like Oscar Peterson. My dream, my goal, was to sound like him—until I had my contract with CBS. That's when I realized, 'Okay, nobody wants to buy fake Oscar Peterson records, so I better come up with my own ideas and style.' That's when I stopped playing standard music and started to write a lot of my own original material. That's when I started to listen to a lot of classical music. I didn't even *like* classical music until then. But in order for me to get out of that cage. I didn't want to be a clone of Oscar."

"Do you have a classical background?"

"No, I don't."

"Really? Your technique is superb."

"I did take classical lessons for about six months. From a French priest in Japan. He was, and still is, a wonderful teacher. He taught me the basic finger exercises, and then after six months of lessons I broke my left arm. It took me about six months to heal, and after that I couldn't get in touch with him. He was such a busy teacher, his schedule was completely filled. I was about twelve or thirteen and started to transcribe Oscar Peterson's records. Transcribing is one thing, but after you've got it all down and try to play it—well, that's another challenge. I forced my fingers to go faster and faster and faster, but my teacher had always told me, 'If you want to play fast, you always have to practice *slow*' . . . you know, frankly, I don't know exactly what I meant by 'I try to improvise with consonance.'"

When I reread the quote to him, he said, "Actually I do still feel that way to a certain extent, but now I go back and forth between dissonance and consonance. I have a wider range now, I guess. At least I *hope* I do."

I said I'd been listening to lots of his recordings, including those made in Japan that friends had brought me that weren't available in the States, and I found the range of forms and styles amazing. On "Monk's Dream," on *Face to Face,* he comes up with a boogie-woogie pattern that begins as a walking bass.

"That just kind of happened there. That's one of those spur-of-the-moment things. You do it and it works, but then you try to do it again, because it worked before, and it *won't* work. I always try to play what I *hear*."

I read another quote I'd found of his: "I always have trouble doing just one thing. I always want to try out *everything*." Yet, I pointed out, the various styles don't seem to conflict at all. Makoto moves from one to another with ease: stuff that sounds like lush film scores, pieces with a decidedly classical feel, then hard-driving bop.

"Yeah? I'm glad that I'm doing it okay," he said, laughing. "These days it's so hard, as a jazz pianist, to pick what your favorite music is. Everybody calls me a jazz pianist, but I like to do a lot of different things. If I see something I *don't* know, that really bugs me to learn it. For instance, this coming June, for the first time in my life, I have a chance to play with the New Japan Philharmonic. We will perform 'Rhapsody in Blue,' the whole piece. I got the music to it and I said, 'Oh, my God, there are a lot of notes on this, and I have to *practice!*' I finally bought a piano. For thirty years I never owned a piano. When I was growing up, my father always had a piano. When I moved into an apartment here, I never wanted to buy my own upright. Why bother when I could use the grand piano at Berklee? So I always went to school, even after I graduated. I would call up Gary and he set up some room for me to practice in when I wanted to, which only happened once a week. But to try to play something like 'Rhapsody in Blue'! I'm also working on a Mozart piece right now. Chick Corea got me into this. He told me to learn the Mozart double piano concerto. It's a lot of fun. It's a totally different context, and I hope I'm playing it right. I took Chick's advice. He said, 'Don't worry about what people might say about your Mozart. Just play the notes, and then just play as you *feel.*'"

I mentioned Kotaro Tsukahara, who's played "Rhapsody in Blue" in concert.

"Kotaro. I know him very well. He's played 'Rhapsody in Blue'? The whole thing? That's quite a hard piece. I haven't seen any jazz player, except somebody like Keith Jarrett or a classically orientated player, perform the whole thing. I've seen Yosuke Yamashita do it, but he rearranged it. To more of a jazz style."

"If you can play 'Opus Half,' you must be able to play *anything.*"

"I don't know. There are different techniques that are required. 'Rhapsody' is more precise."

I read another quote of his: "I want to be a melody player. That's the most important thing."

"I still am. The melody . . . a strong melodic idea is always the key to my playing, yes."

I commented on the rich melodic sense I found in traditional Japanese music, its seeming importance.

"Yeah, I'm sure it is. The only thing that seems to be missing in Japanese music is the *rhythm* that we have in jazz—the backbeat feel, you know? These days I sometimes am shocked to see American people clap their hands on *one* and *three.* Younger kids do that nowadays; they don't really go for *two* and *four.* But the backbeat feel is always the basic element in swing. They hear the bass drum, which is always way too loudly recorded."

"I mentioned film work before. Have you done any?"

"No, but I would really love to do that, someday. One, I have no experience doing it, and, two, I just don't know how. Dave Mash is a wonderful film-score writer from Berklee. In fact I took his course when I was a student there. That was 'Introduction to Film Scoring.' It was so basic we didn't even write music, so I dropped out." He laughed. "He remembers that! But I would really love to write something for film. I'm getting into technology with my Macintosh. How to synchronize and all that."

I mentioned two recordings friends had brought me from Japan, recordings apparently not available in the States: *Walk Alone* and *Break Out*.

"Oh, you've got *Walk Alone*! That's one of my favorite records. I'm so sorry it's not available here. You can't go wrong with *those* rhythm-section players: Marc Johnson on bass and Peter Erskine on drums. Literally, each of them had only about eight bars of solo on the whole record, but they didn't complain. Usually jazz players say, 'Hey, man, let me solo more!' We did a live recording, in nine hours, in New York. Usually, these days, the strings are always overdubbed, but I said, 'Come on, this is a *jazz* record, man. We've got to do it *live.*' That's what I'm paying all this big money for!" He laughed. "I want to play with the fuckin' strings, you know?! It's all a business deal in Japan. JVC had split up into two different companies, and I ended up with the domestic division. So I said, 'Well, okay, if you can't release my album in the States, or Europe for that matter, I'll have to go somewhere else.' *Break Out* was a solo album. Yeah, that's on Verve. It was released in Japan, and Europe, and everywhere else, *except* the United States. I don't know why."

"What a shame," I said.

"I guess they don't have the incentive to bring it out here and make a promotional push behind it. I did just put out another recording called *Nature Boys*. Once again with Peter Erskine on drums, but John Patitucci on bass. Everyone knows who *he* is. This is a record of standards. I did 'Nature Boy,' solo, 'All of You,' 'But Beautiful,' 'Lover Come Back to Me.' Like *clap clap clap clap clap*—real fast! Peter was really cooking on that. Interestingly enough, I only wrote one tune on this recording. It's called 'Before I Was Born.' It's a ballad. And I did a couple of tunes that are not well-known jazz tunes. One was 'Laughter in the Rain.' It's a pop song by . . . I think Neil Sedaka may have written it."

I asked Makoto about his own compositions. Most of the tunes on

Walk Alone, Break Out, and another album, *Starlight,* are his. And I was curious about "Bento Box" on *Face to Face*—just how it had come about.

"Two of my original tunes on *Face to Face*—'Bento Box' and 'Times Like These'—were written for Gary's first record for GPR. That was about eight years ago. When he moved to GPR from ECM, he asked me if I would write a couple of tunes for a record without knowing whether he was going to use them or not, because he has to *like* the tunes in order to record them. That was back in the days when I didn't have a piano. He called me up one day and he said, 'I'll be doing my errands in the next couple of hours. Do you want to use my piano in the basement?' I said, 'Sure.' So I drove over to his house and he locked me in his basement. When he came back I had those two. In fact, 'Times Like These' is still one of my favorites. It's so simple, yet so strong. When I finished writing it he came back into the room. He heard whatever I was playing and he said, 'That sounded *nice.*' If he hadn't heard it, I would have kept it for myself! No, I'm glad he heard it, because I wrote it for Michael Brecker. I was just hearing Michael Brecker playing the melody on tenor—that wild gorgeous sound that he gets."

"So when you compose, you're hearing specific people you want to play that piece?"

"Yes, you always have to. This is interesting. I was talking with Chick Corea about this, and he does the same thing. He can't write tunes unless he knows what the instruments are and who will be playing them. I feel the same, always. When I'm asked to write a tune, I say, 'Okay, what's the personnel?' Or 'What's the instrumentation?' You have to first pick the key that is best for the instrument, especially if you are going to use a horn. That's how I write."

When I asked Makoto about the current jazz scene in Japan, he mentioned the large number of "younger players who are really talented coming out. I just hope they get the exposure they deserve. We have this tradition in Japan of paying an incredible amount of respect to older people. I think it's a great tradition, and as far as some artists are concerned I believe it's good, to a certain extent. But sometimes, just because they have a right to say what they want and the younger people *don't,* the older musicians tell the younger that they're not old enough to play a certain tune. 'You are too green,' etc. Young players should be able to experiment. *All* musicians should experiment in any way they want. They should be able to *exchange* opinions. But it's taboo for younger people to offer suggestions or state an opinion to older people in Japan. When you are fifty years old, you have a lot of experience that will naturally project into your performance, especially when you play ballads or medium swing; but these older performers make comments like, 'You've got chops, kid, but don't get drowned in them.' I pay a great deal of respect to older musicians. I'm not saying it's *their* fault. Part of it is the younger musicians' fault because they keep their mouths shut about it. But some musicians are *different*. Like Junko Onishi, the piano player. She was my student for a while at Berklee in Japan. She's always played the way she does and I've always thought, 'Wow, this is something *strange*.' This is definitely not my kind of pianist, but this is something I *can't do*. You know it's a Monkish style. That Thelonious Monk style . . ."

"Not much consonance."

"Yeah, not much consonance! It's not *polished*. But so what? That's her style. She means to play it that way. And then it really comes across very well. I enjoy it, even though I don't want to play like that."

I asked Makoto about another fine female pianist I'd heard on recordings, Aki Takase.

"She's more avant-garde I guess," he said, "to a certain extent. Like Yosuke Yamashita's stuff. And that's a style I can't stand." He laughed. "To me, it's almost *piano abuse*." He laughed again. "Playing with the elbows and all that. I always think, 'Oh God, that *hurts!*' There are a few avant-garde players, but I don't go listen to them. I'm not saying they're bad, but it just doesn't do anything to me. For me."

I asked about the possibility of an emerging, uniquely *Japanese* style of jazz: is there such a thing?

"I don't know. I just don't know *what* Japanese jazz would be. If it's called 'jazz,' I don't know why they even say 'Japanese jazz.' To me that's just an excuse, a way to get away with something that's not real. I shouldn't be saying that, but . . . you're talking about Japanese musicians going back home? For one thing, now, in 1996, the yen is very strong, so they'd rather work over there. I'm sure that's one of the reasons. And quite simply: there aren't as many jazz venues available as there used to be in the States, whereas Japan still has jazz forums growing—which is true also in Europe."

I said that Kotaro Tsukahara had said, "It's Bud Powell for me. I have no interest in using traditional Japanese music."

"Good for him, yeah! Growing up, I was always surrounded by *jazz*, not traditional Japanese music. I grew up with Benny Goodman, Dixieland, Louis Armstrong. My father was always playing this music."

Recalling his father's club was in Kobe, I asked about the effect of the earthquake.

"My father's club is gone. After the earthquake in Kobe, yeah. We lost three buildings. But he managed to buy something new, so they're okay."

There was a respectful pause. We both stared out the window for a moment. I thought about the newspaper and magazine photos I'd seen of Japan's "quake-proof" second-largest port city demolished in twenty seconds (a landscape of rubble; 1,650 feet of a four-lane freeway folding like an accordion and falling on its side, tossing cars in the air; the city's death toll surpassing five thousand), and I couldn't help contrasting *that* scene with the bright California seascape outside the glass, this placid place itself (we've been told) another disaster just waiting to happen.

When we began to talk again, it was about the existence of a strictly Japanese aesthetic. When I mentioned *biteki kankaku* (aesthetics), Makoto asked me to clarify what I meant. I defined it as a distinctive *native* approach to art that would make its way into one's music. I mentioned that, in articles I'd read, Toshiko Akiyoshi talked about a time when she *wanted* to incorporate Japanese elements in her writing, actually using traditional instruments such as the koto and *shakuhachi*.

"*She* does that very very well. But I had a chance to talk with a traditional Japanese performer, a Japanese musical artist who plays an instrument called a *tsuzumi*, a small drum . . . like this." Makoto held an imaginary *tsuzumi* drum before him. "They hold it *here* and they have a small plastic thing on their fingers, and they go *bowwwmm bowwwmm*, with the Japanese flute also going. This man said he had a chance to play with an avant-garde jazz pianist who wanted to play with him because he's a legend on the *tsuzumi* drum. I said, 'How was it?' And he said, 'Oh, he was just all *bullshit*.' I said, 'Wow, that's what I thought too.'"

This reminded me of what Tiger Okoshi had said in Honolulu: the same disapproving stance. Makoto continued, "When you try to play avant-garde there's a fine line between actually hearing the notes and communicating or just playing whatever notes you *see*. It will probably sound the same to you, but the vibes that come across to an audience will be completely different. Chick Corea gave a solo piano concert once, pulled out another piano, and called me up on stage. I sat in. We played together. We started out doing a kind of avant-garde thing that led into 'Green Dolphin Street.' We tried to communicate, but it was right on the edge. You can fall off so easily if you are not really hearing each other. So the *tsuzumi* player was saying the pianist didn't really know our music too well. I'm sure that Toshiko has done an incredible amount of study of Japanese music, because she includes it in her big band writing. I've heard her big band with a *shakuhachi* and *tsuzumi* and other stuff, and she uses it all extremely well. And of course she uses Japanese harmony, and it all blends so well together. I really have a great respect for her doing that. So when that *tsuzumi* player said, 'Oh that was bullshit, because you really have to know Japanese music,' I said, 'Okay, I was right about this,' because at one time I thought about using some of the Japanese instruments, and I thought, 'Oh no, I don't know anything about Japanese traditional music, so I'd better not do this until I study some of it. I haven't done that *yet*. I'm doing so many other things that I want to do now, like Mozart and 'Rhapsody in Blue.'" He laughed. "And I'm very interested in and studying . . . the *tango!*"

"Right on!" I said. Then, thinking *Japanese* again, "Isn't 'Bento Box' pentatonic? The theme at the beginning sounds it."

"It's pentatonic, but we also have a minor scale, a Japanese minor scale. I don't know what we call that in English, but . . . not only that but you have to understand the *breathing* of Japanese music. It's like when you groove or swing, there's got to be some kind of groove in Japanese music too—which *I don't know*, even though I'm Japanese. The rhythmic thing is very important. If you try to go *one-two-three-four* in Japanese music, it won't work. You just have to breathe with it another way, which is true when you play jazz also. You breathe in a certain way, and you tap your fingers in certain ways, and your body sort of reacts to that with a certain response, the natural body response. The rhythm and the groove have to come out of your body naturally. In order for me to *play* Japanese, I would have to first study and then *experience* it, playing with good musicians, Japanese musicians. But I don't have a particular interest in mixing my music with traditional Japanese music yet. However, if you are going to see Toshiko, you can tell her what we talked about and that I have great respect and admiration for her music, always. The reason I wanted to go to Berklee was because I saw Toshiko's big band with Lew Tabackin. This was when I was about twelve years old. I saw this Japanese lady with such hip compositions and arrangements, and when she did *this*"—he gestured emphatically, the way Toshiko does when she directs her band—"and all those *big* American guys were following *her* fingers, I thought, 'Oh my God, this is *unbelievable!*' I've always loved her music. In fact she cooked scrambled eggs for me one morning.

Toshiko did. I went to her apartment in Europe, right after she moved over there. A friend of mine was going there to rehearse with Lew, so I walked in and I shook her hand for the first time. She said, 'Oh, are you hungry?' I said, 'Yeah,' and she said, 'How 'bout some scrambled egg?' 'Great!' I said."

It was time for Makoto's second set with Gary (one that proved every bit as rich as the first), so I thanked him for his time. In Japanese, the word *makoto* means truth, sincerity, an important ideal of former court poetry as penetrating to the heart or truth of things, treating nature and human experience with intense yet respectful observation of detail so as to capture the essential reality. Having met Makoto Ozone, I was tempted to add words like "hip," "sharp," "smart," and "honest" to this meaning. And, of course, "gracious," "considerate." At the very close of our conversation, he smiled and said, "I hope you got what you needed. And I hope I didn't say anything rude. Some Japanese think I have a big mouth. I hope I didn't offend anybody."

THE TOKAIDO ROAD AND BEYOND: THE MONTEREY JAZZ FESTIVAL IN NOTO

BETTY AND I STOOD BEHIND a severe yellow line made up of six stripes, watched by an equally severe railroad attendant in his impeccably pressed blue and white striped shirt, white gloves, and visored military hat with red band. Betty was poised to break beyond both barriers and snap a photo of the *shinkansen* (new trunk line, or bullet train) as it roared into Tokyo Station. When it did, somewhat shy of its advertised two hundred kilometers an hour but fast enough to activate the severe railroad official, Betty got her picture, then stepped back behind the yellow lines. The photo is interesting not because of the nose of the distant train but the look on the face of the railroad official. Needless to say, that face does not register approval of gaijin who step over yellow lines to take photos of approaching trains, bullet or otherwise.

We'd be traveling on what's left of the old Tokaido Road from Edo (Tokyo) to Kyoto. I'd dreamed of setting out along this famous "way" from Nihonbashi Bridge, as depicted in Hiroshige's series of prints, *Fifty-three Stations on the Tokaido*. Nihonbashi was the point from which all distances were once measured in Japan—as Hiroshige depicts it, a curved wooden footbridge no more than fifteen or twenty feet wide supporting porters bent beneath large red crates, another group carting round flat buckets suspended from poles on their shoulders. Unfortunately, we made the mistake of going to Nihonbashi Bridge, which is now a contemporary cement structure beneath a freeway (built to accommodate excess traffic during the 1964 Olympics), complete with large ornate lamps so fierce they resemble temple guardians. At the road's end, Kyoto, we would transfer to a train that would transport us to Wakura Onsen (Wakura Hot Springs), site of the eighth annual Monterey Jazz Festival in Noto. I was curious about what we'd find in the countryside we would pass through, what resided out there to pull jazz so far from the "Big Apple" of Tokyo.

The *shinkansen* accommodations were cool and comfortable; Tokyo's heavy heat and humidity, which had left us drenched with sweat after carting our luggage to the station, were now shut out. We weren't instantly transported to the *inaka* (countryside or rural areas), a world of thatched roofs and rice paddies, however, for the city remained very much in sight, looking now more of a piece than it had when we wandered amid its particulars. We saw an array of blue-, gray-, copper-, ochre-, and orange-tiled rooftops when we hit the suburbs, plus more of those tall green screened-in driving ranges. We would see *them* in cities all the way to Kyoto, but never an actual golf course. What were people practicing *for*?

The Tokaido Road, circa 1996, struck us as one continuous city, and what wasn't city was tunnels (the original journey must have been somewhat mountainous). As we drew near Odawa, I kept asking about, and was promised, a splendid view of Mt. Fuji, but we cruised right on by, the famous site shrouded in clouds or fog or smog, or all three. I had ample time, throughout this journey, to think back on the music I'd heard in Tokyo and what I'd learned—from Yozo Iwanami, Yoichi Nakao, Bunichi Murata, and Yasuhiko Shimazaki—about the cultural climate that made jazz possible in Japan. In his Harvard thesis, Akira Tana claims that a majority of Japanese performers, unlike their American counterparts, come from "fairly stable social and economic backgrounds that are characteristic of the middle and upper classes," that the study of jazz in Japan is "a leisure activity that becomes a professional occupation for those who succeed." What I'd seen in Tokyo confirmed this observation, although it appeared that both Toshiko Akiyoshi and Kiyoko Ami had literally been forced to "run away from home" in order to play jazz. Stable social and economic background might produce less of an "edge" to the music, perhaps, less anxious hunger, less open competition. From Tokyo on, the most frequent complaint I would hear from musicians themselves would be that they weren't "aggressive" enough in their playing, but I was tempted to ask, "Why do you *want* to be?" I had enjoyed the relaxed, genial, even joyous atmosphere of the clubs, devoid of the somewhat superciliously super-serious (occasion-

147

ally even rancorous) contestation one finds in the States—or the church-like (occasionally hypocritical) tone of jazz as High Art there. In his *Japan: A Short Cultural History*, George Sansom comments, "What interests [Zen artists and poets] is not the restless movement on the surface of life, but . . . the eternal tranquility seen through and behind change. So Noami [painter, 1397–1476], a fine judge, approved highly of a critic who said in esteem of a Chinese painter's work: 'It is a quiet picture.'" If much of the music I'd heard seemed "quiet" or even a bit tame, that did seem to be in keeping with a Zen aesthetic.

Actually I'd been exposed to a wide variety of music, but the common element that ran through Masahiko Satoh's intelligence and intentionality, the overt joy of Kotaro Tsukahara's practice, Ami's more laid-back approach, Yoko Sike's smooth vocalizations, or Benisuke Sakai's proficient and imaginative bass work was a prevailing sense of culturally sanctioned ease of craftsmanship: deceptive, I know, when one realizes the arduous discipline and dedication required to arrive at that state, but very much in keeping with the nature of Japanese art. So many artists in America seem condemned to *fight* for lives in art, for their existence as artists, and not just in the early stages of their careers. America's natural urge seems mostly pragmatic, survival oriented. On the other hand, even if it's not conscious, there seems to be a *natural,* not forced, context for "art" in Japan that's a given, in spite of the fact that a genius like Masahiko Satoh feels he may be regarded as "a strange person" by his fellow Japanese. Even if it lacks the American historical/social context, as Akira Tana felt it does, jazz in Japan *is* actually regarded as an art.

When we checked into the Alpha One Hotel in Wakura Onsen, we were given a *futariyo no heya* (double room) richly furnished (for a modest hotel like the Alpha One) with radio, alarm clock, blow drier, electronic ironing board, and a toilet with a seat that warmed up to whatever degree of satisfaction you desired. However, we couldn't get any of these things to work. I refreshed my knowledge of the words I would need to complain (*ariari o tsukeraremasen;* the lights don't work). Fortunately, before I went back downstairs and made a fool of myself, Betty discovered a sign that said "Please deposit your key here." Suddenly, all the lights, the radio, alarm clock, blow drier, electric ironing board, air-conditioning unit, and even the toilet started up at the same time.

On our way out to check out the town, Betty and I ran into Richie Cole in the elevator. I'd interviewed the American alto saxophonist by phone before but never met him face to face. He was one of the "stars" appearing at the Monterey Jazz Festival in Noto. Richie had also appeared on the cover of the book I'd written about jazz in the Soviet Union. I told him this now, and he said he'd never seen the book. A jam session party was scheduled at another hotel that evening, so I said I'd bring a copy. Richie, a somewhat rumpled-looking man, was quite friendly. In *Unzipped Souls,* I'd described him, of the American musicians who'd performed in the USSR, as the one most akin to the Russians "in his madness," for even our phone calls had turned out to be slightly wacky adventures. He'd said then that jazz music was "the music of world peace" and gone on to tell me that in South Africa, in Soweto, where he'd made a music video, he'd played with a Mau Mau on bass and a Zulu on drums, adding, "Traditionally, you know, man, those cats *eat* each other!" Richie was only slightly more subdued now in the elevator, and I was happy that we'd run into him.

Outside, the day was hot, and Betty and I ambled up Wakura Onsen's main street, which boasted a row of fairly fancy hotels, the Notoraku, Juen, Biwansho, and Sun Kagaya (where a woman in kimono was playing koto at noon, on a raised platform; she'd still be there when we returned that night), all leading up to the jewel of them all at the street's end, the resplendent Hotel Kagaya complex, where the jam session party was to be held. The festival itself would take place the next day at the Wakura Spa Seaside Park.

While we were eating dinner that night, at a second-floor restaurant we'd picked out, everyone jumped up and ran to the window to watch a parade go by below: a large float embellished with an expressionist scowling samurai with angry eyebrows that could easily have been carved by Munakata (except it had been painted), fiercely black/white/orange/gold in design, the float surrounded and followed by children in brightly colored kimonos. Another *matsuri*! I was beginning to think that all of Japan was one large festival leading up to jazz, several forms of cultural delight flowing into another, merging seamlessly.

After dinner, we walked down to the pier, where the *matsuri* was in full swing. Families dressed in light summer *yukata* strolled percussively on *geta* (wooden clogs); vendors sold soft drinks and Kirin beer from kegs out on the street. A large stage had been erected. The giant lantern-lit samurai figure we'd seen now sat beside it. Booths offered just about any type of food or drink you desired, plus games for children. Overhead, wires held red and white lanterns that bobbed in the night breeze.

On the pier itself, thousands of candle-lit paper cups had been lined up, some sort of pledge or prayer or message inserted in each. Kimono-clad local "beauty queens" (hands clasped in front of them, eyes lowered with demure allure) stood by while the mayor and other local officials, decked out in suits or *happi* coats, gave speeches. A *taiko* drum contest began, the heads of the participants bound with sweatbands.

Back in town, a parade commenced, winding its way through the streets. To our surprise and delight, the members of the California High School All-Star Jazz Band (slated to perform at the festival the next day) came prancing by, proud and somewhat ridiculous looking in their hotel-provided *yukata,* some in more fancy dress provided by host families, but conspicuous either way by their blond hair (some) and open laughter. They were accompanied by camp followers or "groupies," pretty Japanese girls in gold and black kimonos who were attracted to these aspiring young jazz musicians like flies to tofu.

The Hotel Kagaya, my destination for the jam session party, which I would attend alone (I had only been granted one pass to this lavish affair), is a rather spectacular edifice, inside and out. Four glistening elevators ascend and descend outside, and the interior—once you have managed to outdistance the row of bowing women in dark blue kimonos greeting you at the door with "Irrashimase!" (Welcome!)—hosts a pink and crimson carpet as large as a soccer field, with rows of ornate chandeliers above. The jam session party was held in an immense ballroom upstairs. Individual tables, well stocked with hard liquor, had been set up, tables at which people did not sit but stand (convenient for roving from spot to spot and making friends). Tables set against the walls served everything from a universe of sashimi to tureens of French soups.

The party was in full swing by the time I arrived. A quintet called Vivace, made up of five young women, was performing: alto sax, vibraphone, piano, bass, and drums. I saw Monterey Jazz Festival general manager Tim Jackson and production coordinator David Murray, who introduced me to Masahisa Segawa, a distinguished gentleman with white hair, the *other* "Leonard Feather of Japan" I'd been waiting to meet. We stood and listened to Vivace a bit, and Segawa said he admired them but didn't feel they were quite ready for a CD recording. Various spontaneous musical groupings began to form, individual members of Vivace performing with soloists from the High School All-Star Band or members of two Japanese big bands, the Field Holler Jazz Orchestra and the Moonlight Jazz Orchestra, both of which would be performing the next day. The tunes they played were familiar, standards, accessible to relative strangers for improvisation, so the night turned into a legitimate "jam."

Richie Cole, when he appeared, brought the house down with his Alto Madness flare and energy. After his performance, I showed him the copy of *Unzipped Souls* I'd promised to bring, with his photo on the cover. He, in turn, began to show it to any and everyone who passed by. An older Japanese woman, no doubt the wife of a local businessman, looked surprised when Richie ran up to her and said, "Look! I'm on the cover of this *book!* And my mother told me, 'Richie, you'll never be anything but a *bum,*' but look!" When I later told Tim Jackson about this incident, he smiled and said, good-naturedly, "Richie's *still* a bum."

Masahisa Segawa came and told me that the women from Vivace had agreed to let me interview them, so we all stepped outside the now musically charged ballroom. While fans came up and asked them for autographs, I talked individually to the members of the group. Tomako Narumi, who plays alto sax, has lived in the United States and speaks English well, so she graciously agreed to serve as interpreter for the rest. She graduated from Tokyo Musical College, attended Berklee College three years ago, graduated, and played with Gunther Schuller's and George Russell's big bands. Tomako then went to New York and lived there for a year, playing in a number of salsa bands.

"I like Latin music," she said. "And I *really* like Brazilian music. My parents enjoyed dancing, so when I was young I listened to many big bands. I studied that music in a clinic here, but it wasn't much fun, so that's when I decided to go to Boston."

Because of family obligations and limits on her visa, and her feeling that "it was time to do something in Japan," Tomako returned in 1995 and joined Vivace. "I don't know what kind of music I will end up playing," she told me. "I just do everything I can now. This, jazz big bands, even musicals." As a child, her tastes displayed a certain measure of catholicity also: Prez Prado, Benny Goodman, Nat "King" Cole, Bing Crosby. At thirteen, she played clarinet and flute in her school marching band; then she heard Cannonball Adderley and Phil Woods and switched to alto saxophone.

Pianist Ayako Shirasaki started playing classical music at five, was an amateur jazz pianist at ten, and is now twenty-six years of age. Ayako's musical heroes are Bud Powell, Barry Harris, and Tommy

Flanagan. She likes the latter's "touch and natural phrasing." She turned professional when she graduated from Tokyo University of Arts with a degree in classical music. When she first performed at the J Club in Shinjuku, she was said to be a "genius." In 1983, Ayako won the Grand Prix at the Asakusa Jazz Festival and, in 1985, the same prize at the Piano Ensemble Festival. In 1992, she studied with Barry Harris in New York. When she returned to Japan, her manager asked, "Why don't you form a women's group?" The women do not work exclusively together but perform at other gigs, with other bands. "We are trying to see how much we can do, how far we can go as a women's group."

Nobuko Ariake plays vibes. She started on piano but heard a performance by Gary Burton and Chick Corea at twenty that "really shook me up, they were so great." She was a music major at Tokyo Education University. Nobuko is regarded as the *ichiban* (number-one) vibraphonist among young musicians. She hopes to become a teacher and aspires to play jazz, not pop or rock music. Her musical heroes now are Milt Jackson and Bobby Hutcherson. When she turned twenty-five, she joined Vivace. Nobuko has two children and admits that, while "jazz is my life," it is "not an easy life here, very difficult." She's paid her dues playing with men, "had a good time," does not feel as if she is being looked down on, although she admits that, in Japan, "jazz is a man's world." About Vivace, she says, "We don't care if we're men or women; we just want to show our music. And so far, everybody's said, 'They're women; that's fine.'"

If you saw Rumi Sato waiting at a subway station, you would never guess she is a bass player. Short, demure, elegantly dressed in a black jersey with a crest and a satin-sheen russet skirt, she offers a somewhat pinched, wry smile. She "likes the low notes," and that's what attracted her to such an overlarge instrument. She also liked folk songs and started on guitar, switched to electric bass in a blues band, and then began listening seriously to jazz. Largely self-taught, she studied electric bass at a private school of contemporary music in Roppongi in Tokyo. She first worked professionally at twenty-one, in another women's group, for weddings and parties. Then she took up—or stood up to—the contrabass. Her influences are Ray Brown, Paul Chambers, George Mraz, John Patitucci, and "next and next and next—*everybody!* And not only bass players. Everyone's my teacher." She confesses that, given their varied backgrounds, conflicts exist within Vivace, but the women discuss everything. "We work with it and that gives us strength." Pianist Ayako

Shirasaki selects the music the group plays, Rumi said. She closed with the straightforward, smiling declaration, "I love music!"

Drummer Satomi Onishi wanted to play flute when she was in her junior high school brass band, but the teacher said, "percussion." She studied classical music and percussion rudiments in a Kanagawa prefecture music school and then studied privately with Akira Tana's friend Takeshi Inomata. "He had a large effect on me." Later, she continued to play in brass bands and played tympani with a symphony orchestra. She began to copy classic-rock licks from groups like Deep Purple and then, as a chemistry major at the Science University of Tokyo, joined a jazz club. In high school, she'd listened to Max Roach, his melodious "Drum Sound" solo. She played with a group called Jack Pot and won Grand Prix at the Asakusa Jazz Contest in 1994. She's also performed at the Austria Jazz Festival in Europe. Satomi, now thirty, worked for several years as a chemist, not playing music professionally. Then last year, a phone call came from pianist Shirasaki. "She didn't like the others [drummers] she'd heard, but she selected me."

The group had been together for six months. They appeared at an all-women festival held in Tokyo in April of 1998, one that featured American performers Terry Lee Carrington, Dorothy Donegan, and Ann Patterson and Maiden Voyage, and Japanese pianist Junko Onishi. I looked forward to hearing them in concert the next day.

Russian and Japanese jazz festival crowds—as you might expect—are not at all alike. The latter audience is predictably attentive, reserved, polite. They are not effusive, rude, or abusive the way the former can be: the Russians entering and exiting a concert hall at will; stamping their feet in impatience (remember Khrushchev and his shoe at the United Nations?) if they are forced to wait too long between acts; yet discerning, musically sophisticated, and fully demonstrative when pleased by what they finally hear. The Japanese are more restrained in their perhaps generic rather than specific appreciation. And they tend to be *young*— something that, unfortunately, an American jazz festival crowd is less inclined to be.

Folding chairs had been set up in tidy rows throughout a large open area that flanked the turquoise twists and turns of the Water World pavilion at Seaside Park. Outside the seating area, a row of canvas-topped booths provided everything from large slabs of dried squid to teriyaki chicken skewers to soft drinks and beer.

The festival's emcee was a spunky young woman named Kyoko Muraguchi, a disc jockey on Station FM Ishikawa, who also serves as what's known in Japan as a "television personality" or *bijin* (a beauty or "cute girl," somewhat in the manner of an American anchorwoman), a role that, transferred to a jazz concert stage, seems to consist of keeping nearly inane verbal patter running nonstop whenever there is an absence of music. Ms. Muraguchi inaugurated the Monterey Jazz Festival in Noto by introducing Tim Jackson. She kept asking him if Richie Cole was going to play "Quando Quando Quando" (translated as *itsu itsu itsu*—where where where?—for the Japanese audience), Jackson replying, "If you *ask* him, I'm sure he'll play it." What we got in the meantime was the Field Holler Jazz Orchestra, from Toyama, a good, tight big band I'd heard in Monterey performing with American trumpeter Bobby Shew, for whom the leader, bassist Katsuyuki Okamoto, showed his respect by saying, "We purchased American postage stamp and wonder why he is not on it! Because he is still *alive*, I guess."

The Field Holler Jazz Orchestra immediately plunged into Dizzy Gillespie's up-tempo "Tour de Force." Their version of the tune contains a lively sax exchange featuring a young woman I recalled from their Monterey appearance because, wearing an ankle-length flower-print granny dress and sporting a dainty Ukiyo-e smile and amazingly large feet, she had entrusted her baby to the care of a friend or relative in the audience (a woman wearing an honest-to-God leopard-skin pillbox hat); *okāsan* would hop down off the bandstand between each number to make sure the baby was all right. Her musical "opponent" now was the man seated next to her in the sax section, where—this time without the baby—she remained throughout the set.

In many ways, Field Holler is typical of Japanese amateur big bands, which, as American trumpeter Bobby Shew said in Monterey, "there are literally hundreds and hundreds of; they don't play for a living but because they *want* to play!" The band hosts a wide range of ages (twenty-four to forty-seven), as reflected in its charts: Woody Herman's "Hit Parade" and "Four Brothers"—the latter offered and expanded by a three-brother and two-"sister" sax section—side-by-side with John Coltrane's "Moment's Notice"; Herman's "Early Autumn" (with a Getz clone solo)—balanced off by "Up Jumped Spring." After its California performance, the entire group (band, friends, Japanese fans, even the baby) had posed out on the lawn for the customary group photo, with the innocent abandon and glee of a scout troop. I learned that lead trom-

154

bonist Yoshiuki Tamimura is the husband of Tomoko Tamimura, the saxophonist mom; that trombonist Kikia Makimoto (for whom Lee Morgan's trumpet solo on "Moment's Notice" had been arranged) is a computer engineer; and that the group's leader is a journalist.

In Noto, Kyoko Muraguchi next introduced the Moonlight Jazz Orchestra, another amateur big band, a group that the pianist, Masahiko Abe, kicked into high gear with a spunky lead into Duke Ellington's "Rockin' in Rhythm." In contrast to the Field Holler Jazz Orchestra (which, ordinarily very much in synch, had sounded—in spite of its fine soloists—a bit complacent or even tentative as a group), the Moonlight Jazz Orchestra was truly tight, together. However, *their* tenor sax duel and a slightly tired trombone on "Johnny Come Lately" called attention to their weakness (and that of other Japanese amateur big bands, no matter how much communal zeal they bring to their charts): a dearth of confident soloists. The unison work was compact and forceful enough, and the band *looked* great, but a short Sarah Vaughan–influenced vocalist with red-tinged hair, introduced as a "*dynamito* singer," waxed a shade too enthusiastic on "A-Train." A literal translation of "Green Dolphin Street," *midori no iruka dori*, sounds funny in Japanese and drew laughs, and "All of Me" called too much attention to the fact that the singer was eating up most of the band's set time.

Next up was Vivace. After Kyoko Muraguchi stopped bugging Tim Jackson about how much he liked, or disliked, the Moonlight Jazz Orchestra's Hawaiian-style shirts (he replied, "Very fruity"), pianist Ayako Shirasaki was introduced. She began by saying that "to know music is the essence of life" and explained the group's name (OED: "*vivace, vivacemente* (It.) Vivacious, from *vivacita, vivacezza*, vivacity. Fast and lively") as "life combined with spirited performance"—all of which they provided. On "Yardbird Suite," pianist Ayako Shirasaki was on top of things all the way, and bassist Rumi Sato provided steady time (her solos a bit "studied" perhaps, but she kept the momentum going), drummer Satomi Onishi starting out somewhat timidly (four/four straight-ahead with occasional, and predictable, cymbal crashes), and saxophonist Tomako Narumi and vibraphonist Nobuko Ariake both highly professional and strong.

Two American girls sitting next to Betty and me began a conversation that threatened to drown out the music, but fortunately some of it actually related to Vivace.

"This surprises me," one said, "that it's an all-girl band in Japan!"

"That really surprises me too," the second replied. "And they're *good.*"

"I know, yeah. It's about time!"

Ayako's piano seemed to provide the most dynamic, interesting moments, but Satomi counted off a blues beat, and—good vibes harmony above the piano, sax easing into steady if not stomping blues—the tune turned out to be "Bag's Groove." When the set ended, Tomako introduced each of the group's members, to much final applause. Vivace—I believe—was a success. Certainly in the eyes (ears) of the audience, and Betty's and mine. However, a Japanese man seated in front of us, with whom I had chatted during one of the interminable intros, telling me his sister was *ima* (now) going to school in Pittsburgh, also asked me—when I told him of my reason for being in Japan—what I honestly thought of Japanese musicians. When I mentioned the women's group and praised their skill, he countered, with great authority, "They need more *power,* especially the saxophonist." I didn't agree, but I wasn't there to argue, so I nodded politely, in the local manner, and kept my mouth shut.

The California All-Star Band followed, and on "Love for Sale" you could sense the immediate vigor, the punch, the dynamism and dynamics (buildup and release), the poise of these "kids"! The Japanese audience responded with reverent amazement—"Hontō de!" (Wow!); "Sō desu ne!" (Can that be?)—when pianist Milton Fletcher, all of thirteen, *jū-san sei,* at the time was introduced. Billy Strayhorn's "Daydream" displayed the inspired leap (led by cornetist Bill Berry) this aggregate has made over the years and the beyond-the-charts depth and skill of its soloists. Berry himself kicked "A Night in Tunisia" into high gear, sharing solo chores with the entire trumpet section, which acquitted itself with pride.

The day's heat at peak force now and a smattering of the crowd dozing off, the sudden appearance, prancing out on stage with aplomb, of Arturo Sandoval—his screeching-assault, Cat Anderson high notes on "Caravan"—brought everyone back to alert, full life again. There was only one means, one man left to top Sandoval, and that was Mr. Richie Cole.

"Will Richie play 'Quando, Quando, Quando'?" Ms. Muraguchi asked Tim Jackson again in her introduction.

"You just can't wait to hear that song, can you?"

"Is it true that Richie likes alcohol?"

Jackson, generally Mr. Cool but momentarily nonplussed, replied, "No comment."

The intro was saved by a pitch for Richie's *atarashii* (new or latest) recording, and then the man himself was on stage, wearing the same baseball cap he'd worn to the jam session party. And he did play "Quando, Quando, Quando" (I could imagine Ms. Muraguchi squealing with delight backstage), somehow even managing to fit a quote from "Stranger in Paradise" into it. Richie Cole was joined by two Japanese percussionists, Tatsuzi Yokoyama and Yoichi Okabe. The saxophonist threw his hands up in exultation, his face a grandiose grin, when one switched from conga drums to the Brazilian bead-strung gourd, *shekere*, and then timbales, Cole singing "Let me do the dance of love!"—prancing about the stage, all showman, delighting the crowd.

"You guys are *dangerous!*" Cole shouted to the percussionists. "The dangerous duo!" Then turning back to the crowd, he cried, "We just *met*, you know! Let's hear it for my man on congas! Let's hear it for my man on timbales!" Cole turned in a fine performance on a tune that he introduced as "one of my favorite songs, 'Green Dolphin Street.'" It was a tune the Moonlight Jazz Orchestra had played, and unfortunately it afforded too much room for comparison.

"I'll miss you!" Richie Cole cried when the set ended. "I want to *marry* you!"

He hoisted his arms with pugilistic pride and sang, "It's so wonderful to be in Japan . . . Noto, Noto, Noto, oh; I got those Wakura Hot Springs blues!"

NARA, KYOTO, AND THE RAG CLUB

When our train pulled into the Nara station, an entire family was there to greet us: our daughter-in-law Yoko's sister Kazuko, vivacious and pretty in a pink dress; her husband, Katsuyuki; and all four of their children: Akimi (age ten), Ayako (age eight), Haruna (three and a half), and the baby of the bunch at two, Yohei. Akimi and Ayako (sporting a baseball cap) had black money belts at their waists.

We spent our first night in Nara at Katsuyuki and Kazuko's home. Due to a self-conscious concern over lack of space, the Japanese are shy about such invitations. In a small "living room" in which we would eventually eat, a room that also housed a *butsudan* (a shrine or altar above which photos of Katsuyuki's parents stood), a shiny black Yamaha upright sat proudly against the wall. Ten-year-old Akimi, I found out, had commenced lessons at age six, and she showed me the results, which were fairly impressive. Betty and I slept in a room on the second floor, next to that of Akimi and Ayako. We closed the shōji doors that separated the rooms, but the girls kept reopening them. Lying on their stomachs, propped on their elbows, they stared at us with infinite curiosity until I fell asleep—just before which Ayako flashed me the peace sign.

The next day, we met Yoko's other sister, Minako, and her husband, Noriyoshi, plus their children: "hip" Issei (he would instruct me in essential Japanese etiquette, such as pouring Kirin beer for the person across from you before you pour your own) and ever-zestful, nonstop-talking Mariko. Noriyoshi led us through the temple grounds at Horyuji, which he said contain "some of the oldest wood structures in the world."

Passing beneath one of the tall torii gates, I couldn't help but think of the traditional Japanese children's song "Toryanse, Toryanse" (Please, My Child, Go Through), as interpreted by Elvin Jones on his *Live at the Village Vanguard* CD I'd discussed with Toshiko Akiyoshi. About the song, Jones said, "This is one of the most beautiful tunes I've ever heard!" The hundred-year-old folk song commemorates a rite of passage (literally) for a seven-year-old child admitted to the Ten Jin Shrine to offer prayers ("Ko wai na gara no, toryanse": Go through with no fear now).

That evening, Betty and I were treated to a *kaiseki* dinner, a full seven- to eleven- (I think we got all eleven) course meal that included everything from ginger shrimp on ice to something gelatinoid that might still have been alive. But I ate it, smirked, and said "Oishikatta!" (Delicious!), the faces of our relatives concerned that we approve of all that was offered. And at the meal's close came—and you never get, as I've said, too far away from it in Japan—music! A giant karaoke machine sat in a corner of the room, one that declined to play any of the *many* Ray Charles and Willie Nelson songs offered in English, so I settled for the Japanese pop tunes I'd tried to learn before the trip: a 1980 hit by singer/composer Tsuyoshi Nagabuchi, a sentimental favorite of the Japanese called "Kanpai," ordinarily sung at marriages and other "rites of passage" ceremonies, ending with upbeat hope for the future—"Kimi ni shiawase are" (May happiness be yours). This song turned out to be a collective rouser. Kazuko's husband, Katsuyuki, is shyly affable, but Minako's husband, Noriyoshi, turned out to be a veritable tiger of a performer once he had a mike in hand. We sang "Sayonara," by the rock group Off Course, and Ozaki Yutaka's "I Love You." Yutaka was an angry rebel who became a cult figure for many of Japan's disenchanted youth when he died of a drug overdose in 1992, young girls mourning at a Tokyo plaque that bears his name just as fans wept for Kurt Cobain or flocked to Jim Morrison's grave in Paris. We also sang "Itoshi no Eri" by the Southern All-Stars, one of those rare cases when a Japanese song caught the fancy of an American singer (none other than Ray Charles) and became a hit abroad, a tune whose sprightly chorus, "Utsutte motto, baby" (Convey more of yourself to me), is fun as hell to sing.

Late that night, we all exchanged gifts, and I made what Betty in her diary called "a little speech in Japanese" (which seemed to come across okay). Next morning everyone came to the train station to see us off to Kyoto, waving *baibai* and *dōzo gobuji de* (bye-bye, come back safe and sound).

To get to the Rag Club in Kyoto, you get off at the Seihan-Sanjo subway station and cross a bridge over the Kamo River, one spanning that same dry riverbed where, on open-air platforms, early Kabuki troupes composed of "lewd" women had lured men by singing, dancing, and performing humorous skits. Fortunately (or unfortunately), no one attempted to "lure" me, but I did see, below me, a *matsuri* whose canvas booths stretched far into the distance alongside the river. I even saw a full set of drums, which tempted me to go down and check it all out. But I was headed for Kyoto's major jazz spot, the Rag Club (just past the Grizzly Bar): another of those tucked-away but packed jazz "live houses"—although this one was more spacious than most I'd found in Tokyo.

I was there to hear guitarist Takeshi Yamaguchi, advertised as appearing with pianist Takehiro Honda, an older musician Leonard Feather and Ira Gitler had included in their *Encyclopedia of Jazz* and whose CD *Minton Blues,* with Sadao Watanabe and guitarist Yoshiaki Masuo, I'd listened to at home. I found out that Honda was indisposed and wouldn't show that night. He was replaced by a somewhat grizzly-looking pianist with a goatee and a flamboyant head of hair that seemed to splay in several directions beneath the baseball cap that attempted to contain it. His name was Hatsuho Furukawa, and he would turn out to be good.

I did see evidence that guitarist Masuo had performed at the Rag Club: the words "Yoshiaki Masuo was here! June 18, '90," along with "Stay Peace Full, Stay Music," scrawled on a wall. When I entered I heard Nat "King" Cole singing "Sweet Lorainne," then June Christy doing "It Could Happen to You" and Billie Holiday on "Lover Man." I hadn't suffered a stitch of homesickness so far and wasn't about to (fully enjoying our steady diet of Japanese jazz, shrines, temples, relatives, and *kaiseki* dinners), but I did pause a minute, contemplating this music so far from home—even though it was clear by now that jazz was in Japan to stay, had truly become an international language, one the Japanese had assimilated as their own.

Following a brief final sound check—"Daijōbu?" (Okay?)—Takeshi Yamaguchi's quartet came on with a smash, the tempo and volume belied by the guitarist's laid-back stance—literally, a sort of comfortable tilt he would maintain most of the night, slyly stoic, no grimace of exertion at all. Pianist Furukawa proved solemn yet imaginative in his solos. A baby-faced drummer in a leather hat provided fit, fat accents on a turquoise full kit with two large ride cymbals and a small one for smashes, which he proved to love. Yamaguchi kept the sleeves of his shirt down and buttoned all night (as did the pianist). No speed merchant, he was a tasteful player with a penchant for crisp, clean, single notes. Only an occasional knee pop afforded any indication that he was much absorbed in the rhythm. Next, pianist Furukawa offered a solo piece he'd "just finished a chart for that day," a tune called "Moon on the Lake," *shizuka na* (quiet, calm), *suzushii* (cool), impressionistic, taking me back to the spacious raked temple grounds we'd walked on beside Lake Kashihara the previous day in Nara, complete with lily pads and acquiescent ducks. Yamaguchi's shuffle-rhythm guitar solo was made up largely of arpeggios, quick runs, then thick "choir" chords that provided a close.

I talked with Takeshi Yamaguchi between sets. Quite personable, he told me he'd lived in New York for four years (1975–79), worked with drummer Charles Moffett (and family) there, returned to Japan, gone back to New York in 1988, worked as a street musician, and studied Uesu Montogomeri (Wes Montgomery) "completely." He came back to Japan again in 1993 and made an extensive, and successful, duo tour with Ron Carter in 1995. He's recorded four CDs on Paddle Wheel Records: one with Carter alone; another with Carter, Renee Rosnes, and Al Foster. At the Rag Club, I saw his CDs for sale, and I'm sorry now I didn't buy one, but they were going for 3,000 yen apiece (close to thirty dollars!). Drinks at the Rag Club were 750 yen, the cover charge 3,000. I decided that a jazz night on the town in Kyoto was a bit more expensive than I'd anticipated.

I was also introduced to Hikaru Kawakami, office manager of Rag International Music Co., Ltd., a pretty, gracious woman I would interview later with pianist Yosuke Yamashita, the "Cecil Taylor of Japan," before we left Kyoto. It was Hikaru-san who told me that Furukawa was filling in for Takehiro Honda because the latter was ill. She said that Furukawa, born in Osaka, lives in Tokyo, is forty-one years old ("maybe"), and that "this night's session may be the first time they've all played together."

The second set commenced with a riff tune, the guitarist's eyes closed now, chin jutting, the piece turning into an honest-to-God twelve-bar blues stomp complete with a lusty rock beat and a wild gliss at the end. "Goodbye Pork Pie Hat" started out as a guitar solo executed with fierce concentration, Yamaguchi truly into it now. "Humpty

Dumpty" was taken up-tempo, the group falling firmly into sync as the night ended, although the drummer left me with a thirst for more dynamics on his somewhat unimaginative "fours." I would discover another side of Takeshi Yamaguchi when I returned home and played the King Records *Jazz Restoration* CDs I'd been given in Tokyo, his recording—with Ron Carter—of "Fly Me to the Moon" disclosing an acoustic, somewhat formal, "classical" precision combined with light easy swing, offset by Carter's stately counterpoint. Yamaguchi's solo, once again, was made up of cards held close to the chest, classy baroque lines, discreet but not overly cautious.

I had lots of time, and impetus, daily (discovering the same excellence in craftsmanship throughout our temple tours in Kyoto) to think about Yamaguchi's music, which resembled much of the mainstream music I'd heard in Tokyo. That music was delightful and highly digestible (again, like the small separate "units" of a *kaiseki* dinner), handsomely executed. Its demands might be somewhat slight or slender compared to the fierce, cutting-edge music I'd left behind in the States (David Murray, Tim Berne, Matthew Shipp, or John Zorn) or even heard in the former Soviet Union, but I didn't want to start sounding, or thinking, like those I'd criticized for their ethnocentric condescension before I'd left on the trip, even though I could sense the temptation. Was I falling into the "origami" trap too (how quaint! how *nice!*), finding the music emotionally hamstrung, too discreet or polite for its own good? If so, why was I enjoying—truly digging—it so much?

I recalled something else G. B. Sansom had written in his classic *Japan: A Short Cultural History,* addressing the artistic merits of the Noh theater, which was heavily influenced by Zen, among other schools of Buddhism, and presented in accordance with Zen canons of taste: "Everywhere there was a careful avoidance of the trite, the obvious and the emphatic. The most powerful effects are those which are obtained by allusion, suggestion and restraint. . . . The rigid convention, the hieratic mode, the deliberate avoidance of excess, all these guard against lapses from pure taste; but in another aspect they are the expression of a timid orthodoxy and if they refine they also attenuate." Sansom feels that Western students may find Japanese art "undervitalized" and may prefer "a more impulsive squandering of effort, an heroic if unregulated luxuriance." I thought of the "firefly hunt" scene in Junichiro Tanizaki's *The Makioka Sisters,* in which a woman named Sachiko reflects that the firefly hunt is "dark, dreamy," containing "something of the child's world, the world of the fairy story . . . something not to be painted but to be set to music, the mood of it taken up by a piano or koto"—and I realized that I *liked* what Sansom calls the "kindly Japanese touch" and was growing favorably accustomed to it.

Our daughter-in-law Yoko's uncle, Katsunori Matsumoto, arranged for a young woman, a high school student who lived there, to show us around Kyoto. Over the phone she'd been shy and typically giggly, but the young woman I met in the lobby of our *ryokan* was a beauty: demure, self-effacing, accomplished (we would discover that she'd taken piano lessons since the age of five and performed Brahms, Chopin, and Satie like a pro), highly—in spite of the mandatory schoolgirl giddiness—"refined." Her name was Hisayo Oshima, and she took Betty and me, by bus, to Kiyomizudera, its main hall supported by 139 giant pillars and reached after you climb a steep hillside that affords a fine view of the valley in which Kyoto resides. (*Fodor's* says people came here to escape "open political intrigue" in the city and "to scheme in secret.") Our favorite spot—although I took photos and didn't participate—was a pavilion from which you reach out with long-handled tin cups to three "waterfalls," streams of deliciously cold (I was told, and would return two years later to find out for myself) *mizu*—water—that rewards you, depending on which fountain you drink from—with health, wealth, or *kōfuku* (general well-being or happiness). Hisayo and Betty drank from the latter.

I came to think of Hisayo Oshima as a representative Japanese jazz fan, admirable in her ability to blend knowledgeable appreciation of the music (it was she who had heard Yosuke Yamashita in concert, twice, and had learned of his forthcoming appearance at the Rag Club), respect for cultural tradition (represented by sites such as Kiyomizudera), and her own life as high school student and classical pianist. When it came to jazz, she was *not* a fanatic, a snob, or even an aficionado in the American sense of having found her "thing." She was not a convert, curator, cognoscente: an exclusionist who felt it was "hip" to dig jazz and make a big deal of it. She just happened to like the stuff; she just, in her refined way, *dug* it. She was a sensible young woman who admired jazz as an art form, but also as music very much at home within a more inclusive domain of ceremony or social ritual, music that took its rightful place in a larger cultural context.

Writer Annie Proulx has defined the American character as "aggressive, protean, identity-shifting, mutable, restless and mobile." If there's truth in this definition (and I believe there is), it's hard to imagine anything more diametrically different from—opposed to—"the Japanese." Even the paying of heavy "dues" in Japan seemed laced with beauty, for when Betty and I visited Higashi-Honganji Temple, I learned that its monstrous wooden beams had been hauled by way of thick strands of rope made from the sacrifice of a most prized possession in medieval Japan: a woman's long blue-black hair. Not that I'd lost touch completely with Japan's "hard struggle against the pressure of mechanized civilization," evidence of which was not hard to find at all, within and outside the music. On our way to my very favorite temple, Nanzenji, headquarters of the Nanzenji school of the Rinzai Zen sect, I saw a hotel called the Luminous Nose.

By contrast, Nanzenji is so stark in its purity and simplicity that it seemed to sum up what I had come to feel is the Japanese aesthetic. A sliding shōji door disclosed an opulent green exterior set against the barren geometry of a dark interior: a garden in which bamboo sticks dropped water from level to level, transporting impulses across a synapse in which blossoms were suspended. I became convinced that the jazz I heard, especially in Kyoto (a city that overwhelms you with its ancient architecture), was a product of the total culture from which it emerged, whether such influence was intentional or unconscious.

One of these side trips—to Sanjusangendo Temple—prepared me for a meeting with a musician, pianist Yosuke Yamashita, who would challenge any theories about the complacency or placidity of Japanese jazz. There we saw 1,001 statues of thousand-armed Kannon, metal sun rays emanating from their heads, defended by a host of jazzy "demons": Kin-nara with his flaming head and handheld drum; Karurao, a deity who "eats up every evil and wickedness" but also has time to blow some fine flute; and Magorao, a god with five eyes who wields a large lute he plays with a plectrum.

YOSUKE YAMASHITA

O ur new friend Hisayo Oshima had invited Betty and me to the Rag
Club the previous night to hear pianist Yosuke Yamashita, whom
she'd heard twice before in concert. It seemed we'd no sooner taken our
seats than the band, quickly assembled and with not so much as a hint
of an intro, plunged into a tune. Yamashita was joined by drummer
Akira Horikoshi and tenor saxophonist Nariu Shichijiki. A hyperactive
child set free to romp to his heart's content on its long narrow room,
Yamashita was all over the keyboard, exploring every inch of its terrain.
The tenor sax sliced into this wild edifice of broken angles as if deflect-
ing Yamashita's "attack" with a knife. The performance was physical,
percussive, very dynamic or "exciting"—as Hisayo had said of her first
exposure to Yamashita's music.

Propulsive with no letup, Yamashita even massaged the keyboard
with his wrists, provoking vivid clusters. Drummer Horikoshi provided
set rhythm for a time, but not for long. Yamashita's bacchius meter
(short-long-long accents) was offset by unpredictable but agile gymnastics. A tune called "Echo of Greatness" found Yamashita exploring
polyphony with himself (he is decidedly a two-handed pianist), the
tenor sax joining in on what turned out to be a Bach-based baroque
romp, playful, fun for the sake of fun, parody for the sake of parody.
"Forces Straight Up" started out wild and free, Yamashita indulging his
backhanded crunch of keys, then providing impressive single-finger
runs that exploited the entire keyboard. A melodic a capella sax interlude followed, plaintive, full of high drama, a sort of cruel parody of "As

Time Goes By." When Yamashita took over again, he introduced wild two-handed silent-movie tremolos converted to anger. A solid drum solo made *omoshiroi* (interesting) use of Chinese "splash" cymbal effects; the full group was back in for the ride out.

"Chigaimasuka?" (Different?) I asked Yamashita in the restaurant at the Royal Hotel, where we met the next day for brunch.

"Hai, chigaimasu," he replied, smiling.

We'd been discussing the Japanese educational system and Masahiko Satoh's view that Japan produced fine, disciplined jazz performers but did not encourage them to become *exceptional*. Yosuke Yamashita agreed.

"The Japanese way," he said now, "is to produce a very *normal* person. Not just in the music system, but education as a whole. If some guy says things that are very different, they do not applaud or reward him. Instead, they want to pull him back in or down."

"Deru kugi wa utareru" (The nail—or stake—that sticks out gets hammered down), I said, remembering an old precept I'd learned at home.

"But if a person is stubborn enough," Yamashita said, laughing, "he can break free."

"Gaman?" (Patience?) I said.

"Gaman. Holding on to some strength, some power, telling yourself, 'Keep playing, keep playing.' You just have to be yourself. Then finally people say, 'Well, okay.'"

"Are there recording opportunities for your kind of music in Japan? Or do you have to go to Europe to find them?"

"I record here. That has been a very fortunate, lucky, situation for me. I think, from the start, I was somewhat accepted as *one* kind of possible exception. I don't know."

"Well you were certainly doing some amazing things last night at the Rag Club. I've seen back of the hand and knuckles before, but that was my first *elbow* glissando! And you were playing flat-handed at times."

I asked Yosuke Yamashita about the free-jazz scene in Japan. Having been to King Records and the *Swing Journal* office in Tokyo, having visited four clubs there, and having attended the Monterey Jazz Festival in Noto, I had—outside of Masahiko Satoh's contributions—been listening mostly to mainstream jazz, swing, and bop, in either a big band or small-combo context, albeit music of a high order. I had, however, heard lots of "free jazz"—a spacious, liberal mix—in Yamashita's performance the previous night. But he surprised me when I asked him to tell me about the free jazz scene in general in Japan.

"Can I tell you about *myself?*" he asked. "In the middle of the 1960s—well, in 1965 exactly—Sadao Watanabe, the great alto sax player, returned to Japan from the States, from Berklee College, and formed his first session band here. I was one of its members. At that time I was playing like a 'straight' musician. But even before that, when I was twenty or twenty-one years old, I had—together with trumpeter Terumasa Hino—joined a very experimental group that was led by bassist Mr. Hideto Kanai and a very avant-garde guitarist, Mr. Masayuki Takayanagi. They brought many theories and musical elements from modern classical music—such as those of John Cage—into jazz. I was told that you could do *anything*. That was when I was twenty or twenty-one years old. But I was still a straight jazz student. After I played in Sadao Watanabe's group, I formed my own trio, together with bass and drums. We played like late John Coltrane. However, I had to stop playing because I became sick. My lungs. I returned to the scene after one and a half years. That was in 1969, when a new *movement,* now 'old,' seemed to be happening everywhere."

We discussed the Pit Inn scene Masahiko Satoh had described and his participation in it.

"Nineteen sixty-nine was my 'turning point' year. I was twenty-seven and I started rehearsals with my own musicians. We had piano, bass, drums, and tenor saxophone. The saxophonist was Seiichi Nakamura, who plays with drummer George Kawaguchi now. Our drummer was Takeo Moriyama, who is a very very great—a 'monster'—drummer. He's not so active now, but he was a genius. One day we just started playing very *free*. I said, 'Let's try it, everything free,' so we did. At the time I was listening to late Coltrane, and Ornette Coleman of course. And finally Cecil Taylor. I believed we could make some music in that direction. And we discovered, when we finished rehearsing and listened to the music we had recorded played back, that it was very *interesting!*" He laughed openly. "We felt, 'Hey, that's *right!*' In the beginning, not many people came to listen to us, just a few, but they were *great* people! A famous novelist came to listen to our music, and then brought other writers with him. Some of them were very young at the time, and very sharp jazz critics, like Satoh Ikara or Masahaki Iroka. They were very different from the established writers at *Swing Journal*. And they liked our music! At that time, many students from the university also wanted to hear us, because what we played was expressionistic, very aggressive, and that caught their interest in some way. Then, in 1974, someone from Germany named Horst Weber, who ran Enja Records in Munich, liked our music very much and made an effort to get us invited to Europe. Horst Weber booked us at many jazz festivals and club gigs in Europe in '74. That was our *debut* there. There was a Merce New Jazz Festival. Merce is a small city just a little bit north of Dusseldorf. We played there and got such a great response. And that encouraged us very much."

I mentioned that my wife and I had come to the Rag Club the previous night with a young woman named Hisayo Oshima; that she'd played classical piano since the age of five, had heard him in concert twice, and that he was her *idol*. I said it was obvious he had *lots* of fans, among them a Buddhist priest sitting behind us who was richly appreciative. I said it had been interesting for me to see how responsive the Japanese audience was, relishing the music.

"I've continued to play *my* way for more than twenty-five years," Yamashita said. "People finally came to think, 'Let him go. It's okay.'" He laughed. "But when we came back from Europe in 1974, the situation had not changed that much in Japan, even though more and more people started to understand us."

I told Yamashita about a CD that got excellent reviews in the States, Sachi Hayasaka's 2.26, with the group Stir Up. I read a portion of one: "[Hayasaka's] alto solos are a highlight of the stimulating set, but pianist Yosuke Yamashita, whose percussive style recalls Don Pullen, and the rhythm section are also quite inspired." I said this critic, Scott Yanow, considered the CD "one of the more significant jazz releases of recent times."

"Hmmmm," Yamashita replied, granting a sort of moan-groan approval, the nonverbal equivalent of "Sō desu ne?" (Is that so?) "That session came about in a very funny way. It has something to do with our birthdays. Together with musicians who shared her birth date, Sachi started a birthday concert. Sachi was born on the twenty-sixth of February, drummer Ken Tsunoda was born on the same day, so these two musicians started the '2.26' concert, which is held each year. *I* was born on the same day, so Sachi called me and said, 'Why don't you join us?' This was before I knew how well she could play. I said okay, this will be a once a year session. This is the only concert where I play as a sideman, but I'm very happy to do it."

168

All but one of the pieces performed on *2.26* (bassist Toshiki Nagata's "Heso") are compositions by Sachi Hayasaka. "Bubble Net Feeding" is a "shocker" somewhat reminiscent of John Zorn's "unremittingly violent" (in one critic's words) CD *Spy vs. Spy: The Music of Ornette Coleman*. Hayasaka's piece is a sort of feeding frenzy throughout, the percussion marked by stark cymbal splashes and march-time *taiko* drumming gone berserk. Hayasaka herself seems a possessed shaman whose tonal effects range from grinding banshee screeches to deep bass growls, stuttered seven-note configurations mixed with nimble triplets. Her "Children Children" starts with a tocking percussive ambience, birdlike chirping, and small sounds moving to a bass-led "Bolero" buildup, then Gaelic quickstep sax work, an alto sax howl, and the screech reach is on. The piece subsides to distant, ruminating Yamashita piano, until he too unleashes his own huge sweeps and clusters. Other Hayasaka tunes are "Yellow Monk" (with unison sax work that suggests the World Saxophone Quartet) and the title tune, "2.26," which pulls out all the stops and includes R&B and Latin/rock cacophony—the participants delightfully unruly on the occasion of their joint birthdays.

Sachi Hayasaka is a formidable talent in her own right, an artist who took classical piano lessons in elementary school, joined a brass band (hoping to play flute but assigned alto sax), and spent her "entire childhood savings" on a soprano sax ("not a popular instrument" at the time, but she wanted something "that no one else had"). She confesses that, like Yamashita, she felt a fascination for "doing what no one else was doing." Hayasaka made her musical debut at the Pit Inn in Shinjuku and claims to have learned lots listening to Wayne Shorter, Ornette Coleman, and Monk. She says she has never been conscious of herself as a "woman" performer, that jazz is "definitely a mode of individual expression, exclusive of male or female. There is either a good or bad performance. What I play is an extension of myself and if the listener senses something 'feminine,' no problem."

Yosuke Yamashita has also recorded with tenor saxophonist Joe Lovano, in the excellent company of bassist Cecil McBee and drummer Pheeroan akLaff.

"I met Cecil and Pheeroan in New York in 1988," he told me. "I was a newcomer in the city, and it seemed very very *far* away to me at the time. I wanted to start over again; I wanted to go back to a very ordinary piano feeling, with just bass and drums. I wanted to express myself within that trio formation, to see if I could pull all the music I had made in twenty-five years together in that format. It was a challenge to me, and from the very first rehearsal we did very well together. We played at Sweet Basil's, and the response was good. We were genuinely happy with the result—not like going backstage after and breaking out in a fight." He laughed. "Nothing like that ever happened, as it sometimes does! Then, four or five years later, I felt as if the trio was ready to add a horn player. I went to a very good friend of mine who was then floor manager at Blue Note and is now floor manager at Iridium in uptown Manhattan. He recommended Joe Lovano, who was really coming up then, working with Paul Motian and John Schofield, before his name grew and he went *past me*, you know? At that time I could still catch him!"

Yamashita's New York trio recorded *Kurdish Dance* with Lovano in 1992 and returned with *Dazzling Days* in 1993. All of the tunes—aside from "My Grandfather's Clock" on the latter—are Yamashita compositions. The title piece on the first CD features the pianist's sprightly, staggered, stop-time rhythms; an agile boxer's bob-and-weave patterns; and Joe Lovano's subtle statement of theme. Yamashita shows that he can play with considerable tenderness on "Back Yard." "Act 3–8" is fugue-like, contrapuntal, filled with nearly "drunken" dialogue, the tension enticing. Lovano comes up with whirlpool interactive fury with the pianist on "4th Street Up."

Dazzling Days, with the same personnel, is somewhat more relaxed but no less impressive. "Parallel Run" contains subtle bop-oriented lines that converge and scatter with almost mathematical precision. "Promenade" is just that: a leisurely Sunday stroll (somewhat reminiscent of "Waltz for Debby," and Bill Evans is not a reference point that readily comes to mind with regard to Yamashita). Both Yamashita and Lovano unleash their full bag of tricks on "Dazzling Circle" (flippant triplets, quick cocky accents, and sudden declines). "Lullaby of Color" is a sweet, simple, songlike waltz, a child discovering his fingers one by one. The only tune not written by Yamashita, "My Grandfather's Clock," offers wide-open keyboard "grandfatherly" grandiloquence.

Joe Lovano enjoyed the sessions, saying that Yamashita's melodies were much like those of folksongs, "and that was very new to me." He also found a lot of "vacant space" within the pieces, and he was allowed to do "what I wanted to do with it."

We talked about the use of traditional Japanese instruments in jazz, and I mentioned Yamashita's CD *Sakura* (Cherry Blossoms; "Yayoi no sora wa / Miwatasu kagiri / Kasumi ka kumo ka": Cherry blossoms in the March sky / As far as the eye can see; / They're like mist or floating clouds), which makes use of several Japanese folk songs.

"Yes, that was my response to traditional Japanese music. You could say the 'old music' that every Japanese child knows. I tried out many pieces, and I chose what appealed to my ear and my feelings. I looked for elements I could improvise on easily, or not at all. After I chose, I discovered that many of these tunes were written by Mr. Shinpei Nakayama, a very old composer. I didn't realize that at the time. Anyway, that CD was one result of my interest in Japanese music. One more thing is: I have, many times, had an opportunity to perform with traditional Japanese instrumentalists. There is an excellent *taiko* group called Kodo, from Sado Island. They go on a world tour every year, with large drums, small drums, about fifteen to twenty people."

We discussed Sumi Tonooka's *taiko* drum project, the one featuring Kenny Endo and Akira Tana. I said that elements I'd heard the previous night reminded me of *taiko* at times.

"Akira Tana, ah, yes! As far as influences go, I've surely studied and learned from *taiko*. It was many years ago that I became specifically interested in traditional Japanese music. I wanted to know exactly what our sense of the music had come from. And that finally got me interested in ethnomusicology, into theory, so I studied that. I connected what I learned to the 'blue note' phenomenon, the blue notes in jazz: what is not ordinarily expected in a specific key, something unexpected. The behavior of those notes is very unique, very particular. I could catch on to it in jazz because it was similar to what I'd found while studying traditional Japanese music. Some Japanese traditional melodies do behave in the same way as the blue notes in jazz. When we first started to play freely, I believed that if you played that way, you could express *everything*, including the entire history of your own nation, of your own land. *All* history in fact!"

Yosuke Yamashita's *Sakura* CD offers an inventive, seamless, rewarding marriage of traditional Japanese elements and jazz. The title tune gets off to a prankish, craggy, Monkish start, not at all in keeping with the song's customary soft, fluttering notes, although the melody does get inserted within this context. The tune's three prominent notes (*sa-ku-ra*) become as pronounced as those four in Beethoven's Fifth Symphony, and Yamashita mixes them with slices of Monk's "Well, You Needn't," the entire construction clever, good fun. In the recording's liner notes, Yamashita says, "It may be because of my cultural background, but some European critics say that I play in a Zen manner, although I don't really know that much about the spirit of Zen. People imagine a lot into my music, which is great, but I'm not concerned how they listen as long as they accept it."

Another Yamashita original, "Haiku," adopts—appropriately enough—a five/seven/five-beat (or syllable) format, then turns free as akLaff dismantles the too-tight pattern, as if to say, "What's with all this dainty frog/jump/splash shit, man? We're out to getcha!" By way of contrast, "Amefuri" is just what the title suggests: a slow drizzly day stroll spent beneath a parasol. Again in the liner notes, Yamashita says, "The reason I play these Japanese traditional and folk songs is that I have wanted to emphasize my Japanese character as a musician. Jazz is an American culture, but I have my own way to express myself to the American audience. I like these old Japanese songs, and by combining the two different cultures I can create *my own* jazz expression."

Another fortunate collaboration occurred *within* the Japanese context: the previously mentioned work with the Kodo *taiko* drummers from Sado Island. Their CD collection is called *Kodo vs. Yosuke Yamashita: Live,* but there's nothing combative in the juxtaposition. The cover shows the pianist in an immaculate white suit, looking a bit like Jay Gatsby, while a naked (aside from headband and loincloth) percussionist strikes the large *ō-taiko* drum. "Monochrome." begins with *kakko* (small-drum) tap-a-tap-a-tap-a-tap-a-tapping, increasing in volume until it resembles August screeching—the *semi no koe* (voices or song of cicadas). By way of contrast, Yamashita offers some frisky boogie-woogie, the small drum in a holding pattern now. Yamashita's piano work then explodes as all the drums join in for an avalanche of steady thumping, the *kakko*'s persistent irritation still there, its small power and pride—all of this a powerful corrective to any stereotypes of Japanese lack of passion or "inscrutability."

Yosuke Yamashita had come to the Royal Hotel accompanied by Hikaru Kawakami, manager of the Rag Club in Kyoto. During our conversation, she had sat very still, listening intently to the pianist, never saying a word herself. Finally, I asked her about the club scene, what it took to run a club successfully in Kyoto, to make it work. With bookings each night, there seemed to be a very active jazz scene in the city. *Sonna koto ga hontō ni aru daro ka?* (Is such a thing actually possible?)

Yamashita translated for me: "Well, about half of the month it's like it was last night. Full of people. But other days, not always so great!

Her place does not just offer jazz, but rock and fusion. By comparison, a fusion band can attract a large audience. But it depends on the musicians. Their names, if they are well known or not."

Thinking of all the jazz clubs I'd seen converted to *sports bars* in the States, I asked just how one kept a jazz club alive in Japan.

"Muzukashii desu!" (It is very difficult!) Kawakami said, laughing. "Maybe five clubs in Kyoto offer jazz. Sometimes jazz, sometimes not. There is a club called Blue Note, but it has nothing to do with the other Blue Notes in Japan, in Osaka and Tokyo. It's not part of that franchise. It's a small club. Just jazz. Solo piano. Every once in a while they have midnight jam sessions there, but it is not like the Rag Club. There, people just show up and play."

"And the Rag Club is best?"

"Yeah!" Yamashita said. "She wants to say that, but she is a Kyoto *lady,* so it would be impolite to say, 'Yes.'"

"I think I might say that not only in Kyoto but in the whole Kansai area, I might be able to say with confidence that the Rag Club is best because we invite the best performers to play here, and they like to come. There is no other place like our place."

"Omedetō gozaimasu" (Congratulations), I said. "Yosuke-san is obviously a strong draw, but you must have to retune the piano each time he plays!"

"Ah, *hai*! It is necessary to do that!"

"She has a very good tuner," Yamashita added, laughing.

I thanked Yosuke Yamashita and Hikaru Kawakami for their generous gift of time; then I took a photo of them standing by an elaborate vase of flowers in the lobby of the Royal Hotel and went back to our *ryokan.* If you stick with it, if you persevere, as Yosuke Yamashita has, there are tangible rewards for being *chigau* (different) in Japan, the consensus society. There's a recompense for *not* letting your nail get slammed down, or back into the board, with all the rest. At the *ryokan,* I went through some information I had assembled on Yamashita back in the States. Not only has he performed at the foreign festival he mentioned to me (the 1974 Berlin Jazz Festival), but he was "an overwhelming success" at his 1979 U.S. debut at the Newport Jazz Festival, played solo at the Chicago Jazz Festival in 1991, was part of a Japan Foundation mission tour throughout Latin America (Brazil, Paraguay, Argentina), toured Europe in 1993 with his New York trio (Montreux Jazz Festival, North Sea Jazz Festival), and performed at Verve's fiftieth-anniversary concert at Carnegie Hall (offering a tribute tune to Bud Powell). In 1990, he joined the Toronto Symphony (conducted by Michiyoshi Inoue), and he has performed George Gershwin's "Rhapsody in Blue," as well as Bach, Ravel, and Dvořák, in concert settings. In 1993, he received a three-year grant from the Marantz Music Foundation for his "international activities."

His new trio completed an "eighty-eight places survival tour" of Japan, and he has been awarded the Celebrated Japan Jazzist Award by *Swing Journal* magazine. As if all this wasn't enough to take up his time, Yosuke Yamashita is also a popular essayist with over ten books to his name. And a role model and spiritual support for many ambitious young Japanese jazz and rock musicians who seek to play internationally. The article I consulted said Yamashita is a household celebrity in Japan who is constantly "trying to enlarge and enrich his domain of jazz music."

18

ZAKONE

The Japanese word *zakone* means "sleeping together" but has no sensual or sexual connotation. In our case, it meant sleeping with relatives. We spent a delightful evening at the seaside resort town of Shirahama, where—lying side-by-side like sardines in a tin—Betty and I shared two very small rooms with our daughter-in-law's parents, Shigehumi and Sumako Takitani; her sister Minako; Minako's husband, Noriyoshi; and their two children, talkative Mariko and "way cool" Issei. This warm autumn night in Shirahama, awoken at three in the morning not by some dark night of the soul but by a common call from nature, I tiptoed my way to the john in the dark (no moonlight spread out) and, with *miyabi* (courtly poise) and a strong sense of *koishisa* (romantic yearning or lovingness) and mostly *nagame* (sleepy, distant reverie), I attempted *not* to step on any of the recumbent bodies that lay about.

On the long road from Shingu to Shirahama (which *Fodor's* hails as "one of the three best hot-spring resorts in the country"), the hot, grueling drive had forced Shigehumi-sama to smack the side of his head with the palm of his hand, frequently, in order to stay awake. Commiserating (I don't drive, I'm ashamed to say in this one case, but even if I did he would, out of courtesy, have insisted on assuming the chore himself), I had ample time, taking in the sights (churning surf and immaculate bays), to think about and summarize whatever I'd discovered about jazz in Japan at this point in our trip.

Most of the music I'd heard so far—aside from that of Masahiko Satoh and Randooga, Sachi Hayasaka and Stir Up, and Yosuke

Yamashita—*was,* admittedly, largely mainstream. But knowing what I'd known about jazz from Japan before I left the States, this was no surprise. Besides, I'd been "raised" on swing and bebop myself, first introduced to the music by way of Chicago-style trad jazz, a first love and music I still enjoy, and then big band swing and small-combo bebop, so what I'd heard so far was music I could respond to in terms of familiarity. I'm not one of those jazz aficionados convinced that all mainstream music suffers from overuse, outright abuse, fatigue, or senility—its capacity for honest artistic invention depleted. I can still appreciate fresh, unique voices at work within the genre, such as those of Eiji Kitamura and Kotaro Tsukahara. On the other hand, I had little patience with purists: people with a fixed notion that there was one story and one story only, One True Church of jazz, be it right or left, in or out. Such proclamations—factions with agendas galore, Neo-this and Neo-that, the politics of art that I feel contaminate the American jazz scene—leave me cold, and I was grateful that I was not finding much of *that* sort of thing going on in Japan.

Japanese jazz artists have worked long and hard at absorbing and assimilating the music they heard after the war. They have "grown up" with and into jazz in a manner quite different from Americans, who—surrounded by it—can, if they've been lucky, nearly take the art for granted. This being the case, I could understand why the Japanese were less anxious to grow up from or *out of* a mainstream context, less in a hurry than some Americans, less compelled to wean themselves from a genre they had so recently discovered and embraced.

If I could feel comfortable, *at home,* with the music I had encountered in Japan so far, I also understood, and loved, the work of innovators in America the Japanese might be less eager to "imitate" (or follow) because they are largely inimitable: artists such as Muhal Richard Abrams, Horace Tapscott, Henry Threadgill, or Anthony Davis, all of whom have expanded the imaginative possibilities beyond or *outside* conventional forms. These performers/composers were fed from a wide diversity of sources that include, in the case of Threadgill (who experienced it all firsthand), gospel, blues, ragtime, academic study (in musical theory), classical music (Prokofiev, Poulenc, Beethoven, Hindemith), VFW post marching bands, circus gigs, and collective improvisation. As Abrams, who defines himself as a "musical historian as well as a practicing musician," has said, "I feel it's an all-in-one thing. When you grew up in the Black Belt, especially during the time when I

176

grew up, you hear it all. . . . Reaching back did actually propel [my] move to more original approaches. . . . The past gets further in front and further behind at the same time. So I'm looking in all directions."

The Japanese jazz musicians I had encountered so far had not avoided or evaded the rigors that reside outside the sphere of "mainstream" jazz; in fact, the ambiguity of exposure (their position as a midpoint between East and West, a sort of cultural conduit) places them smack in the center of the wealth of resources available to someone like Henry Threadgill. But they have dealt with this ambiguity, this very availability, through assimilation and refinement. Modesty and humility are not highly prized attributes in America; self-assertion is. Yet even given the grand ambitions of American composers such as Duke Ellington and Charles Mingus, or the work of an extremely gifted composer such as Anthony Davis, jazz—from whatever nation—seems to remain a limited, modest art compared to the complex musical order of, say, an opera such as Alban Berg's *Wozzeck*. In an article called "Earthly Laughter," John Ardoin lists the extraordinary range of forms that Berg employed: dance music (garotte, gigue and pavane); passacaglia; bitonality; nontonality; diatonic tonality; compound chords (ninths, thirteenths, even fifteenths); chromatic harmony; triple fugue; canonic variation; stretto, augmentation; diminutia; and a host of rhythmic patterns (two/four imposed over three/four, followed by four/four over six/eight); plus the voice effects of *sprechstimme* (a form of speaking on pitch pioneered by Berg's mentor, Arnold Schoenberg). And throughout it all, Berg somehow managed to keep the musical drama *organic* and alive! By comparison, even the most complex jazz—the most ambitious "suites"—remains relatively simple, or "mainstream."

If the majority of Japanese performer/composers I'd heard so far had shied away from the more adventurous, ambitious undertakings of an Abrams, Threadgill, or Davis (or Berg!), they *did* have unique resources to draw on that are not available "by birth" to American artists—such as the unique form of breathing pointed out by Masahiko Satoh and Toru Takemitsu. One could also add a sort of Zen-based sensibility that—mistrusting the obvious gap between ambition and actual accomplishment or "practice" (as it's called in Soto Zen), between "talk" and "walk"—has developed unique methods for training both body and mind *together*, regarding the two as one (*kokoro*, or "heartmind" in this case). I thought of Yoshiaki "Miya" Miyanoue practicing Wes Montgomery's warm thumb sound, "up and down, up and down," for ten years and then telling me, quite modestly, that "not many people are willing to do just one thing for ten years."

Although it was still too early for me to take on some of the questions Akira Tana's thesis had raised before I left the States, I was in a position already—I felt—to answer a few. Were employment opportunities still "abundant"? Yes. Had the level of engagement, of sophistication, on the part of audiences risen? I'd say yes. Had the search for "authenticity" reached a stage where music with "unique Japanese character" had come to pass? To a certain degree, yes—and in the case of someone like Masahiko Satoh (performing with his 998 Shōmyō-chanting monks), definitely. Had *shimpō* (progress) within the Japanese jazz scene taken place? Based on what I'd seen and heard so far—and especially at the hands of exciting new groups like the jazz restoration "young lions," Sachi Hayasaka's Stir Up, and Vivace—I'd say yes.

On the trip from Shingu, where the Takitanis live, to Shirahama, we had stopped at the Nachisan Seigantoji Temple, which resides on the famous site of Japan's tallest waterfall, the Great Falls of Nachi, with its drop of 430 feet. There, the Takitanis purchased a blessing for both our families, or "houses," for eight thousand yen. We all sat in a row on a narrow bench before an altar. A tall lean priest appeared, wearing the traditional Shintō *eboshi* (tall rounded hat). With a fine flourish, he waved a *harai-gushi* (purification wand to which many long paper streamers and a few strands of flax are attached), after which we were presented with wooden tablets that read *fu-sho-den* (may the gods give you grace), our names inscribed in katakana upon them.

The entire family came to see us off at the train station near Shirahama. Minako purchased mineral water for our journey, and examining the brand, I made an unfortunate *jōdan* (joke) about it not being sake— which prompted Sumako to buy us two bottles of *that* beverage, one for the train ride ("To make you dizzy and let you sleep," she said, laughing), the other a large bottle in a handsomely designed carton (of course) to be saved for the road beyond. We said *shitsurei itashimasu* (good-bye) to these fine people in a land where jazz is just a part—but a very important part—of the larger ceremony of life itself.

19

Osaka: The Blue Note, Satoru "Salt" Shionoya, the Over Seas Club, and Meeting Hisayuki Terai

"OH NO, NOT THE BLUE NOTE!" Betty said after Mr. Matsumoto (our daughter-in-law Yoko's uncle) had parked the car and marched us past a horde of young women I thought must be lined up for a rock concert. Mr. Matsumoto was proud. He'd discovered an honest-to-God jazz event for us in Osaka and was leading us there, like the Pied Piper. But . . .

"Oh no, not the Blue Note!" I concurred.

Katsunori Matsumoto, since we'd first met him, had been outrageously generous, and we'd decided that this night would be on *us*. However, arriving at the Blue Note, we could see, or *smell*, just how much such an expensive venue would cost us. The popular artist we would hear was Satoru "Salt" Shionoya: a young pianist with a Latin-inclined fusion group, along with the pop singer Chikuzen Satoh.

Despite the price, the place was mobbed. Even though we had Emi, a high school student, in tow, our party averaged out to being about thirty-five years older than anyone else in the house. The only available table was perched behind a drum set so overburdened with tom-toms and cymbals that it looked like a double (maybe even a triple) kit. The cymbals alone resembled a full-wall Zildjian display in a music store. The kit was miked to the hilt, and I knew we were in for a long, noisy night, an electronic massage I wasn't sure my eardrums—or those of my companions—could survive. But the crowd assembled was obviously up for the ride, open to max-volume kicks—and they got them.

The leader, when he came on stage, turned out to be a poised, handsome, and somewhat shy young man (age thirty) who played acoustic concert grand, backed up by the sizeable drum kit plus electric bass, electric guitar, an additional keyboard player, and, later in the set, the guest vocalist. On the CD he would give me later (the ever alacritous Mr. Matsumoto had arranged an interview), Salt Shionoya stands, hands on hips, chin thrust forward in disdain or outright challenge beneath a sign that reads "Checked by Radar" overlooking what appears to be the most barren stretch of highway in the United States, a Nevada setting that resembles an abandoned atomic test site. His appearance on the night we saw him live was less dramatic (less a publicist's dream), far more modest. He announced each tune in a quiet, self-effacing manner—perhaps a polite gesture or a modest way of easing us all into the ensuing din. The band was *loud,* and I didn't hear much of what it was up to that night—that is, particulars. I did hear much undifferentiated mass or volume, much of it percussive. Fortunately, later, the CD would clarify matters. The group is quite good; the performance was exciting, the music well constructed, enjoyable.

Shionoya's group played many of the songs contained on the CD, all originals by the pianist—tunes such as "Shufflin' City," which truly shuffles. Rippling electric bass riffs set the midtempo pace, the piano supplying a catchy, danceable theme. Synthesized cosmic wisps struck me as a bit overbaked or melodramatic, even corny, but Salt Shionoya's piano work is solid, his themes or melodic lines fetching. "She Knocks Me Out" is charged with both bounce and affectionate shuffle. The other pieces are predictable by title: "For My Lady" a synth-supported slow dance, "Reflections" accompanied by an electric bass vamp and soft ornamental piano. The tunes do bear an unfortunate resemblance to one another. You feel as if you've already heard them as elevator Muzak throughout Japan and probably have. A string section attended "Na-Gi," very pentatonic, and this was one of my favorite pieces. "Earth Beat" is a tune Shionoya wrote as a theme song for a 1994 Earth Day concert held at the Nippon Budōkan, where he performed with Carlos Santana. The song carries the required anthem quality, a New Age piano interlude set against a lush full orchestra, and *lots* of repetition to get the point across. I kept imagining a couple doing a majestic sort of ice-dance routine to this music.

Another attraction throughout our night at the Blue Note in Osaka, aside from Satoru "Salt" Shionoya himself, was guitarist Yoshiuki Asano, whose lavish licks prompted the heads of the young women in the front rows to bob like corks in rough water, their hairdos tapping in time.

Asano also got them clapping—fortunately on two and four. Much of the music had a Latin beat, the group as a whole very physical and very percussive, as I've said—or complained, situated as we were just behind the drums. At the close of each song, Salt would stand up and, receiving raucous applause, bow like an obedient schoolboy and smile in a mode I'm sure the women found charming.

A third attraction was vocalist Chikuzen Satoh. He strolled out with his arms hoisted in a victory salute before he'd even sung a note, and his many fans cried out clamorously. His first tune spoke of going for the "magic" in love but reminded the girls that magic, unfortunately, cannot "last forever." This was not the first song, obviously, to ever expound on *that* theme, but the young audience responded as if it were. Satoh had a nice voice, favorable guitar and piano backing, and–obviously again—a substantial following. For his second song, the house lights dimmed to fragile blue (temporarily extinguishing my dinner from view, the meal itself quite good, although I can't recall what it was other than expensive). Satoh sang "Let Love Lead" with breathless occasionally falsetto sincerity (in English: "If you know what is real from the start / you can feel it in your heart"), and the girls ate it up.

Katsunori Matsumoto was a man on a mission. He was determined that I would not leave Osaka without maximum musical exposure or material for my book. And I had to admit that I could no longer complain about a lack of musical variety, for I'd heard just about everything now, from mainstream jazz and avant-garde or "free" music to Latin-fusion. After the close of the set, I took advantage of the interview opportunity Katsunori-san had orchestrated for me. Shionoya's wife, who'd lived in New York, served as translator. I learned that Satoru "Salt" Shionoya's father had been a jazz fan, fond of Oscar Peterson and Bill Evans, yet the family was strongly opposed to their son's desire to pursue a career as a composer. That didn't stop him though, his musical interest kindled at age five (electric organ was his first instrument), composing his first piece at nine. Later he attended the prestigious Tokyo National University of Fine Arts and Music, where he studied composition.

Salt Shionoya introduced the members of his group to me: keyboardist Akira Onozuka, bassist Hideki Matabara, guitarist Yoshiuki Asano, drummer Takeshi Numazawa, and percussionist Gen Ogimi. Shionoya joined the latter's salsa band, Orchesta de la Luz, in 1986 and also played keyboards with a pop group, Adi. Orchesta de la Luz went to New York in 1989; released an album, *Salsa Caliente del Japan* (BMG Victor); and toured a host of cities in North America, Central and South America, and Europe. In April of 1994, the group appeared at the previously mentioned Earth Day concert in Japan with Santana. Carlos Santana's admiration for Shionoya and Orchesta de la Luz led him to invite them to perform with him in Santa Barbara and San Francisco. Salt's last performance with Orchesta de la Luz was in Hawaii, at the Honolulu Musical Festival. By that time the group had garnered a number of awards: number one on *Billboard*'s Latin chart for *Salsa Caliente del Japan*; New York's ACE Award; Best Band of the Year in Japan in 1992; Best Album of the Year at ACE; and the United Nations Peace Medal.

Not bad credentials for a young man who, at age twenty-nine, had also established a sizeable reputation as solo artist, composer, and arranger. In October of 1995, he released his own second album, *Salt II*.

I rejoined Mr. Matsumoto and Emi. I saw, standing beneath the stage lights in a now nearly empty nightclub, my wife, her face turned ashen white. She handed me the Blue Note bill she'd just paid. The 8,000-yen cover charge was listed at the top, the entire bill having come to 36,500 yen (roughly, $365). Not bad for a single night's "work." I mustered up my best samurai-stoic grimace, nodded *hai,* and restrained the impulse to add, "Shiyo ga nai" (So what; it can't be helped).

I still have, to this day, an *omiyage* I carried away from the Blue Note in Osaka: a handsome envelope with "Thanks for Everything!" inscribed upon it (you bet!) that contained Blue Note's sixth-anniversary original calendar, with the photos and signatures of Natalie Cole, Fourplay, Roberta Flack, Kool and the Gang, and Al Jarreau—plus a cute little punch-out stand that allows the calendar to stand up.

In Osaka, we stayed at the Matsumotos' home, and Kyoko Matsumoto proved to be not only a fine cook but an exceptional kimono maker. She had studied with Hisayo Oshima's mother (Hisayo's father owns a kimono-making business). Kyoko brought out a beautiful (and costly!) example of her handiwork: a salmon-colored kimono she let Betty try on, even though the latter would probably have been content just stroking the highly refined material. Other evidence of artistic skill was provided throughout the house: ikebana, or flower arrangements; a handsome sample of Emi's calligraphy mounted on a scroll; and, to my surprise, Fraktur-Schriften (Pennsylvania Dutch illuminated pieces)

Toshiko Akiyoshi conducting, or "sculpting," her orchestra.
(Courtesy of Stuart Brinin.)

Masahiko Satoh.
(Courtesy of Masahiko
Satoh.)

Pianist Junko Onishi and tenor saxophonist Satolu Oda.
(Courtesy of Yozo Iwanami.)

Alto saxophonist Sadao
Watanabe and pianist
Masabumi "Poo"
Kikuchi.
(Courtesy of Yozo
Iwanami.)

Masahisa Segawa.
(Courtesy of the author.)

Kiyoko Ami and Mr. Satoh, amateur vibraphonist. (Courtesy of the author.)

Hisayuki Terai, piano, and bassist Masahiro Munetake. (Courtesy of the author.)

Yosuke Yamashita.
(Courtesy of the author.)

Miya Masaoka, koto master. (Courtesy of Stuart Brinin.)

Yoshiaki "Miya" Miyanoue. (Courtesy of Steve Minor.)

Vivace: Ayako Shirasaki (piano, leader), Rumi Sato (bass), Tomako Narumi (alto sax), Satomi Onishi (drums), Nobuko Ariake (vibes). (Courtesy of the author.)

Vocalist Shiho Sukoi at the Swing City Club in Ginza. (Courtesy of the author.)

The author and Kotaro Tsukahara performing at the Swing City Club. (Courtesy of the author.)

Takeshi "Tee" Fuji of Three Blind Mice Records. (Courtesy of the author.)

Ryozo Sugiura (vibes) and Hideto Kanai (bass) at the Jazzmen Club in Yokohama. (Courtesy of the author.)

Members of the Albatross Swing Jazz Orchestra: Sachiyo Nagata (trumpet), Masao Ishii (tenor sax and leader), the author, Ryoichi Yamaguchi (piano), and Masahiro Saito (tenor sax). (Courtesy of the author.)

Tsuneo Hashimoto, owner of the Jazz Aster *kissaten* (coffeehouse) in Nagoya. (Courtesy of the author.)

Jake Mori and Bunichi Murata, chief editor of *Swing Journal*.
(Courtesy of the author.)

Koichi Osamu, bassist with the Murata Youichi Orchestra, chats with his fans.
(Courtesy of the author.)

Karrin Allyson signs CDs for her fans at the Monterey Jazz Festival in Noto.
(Courtesy of the author.)

The Field Holler Jazz Orchestra on stage at the Monterey Jazz Festival in Noto.
(Courtesy of the author.)

The author and his wife, Betty, with the Kawagishi and Nakamura families in Nara; a Yamaha upright is in the background. (Courtesy of the author.)

Clarinetist Eiji Kitamura when he first appeared at the Monterey Jazz Festival. (Courtesy of Monterey Jazz Festival Archives.)

Hidehiko "Sleepy"
Matsumoto.
(Courtesy of Monterey
Jazz Festival Archives.)

Tatsuya Takahashi and the Tokyo Union Orchestra at the Monterey Jazz Festival.
(Courtesy of Monterey Jazz Festival Archives.)

Makoto Ozone, at the recording session of "Treasure." (Courtesy of Gildas Boclé.)

Tiger Okoshi. (Courtesy of Vera Hørven.)

Satoko Fujii. (Courtesy of Ryo Natsuki.)

Drummer/producer Akira Tana. (Courtesy of Ebet Roberts.)

that Kyoko had sewn—pillows or wall displays with slogans in English: "Heart Club" and "Join Us," a grandfather's clock with "Joyful Time" embossed.

One is never very far from music in Japan, so later, entering the grounds of the Municipal Museum of Fine Art, Mr. Matsumoto directed my attention to a row of men in shirtsleeves or full-dress *sararīman* suits who lined the street, each in a separate spot marked off for karaoke. Each man sported his own microphone and sound box and was singing his heart out, drawing on a repertoire sufficient to last through lunch hour. Mr. Matsumoto also—on Betty's last day in Japan (she had to return to her job as an elementary school aid)—took us on a *fancy* shopping tour, to a craft store that sold beautiful items for, actually, fairly reasonable prices and then wrapped them in paper with one of Munakata's prints on it (paper I saved). I found a seductively shaped sake jar with a dark brown glaze on the bottom and a egg-blue top flecked with black and brown. Betty found great toys for our grandchildren. Mr. Matsumoto also had some method to his "madness" (extravagant lure) in bringing us to this shopping area, for a jazz club, called Over Seas, was located nearby. I'd told him of this club, not knowing just where it was located, as it was owned and run by a pianist whose CDs I'd found and purchased in the States: Hisayuki Terai.

Entering the Over Seas Club, even at noon, you can tell that it combines the best features of a restaurant and a nightclub. A splendid black grand piano, its lid erect at a forty-five-degree angle, sits off to the right, beside a set of tucked-back brocade drapes. Framed photos of visits by Tommy Flanagan—Hisayuki Terai's mentor and hero—dot the walls. Hisayuki was very cordial to Mr. Matsumoto and Emi. His wife Tamae's English is excellent, and she seems shyly proud of the fact that she picked it up from visiting musicians and not at a school. Tamae served as translator while her husband told me a bit about the club they've run for twelve years.

"I turned to jazz from classical music in 1972. At that time in Japan, McCoy Tyner was the most popular pianist. All the jazz journalists talked and wrote about him—only McCoy Tyner. After him, Chick Corea came onto the scene, and everybody in Japan was raving about him. Every Japanese pianist became, first, McCoy Tyner, and then, Chick Corea. This was very frustrating for me. The jazz scene in Japan is really controlled by journalism and the mass communications industry, the record companies. The musicians don't have enough faith in *them-*

selves. So everyone tries to be a McCoy Tyner or a Chick Corea—whoever is *it* from time to time. But when I was young, I really loved the Detroit bebop style. *I* wanted to play in the style of Tommy Flanagan. But nobody would accept that style at the time I began playing piano. I thought, What shall I do? And I decided to open a jazz club by myself." They both laughed. "And that was the start, in 1979."

I mentioned the coffeeshops or bars that Toshiko had gone to in order to listen to and *study* Bud Powell.

"We called them 'jazz coffeeshops,'" Hisayuki Terai said. "That was in the seventies. The early seventies. The jazz coffeeshops were booming. There were lots of them in cities like Osaka and Tokyo. You sat and sipped coffee and stayed for two to three hours, just listening to jazz. It was like Zen practice. Some of the people who listened were *very* serious. Before 1970, there were not so many concerts. American musicians started coming to Japan while the coffeeshops were still booming. They started coming one after the other. From 1972 until 1977, so many groups came to perform that it was known as the Golden Age of American Jazz Musicians. They didn't just play at festivals. They would give concerts with their own groups. Tommy Flanagan. Ella Fitzgerald. Sarah Vaughan. Johnny Griffin. Barry Harris. Jimmy Rainey. I was in college at that time, and I was able to see and hear all of these groups on stage. I was exposed to, and found myself accepting, many different styles of jazz. But from the eighties on, jazz festivals—*that* style of concert—became more popular. The concerts became more like jam sessions. Promoters didn't want to invite interesting jazz groups with more serious styles anymore. So the opportunities for young musicians to see great performances grew less and less. Of course you can always study styles by listening to records, but jazz music is very different in live performance. The musicians are doing very different things on stage and on a bandstand than they do in a recording studio. Much different. Especially the intros and the endings. Totally different."

Unfortunately, we had to cut our conversation short at this time. We agreed to meet again in a few days, after I returned to Osaka, when I would also have a chance to hear him play.

On the trip back from Kansai Airport, where we saw Betty off, I practiced a ruse I had deployed over the past few days. Emi sat next to her father as he drove, and I, seated behind her, took out the cheat sheet I'd prepared: a list of vocabulary words I knew I would need for whatever excursion we set out on (*bijutsukan* for art museum, *mise* for shop, even *kōtsūjūtai* for traffic jam, a state we found ourselves in on more than one occasion). I would slip the sheet from my pants pocket and spout complete sentences. Katsunori may well have wondered why my Japanese was considerably less proficient face to face than it was when delivered from the back seat of his car.

That night we attended the Feast of a Thousand Candles at Tennoji Temple. The impact of this scene was such that an estimate of a million candles seems more accurate than a mere thousand. The candles are arranged on four-tiered stands that, side-by-side, encircle the grounds, surrounding the temple's five-story pagoda, the candles glittering, casting soft golden shadows, attended by acolytes dressed in black *happi* coats with white sashes tied about their foreheads. Emi employed her calligraphic skills to inscribe a candle she acquired for Betty and me, our names written in katakana: *bi-ru mi-no-ru / be-ti*. The brightly kindled rows seemed to spread a blush through the night air. Families stood reverently before their oblational, lovingly inscribed white candles, paying homage to the wind-wafted flames. When you stepped back from the crowd, the sacred enclosure, the effect was overwhelming, the candle-lit rows resembling avenues of light, of ignited hope and love—or the appearance of a city you return to as home, viewed from an airplane. I said a prayer for all the people I love—living and dead—and returned to my new friends Katsunori and Emi.

20

YOKOHAMA: THE MT. FUJI JAZZ FESTIVAL

I T WAS A HEALTHY CROSSTOWN walk from the Central Inn to Yokohama Minato-Mirai, the latter a slice of land extending out into a bay, the site (Rinko Park) where the Mt. Fuji Jazz Festival would take place. The city was obviously geared up for jazz. I passed a restaurant that, along with the customary plastic display of available dishes, presented an array of doll-like figures worthy of Emi's Girl's Day collection, but in this case not the emperor's entourage but seven black musicians, each about a foot high: a bassist hunched over his "ax" (exuberantly, like Milt Hinton); a trumpeter lurching into his mute-crowned horn; a drummer with the tag ends of his tie draped over an impeccably clean white shirt (his trap set alone a work of art, in the mode of netsuke sculpted pieces); a pianist with his hat set at a rakish angle; a vocalist in a white dress with plunging neckline; and a final figure in spats, contorted with musical effort, doubled over an alto sax. Who was the artist responsible for such joyous verisimilitude rendered in miniature? As I would later find out, Yokohama is the doll capital of Japan, hosting an excellent three-story museum devoted to just this sort of craftsmanship.

The line I stood in to hear Shuichi "Ponta" Murakami was made up of people who looked even younger than those who had come to hear Satoru "Salt" Shionoya at the Blue Note in Osaka. Inside, we were greeted by a pop-rock tune screeching over the sound system, while one of those ubiquitous *bijin* (cute girls, or literally, beautiful women) attempted to cut in, saying "Dōzo kudasai," announcing the present time (19:00), and stating that no photographs or private recordings were allowed inside the theater. The rock tune was replaced by a Broadway show tune—full of strepitous frills and strident strings—and I began to wonder just what I was getting myself into. As we'd entered the hall, young women dressed in Heineken green sport coats and miniskirts had passed out the sponsor's "Evergreen Mt. Fuji Jazz Festival 1996" plastic sticks. Once bent and snapped, these sticks glowed in the dark. The young people around me now amused themselves by snapping and waving these phosphorescent wands above their heads in the semidark auditorium.

A sudden, crushing electronic tremolo served as harbinger of the show to come, followed by the lacerating steady sound of rock guitar and bass. A man wearing a massive black Afro wig, his face puffed and blackened to make him look like James Brown, materialized on stage, accompanied by a guitarist dressed in skintight red pants, red and black shoes, and an oversized padded leopard-skin cap whose elastic band nailed his ears to his face. The bassist's hair was streaked red and green, and he wore sunglasses and a pink shirt generously bedecked with flowers. Strobe lights minced the trio's movements. James Brown, or the unreasonable facsimile thereof, took a seat behind the drum kit nearest the piano. Sounding more like Austin Powers than the Beatles, the group launched into "Come Together." This was followed by an equally unsettling "Back in the USSR."

A manic medley of Beatle songs now blared, burped, buzzed, and blazed, each piece dreadful to the core, ending with a truly repellent "Get Back." All of the songs were sung in English, or a replica thereof. Just as the music reached a nearly intolerable peak (for me—the young audience was laughing its collective ass off, cheering with approval), a distraught, very official-looking young man in a business suit hastened out on stage, shouting wildly, telling the musicians to stop this outrage at once—or else! Surprisingly, they did. Stagehands appeared from all over, immediately. They snatched the guitarist's "ax" from his hands and even stripped Shuichi "Ponta" Murakami of his drum kit, leaving him standing alone on stage with little more than his James Brown wig.

Murakami, apparently, is a cutup who loves to stage the type of fracas I'd just witnessed. He makes Richie Cole, in his most extreme fit of Alto Madness, seem tepid, tea-time tame by comparison. The audience knew all this, apparently, and had been granted exactly what they'd paid for—an *act* they awarded with roisterous applause. Once things quieted down, following the departure of the "official" and the stagehands,

Shuichi "Ponta" Murakami appeared again, sans wig and outrageous costume. He mounted the elaborate second drum set, now moved stage forward, and a pianist materialized, plus guitar and electric bass. They received a warm welcome from the crowd. Ponta, now wearing a T-shirt and baseball cap (reversed, of course), showed the crowd—and me— that he truly does know his way around a drum kit, even one this extensive, exploring a range of apt accents while the bass player began what turned out to be a tribute to the deceased Jaco Pastorius—no slouch himself, while alive, as a showman.

After the first tune, an up-tempo Latin romp that allowed him a substantial but not sovereign or overbearing display of flashy drumming, Shuichi "Ponta" Murakami apologized ("Sumimasen!") for the first set, saying, "Watashi wa imasen deshita!" (That wasn't really *me* that was here!) The crowd roared in approval and laughter. I was seeing another side of Japan, young Japan, and it was fascinating—if not all that musically rewarding so far. The group swung back into action again with a modal piece that allowed pianist Masahiro Sayano to display a good blues sense coupled with adroit bop runs, impressive parallel hands in octaves, and some dramatic dissonance, supported by a strong four-note electric bass vamp that sucked it all together nicely.

The group grew increasingly hyperactive as the set progressed. Ponta indulged in gymnastic feats that didn't add much—aside from ham drama—to his drumming, but he was an impressive technician. "Sing Sing Sing" commenced with familiar Gene Krupa invocations, and the young audience recognized and applauded the quote. The piece then took off in an entirely different direction, something original but equally familiar to the crowd—an all-out rock offering that allowed the musicians to abandon any subtle jazz effects they'd indulged in for a full-fledged wanton shoot-out; and the young audience seemed to love this too. A man dressed all in black (T-shirt, sport coat, trousers, even a black headband) appeared: a sort of Tony Clifton to Ponta's Andy Kaufman anarchistic bent, his raspy voice and hip inflection a parody of a blues rather than a lounge singer—although I'm not certain parody was intended. His name was Fusanosuke Kondon, and I would learn later— from Jake Mori—that he owns his own blues record store in Tokyo, loves the medium, and is self-taught. "He goes his own way, does his own thing always," Jake would say. I would also learn from Jake that Ponta is about forty-four years of age and that the Beatle onslaught at the start is his stock-in-trade form of absurd comedy, devoid of any social or political significance, just his own—given the popularity of the Beatles in Japan, *still*—special sort of put-on or joke.

After the show, I walked back to the hotel and saw some interesting graffiti on a wall surrounding a construction site: large slashing angular red *rōmaji* (Roman letters) painted on overlapping multicolored kidney shapes and arabesques worthy of Arshile Gorky, letters that spelled out *kane* (money) with the words "Fuck Harm" sprayed next to them. I realized I was seeing (and hearing) an entirely different side of Japan, but an integral part. The Central Hotel, where I stayed, houses businessmen in and out of town and offers delights, apparently, that Betty and I had not seen advertised at the more humble *ryokans* we stayed in. When I got to my room I discovered, sitting prominently on my dresser, a slick brochure for "What a Night: Party Pink Topless Bottomless." Alongside it lay a flier for "Pixy Body Conscious Club" (*ike ike bodei kon*), with photos of long-legged Mari (in yellow tank top and matching miniskirt); Reiko (in a red dress no bigger than a *furoshiki*, a small cloth square used for wrapping or carrying parcels); and other nubile beauties named Rina, Tsubasa, Miho, Ai, and Chika. Not one of these girls appeared to be much older than sixteen. Party Pink's copy carried a Buddhist message in support of its very secular attractions: "The illusionary world rises above time and space; we invite you to take an incredible journey."

Next morning, I walked back to Minato Mirai, skipping across the streets in time to "Comin' through the Rye" (this chime-performed tune—actually a Japanese melody—alerting pedestrians that it is now safe to cross the street) and ended up in Rinko Park, a large greensward that sloped down to Yokohama Bay, grounds on which a wide stage had been erected, two-story plastic Heineken beer bottles straddling each side of it. The day's fare was a "Mt. Fuji Super Jam," featuring Terumasa Hino and the Asian Jazz All Stars; American vocalist Kevin Mahogany; the Jackie McLean Quintet with Junko Onishi and Freddie Hubbard; and the Blue Note All Stars, which featured Greg Osby. The scene that greeted me on the grounds was a delight: spacious, crowd-happy, breeze-wafted. In spite of a long line of jazz fans still waiting outside, the grassy knoll that sloped down to the sea—spotted with bonsai trees propped up with stakes—seemed nearly full, people camping on colorful mats, some shaded (along with their coolers) by small *kasa* (umbrellas). Sections were cordoned off with low ropes, and the Japanese seemed to confine themselves to them, but I found a solitary position just outside one of these official "campsites" and made it my own—a nice spot on a hill above the bulk of the crowd, with a good—if distant—view of the stage. I could see a bridge on the bay, to the left of the stage. I also noticed just how *young* (once again, as in Wakura Onsen) the crowd was: girls with straw hats and giant gold circular earrings, in cut-off jeans or loose-fitting flower-print summer dresses and bare feet; young men in T-shirts with slogans such as "Grand Canyon," "Select Life Under the Stars," "Out of This World," "Dog Police," "Get Off," or—my favorite—"Beans in Tomato Stew." One couple, with wet towels pasted to their faces, sprawled on a crinkly silver plastic mat embellished with pink dolphins and blue jellyfish. The afternoon was not hot—yet. The landscape was bright, cheerful, sunny as I waited for the music.

The first musician to appear on stage—after the customary interminable dialogue between the *bijin* and her male counterpart—was trumpeter Terumasa Hino, with his Asian Jazz All Stars group. Hino, at fifty-four, has long been a part of the international jazz scene, a highly respected musician, and I knew whatever he offered would be good.

TERUMASA HINO AND JUNKO ONISHI

Terumasa Hino's a go-for-it brassman—it's obvious from his stance at the microphone, no less than his sound," a 1990 *Down Beat* article proclaimed. The piece was titled "Bluestruck from Birth," the initial word based on a recording Hino released called *Bluestruck.*

Hino told writer Howard Mandel that he got his first horn at nine years of age. Before that he was a tap dancer. His father was both a trumpeter and a hoofer. Hino grew up listening "all the time to Satchmo," and he recalls seeing movies that featured Harry James. "Nothing Japanese influences. Of course, later I look more inside, and realize I'm so Japanese in identity." Hino finds nothing odd in such an anomaly, claiming that Japan loves the "frontier spirit" of America, its raw energy, and that this was true even during the war. The trumpeter tells a story about a famous Japanese jazz vocalist who—like the former Zero pilot Yasuyuki Ishihara, the record producer I met in Tokyo—"was a telegraph soldier, doing Morse Code," fighting Americans but listening all the while to American jazz radio stations.

Terumasa Hino is self-taught. He started performing at fourteen with the U.S. Army's Camp Drake big band and joined "the American equivalent of the Jazz Composers Orchestra Association" at nineteen. Yosuke Yamashita was his band mate in a quintet determined to make music on its own, "rather than imitate note-for-note solos heard on imported records." The group experimented with such "out" practices as switching trumpet and clarinet or alto saxophone mouthpieces. "I'm a very free musician, though now I play more straightahead. I can go back and forth anytime I want to."

Which is exactly what he did with his Asian Jazz All Stars on that sunny afternoon in Yokohama. The group consisted of Hino, his brother Motohiko on drums (a seasoned and much respected jazz veteran), Tots Tolentino (from Manila) on alto sax, Lee Jung Shik (Korea) on tenor sax, Paul Candelaria on bass, Jeremy Monteiro on piano, Eugene Pao of Hong Kong on guitar, and Filipino vocalist Charito. The opening strains were made up of unique ethnic imperatives but also showcased an ear for the elaborate orchestration of Charles Mingus and the melodic ingenuity of Ornette Coleman. The saxes brawled and howled with canine-hungry inflection, while Hino offset the drama with spare, carefully selected whole notes mixed with quick runs. Truly a "go-for-it brassman," shoulders hunched with pugilistic aplomb, he bent into his horn as if coaxing out its darkest secrets, then fetched fast flight-of-the-bumblebee spatters, his elbows flailing as he soared aloft.

"Konichiwa!" (Hello!) Hino cried after, and then introduced "a beautiful singer from the Philippines, but she's been living in Japan for a long time now . . ."

This was Charito, *kirei na* (pretty) in voice and person. Her inflection was quaint on "My Funny Valentine" ("Valley-on-times-dai"), her range and falsetto reminiscent of Sarah Vaughan's. A tune about "precious secrets" emboldened couples on the lawn, who cuddled up closer. After a moving interpretation of a Latin-flavored "God Bless the Child," Charito gave Terumasa Hino a kiss, a gesture he didn't seem to mind at all. The set lasted for more than an hour but, given its variety, was never sluggish or slow. It was filled with the range of material I'd heard on the CDs by Hino I had at home, beginning with *Bluestruck.* A tune called "Romancero Gitano" features ensemble work very much in the Art Blakey's Jazz Messengers vein. Hino's solo was subtle, well constructed, mixing Freddie Hubbard's reach with Miles Davis's stay-at-home (midrange) savvy. On the title tune, "Bluestruck," Hino stepped in with piercing high notes and remained—with pride and panache—in that register nearly throughout.

In his *JazzTimes* review of *Bluestruck,* Chuck Berg wrote, "Hino's cornet is a wonder. His burnished brassy sound coos and crackles with steely abandon," adding, "Hino, it should be noted, is a terrific writer. From the jaunty 'Hugo' to the balladic poignancy of 'Rain Again,' Hino shows impressive range and depth." That range and depth come through again on a 1992 recording, *Unforgettable,* made in the excellent company of pianist Cedar Walton. Ironically, the title tune seems one of the more forgettable of the set, whereas a lesser-known vehicle, an original called "Blue Smiles," moves from lyrical, lively broken rhythm into double-time, Hino's muted without a mute tone detonating at the close.

One of my favorite Terumasa Hino CDs is *Spark* (Blue Note), an ambitious recording that finds him fronting an eleven-piece aggregate that includes bassist Benisuke Sakai, whom I'd heard in Tokyo and would hear many good things about as I traveled throughout Japan. It's Hino's original tunes that stand out: an exotic, liquid, danceable "Tribe"; "Suavemente," with its "fat" full-tone horn; and a piece called "Art Blakey," complete with cymbal splashes, press rolls, and trumpet flutters and screeches. A Hino quintet recording, *Live!* (Three Blind Mice), features an all-Japanese cast that includes brother Motohiko on drums and Mikio Masuda on piano. "Stella by Starlight" turns minimalist, showing another side of Hino's art, music that seems a reflection in water, musing on itself.

Hino works often with pianist Masabumi Kikuchi (one of those pianists who likes to croon or even gargle encouragement to himself while he plays). Their 1993 *Triple Helix,* with the adventurous Masahiko Togashi providing percussion, offers a mix of originals by both Togashi and Hino. When the trumpeter enters "Trial," it's with anthem flare. Togashi—an exciting percussionist not in the showboating tradition but that rarest of all genres: unconventional, no-nonsense, tasteful drumming—provides *taiko*-influenced fill and is always very much *there* no matter how subtle or understated. This performance was recorded live at the second Yamaha Jazz Festival in Hamamatsu in 1993. On "Twilight South West" (composed by Togashi), Kikuchi chants, or chitters, in the background, but in sync with Terumasa Hino's meandering horn, which resembles the mind attempting to empty itself during Zazen but not quite succeeding—incessant thoughts or images tediously interrupting some larger notion of Self.

Masabumi Kikuchi is an interesting musical artist and deserves space of his own. He was born in Tokyo in 1939 and started playing piano as a small child. He graduated from the composition department of a high school attached to Japan's prestigious Tokyo National University of Fine Arts and Music. His first recital in 1965 was well received and led to work with Sadao Watanabe's quartet, which also featured Masahiko Togashi. Kikuchi attended Berklee College in 1968, then joined Hino in a quintet under joint leadership. A fine trio recording, *Tethered Moon,* made with Paul Motion and Gary Peacock, is a collection of songs by Kurt Weill, the pieces highly abstracted from the originals, but in a manner that is fresh and original. "Alabama Song" makes me think again of Toru Takemitsu's reflections on Japanese "breathing," its gentle single-note excursions very much in the harmony-free Japanese tradition—even Peacock's bass lines reminiscent of koto or *shamisen*. "September Song" is filled with large spaces (these "days" don't dwindle down; they just dissolve over long stretches); the customary rhythm of "Bilbao Song" is handsomely distorted; and the trio does full justice to "My Ship" (made familiar by Miles Davis and Gil Evans), and does so on their own terms, with dramatic gestures, soaring hope, and a solemn close. All in all, a solid, unique homage to Kurt Weill.

At the Mt. Fuji Jazz Festival in Yokohama, Terumasa Hino pulled together all of the experience he'd gained on his recordings, much of it Japanese: "We don't have much harmony in Japan; traditionally, only a melodic line and rhythm. The African pentatonic scale, like John Coltrane played, modes, and the blues scale, remind me of Japanese folk and traditional songs. Also, Japanese drums. The power is the same." The man afflicted with "goose bumps all over" the first time he heard Art Blakey and his Jazz Messengers in Japan in the 1960s—the man who understands and has incorporated, in a subtle way, his own cultural traditions—that man was both at ease and active, in the manner he values. "American music is much more relaxed," he told *Down Beat*. "Always I'm standing up to jump in so hard. When I went to Europe, critics say, 'Karate jazz, kamikaze jazz,' and they love it. But I played a jam session one night with Art Blakey, and he said, 'Hino, you don't have to prove yourself. You're Hino.' I was very shocked. . . . Oh, I still do that karate jazz, that's what I'm fighting. I have to calm down, settle down, take time, relax. That's what I learned from the States."

From the look and sound of his Mt. Fuji Jazz Festival performance, I'd say he's acquired this desired state of American "Zen." Throughout his set, he wasn't forcing himself at any point. He was all Hino.

The second major Japanese musical artist to perform that afternoon in Rinko Park was Junko Onishi. Kyoto-born, raised in Tokyo, she was just twenty-six years old when I saw her in Yokohama, but by then she had already won over New York audiences with a debut engagement at the Village Vanguard, a gig recorded on two CDs in 1994. A *JazzTimes* profile piece praised her for her "flawless technique and facile gift for melody," her suite approach to performance cited as "an intricate series of changes, closer to 'movements' than the typical jazz blueprint of head-bridge-solo." Onishi brought "the romanticism of Chopin and Schumann as well as the orchestral approach of [her hero] Duke Ellington" to her first CD, *Cruisin'* (1993), on Blue Note. She says of Ellington's use of the suite format on *Money Jungle*, 'I really dig that.'"

Moving to New York after graduating from Berklee College of Music (with honors), Onishi was told that she had to confront swing, blues, and bebop more. "Back in Japan, no one was telling me that. I had to deal with the music myself. That's when everything started to open up for me. The concept I want to explore in my music is very clear to me now." She was compelled to return to Japan in 1992 because of illness in her family, saying, "I'm an outsider, 'cause I live in Japan now. But our jazz scene is just growing up. We have a lot of good young players. It's going to be great!" She formed a trio with Japanese friends from Berklee, and her first recording (*WOW* [1993, for Somethin' Else, a division of Toshiba-EMI]) was an unqualified success. For five years in a row, Junko Onishi has been named Jazzman of the Year in *Swing Journal's* Readers' Poll.

At Rinko Park, Onishi appeared with veteran alto saxophonist Jackie McLean, with whom she has recorded a CD called *Hat Trick*. In Yokohama, the group opened with a tune from that disc, "Will You Still Be Mine." Her own solo cheerful, high-stepping, high-strung, Onishi glided through the changes with ambiguous (because offset by tension that kept you attentive) ease. McLean's "Little Melonae" featured the saxophonist's brazen, somewhat raw tone and eager legato lines played off against Onishi's discretion, her solo here a mix of staccato block-chord effects, smooth parallel lines, and steady drive. Holding her own, the pianist functions as much more than just a "guest" with McLean. "Bag's Groove" affords a history lesson on the perennial potential of bop riffs, McLean' s sax quacking with glee at the close.

At the Mt. Fuji Jazz Festival, McLean and Onishi were joined by trumpeter Freddie Hubbard, a little worse for wear because of a bad lip, confining himself mostly to midregister, a zone he hasn't been known—in the past—to dwell in long. Introduced by McLean ("Let's hear it for my favorite trumpet player!"), Hubbard unleashed a sudden bleat and blat to which the saxophonist responded with, "Freddie, save your chops!" The group played "Spirits of Train," and, game if lame, Hubbard gave it his best, providing fine licks. But it was a percussive, nearly barrelhouse Onishi who stole the show for me, showing *chikara* (force or power; also talent or skill), reminding me of a jazz writer's commentary that "almost fifty years after Toshiko Akiyoshi surprised jazz fans by proving a petite Japanese woman could play hard, swinging jazz, [Junko] Onishi is taking yet another step forward."

When McLean said, "Play *your* tune, Freddie," Hubbard responded with "Blues for Miles," a number that got the yin (female) half of a couple down in front of me clapping her hands in time above her head. This spry tune had the crowd on their feet, cheering. The set lasted for more than an hour and included a lovely alto airing of "'Round Midnight"— that interesting edge of irritation in McLean's tone offset by Onishi's highly credible classical chops (she started out that way, doing orchestral chores in high school). Jackie McLean thanked "our very special guest, Miss Onishi, Junko at the piano!" The audience, wanting more, got it: a leisurely, attractive, blues-inflected encore. Hubbard repaid McLean's compliment, saying, "Jackie McLean—what an originator!"— adding, "I love you! Dōmo arigatō!"

I strolled over to a booth selling CDs by all the performers featured at the festival and loaded up on Junko Onishi. I already had her *Cruisin'* back home, along with her *Live at the Village Vanguard* CD (she was the first Japanese artist to perform there with her own band). In Yokohama, I found her 1995 *Piano Quintet Suite* and a CD called *Sextet,* which featured her with a group of exciting young Japanese artists. *Cruisin'* (her American debut recording) features Ornette Coleman's "Congeniality." It's full of both rhythmic and melodic surprise (if it's possible to out-surprise Ornette), moving from sweet to stark, switched on, switched off. "Caravan" is spicy from the start and stays that way, fine drummer Billy Higgins *dancing* throughout, holding it all together, creating a smiling, joyous ambience. The last tune on this impressive American debut is Sonny Rollins's "Blue Seven," a bluesy walkabout that shows that Onishi can cover all the bases—that she has successfully followed the advice of whoever it was that encouraged her, when she first went to New York, to "deal more with swing, blues, and bebop."

There is a Zen tale in which a master named Gutei, whenever asked a question, simply sticks up one finger. Once, when a visitor asks his ambitious young attendant, "What is the Zen your master is teaching?" the boy also sticks up one finger. Hearing of this, Gutei takes a knife and cuts off the boy's digit. When the boy runs out screaming in pain, Gutei calls to him. The boy stops, turns his head, and Gutei sticks up a finger—a gesture that, according to this tale, occasions the lad's enlightenment. In the *teisho* or commentary on this koan, Shibayama Roshi says, "Gutei's finger and his young attendant's finger are the same finger. Still, there is a fundamental difference. While Gutei's finger was Zen itself, the universe itself, the attendant's finger was just an imitation without the fact of his own experience. It was a fake with no life, and should be cut off." So much for fabled Japanese cultural sanctioning of imitation.

Junko Onishi is no imitator. She has absorbed and transformed the ingredients—the basic vocabulary—of jazz in accord with her own experience. An excellent example is the work on her *Piano Quintet Suite,* in which she elicited the fine services of legendary Detroiter Marcus Belgrave on trumpet and Eiichi Hayashi on alto sax. The title tune, an Onishi original, has a full band but a surprisingly ethereal ensemble start. Junko's solo contains embellishment, sass, staccato accents, and solid bop runs—the works! A slow blues interlude reminds you that this *is* a suite and that she is offering the full range of feeling and mood. Throughout the CD, Onishi provides even more variety by inserting brief "Interludes," the first based on Robert Schumann, the second somewhat insane: fifty one minutes of blatant, blaring (horn-assisted) repetition. An Onishi-Hayashi joint original, "The Tropic of Capricorn" reminded me—oddly enough—of the preface to Henry Miller's *Tropic of Cancer,* in which Anaïs Nin compares Miller's work to "a continual oscillation between extremes, with bare stretches that taste like brass and leave the full flavor of emptiness. It is beyond optimism or pessimism. The author has given us the last *frisson.*" Onishi's "Capricorn" achieves the same effect musically. Junko Onishi is one of the major performers to come out of Japan, I feel, although I've heard other Japanese musicians (all male) put her down—perhaps through envy of her upstart success in America? They claim she can't improvise, is dependent on sight-reading. But this is a contention that *seeing* and hearing her live in Yokohama shot down at once.

My day at Rinko Park was delightful. I could probably have spent the rest of my life just stretched out on that lawn in Yokohama, sipping Heineken beer, scanning the crowd of restrained, delighted Japanese jazz fans. Having such a good time, I disregarded those large questions I'd anticipated answering, questions related to "authenticity" and the "unique Japanese character." *Had* there been genuine, substantial *shinkō* (progress) on the Japanese jazz scene since Akira Tana wrote his thesis twenty-two years ago? Were Japanese jazz musicians playing on a level with Americans, as Tiger Okoshi believed (but as some of the people I'd talked to so far doubted)? Certainly in the case of Terumasa Hino and Junko Onishi, the answer to these questions was a resounding *hai!*

But on that splendid afternoon in Yokohama, I wasn't in the mood for comparisons, for judgment—pass or fail. Something *subarashii* (wonderful) was happening, and I just *dug it.* Back in the States, whenever I heard a musician of the caliber of Jackie McLean, I generally simply enjoyed him, instinctively (my appreciation uncompromised by "critical opinion" or evaluation). And now, in Japan, I felt there was no longer anything to *prove* as far as jazz was concerned. Was all the music I'd heard of equal merit? Had I become a mere advocate, blinded by approbation? Was the jazz scene free of music that was flawed, stale, bland, superficial, crude, or vacuous? Hell no. I'd heard some real *kuso* (a vulgar term for you know what)—especially from drummers! But one thing jazz in Japan seemed free of—in a positive, nearly blessed sense— was the petty backbiting, nit-picking, envy, or outright jealousy (feelings of inferiority masking as pride) responsible for the deeply divided, factional nature of the "wars" that take place within the jazz scene back in the States—as later the vitriolic responses to Ken Burns's documentary series *Jazz* would reveal. Perhaps such wars were being waged in Japan also, lurking below the surface, but I trust my instincts and believe I would have sniffed them out. I doubt that such "wars" exist, at least not on the scale they do on the American jazz scene.

TAKESHI "TEE" FUJI AND THREE BLIND MICE

Takeshi "Tee" Fuji is an imposing, animated man. He is a fifth *dan* at Go (expert players' levels ascend from one to nine); sports a bright, engaging, but slightly smug smile; and has an instantly "winning" manner. We met in a coffeeshop not far from the Three Blind Mice studio, which I never saw.

Takeshi "Tee" Fuji first heard Glenn Miller, Benny Goodman, and Louis Armstrong at the age of eleven. When he turned fourteen, he heard *Jazz at Massey Hall.*

"Yeah! That was my first experience of bebop or the new music, and I was deeply impressed. Then, by the time I was high school age, I had to make up my mind about my life: whether to go to a university or something like that. At the time I wanted, if possible, to establish a minor jazz label, because at that time we had no such labels in Japan. Major labels only. But those major labels—King, Columbia, Victor—recorded pop music, or pop jazz: only the big names. They never paid any attention to underrated players. And *these,* I felt, were the most talented musicians: bright newcomers, but because they had no name, the major labels wouldn't give them an opportunity to record, you know? So in 1970, I established Three Blind Mice. It's a funny name. My friends and I—three people—started the label. At this time I liked Art Blakey and the Jazz Messengers. They had an album out on the United Artists label called *Three Blind Mice.* And of course 'Three Blind Mice' is from Mother Goose." He began to sing: "'Three blind mice, three blind mice.' The three of us were amateurs in the recording business. We came into the field *blind.* A mouse is not a regular *rat,* you know. A rat is gray in color, but a mouse is white. So our *flag* was white. No specific color. Do you understand?"

"Wakarimashita" (I understand).

"And of course jazz fans are called *cats,* in slang," he said, laughing. "And a mouse will be caught by jazz fans, the *cats.*"

Fuji graduated from the pharmaceutical course of Nihon University. His father, a "very old man" at the time, controlled a small company that sold drugs, and Tee Fuji had to help him.

"So I am a pharmacist, or was so at first. I helped him for about seven or eight years, and then I established our small recording company. The first musician we recorded was tenor saxophonist Kosuke Mine who, at the time, played alto. He was one of the newcomers. Not yet a big name. And we recorded Sleepy Matsumoto, who was an established musician in Japan. When he returned to Japan from New York, he brought back ideas from the Coltrane school. His first quartet was made up of Isao Suzuki, bass, and Kunihiko Sugano, piano."

Before leaving for Japan, I'd listened to a Three Blind Mice recording called, simply enough, *Sleepy.* On it, Hidehiko "Sleepy" Matsumoto plays both tenor sax and flute and matches an impressive command of technique with a wide range of emotion. An original tune, "Duke's Days," is unabashedly romantic, melodic (Getz-like in tone), then grows assertive, quick runs played off against flicks and flurries of sound. Matsumoto plays flute on "You Don't Know What Love Is," a heavy *shakuhachi*-like vibrato laced with quick "vocal" flirtations with the theme. The final tune is an original entitled "Typhoon." It contains appropriate foreboding, but the storm itself is held under control: a fresh, inspired, well-structured piece.

At home, I'd purchased another recording, *Papillon,* that "introduces" the then sixty-six-year-old saxophonist with the words "Keep your eyes on him," explaining that Sleepy Matsumoto is now "challenging new fields of music." On this recording, that "new" field is fusion (à la highly predictable, heavy-handed orchestration), and Matsumoto sounds trapped, inhibited. The tunes run from "Besame Mucho" to Elvis Presley's "Love Me Tender" to five Matsumoto originals, which are my favorites. "Gissha" has a bon dance feel to it, and "Duke's Days" (his Three Blind Mice quartet version far less syrupy) displays Matsumoto's melodic gift. Comparing the two CDs, I got a clear sense of the service Takeshi "Tee" Fuji has provided for musicians whose work he loves.

Fuji also mentioned bassist Isao Suzuki, another musician whose TBM recording *Blue City* I owned and much admired.

"Isao Suzuki is very talented," Fuji agreed, with relish. Then, pausing, "He has a strong feeling of *soul,* but he's also very eccentric. I respect his playing, but . . ." He paused and smiled.

"Is he difficult to work with?"

"Yeah, very difficult. But it's true that if you listen to Isao Suzuki's first recording, just a single bass solo, you will recognize that player as *Isao Suzuki* and no one else. That's the most important thing. He has his own touch, pace, phrasing, his own soul. He's still active. Maybe three or four times a week he plays in a jazz club in Tokyo. And he usually has some students."

Blue City: Isao Suzuki Quartet + 1 also features pianist Kunihiko Sugano. Kotaro Tsukahara had written me saying that Sugano and Sanpie Ohno gave him a lot of inspiration to play piano, and critic Terry Isono's liner notes describe Sugano as "well known as a piano master with absolute pitch and excellent technique . . . a nervous performer with a quality like delicate glass." Isao Suzuki's group is rounded out by guitarist Kazumi Watanabe, Nobuyoshi Ino on bass (when Suzuki plays cello), and Tetsujiro Obara on drums. On "Body and Soul," Suzuki plays solo at the start with no set rhythm, his stark descending cello line turning tender. His improvisation is unique and engaging. Sugano is impressive (parallel hands in octaves, when the others join in), as is Watanabe.

A Suzuki original, "45th Street" (he lived in New York for six months, where he played with Art Blakey's Jazz Messengers), has a bouncy bop riff, very *urban* with its edge of stimulation, risk, and cagey wit—a spirit Watanabe sustains well. While in New York, Suzuki apparently became a familiar sight in Harlem, a popular habitue at the club Baron. Because Suzuki was not fond of subways (in Tokyo he drives a sports car), Jazz Messenger tenor saxophonist Raymon Morris became his escort, or driver, uptown. Another original, "Blue City," catches the flavor of those days (and nights) well: Suzuki on blues-inflected bass, Sugano's solo somewhat disjointed, quirky in an interesting way, his quick nervous runs accompanied by chords that seem to chant. *Blue City* remains one of my all-time favorite Japanese CDs. Unfortunately, I was not able to meet the "eccentric" Isao Suzuki in Japan.

Pianist Masaru Imada is another unique musician Takeshi "Tee" Fuji has recorded. Before leaving for Japan, I'd listened to a Three Blind Mice CD, *Alone Together,* Imada made with the exceptional Czech

201

bassist George Mraz, and Tee Fuji gave me another, *Now,* on which Imada leads his own quartet.

"Imada he is a fine piano player," Tee Fuji said. "And he's still working, sure. Maybe two-three times a week in a jazz club. He also does studio work; you know, arrangements. And he teaches once a week at one of the music schools."

Alone Together could be used as text for any clinic or seminar. The subject matter might be the instant musical compatibility of two seasoned performers: Imada and Mraz. The bassist was on tour in Japan. He'd never heard of Imada until Tee Fuji lent him some recordings. The two got together at Onkyo House Studio after Mraz finished his final concert with the New York Jazz Quartet in Tokyo. The session "fixed suddenly," Imada said after. "I never saw him until he ran into the studio"—this was not completely true, because the pianist had heard Mraz perform once with the Mel Lewis/Thad Jones Orchestra in Tokyo—"but he understood in advance what I had in mind and freely interpreted it. George has such accurate rhythm—the beat like a stream creeping on the ground. I thought that, in order to stay fresh and tense, we should *not* spend much time meeting or practicing."

They sound refreshingly "tense" (stirred by a challenge, compatibly provoked by it) on the title tune; Mraz's first solo is full of class, the two totally in sync with each other's moves. "Blue Road," an Imada original, contains some sprightly counterpoint, a catchy riff, a tight unison bridge—this road is cool blue and adventurous. The second CD, *Now,* features the Masaru Imada Quartet, with Ichiro Minori on tenor sax. The tunes are all originals. "Nostalgia" is suitably compatible, comforting (drummer Masahiko Ozu provides percussive enhancement by way of *suzu:* a small tree of bells used in Shintō ceremonies). There's no vain striving; the music is very much within reach—and why not? "Shades of the Castle" holds echoes of "Kōjō No Tsuki" ("Moon Over the Desolate Castle") but is taken as a waltz.

Our conversation switched now to big band leader Toshiyuki Miyama.

"Mr. Miyama is seventy years old now, or seventy-one," Tee Fuji offered. "Of course he has maintained the New Herd Big Band, but recently he has performed only at high school jazz concerts or events like that. The band only plays maybe five or six times a month. The individual musicians perform with other small groups. New Herd jobs come first, so everyone comes together on those particular days—or one or two nights. A brand-new album of theirs came out on King Records last year. It's entitled *New Generation.*"

To celebrate the fifth anniversary of the founding of Three Blind Mice, Tee Fuji had commissioned arranger Shuko Mizuno to compose, for Toshiyuki Miyama and the New Herd, a work similar to his successful *Jazz Orchestra '73* recording. "There had been no parties," Fuji says in the liner notes to the result, *Jazz Orchestra '75,* "so presenting one of the best new jazz works seemed to be a suitable method." Mizuno had gone to the United States at the invitation of the Rockefeller Foundation, but upon his return he set to work. Once the piece was recorded, Fuji was "confident we had broken through the confines of the conventional orchestra. I never expected such orchestral jazz: a driven, vibrant, *full* performance. It exceeded my expectations. One reason could be that Shuko devoted all his energies to the work."

It took the composer/arranger four months to complete the score—"no summer holidays!" For the final fifty-four days he stopped only to eat or sleep. The result was a score of over two hundred pages. The composer invites his audience "to listen to my work at the loudest possible volume. It will not make sense without it. The volume is a very important part of the life of this work. So please try to listen to this work only when you are strong and energetic enough to bear such big volume for long time." Bearing his words in mind, I was nearly reluctant to play the CD when I returned to the States, afraid that my ears might not prove equal to the task at hand. But play it I did, and my ears held up. The recording features not only Miyama and the New Herd but all-star guests, including Kenji Mori on alto and tenor sax, Seiichi Nakamura on tenor, and Kazumi Watanabe on guitar. The composition is divided into two parts. Part 1 starts out with rippling, nearly gurgling percussion, the piece at full volume. You feel as if you've stepped into a cauldron of molten lava. The entire sax section plays "solo" together, like Supersax doing Charlie Parker's improvised solos in tandem. The rhythm section remains punishingly propulsive throughout—yet the full frenzy contains a surprising degree of structure: call and response and chromatic ascents. Part 2's tempo is more relaxed, middle range, a steady rock groove enhanced by trombone blats, "middle eastern" sax section work, prominent electric bass, and a cheerful theme with chantlike refrains. This portion has a world music flavor reminiscent of Masahiko Satoh's Randooga group. Watanabe shines on guitar: more Eric Clapton here than Barney Kessel.

Shuko Mizuno is a substantial musical presence, as is guitarist/arranger Kozaburo Yamaki, who contributes six original pieces to a Three Blind Mice CD called *Sunday Thing*. The New Herd was in high spirits because they had just completed a special concert for "the two hundredth anniversary of America's birthday" and had gone on an expedition to the States in 1974 and 1975 "to expand their jazz activities and enthusiastically explore the new world." Yamaki has, throughout his career, composed and arranged more than a hundred works for the New Herd, including *Tsuchi no Oto* (Sound of the Earth), a thirty-minute suite. He makes use of Japanese traditions such as Seijin-shiki (the coming of age ceremony) in his most famous piece, "Furisode Is Crying" (a tune the New Herd played at the 1974 Monterey Jazz Festival—winning "high praise"—and also performed at the Newport Jazz Festival). In the retrospective CD liner notes, jazz critic Masahisa Segawa comments, "I believe [Yamaki's] most valuable contribution as a composer and arranger is the way he assimilated original Japanese concepts and materials into his works. He uses big band jazz as a medium to express his feelings about the general public's daily life and thoughts." Yamaki's music makes use of "materials that evoke a strong emotional response in the Japanese."

The original compositions on *Sunday Thing* bear these claims out. On "Soft Rain" the actual sounds are reproduced abstractly, but are not at all "corny" or brazenly onomatopoetic. Yamaki is known, and praised, for his "immediately recognizable" melodic themes, his "swinging" ballads: "Memories" bounces with a sort of tongue-in-cheek, Dixieland-based funk, a Kurt Weill edge to the self-mockery. "Friends" is a handsome tone poem (the words "intelligent" and "poetic" describe Yamaki's work), and "Plain Song" offers an almost childlike pleasing melody along with a sassy, bratty trombone solo. *Sunday Thing*, overall, offers a rich display of first-class big band composition, arranging, and performance.

According to Tee Fuji, most of the current New Herd band members are young—which brought us to Yoshio Otomo, who seemed to be about the youngest musician on the group of Three Blind Mice CDs I had acquired in the States.

"Yes, Yoshio Otomo is a sexy saxophone player." He laughed. "He plays with his own group and with many other bands. Maybe three or four times a week he works in jazz clubs in Tokyo and near Tokyo."

On a CD called *Moon Ray,* Yoshio Otomo is joined by veteran pianist Tsuyoshi "Go" Yamamoto (who caused a sensation at the 1977 Monterey Jazz Festival when he strolled on stage and, playing "Midnight Sun," stole the show from stalwart veterans Clark Terry, Sweets Edison, Lockjaw Davis, Benny Golson, Cal Tjader, and John Lewis). The title tune, by Artie Shaw, reveals a smooth, accomplished alto above Yamamoto's deft touch. "Emily" was a solid test case for me (it's one of my favorite tunes and the name of my granddaughter), and Otomo passes with subtle colors, his tone just "sour" enough (like that of Jackie McLean) yet plaintive throughout, and even downright *tender* at the close. On "If I Should Lose You," Otomo's attack is bold, brazen. A photo on the CD shows him wearing rough beltless corduroy trousers and an explosively delicate flowered shirt. He's a mustached young man with a heavy head of hair, and his jazz performing style is like his image.

Yoshio Otomo was born in 1947, studied piano when he entered primary school, learned clarinet at thirteen, and switched to alto sax when, in 1963, he first heard Sadao Watanabe at the Gallery 8 in Ginza. He studied under Watanabe at Nihon University and joined the Fumio Itabashi Quartet in 1970 after resigning from school. He received the New Star Prize at the Shinjuku Jazz Festival in 1975. His debut on Three Blind Mice, *When a Man Loves a Woman,* was recorded live at a "Five Days in Jazz 1974" concert, where Otomo shared the bill with such veteran Japanese performers as Seiichi Nakamura on tenor sax, Fumio Karashima on piano, Isao Suzuki on cello, and Sunao Wada on guitar. The title tune shows another side of Otomo's style: heavy-duty funky R&B splatters of bop. Otomo was just twenty-seven at the time.

"At the time you started recording, in the seventies," I said to Tee Fuji, "a number of new, exciting players seem to have been on the scene in Japan. Masaru Imada. Toshiyuki Miyama and the New Herd. Isao Suzuki. Sleepy Matsumoto . . ."

"Tsuyoshi Yamamoto. Yoshio Otomo. Yes. They were all very active. At that time, about three years after John Coltrane died, we (the major influence of American musicians in Japan having ended) began to make our own original jazz. But it was difficult, for at that time almost all of the jazz fans in Japan still liked American jazz only, so the majority of musicians continued to play American jazz standards. However, some of them wanted to try to play their own *unique* music. So I made an album of what was strictly original jazz at that time. That was the first step. I pushed them in that direction, and they began to approach *their own thing*—music that was not imitative. I think that's very important. I tried to sell this new music in Europe and many other places."

He gave me a copy of a handsome catalog entitled "Takeshi 'Tee' Fuji Presents 'One Day with Three Blind Mice': Celebrating the Twentieth Anniversary of Three Blind Mice." Inside, a photo shows "Tee and Company," a full line of musicians on stage that includes alto saxophonist Sachi Hayasaka dressed in a splendidly outrageous loose red kimono, wearing a red headsash, with "chopsticks" in her hair.

"The first half of the catalog," Tee Fuji said, "is about the anniversary concert. And the second half is about the company. If you read these articles, you will understand me and what I was trying to do. This catalog has been distributed throughout the world."

I asked if he could compare the rich 1970s jazz scene he had so successfully tapped into with the present.

"Now? We have problems with many many things now. I would like to make three or four albums a year. That is, I *want* to make them, but it has become difficult recently because the distribution system in Japan is not suited to a small company like ours. Six or seven major recording companies control the record distribution center. It's called NRG. All record store owners order their recordings from them. If they want just *one* CD, NRG will bring it to their shop. But *we* cannot use this system, so it is very difficult for us. Mail orders only bring in 10 percent of sales. Everybody goes to the big shops. We covered almost four hundred record stores in Japan, but we cannot afford large advertising campaigns or promotion. So it is very difficult for us to sell more recordings. Recently, Hong Kong and Southeast Asia musical warehouses—Golden String is our largest distributor—have grown up, and almost all of our customers are either jazz fans or jazz recording audiophiles. Last year, on our twenty-fifth anniversary, I came up with a plan. I made an album, remastered it, and took the lacquer to L.A., to RTI (Record Technology Incorporated). They pressed a very limited edition, but that was good business for us. Yet I have frustration or stress now because it is so difficult to make a *new* album. I *am* recording new people, very talented young musicians I know, but my company has said, 'We have not made so much money over the years,' or 'We have no money for new recordings.' I want to try to continue this label for at least ten more years."

I asked him about the young players in Japan. Were these musicians playing on the same level as the ones he had recorded in the 1970s?

"Same level, yes, but I'd say that twenty-five years ago, the musicians were playing well at maybe eighteen or twenty. Today, a 'young musician' is twenty-eight or thirty. There's a ten-year moratorium because their family lifestyle is a little bit high and both father and mother must work now, so if a person has some talent for music he or she must practice until they are twenty-seven or twenty-eight. Now, a twenty-eight-year-old musician is at the level that an eighteen-year-old was before. Now, they can learn jazz method or technique at a school such as Berklee, so they are . . . how shall we say? They play very nicely as far as *technique* goes. But they forget the most important thing about jazz—and that is having *tone*, having your own *sound*, not just imitation."

I mentioned talking with Masahiko Satoh.

"Masahiko Satoh plays every kind of music," Fuji responded. "He plays *everything*. And he has his very own style. *That* is very important. He is a very talented musician. Some of our musicians play on a major league level, but not so many. Most musicians here are three-A or two-A, or one-A maybe. But I want to work with both very talented three-A musicians and major league." He laughed. "Do you have this double CD album?"

He handed me *Sonnet and Spanish Flower* by the original Tee and Company all-star group, major leaguers indeed ("all eight musicians band *leaders* in their own right")—including my old friend from the Mt. Fuji Jazz Festival, Shuichi "Ponta" Murakami on drums! The double CD contains some of the most adventurous, free jazz performances I'd run across. "Sonnet," a full-scale blowout, starts with Masaru Imada's brooding piano, increases in both pace and volume, and then gets outrageously "Coltraneish," two tenors adding their own intonations and inclinations to that era's most obvious influence.

We discussed three other musicians Tee Fuji has recorded: trumpeter/flugelhornist Shunzo Ohno, tenor saxophonist Mikinori Fujiwara, and guitarist Takayuki Kato. And of course he loaded me up with their recordings, the profusion of gift CDs delightful but embarrassing (my emotional indebtedness, or *on,* growing by leaps and bounds). On *Maya,* all of the tunes, except Steve Wilson's "The Epicurean," are originals by Shunzo Ohno, who works in a tradition of restraint and discretion (he's smooth and spare, like fine Japanese lacquer craftsmanship), quite the opposite of the more extroverted approach of a Tiger Okoshi or Terumasa Hino. Introducing him in the liner notes, Tee Fuji claims that Ohno's "solo work on this album is brilliant and significant, as you will hear." Fuji also cites his "talent for composition." When Ohno moved to New York in 1974, he felt quite comfortable ("Many Japanese in foreign countries live with their eyes turned back to Tokyo," the record producer observes), until he cut his lips badly in a traffic accident. Healed (after a full year), he joined a group led by bassist Buster Williams. "Overcoming the accident has made him a more powerful artist," Fuji claims.

In 1989, Fuji called Mikinori Fujiwara "the most exciting tenor player on the present jazz scene. His style is deeply rooted in traditional mainstream jazz but is progressive in feeling." Mikinori Fujiwara was born in Omura, Nagasaki, and began to play at seventeen. He joined the Hideto Kanai Quintet in 1978, when he was just twenty-four years of age. After Kanai's group, he went on to become a member of Toshiyuki Miyama's New Herd and also played with Takeo Moriyama's quintet, the Native Sun. He is now a member of Three for Duke, a group that meets every Tuesday at the Jazzmen Club. Vibraphonist Ryozo Sugiura and Kanai join Fujiwara on his *Touch Spring* CD. The "exciting big tone" that Fuji praises is immediately apparent. Fujiwara can be both bold and bashful (whatever is called for) and seems at home with honks and ceiling screeches, pianist Hiroya Miyakawa providing wild excursions reminiscent of Don Pullen—the whole a balance between quite free and mainstream hard bop play. Although the tunes are mostly standards, Fujiwara can turn manic, even furious on occasion, and I liked the risks he was willing to take.

On *Guitar Music,* Takayuki Kato, with Hideto Kanai serving as guest artist on two numbers, also presents an impressive, near virtuoso account of himself. Jazz standards—Chick Corea's "What Was" and Monk's "Straight No Chaser"—are mixed with originals: "For Evans," "Autumn Now," "Life Force," and "My Sanctuary." The last four tunes show once again the Japanese—Tee Fuji–encouraged—proclivity for original composition, successfully carried off. "What Was" is acoustic, flamingo-orientated, and reveals virtuoso speed and taste, a sustained gypsy mood. "For Evans" must be for pianist Bill, given its introspective ease and grace, its unique harmonies. Listening to "Straight No Chaser," I wrote down, "Wow!" Fuji regards Kato as "one of the most noteworthy musicians on Japan's jazz scene." The Tokyo-born (1955) artist wanted—on this CD—to combine three elements: extensive improvisation on acoustic guitar, a solo track ("My One and Only Love"), and "free-form playing." Fuji notes that "unlike guitarist Kazumi Watanabe, who consistently makes honors with over 95 points on any musical problem, Takayuki sometimes achieves 100 points and sometimes nothing"—which means he is not wary of risk, which he takes, with bassist Kanai, on the CD's free-form piece, "Life Force."

Tee Fuji now asked me who my favorite Japanese jazz artists were, and I'll confess that—with the flood of practitioners I'd recently encountered—I was, for a short time, stumped. I mentioned the musicians I'd first heard in the States: Eiji Kitamura, Toshiko Akiyoshi, Makoto Ozone, Tiger Okoshi.

"And I liked, very much, what I heard of Isao Suzuki on CD before I left. Masahiko Satoh, of course. Junko Onishi. Masaru Imada. Kunihiko Sugano. And there were musicians I heard with Eiji. A young guitar player named Yoshiaki "Miya" Miyanoue. Kotaro Tsukahara. I heard him with another young pianist, Hideaki Yoshioka, before I came to Japan. I heard Kotaro and Hideaki play a duet. They kept running around, switching sides on the piano bench, enjoying themselves as much as the crowd enjoyed the exchange. I love piano music and I'm always looking out for good pianists . . ."

"I see, I see. Frankly speaking, Yoshioka and Tsukahara are very good players, and I like them, but—along with Yutaka Shiina, who is a newcomer, maybe twenty-eight or twenty-nine years old—they all seem to play the *same.* They are very clever, yes, but sometimes they sound like blues pianists, sometimes like McCoy Tyner, sometimes they play in other styles. I'm sorry to say this, for it seems they have genuine jazz *hearts,* but they haven't really found their own styles—so they are, to me, only two-A or three-A players, but not major league." He laughed. "I would recommend pianists who I feel have their very own style, who have originality, like Tsuyoshi Yamamoto, Masahiko Satoh, Fumio Karashima, Yosuke Yamashita, Masaru Imada. And there is a newcomer . . . Yuichi Inoue. He is not now in the major class, but I feel he has something original to offer."

"How about horn players? Mine?"

"Of course Kosuke Mine. And Ms. Sachi Hayasaka. A very strong lady saxophonist. Yoshio Otomo. Mikinori Fujiwara. And Joh Yamada."

"One last question," I said. "A critic writing in *Cadence* magazine suggested that, given the large number of Berklee College of Music graduates returning to Japan, a unique, and original, style of *Japanese* jazz is likely to emerge. Do you agree?"

"It's already a fact. That's my answer for you. Three Blind Mice recordings are heard all over the world. Only 35 to 40 percent of our LPs and CDs are sold in Japan. The rest—60 to 65 percent—are sold to consumers outside of Japan. In Asia, Europe, America. So perhaps some European jazz fans do not know the correct pronunciation of Tsuyoshi Yamamoto's name—I realize it is very difficult for them—but they recognize his sound. When they listen to our albums—good performance *and* fine recorded sound—they then associate that music with Japan. So *yes*, it is very possible for our musicians now to play with American major league musicians."

Because I had just one night left in Yokohama and wished to spend it listening to jazz on the town, I asked him about jazz clubs available. He said there were about ten clubs in Yokohama, and he gave me the names of some of them: Airgin (in Kannai), the Jazzmen Club (Yamashita-cho), Yoidore Hakushaku (Isezaki-cho), 491 (Yamashita-cho), Bar Bar Bar (Kannai), the Windjammer ("Chinatown"), and Little John (Isezaki-cho). So I was all set for some "cruisin'." Takeshi "Tee" Fuji said he'd like to join me, but that a previous family commitment stood in the way. I thanked him for his generosity of time granted—and CDs!—and I parted from one of the more interesting and delightful jazz aficionados I'd met so far in Japan.

23

THE FOREIGN CEMETERY, AN ART MUSEUM, AND A NIGHT ON THE TOWN WITH TEE FUJI

F OLLOWING MY CONVERSATION WITH TAKESHI "Tee" Fuji and before I left Yokohama, I managed to pack in a visit to the international cemetery located there, a trip to the art museum, and—much to my pleasant surprise—a night on the town with Tee Fuji. When I returned to the hotel on the day I talked to him, I found a message saying that the family obligations he'd mentioned were cancelled and that he would be happy to take me to his favorite jazz clubs. I eagerly accepted the invitation.

After we'd talked that first morning in the Kannai district, I'd followed the Nakamura River, which empties into Yokohama harbor, and climbed a hill that leads to the international cemetery. It is a stark reminder of the port city's curious history. Japan's doors were closed to most gaijin for more than two hundred years, but not long after Commodore Perry's black ships compelled the Tokugawa Shogunate to open them (reluctantly, in 1853), Townsend Harris, America's first diplomatic representative in Japan, set up a residence in the Hangakuji Temple in Kanagawa. Unfortunately, the site was one of fifty-three relay stations on the much-traveled Tokaido Road. The "unclean, long-haired barbarians" were not safe there, faced with the hostility of samurai who were willing to die in order to get rid of what they regarded as an "alien pestilence" (which is interesting in light of the warmhearted embrace of, and near reverence for, American jazz artists now in Japan). The Shogunate had its vulnerable guests moved to Yokohama, where they established a trading post in what was, at the time, a small fishing village suspended on mudflats.

The foreigners were confined to a compound guarded at checkpoints. One American took up permanent residence. A sailor with Perry's fleet, he chose a site for his grave and, when he died in 1854, was buried there. Since that time, the spot has been confined to non-Japanese graves, and four thousand, representing forty different nationalities, can be found. The compacted graves, set on a sloping hillside, many bearing stone crosses, sit solemnly in the sun. I paid my respects to these gaijin dead, then headed back to Minato-Mirai to visit the art museum I'd passed daily on my way to the Mt. Fuji Jazz Festival. I was intrigued by a large sculpted piece representing five grossly fat gaijin women with arms linked, frazzled hair flying (one sported a baseball cap), their breasts prominent in the toll gravity had taken on them or, in the case of the younger women, their flouncing jocularity. I thought of the warm reception jazz musicians now receive, realizing just how complex the Japanese perspective on *us* (Westerners) is, and how interesting.

That night I walked into the Jazzmen Club with Tee Fuji and was introduced to vibraphonist Ryozo Sugiura, owner of the club, then bassist Hideto Kanai. The former is loose and lanky. He wore a neatly pressed blue and white striped shirt and a gray golf cap. Kanai is short, squat, muscular, and wore a knit beige skullcap. I had heard both men on the *History of King Jazz Recordings* that Akira Tana had lent me back in the States. Hideto Kanai, a legendary artist, was well represented on a 1957 Midnight in Tokyo All-Stars performance of "Plug and Connector," with the Modern Jazz All-Stars (again in 1957), and with the winners of the *Swing Journal* Critics Poll 1958 All-Stars. He's also appeared on a large number of Three Blind Mice recordings. Sugiura is a less conspicuous presence on the *King Jazz Recordings,* but he does display his skill with the Midnight in Tokyo All-Stars in 1957 and with his own New Direction Quintet on "Citrus Season" in 1958.

Before their first set began (with a quartet fleshed out by pianist Hiroshi Tamura, whom I'd also encountered on Three Blind Mice Recordings, and drummer Hiroshi Yamazuki), Kanai, Tee Fuji, and I chatted for a while over scotch. Kanai seemed quite eager for conversation, asking many questions about my trip to the former Soviet Union (he had an upcoming gig with saxophonist Keshavan Maslak—also known as Kenny Millions—in Tokyo) and the professional jazz scene in the United States ("Are you free to play whatever sort of music you want?") and expressing his hope for a more "open" approach to the music in the future—some guarantee that artists will be able to do things their own way and still *survive*. It became obvious that Kanai had paid some heavy dues for his own predilections. He told me that he has "tried everything," performing all forms of jazz, all genres, from "free" to music employing traditional Japanese instruments, but that he's found—throughout his long and distinguished musical career—that "market considerations" too often prove to be "overwhelming."

"Muzukashii desu ka?" (Very difficult, no?) he said.

I couldn't have agreed more, although I may have been thinking of the solitary and occasionally seemingly thankless trade of *writing*, as well as playing jazz. I liked the man immediately. Throughout our discussion, Tee Fuji added to what we had talked about the previous day, how difficult it is "to make a new kind of music." He also said he felt traditional Japanese instruments were so set apart from "the jazz mainstream," so different from "the jazz spirit," that the two—"although it may be possible"—more than likely do not "mix." He said he loved "jazz blues" but asked, "How can you play *that* on a traditional Japanese instrument?" Such an attempted blend might provide a "subculture" in the jazz field someday but was not likely to enter the mainstream. Tee Fuji repeated his belief that in jazz "performance comes first, technique second." He bemoaned the fact that if he made a recording with someone like trumpeter Shunzo Ohno, he wanted to make a album that represented *him* and him alone. But because so many people place technical considerations above artistic, the results of the project would more than likely satisfy *audiophiles* more than musicians. Fuji kept pointing to his own head (with its flamboyant crop of white hair), suggesting the overriding importance of originality, of genuine feeling or *voice,* and he pledged again that he would continue his "life's work," attempting to represent the finest artists—such as Ohno and Kanai—until he was "sixty or sixty-five" (can one retire from the jazz trade?).

"Ganbatte!" (Never say die!) I said.

"Ganbatte," he repeated.

Hideto Kanai excused himself to go play some music.

The tunes the quartet played were mostly standards: "I'm Getting Sentimental Over You," "Don't Get Around Much Anymore," "Softly as in a Morning Sunrise," "There'll Never Be Another You." Kanai, no matter what he played, displayed the skill for which he is respected: unswerving rhythmic support yet solid invention (composing his own melodic lines on "Softly"), clever slapped accents, ostinato vamps, dynamics, color (a full palette of sound, from subdued or plaintive to exuberant double-stop strum or a nearly metallic "walk"). Sugiura, too, exhibited a fine range: four-mallet finesse coupled with a sharp sense of when and how to *swing*.

Tee Fuji's request for something *atarashii* (new), something outside the sphere of standards, sent the vibraphonist scouring through his "book," and the group played a piece with intricate broken rhythm (handsome drum fill, genuine shading, nothing overriding), Sugiura providing a thick (stony), tocking marimba sound on vibes. The group was good, and I had enjoyed talking with Hideto Kanai, but Tee Fuji wanted me to see, and hear, *all* that Yokohama had to offer in the way of jazz, so we said sayonara and headed for the Airgin.

When we walked into that nightspot, who should be performing there but guitarist Yoshiaki "Miya" Miyanoue, my friend from his visits to Monterey with Eiji Kitamura's various combos! Tee Fuji had kept this as an *odoroki* (surprise) for me and glowed now with pleasure. Miya was performing with his group Smokin', and when we walked in, they were deep into "Summertime," a tune they followed up with "'Round Midnight" (which I think, by that time, it was). Miya endowed the piece with a set of unique chords, even beyond those already ordained by Monk. Hideaki Yoshioka, the pianist I'd also heard in Monterey (playing duets with Kotaro Tsukahara), was part of the group, along with drummer Dairiki Hara, bassist Kiyoshi Ikeda, and a good trumpet player, Yasushi Miyamoto, I'd never heard before.

Never far from his warm thumb signature sound, Miya—on the up-tempo bop tune that followed—provided nimble octaves, slicing chords, bedazzling runs, all his customary magic, taken at a seemingly inhuman pace, then switched to a battered old Guild acoustic guitar he held flat in his lap, plucking it koto style, on a blues-inflected "When a Man Loves a Woman." If you ever want to hear Yoshiaki "Miya" Miyanoue at his best (a mark he's seldom far off of), treat yourself to a Paddle Wheel CD called—simply enough—*Yoshiaki!!* It features *two* guitarists: Miya and Yoshiaki Okayasu, a young artist—born in Tokyo in 1962—who once took lessons from Miya. They perform instrumental pieces written by musicians themselves (Kenny Dorham, Benny Golson, Horace Silver, Hank Mobley, Juan Tizol), tunes that afford them maximum improvisational opportunities. Dorham's "Lotus Blossom" contains quirky Asian rhythms, and the exchange between Miya (with his warm, visceral, slightly behind the beat, percussive, virtuoso style) and

Okayasu (with his pick-quick, precise, disengaged or "cool" in the manner of Kenny Burrell style) is fascinating. The "master" does not attempt to outclass his former pupil. This duel is conducted at ease. Out of mutual respect, the two echo, paraphrase, and parody one another, and the results are delightful. They do chase each other (aptly enough) on "Chasing the Bird," and that's delightful too. A Miyanoue original, "Touch of a Little Dream" (a, yes, *pretty* piece), is shared by both guitarists, Miya comping Okayasu's improv with a nearly Hawaiian (ukulele) strum, the melodic configurations of each player handsomely laced together at the close. The CD itself closes out with a spunky "Funk in Deep Freeze" (a Hank Mobley tune), featuring Yasushi Miyamoto of Smokin' on trumpet, and a JATP-influenced romp on "Perdido." The two guitarists pull out all the stops on the last tune, taken at a breakneck pace. Their question and answer chase scene, both jeering and gentle, contains some wonderfully unruly counterpoint.

It was great to see and hear Yoshiaki "Miya" Miyanoue again, especially in the intimate Airgin setting—on his own turf—in Japan. The crowd loved him and his group, and it was good to see that too! After his last set, we chatted, and then I thanked Takeshi "Tee" Fuji once again for his generosity of time and friendship. I was grateful to be spending my last night in Yokohama with two people who, each in his own way, had contributed so much to jazz in Japan. But I was already thinking of the train I would catch for my trip to Nikko tomorrow.

NIKKO AND THE ALBATROSS SWING JAZZ ORCHESTRA

Arriving in Nikko by train, I took a cab from the station to the Annex Turtle Hotori-an, a *ryokan* a few miles outside of town. My room was small and simple (tatami mat, futon, tea set) and offered a view of a cemetery on a hillside across from a river. The latter, mildly torrential, roared agreeably, and I dubbed the sound *kawa no uta* (the song of the river). The walk into town was delightful. A Japanese proverb states, "Nikkō wo miru made kekkō to iu na" (Think nothing splendid until you have seen Nikko), and I could see why. The river nested among green hills, mist-laden ghostly mountains in the distance, yellow flowers in bloom alongside the bank. The river picked up momentum, its color now a turgid dark green. Just outside of town, the brilliantly vermilion Shinkyo, or sacred bridge, stands. It was built in 1636 for shoguns and imperial messengers to cross on their way to Toshogu Shrine, the home—or eternal resting place in this case—of Ieyasu Tokugawa, the man who succeeded in uniting all of Japan in 1600. Ordinary mortals were not permitted on the bridge, but today you can trade your mortal status in for divinity at three hundred yen a pop and walk across.

I visited Toshogu Shrine and paid homage to Gohotendo Hall (which houses Benten, patroness of music and the arts) and saw the Holy Stable (its carved panel containing the famous "Hear no evil, see no evil, speak no evil" monkeys) and Kaguraden, a hall where the ceiling hosts paintings of *tennin* (Buddhist angels) playing harps. Another hall called Haiden (the Oratory) contains paintings of thirty-six great poets. If you pay 430 yen (which I did), you can climb the two hundred stone steps that lead to the tomb of Ieyasu Tokugawa, a remarkable man and genuine hero in my eyes.

But I had come to Nikko primarily to see Masao Ishii, leader of the Albatross Swing Jazz Orchestra (a group I first heard in Monterey, where they appeared with Eiji Kitamura). I planned to meet him and some members of the band at the Kanaya Hotel—"the oldest hotel in Japan," I had been told by at least one source. *Fodor's* doesn't mention this but does describe the hotel as "a little worn around the edges." I was greeted by five people: Masao Ishii, a handsome, well-dressed man who is leader, tenor saxophonist, and emcee for the big band; tall, lanky pianist Ryoichi Yamaguchi; another tenor saxophonist, rather shy, Masahiro Saito; trumpeter Sachiyo Nagata, pert and pretty in a summer dress; and a very pleasant female interpreter whose name, I'll confess, I did not jot down and have forgotten. After a suitable period of bowing and exclaiming "Shibaraku deshita!" (So good to see you; it's been a long time!) we went into a large room where, not far from a grand piano, we sat in comfortable chairs. Because I knew Masao Ishii and had heard the others play but had just met them, I suggested they tell me a little about themselves. Pianist Ryoichi Yamaguchi, in real life, turns out to be a teacher. He teaches, he said in English, in a junior high school. Then, in Japanese, he said, "Yoroshiku!" (Pleased to meet you!) The others laughed, as did he. Masahiro Saito said he played tenor saxophone and worked as a public servant. When I asked in what capacity, he turned shy and simply handed me his *meishi,* one that showed a photo of a country road ambling between lush green vegetation and tall trees. It read, "General Affairs Division, Imaichi City Hall."

"My name is Sachiyo Nagata," the woman in the summer dress said. "I play trumpet."

"Anata no shigoto nan desu ka?" (And what sort of work do you do?) I managed to get out.

"I am a piano instructor and a housewife," she replied.

Masao Ishii, too, works as a "public servant," but the card he gave me only says "band leader," so I never discovered exactly what, outside of that capacity, he does. He was clearly the leader, and, maintaining his high public profile throughout our time together, he served as primary spokesperson for the group. I asked how the Albatross Swing Jazz Orchestra got started, and Masao Ishii replied.

"The band was started about fifteen years ago, with only four or five members. The music we played together was Japanese music only, but one day we all started listening to jazz. We changed our direction and decided to try to make our own music of this jazz. The members were able to understand what to play because we had the *papers* [charts]. Having these papers, we decided to make our group a big band, so we asked around, 'Who can play instrumental music in this area?' We eventually all came together to make up a big band. There was a group in this area and they were playing Count Basie's music—from his original charts. Most of our music comes from 'record copy' [transcriptions]. *Tokidoki ano* [Well, sometimes] we use arrangements done by professionals."

"Does anyone in the band do any arranging?"

"No one." They all laughed. "They cannot do that."

I was curious as to how these dedicated amateurs—all of whom play on a very professional level but also have amateur status, holding down day jobs—first got interested in jazz. Pianist Ryoichi Yamaguchi offered his story first:

"When I was at the university I got interested in, and wanted to play like, the Eagles, a rock group. But I could not find any written music of theirs. Then I wanted to play more in the jazz vein, not just *light* music. I was first influenced by Bill Evans."

When I asked if he'd studied music formally, Yamaguchi said, "Oh no. Only myself."

I turned to Sachiyo-san. "I'm curious as to how a piano teacher ends up playing trumpet."

"When I was in high school," she replied, "I was a member of the school band. At that time I already played trumpet. It was a brass band and we did not play jazz. I played jazz by myself. I was playing some jazz music on the piano. I do like Oscar Peterson."

"Some music is very *muzukashii* [difficult] to try, so she tries it," said Masao Ishii, and they all laughed. "And sometimes she plays piano *here,* at the hotel."

"How long have you been with the big band?" I asked Sachiyo-san.

"Fourteen years."

"The band has not changed since you heard us in Monterey," Masao Ishii said.

I asked Masahiro Saito about his discovery of jazz.

"There were many musicians I liked listening to: Michael Brecker, Johnny Griffin, Sonny Rollins, John Coltrane . . ."

I asked if both Mr. Saito and Mr. Ishii took solos on tenor sax with the band.

"We both solo," Masao Ishii replied, "but I play by charts, and he plays ad lib. As a band, we give one concert a year. It is in a concert hall and around a thousand people attend. It's in the next city over. The members of our band come from five or six different cities. We rehearse *shū ni kai* [twice a week]. We introduce about twenty new pieces each year. *Minna hanashiamashita* [Everybody discusses this]. But, because of their various work schedules, it is difficult to get *everyone* together at one time. Our problem is, we almost *never* have all the members there."

How did the trip to Monterey come about?

"Eiji Kitamura arranged that for us. He invited us to accompany him on Mr. Bill Berry's International Jazz Party tour. We really like to go to the United States, because jazz is *real* there!"

"Is that so?" the translator said, turning to me.

"I *hope* so!" We all laughed. "It's not real in Japan also?"

Masahiro Saito: "I was in America in 1992, and I listened to bands there, amateur bands such as ours. The most important thing, I think, was they seemed to be *enjoying* themselves so much when they played. That seems to be the major difference between amateur bands there and here—and they played very well. Although they did sound too loud for me."

Sachiyo Nagata: "The sound of the American big bands comes *together*. It is as if it is just *one sound*. When I listen to big bands in Japan, the sound doesn't seem to come together at one point as it does in the American bands."

Masao Ishii: "I feel there isn't a big difference when we are playing music from a big band chart. The American and Japanese bands are *onaji* [the same]. But when you think about how much the Americans seem to be enjoying playing jazz, you realize that most Japanese have just *started* listening to this music, or learning the music from Japanese popular music bands, but not jazz. They are just entering this music; they are really just beginning to study it. Americans are *born* as jazz musicians, so that's why the feeling is so different. That's why they can relax and simply enjoy the music so much."

Ryoichi Yamaguchi: "What I heard in America is not like what I listen to in Japan, but maybe that's because the level of sophistication in a concert is, because of the demands of my *shigoto* [day job], so different from all the difficulties we went through in our rehearsal or practice sessions."

Ishii [smiling]: "The situation is complex."

Yamaguchi: "When you hear jazz being played in a foreign country, strictly by *foreigners,* there's bound to be a big difference! I have so many different impressions of America. And I always feel a little bit *dumb* there."

Ishii: "We have *inai* [no one] with actual professional experience. Such people are affiliated with a school of music. Or a university or high school. They do not take courses in music. They just enjoy participating in what is like a musical society or club."

I mentioned that, in amateur bands in the States, there might be good *tight* section work—saxophone and brass sections—but that improvised solos were not always so strong. Was it difficult to find people who have experience playing solos in Japan?

"Here, when they start out, amateur bands only play from charts," Masao Ishii said, "practicing and practicing and practicing from charts, so that is why they do so well in an ensemble. But playing a solo is so much more *complex*. When I'm playing a solo, I don't really know what I'm doing! I just follow my fingers as they move."

As we talked, Masao Ishii handed me programs from Albatross Swing Jazz Orchestra performances over the past three years: handsome programs that contained considerable evidence of sponsorship (advertising)—the big band's name embossed, on a slick black cover, in slanting, white, calligraphically appealing English letters, beneath which soared a spotted bird that bore a more striking resemblance to Jonathan Livingston Seagull, perhaps, than to the creature that hounded Samuel Taylor Coleridge. He also gave me the complete score for an original work by composer Kenichi Tsunoda, untitled as of yet, an immense manuscript with all instrumental parts included.

"We wanted to do some original music this year," he said, passing this "baby" to me with the concern and care of a doting father. Once I'd received it, I held the thick score as delicately as I could. "So we asked a professional musician to compose an original piece. The composer is

Mr. Kenichi Tsunoda. He was playing with the Tokyo Union Orchestra, one of the famous big bands in Japan. The piece doesn't have a title yet."

"Muzukashii desu ne?" (Is it difficult?)

"Hmmm, *mada ne* [as yet] we have not played it. The score just arrived yesterday, and even the members of the band do not yet know about it." They all laughed. "I would like you to have this score, please. In America, *daijōbu* [okay]. In Japan, not yet published."

I asked if the band would perform pieces other than the commissioned work by Kenichi Tsunoda at its October concert.

"We will play a lot of Count Basie, because Japanese fans think he's *ichiban*," Masao Ishii said. "They love his music. We have original Japanese arrangements, and we will have a Count Basie special. We do that. Sometimes it's for a particular musician, sometimes for a composer, like Duke Ellington."

"Will you do 'Shiny Stockings'?" I asked. It's one of my favorite Count Basie tunes.

"'Shiny Stockings.' Yes. We do that piece very well, I think. That's *our* kind of music. Do you know 'Wind Machine' by Count Basie? That's the piece I think we do best. Very *fast.* It's our specialty. Enjoyment is the most important part. If we couldn't enjoy what we are doing, we wouldn't continue doing it."

I mentioned that, in the States, professional musicians need to find work as often as they can just to stay *alive,* then added that it was great that the band could get together two or three nights a week, play serious music and give concerts, and have a solid public following. I told them about Mr. Satoh, the *sararīman* amateur vibraphonist who had sat in with the pros at Kiyoko Ami's Scotch and Jazz club. He had been studying for ten years, I said, and sounded very good.

"Eiji Kitamura often says that in Japan," Masao Ishii responded, "we don't have any line between the amateur and the professional. The only real distinction is that one group gets some money for what they do. That's all that makes them professional. If he doesn't get paid, he's an amateur. That's all."

Thinking that this is a healthy approach, and that in the United States, if you're a performer with amateur status, professionals tend to feel you're taking up space where *they* ought to be, I mentioned that at the Swing Club in Ginza, Kotaro Tsukahara had invited me to come up and say a few words about my project in Japan and then had actually let me play a duet on "Ain't Misbehavin'" with him. At the time I'd thought, "Wow, man! I've just played in a club in Tokyo!"

"Sometimes," Masao Ishii said, "Kotaro-san has said to us, 'Please come to the club, and bring your instruments too!' We become a jam session band!"

I asked them about the future. What will the Albatross Swing Jazz Orchestra be doing in another fifteen years (the period of time most of the present members have been with the band)?

"We would like to practice much more and come as close as we can to the professional level of musicians in America," said Masahiro Saito.

"Do you practice often at home yourself, or is your job too demanding to make that possible?"

"I don't get to practice at home at all." He laughed; they all did. "I just come to rehearsal twice a week! I don't have any other free time."

"This is a very difficult time for professional big bands in Japan," said Ryoichi Yamaguchi. "Most of them find it very hard to continue. So the professional big bands in Japan are actually *supported* by amateur bands. There are over two thousand amateur bands in Japan, so perhaps *this* is what will become our Japanese music. Perhaps jazz is no longer just American music but is becoming true Japanese music."

"That's been my feeling for some time," I said. "When I was traveling in the former Soviet Union, I felt that jazz had truly become an *international* language—a language for each nation that plays it."

"Yet *swing* music is a very different thing for us," said Yamaguchi. "Japanese *counting* is very regular. The emphasis is even: one, two, three, four. But swing music has a very different rhythm." He clapped on the off beat, on two and four, the "secret" or trick of syncopation. "Japanese people tend to experience swing in the mind, rather than in the body."

"Of course swing music was *dance* music when it got started in America. That explains the popularity of Fletcher Henderson, Chick Webb, Jimmy Lunceford, Duke Ellington. Of Benny Goodman, Artie Shaw, and Glenn Miller. They were all popular dance bands. Is that why swing music is so popular in Japan? Is it dance music, or is it more like concert hall music?"

"Only concerts," said Masao Ishii. "In Japan now, we tend to divide big band music into that which is strictly for dancing and swing music for listening, as in a concert hall setting. There is a definite division between the two, so they do not come together. Dance music is played only by what we call a 'dance music band.'"

222

When our interview was over, after an extended round of bowing, choreographed thanks, the five members of the Albatross Swing Jazz Orchestra escorted me outside, where, standing in a row on the steps that led up to the Kanaya Hotel, we had our group photo taken by the translator.

A videotape that Masao Ishii gave me of an Albatross December concert opens with the view of a stage bathed in blinking blue lights. The words "Albatross" and "Jazz in Yiata" are inscribed on a wall behind the band, which is decked out in white, except for Masao Ishii, who wears a black tux. He comes down front to say "Konban wa" (Good evening) to the audience and then greets the inevitable *bijin* who strolls out on stage and, in the prescribed jovial manner, introduces the band leader as such. The Albatross Swing Jazz Orchestra then launches into its theme song, "Take the 'A' Train," on which trumpeter/piano instructor/housewife Sachiyo Nagata stands up for the plunger mute break made famous by Ray Nance. The tunes that follow include Bobby Timmons's "Moanin'," "Wind Machine," and "On the Sunny Side of the Street" (announced in Japanese as "Akarumi no dōri," which translates roughly as "Lighted Spot of Street")—jazz standards, but with an interesting touch added, one an American audience might find strange.

The female emcee introduces and explains each section of the orchestra to the Japanese audience, starting with the trombones, asking one musician to reenact the instrument's most prominent action ("Slide, damn you, slide!" although that's not the way she says it), which he does to her satisfaction, the *bijin* laughing, saying, "Kekkō desu!" (That's enough!) A trumpet player stands up and does his thing; then the rhythm section does theirs, the drummer smiling as he cuts loose with a vivid march pattern. Last but not least come the saxes: Masao Ishii holding his tenor aloft, the baritone sax player blowing a single deep scruffy note that makes the emcee giggle as if she's being tickled. She then says thank you (in Japanese, of course). It's a remarkable performance and makes me think of Akira Tana's statement about the failure of Japanese jazz education. There may not be a college such as Berklee for individual players, but I've never seen an American audience subjected to this sort of exegesis before. Perhaps they wouldn't sit still for it, even if they needed it. I thought of all those people—myself included—who attended operas for years pretending they knew what the hell was going on in Italian or German but really didn't until subtitles came along!

Following my interview with the members of the Albatross Swing Jazz Orchestra, I walked back through the town of Nikko and found a noodle shop open, one advertised as "The Best in Nikko." It *was*. The shop was owned by an overtly friendly woman who not only fed me delicious udon noodles but with whom I had—much to my surprise—my most successful extended conversation, totally in Japanese, so far. The shop was a small, dark, but cozy enclosure with no more than four tables, a sort of cottage or hut, but its walls were decorated with signatures of which the matron was immensely proud. She pointed out those members of the Boston Symphony who'd performed in Nikko, American opera stars who'd appeared here, and various other international luminaries—musical and otherwise—who had once partaken of her noodles. The walls also displayed fierce woodcut-print black and white faces of Kabuki actors and samurai. The owner seemed genuinely interested in my jazz quest in Japan (especially whatever had drawn me to an outlying spot such as Nikko), and I was sorry to have to leave her excellent company, and noodles. We parted outside a woodcut-adorned *noren* (a half-curtain in the doorway of the shop).

On the walk back to my *ryokan,* I had the voice of the river—*kawa no uta*—for a companion. Its song stayed with me through the night, even in sleep. I had answered, first with the Monterey Jazz Festival in Noto and now with my visit to Nikko and the Albatross Swing Jazz Orchestra, another of the questions suggested by Akira Tana's thesis. Did jazz exist, and was its "expressive value recognized even in quite remote areas"? The answer was affirmative.

25

Nagoya: "Love Rescues the Earth," the Castle, Donny Schwekediek, Star Eyes, Jazz Aster, and Swing

When the train entered Nagoya I saw, posted on the side of a building, large letters that read "ENGLISH WELLNESS PREP SCHOOL." This became my favorite use, or misuse, of English in Japan, although I had collected others in my notebook that would, I felt, make fine titles for bebop tunes or perhaps even the names of jazz groups: Hotel New Yours, the Mix-Up Club, the Luminous Nose, Music House, Mary and Lamb, Sugar Ray, the Sing, Cool Jo Jo, Chat House, Lounge NASA, Joe Cool, Monkey Banana, It Inn, Heart-Inn (definitely a love hotel, very popular places for assignations in Japan), Play City Carrot (perhaps the same?!), Fit Cave (no comment!), Creative Catch Surf Gear, Bar Ber (the English words separated by a pair of scissors), Salty Sugar Tea Spot, Coffee Shop P.P.

When I arrived in Nagoya, strolling through a park on my way to Nagoyajo Castle, I stumbled upon a "24 Hour Television" public rally in an area called (in English) "Central Plaza." Once again, Japan's gift for extraordinary juxtapositions didn't let me down. A vocal rock group made up of what appeared to be three teenage girls performed on a huge stage, aglitter in daylight (illumination that might prove sufficient for an NFL *Monday Night Football* game) with tiers of red, orange, and blue lights. The sizeable crowd gathered was in a festive mood, sampling food offered at several booths, strolling or just standing about, watching the proceedings. A group of young people wearing "TV Staff" orange T-shirts was setting up a "ONE LOVE" display, surrounded by a battery of cameras; another group was stringing up signs that said "Love Rescues the Earth."

Just outside the castle, I discovered an impressive statue of Kiyomasa Kato, a man so honored because, having been commanded by Ieyasu Tokugawa to construct the walls of this impressive edifice, he supervised the task standing atop one of the many stones being hauled, waved his war fan, and—music everywhere in Japan as usual—personally "called the tune," inciting the men drawing the carts to *sing* a lumber carrier's chant. In Nagoya, I followed the pattern I'd set up elsewhere: temples, shrines, museums (or castles) by day; jazz clubs at night. The sightseeing allowed me time to reflect on my entire "jazz journey to Japan" thus far. A quiet tree-shrouded walkway led to Atsuta Jingu Shrine, one of the three most important shrines in Japan, housing—as it does—the Kusamagi-no-tsurugi (Grass-Mowing Sword), one of three items that make up the imperial regalia. Tucked away in another residential area, I found the Arako-Kannon Temple, a small, modest complex designated a "National Treasure" because it houses twelve hundred wooden Buddhas carved by an itinerant monk named Enku. I also found a fairly large complex, Osu-Kannon, a colorful site with steps leading up to a sanctuary covered by a silver two-tiered roof, the buildings bright red, tall white banners inscribed with black kanji crackling in a not-so-gentle wind. I felt as if I'd stepped into the setting for a film by Kurosawa. Wandering through a shopping mall not far from the temple, I found a handsome *shakuhachi* for forty-five hundred yen, but I didn't buy it (and later of course, at home once more, I wished I had!).

That evening, I went to the Star Eyes Club to meet American pianist Donny Schwekediek, who's made Japan his permanent home. Walking into the club, the first thing I noticed was a substantial list of musicians who'd performed there, posted on the wall: Art Farmer and the Great Jazz Trio (Hank Jones, Eddie Gomez, Jimmy Cobb), Mal Waldron, Duke Jordan, Mulgrew Miller, Danny Richmond, Michel Petrucciani, Joe Henderson, Ray Drummond, Niels-Henning Ørsted Pedersen, and many others. Donny, bassist Hiroyuki Kitagawa, and drummer Yasuyuki Sawatari were playing "Come Rain or Come Shine" when I came in. Donny is a large man with a fleshy face, substantial jaw (somewhat shy of Jay Leno's), and a full mane of black hair. He was dressed in jeans, black T-shirt, black sport coat. Hunched over the piano, he played a mix of lush block chords and intelligent runs, his touch reminiscent of Red Garland's (one of my favorite jazz pianists and, as it would turn out—not surprisingly—one of Donny's too). Bill Evans's "Waltz for Debby" was next, the bassist, perusing a chart, providing fine, spontaneous support and a solid solo the drummer might have backed off on a bit more, as Donny did. Announcing tunes, Donny spoke in English, even though his Japanese—after nine years—is excellent. "We'd like to play a beautiful ballad for you now," he said, "'Never Let Me Go.'" The trio's smooth groove elicited a piercing whistle of praise from an appreciative—and slightly inebriated—customer. When the set ended, Donny came to my table and introduced himself. Tracing his personal history, he mentioned his daughter, and I asked if that was the polite, charming girl I'd talked to that morning on the phone.

"Yeah. She'll be eight next month. She was born in Nagoya, right after we got here. So I was more or less *entrenched,* as it were."

"Tell me when you came, why you came, and why you stayed . . ."

"I first came to Japan about nine and a half years ago," Donny said. "I was in southern Japan, in a town called Kumamoto. There was a jazz club there, and the manager decided to hire American musicians. He was a drummer, so he went to San Francisco looking for a pianist and bassist, and he bumped into me. I was playing in various places on the, you know, 'local scene.' Not big stuff or anything like that. I lived in Berkeley, so I played a lot there and in San Francisco. I came to Japan on a four-month contract, and we ended up extending it to six months. And I ended up getting married during that time!"

"I've heard that story often from Americans in Japan."

"Well I really fell in love with Japan—if for no other reason than the music scene. Not individual players so much, but the fact that the people here sort of got *stuck* in the stuff from the mid-fifties to the mid-sixties, the hard bop era. And that's what I like, so I felt really comfortable. I wanted to live in another country anyway—just to experience that. At the time, to be honest, I didn't really care which country it was. My wife and I got married, went back to San Francisco, but I knew I wanted to return. A club in this city, Nagoya, offered me a two-month contract, and I thought, 'Well, that will get my way paid back to Japan and then maybe I can put something together.' I ended up working at that club for three years. It's not around now, but it wasn't far from here.

It had a great name: the Shanghai Ja Ja Club. I ended up being the house pianist. We booked singers and bass players out of the San Francisco Bay area. I did most of the booking myself, and I got people I knew."

"And the club was willing to foot the bill for that?"

"Oh yeah, sure. It was at the time of the bubble economy. Right before the bubble burst. The club was actually owned by a Korean barbecue chain. They were making money hand over fist with their restaurants. The owner had a place in San Francisco and also lived in L.A. for a couple of years. So she liked the States and she liked things American. She opened a club in Nagoya, and that's how I ended up in *this* city. Unfortunately, they were on the bottom floor of an apartment, and they kept getting complaints about the sound. The club was running just a bit below the break-even point, so they had to bag on live music. After that, I came to Star Eyes. I've been here for three years."

I asked Donny about the number of jazz clubs in Nagoya.

"At this point—programming live jazz every night, with groups— I'd put it at *three*. There's Jazz Inn Lovely. Star Eyes. And the club I was just talking about, Swing. There are numerous other small places, tiny, with just a piano. They may do piano and a singer a couple of nights a week. And there's another place down the road from here which has bass, piano, and vocals—stuff like that. So that might bring it up to, say, *ten* places to play. The drummer this evening has his own jazz club in Gifu city, which is close by."

Donny mentioned two other cities not too far away in which he'd played: Okazaki and Yokaichi ("about an hour's drive away—a nice jazz club"). I commented, once more, on what appeared to be a very healthy jazz scene in Japan.

"It is. Another club in town I wish I could take you to is the one called Swing. It's run by the granddaddy of jazz guitar in Nagoya. He's actually known all over the country. His name is Wada Sunao. He's really good. He's considered a blues guitar player, but he's straight out of the Wes Montgomery–type thing, and bebop. He's got his own place and it's a really interesting place." (Actually we *would* go there before the night was out.)

I asked if he were house pianist at Star Eyes.

"Oh no no no. I play here three or four times a month. And every time I play it's in a different setting. I book under my own name for about three of those nights, but I also work with different singers. One singer once a month. On other nights I play with either a trio or quartet. Tonight just so happens to be the drummer's gig. In spite of the healthy scene, and not unlike the States, it *is* difficult to support yourself playing jazz here, but I'm doing it. Again, as in the States, the first person who's going to be able to pull it off is a pianist. Because you can do gigs by yourself. There's always the piano there, usually. So that makes it easy. But it's tough for bassists. And for drummers it's pretty much impossible."

I said that the young bassists I'd heard so far had impressed me but that the musicians who'd impressed me the least, I was sorry to say— especially if it's rough for them to find gigs—were drummers. I hadn't heard any who could compare to a Billy Higgins with his subtle sense of "shading" (supporting other players, truly interacting with them), dynamics, and genuine taste.

"There are a couple," Donny said, laughing, "but they *are* few and far between. As a matter of fact, one is a drummer I'd been working with for the last three years. He's a branch manager—or something like that—with Yamaha. You know how Japanese companies are: always transferring their employees after about two or three years. It's standard procedure. They no longer let people stay in one place forever, or it's rare that they do. This guy was a branch manager, but he was also a drummer in town, and we'd been working on and off together for three years, in various settings. But he just got transferred to Tokyo! We played our last gig last week, and I'm really in a fix right now. There are a couple of other players I can work with, but they don't have a broad enough *range* to do all the things I'd like to do. This guy was a really good player and had a wide spectrum, but such players *are* few and far between."

I mentioned that I'd gone to the club Jazz Inn Lovely the previous night and that I'd heard a trio with smooth Nat "King" Cole Trio rapport but that when a drummer sat in for the second set, he was totally out of sync with them.

"It's funny you say that, because I had the exact same experience last week at the place I mentioned, Swing. I was playing with Wada-san, the guitar player. Him and a bass player, a young guy I really like. We played a first set and it was *groovin' so hard*—really swingin'! No drums. Again, as you just said, I immediately thought of the Nat 'King' Cole Trio. Maybe Ahmad Jamal's guitar trio, stuff like that. But then, for the second set, a drummer came and sat in. The bass player got so bummed out, he said, 'I wish that guy hadn't come!' He was an okay drummer, but, but . . ."

"How about Japanese musicians in general?" I mentioned Tiger Okoshi's baseball analogy, his feeling that Japanese jazz artists—because jazz has become an international language—were now playing in the major leagues.

"There's a smaller number of major league players in Japan, compared to the number of people who play. But I'm sure that's probably true in the States too. Yet in the States I find that, on the local level, there are a lot of really good players that just never made it in the major leagues. And they're never going to because there's just not *room*. Here, I think there's a really large gap between the number-one cat and the other guys on the local level. Of course jazz was born in America and it will always be an American art form, as it were, but the players here have . . . well, they have quite a bit of a complex about that, okay? 'Well, we weren't *born* listening to jazz, so we have this handicap that we will carry with us for life.' And I always tell them, 'Hey, that's a big mistake.' In *my* case, I grew up listening to country-western music, because that's what my dad listened to. I didn't even hear jazz until I was maybe sixteen or seventeen. So I don't claim some sort of *right* to jazz. Most of the Japanese players have been listening to jazz longer than *I* have!"

"Have you heard musicians like Masahiko Satoh and Yosuke Yamashita? They seem to be very unusual in that they're truly doing *their own thing*."

"Oh yeah, cats at that level aren't trippin' like the others are. At least the ones I've met. But a lot of the musicians below that level are."

I mentioned Masahiko Satoh's ideas on the American educational system as opposed to the Japanese: you can get an A+ in music and an F in History in the U.S., whereas in Japan, education is more across the board—they're not out to produce the exception.

"Right, right. And you can see that when you look at sports. Baseball, for example. I think that if you sent a Japanese high school team to the States, they'd be kickin' butt, because everything would come down to the *technical* level. But from that point on is where the physical and mental kicks in. I think of athletes the same way I think of artists. In the long run, you have to do what you *feel*. You build your technique, and when you mature, you go with your instincts. The technique is already there, but there's that *leap*, that really difficult leap you have to make, and some people can't do it. It's a function of the educational system. No question about it, there is this quelling of originality at the early stages in Japan. People are afraid to be thought of as different. Really afraid. Of course there are exceptions . . ."

I said that, after being there for a month and a half, I had just discovered that in front of the spot, the *exact* spot, where each car stops in a subway station, there are *footprints* painted to show people where to queue up. An ex–New Yorker (from Brooklyn, no less), I'd been standing off to one side so I could make my rush to the door. But the Japanese match their shoes up with those marks exactly and *wait*. Of course there's that rush-hour exception in Tokyo of getting crammed into cars . . .

"Right, right. People here won't cross against a red light, even if there are no automobiles coming. *I* do it all the time. I call it the 'gaijin strut.' I'm going to do the gaijin strut! Speaking of which, hey, I've got to go back and play, okay? I'll be back."

The audience at Star Eyes consisted of two seemingly drunk *sararīman* slackening off on coffee, a man sitting at a table next to mine (he was nursing a bottle of Jack Daniels), a talkative couple, and two young women, one of whom, quite attractive with long smooth blue-black hair, would provide a surprise performance of her own before the evening's end. The trio opened the second set with "Speak Low," the drummer breaking into a wide smile when Donny slipped into a compelling Gene Harris groove, the piano rocking beneath the weight of thick blues trills and percussive chords, no fragile touch on this one. After, Donny announced the tune as " 'Speak Low' . . . which is exactly what we didn't do," but they did on the next tune (a request), "You Don't Know What Love Is." The young woman with her friend with fine long hair clapped in glee. After saying, "Here's one of my favorite tunes, and it just happens to be a request," Donny played Cole Porter's "Every Time We Say Goodbye"—for me.

When he returned to my table, we discussed the jazz coffeeshops, or what he called *kissaten,* popular in Japan in the 1960s and 1970s.

"Records were too expensive to buy," Donny said. "In the Japanese lingo, the shops were called *jazu kissa.* They were all equipped with those huge speakers you see over there."

He pointed to a large pair of speakers over by a shelf that housed LPs. I mentioned the impressive collection.

"Oh yeah," Donny responded. "The owner has probably got five times that many at his house. When he started out, about thirteen years ago, half of this place was a jazz *kissaten,* and he had live music only a couple of days a week. The musicians would come to these coffeeshops, and regular listeners as well, because you couldn't find live shows or music. So the mood, or atmosphere, in these places was just like that of a live performance! Also, a cup of coffee cost three hundred yen, which it still does today, but at the time that was a huge sum of money. You'd sit at your table and drink *one* cup of coffee, quietly listening to the music. The musicians would be transcribing solos, but only from a record! They didn't have anything else. They couldn't afford to buy the recordings. They couldn't even listen to them *twice.* They had to get it *just that once* [excellent ear training!]. Some of those jazz *kissaten* are still around today. If you're game, we can hang out after and find one. I don't know what your schedule is . . ."

I told Donny I was scheduled to leave at ten in the morning—still, I was game!

"I'll take you to the granddaddy of all Nagoya *kissas.* It's been in business now for over thirty years! To be honest with you, I've never been there myself. It's famous. When I was in Kumamoto, after we played the first night, the drummer did take me to a place just down the street. Kumamoto is a town of about five hundred thousand. In the States we'd consider that a halfway decent *city,* but in Japan they consider it *country.* He took me to this little place down in a basement, and all of a sudden there was this *wall* covered with LPs. When I walked in the guy was playing the Three Sounds, with Lou Donaldson. *L. D. Plus 3*—one of my favorite records! I thought I'd died and gone to heaven."

I mentioned that Michael Cuscuna said that he thinks Japan kept jazz alive in the 1970s single-handedly when it was dying out in the States.

"No question about it! That brings me back to a point I'd like to make. In that same period, Art Blakey came over to play here. He brought over that *killing* band with Bobby Timmons, Wayne Shorter, Lee Morgan—the one that made *The Big Beat* and all those other great recordings. They were doing 'Moanin',' and the timing was perfect, because it was after Elvis had died out and before the Beatles hit. 'Moanin'' in Japan was like a number-one hit tune! In America, nobody outside jazz circles has heard of 'Moanin',' and even a few people there

232

don't know who Bobby Timmons was, or at least not as much as they should. But there's not a person in Japan, young or old, who doesn't know 'Moanin'.' Even kids in their twenties, because to this day it's still used on radio commercials and stuff like that. Art Blakey was like a *pop star!* That song was on the radio every day, and *that* put jazz on the map here—on a huge 'pop hit' level in the early and mid-sixties, just the time when the music was taking a nose dive in the States. Late fifties, early sixties hard bop is still the major image of jazz here. One backlash of that is there's just a very small body of work, a small group of tunes known, and lots of times they're tunes that were never big in the States."

I asked if he could give me some examples.

"Sure. Two really huge tunes on the scene here are Mal Waldron's 'Left Alone'—a monster jazz hit in Japan—and Helen Merrill's 'You'd Be So Nice to Come Home To.' Helen Merrill was a major hit here. Another tune is Bud Powell's 'Cleopatra's Dream.' *That's* a huge hit here. When I first arrived, someone requested 'Left Alone,' but I'd never even heard it before! I got so many requests for it that I went out and bought a Japanese fake book, one I found in a little music store in Kumamoto. Mal Waldron was Billie Holiday's last accompanist, right? And he wrote 'Left Alone' for her. She composed the lyrics for it while she was riding on an airplane, but she passed away before she could record it. As recorded by Mal Waldron, with Jackie McLean on alto saxophone, it's a beautiful tune, but nobody told me it was a ballad. I just looked at the melody and the chord progressions, and my impression was it was a medium-swing minor tune. The melody goes"—he hummed it: a stately theme but, yes, very sad, a dirge—"but I took it"— he snapped his fingers, lifting the tempo, singing scat—"and everybody said, '*What* are you doing?' I said, 'I'm playing "Left Alone,"' and they said, 'That's not how it goes.' But I didn't know that. Another tune that is a big hit here is Duke Jordan's 'No Problem.' I met him in Kumamoto. He was playing in a tiny coffeeshop. I can look at a CD now by one of those cats—Ray Bryant or Kenny Burrell or Duke Jordan, even Jackie McLean—and just by the selection of tunes, I *know* it's a Japanese production . . ."

I said I'd heard "You Don't Know What Love Is" played often in Japan.

"'You Don't Know What Love Is'! That's huge because of Sonny Rollins. His *Saxophone Colossus* album is etched in stone in everybody's mind here. Another thing about Japanese audiences—and you've probably noticed this already—is that they really lean toward melodies in a minor key. Like 'You'd Be So Nice To Come Home To.' Or 'Summertime.' And also 'Softly as in a Morning Sunrise.' "

I mentioned the irony that there were Japanese players known in the States who did not seem to be known in Japan at all; then people like Tiger Okoshi or Makoto Ozone who go back and forth; and a third group who record and play in Japan exclusively—such as pianist Hisayuki Terai, whom I would see again in Osaka—yet are hardly known in the States at all.

"It's true. Players in the States hear that Japan is jazz *Mecca,* and in some ways it *is,* but the Japanese are very much geared to big names. Musicians think they can come over here and tour, but if you're someone with no name, you just can't do it, even if you do have a CD out. If it's not on a major label and if you haven't played with some major people, you're not going to get the time of day. In my case, I had that steady job for three years, so that allowed me to *gradually* ease myself into the scene. But in some ways, that scene is very closed. We were talking earlier about the Japanese—to put it bluntly—inferiority complex, as far as American musicians are concerned. That has another effect. Whereas the customers, a Japanese audience, will accept anything if it's by American musicians, the Japanese musicians themselves are more wary of American players. They're going to put them to the test, as it were. I don't like to step on people's toes: that's just not my nature. And that's the Japanese style too. You are *always* very careful in your relationships here, especially in the beginning. You don't want to seem arrogant. You want, always, to be deferential."

"It's the old networking thing, but with a different cultural basis."

"It's *networking!* And there's also a thing about learning the language. An excellent bass player I know hasn't gotten called once, and he's been around here as long as me, because he still hasn't learned the language. People tend to put you off because they don't feel they can communicate. Being able to speak the language has definitely been a social lubricant. So I haven't experienced any very bad situations myself, but there are other people who have. There's a lot of politics involved here. More so than in the States. For instance, I recently started working with another bassist. He's my regular bassist, as it were, so for me to use somebody else would be even more difficult than doing that in the States. People get their feelings hurt in the States too, but Japan is a much *smaller* world. People know what's going on."

I mentioned Yoshiaki "Miya" Miyanoue's overtly polite, very self-effacing reaction when I spoke to him about his guitar "duels" with Bruce Forman.

"Oh yeah," Donny responded, "but that old samurai spirit . . . it's still burnin'!"

I asked about recording opportunities. Had he recorded in Japan?

"I've had nothing. Which is definitely not sour grapes, because there are so many people much much better than me on the scene. Nonetheless, it *is* one step more difficult for a foreigner to get over on the Japanese scene on that level—like the *national* level. Because at that level they're thinking, 'Hey, if we're going to make a recording with a foreigner, we'd just as soon make it with a big name. And the opposite thing happens: if they want to sell a record by the top Japanese players, they have them go to the United States and make a recording with the top players *there*. The record companies have the money, and it doesn't take all *that* much money to get the top American players to play."

After completing the second set, Donny told me about a gig coming up: playing on a cruise ship, or what he described as "a huge ferry."

"It's a trip that leaves from Nagoya at 8:00 in the evening and stops at Sendai the next afternoon at five, then on to a port in Southern Hokkaido called Tomakonai. The boat has a really nice large lounge, but the customers are truck drivers, and they're mostly older people on packaged tours. People from the country, in their sixties and seventies. And no one knows jazz whatsoever, so when I first started playing on the boat it was the most difficult gig I had here. Eventually I figured something out for myself, and one night I said, 'Look, I know I've got *the* set for these people.' I did all this *movie music*, because they seemed to like it. I did 'As Time Goes By.' I did 'Love Is a Many-Splendored Thing.' I think I might also have done 'Charade.' Old movies are very popular in Japan, and they know the music. I closed the set with 'You Are My Sunshine.' I had an arrangement on that tune that I really enjoy playing. My wife happened to be with me on this trip. She was sitting in the audience among all these little old ladies, and when I kicked into 'You Are My Sunshine,' the lady next to her said to her friend, 'Well finally there's a song that I *know*.' When my wife told me that, I thought, 'Wow, they're just coming from a totally different place. One of my policies is: never come down on this or that tune for not being *hip*. I don't dig that attitude. Any tune is hip; it's how it's played that's not."

Donny said that, in order to maintain this common ground with his audience, he'd accumulated his own little fake book, with about thirty tunes or so, mostly "corny."

"And I've begun to arrange some Japanese children's songs. They've got a song about spring called 'Haru ga Kita' [Spring Has Come]. And there's a very popular spring song that's not a children's song. You've probably heard it: 'Sakura, Sakura.' I've got another tune about snow. It's snowing and the pet dog is very happy and running around the yard and the cat is rolled up in a warm place in the house." Actually, I was familiar with this song, "Yuki": "neko wa kotatsu de maruku naru" (cats curl up snug and warm by the fireside). "All of these tunes are seasonal, as you can tell. Snow and acorns and spring! Unfortunately I can't play that gig year-round. I have to choose my season and play *those* songs. I also do 'Battle Hymn of the Republic.' And I do 'Love Me Tender,' 'Danny Boy,' 'Tennessee Waltz.' It's the way you approach a tune. I do everything *swinging* if I can. I've gotta swing, if I really sink my teeth into a tune. But since I've started doing what I've been doing on the boat, the response has been good. *Really* good. I've got those people in my hip pocket now. But you have to realize where I'm coming from. I'm trying to appeal to people on a very *local* level. I want to let everybody in on the music, rather than trying to blow them away strictly with all this highbrow stuff. I want to let them know, 'Yeah, you're a part of it too.' "

He told me that some people from one of the schools run by Yamaha came to listen to him play and said, "You should teach over there." But Donny felt that, not trained formally himself, there were "a billion people in the community alone" who could teach the Yamaha system. One of the gentlemen wouldn't take no for an answer, however, and he put together a program for Donny and even suggested a name: "Jazz and Popular Piano."

"I said, 'Well, I don't play *popular* piano.' We discussed this, and it turned out to be a *semantic* thing. In Japan, they consider songs like 'Misty' and 'Summertime' and 'Take the "A" Train' *popular* tunes. So I said, 'Fine.' They said, 'What text are you going to use?' And I said, 'I'm not going to use a text.' They said, 'That's fine,' but when they made up the advertisement for the course, they said, 'original text.' Over the course of the last, say, seven or eight years I've had—easily—sixty people or so come through the door. But out of all the people I've taught, there are only *three* that would ever have a slight chance of playing professionally. And I would say that no more than that came to me with any ideas of doing anything except just to *enjoy* it. I've put together recitals. We learn the tunes and I hire a professional bassist and a drummer. We rent out a club like this, and the students get to go up on stage and play two tunes in front of friends they invite. It's so *cool!* I'm so happy about it! To see and hear some sixty-year-old woman or these high school girls or *sararīman,* people from *all walks,* doing that. They want just a small taste of playing jazz piano. It's assumed that a girl will study piano in Japan. I think it may even be understatement to say that, here, 75 percent of all girls have taken piano. For boys, it's different. A lot of them take piano lessons, but out of all the students I have—and at this point, with my private students and the students at Yamaha—I've got just *two* men. The rest are women. And *older* women. Sometimes they get really frustrated, saying, 'My solos always sound the same to me; I don't seem to be able to *break through!*' And I say, 'Look at where you were a year ago! Could you sit down with no notes written out at all, just these chord progressions, and *play* something—anything, good or bad?' And they say, 'No [which in this context means *yes*], that's true.' And I say, 'Okay, now look at this. In this prefecture of Aichi, there are six million people. Of those, do you think that even 1 percent of those people can play a solo on "Take the 'A' Train"? Good *or* bad? You are in a very *elite* group.'" He laughed. "And it's true. It's so cool to have that hands-on thing, to be able to play *one* tune! In the States, it would be very difficult to get forty students—housewives!—who want to play jazz. Housewives! *Improvising?!* It's funny how this country works."

"You're here for good . . ."

"I'm here for good. For various reasons, not the least of which is I can't leave now. I've got a house, two cars, dog and cats and daughter and this and that and the other thing. My parents have always wanted me to come back. I've been away from Atlanta—where they live—for twenty years, and they tell me the city has turned into a very cosmopolitan place. I'm sure it's quite a bit different from what it was twenty years ago, but my wife says, 'Look, if you can support us in the style to which we have become accustomed, that's fine.' But there's no way in hell I could *there*. She doesn't work, and I'm supporting the family doing exactly what I like to do. And that's not the only reason I like being in Japan. Of course, after having been here this long, there are tons of things I *don't* like about Japan too. Things about the society. Its very restrictive customs."

I mentioned the *sararīman,* housewives, kids, college students—

everyone!—on subways reading their *manga* comics. Ingesting all that fantasy. There seemed to be a lot going on, *kokoro ni,* in the heart below the surface.

"Right, right, right. But *expressing* it has been suppressed for so long, and many people just don't know how to *let go* and have a good time. Or else they have to get totally *blitzed* in order to do that. I've never been in a place that is as forgiving of drunks as Japan. It's just standard course here. I'll have to say I've seen more public drunkenness here than I did in the States. In a way it's like nobody is putting any sort of big judgment on it. If someone's lying there who just got through throwing his guts up"—he laughed—"everybody else is just, well, nobody sees a trip on it."

As if to prove his point, during the second set, the pretty young woman with the stunning long hair became so intoxicated that she fell off her chair. Her friend took her to the restroom for a prolonged period of time, so long, in fact, that I thought they'd left. When she returned, she sat demurely in her seat for a few moments, then threw up all over the floor. Her friend escorted her to the rest room again while the cocktail waitress who'd waited on me cleaned up the mess. When the two friends emerged again, the less intoxicated had to carry the indisposed one out, the latter startling the large flat fish when she crashed into their bubbling tank. Nobody blinked an eye. A half-empty bottle of Canadian Club remained on their table.

Donny's gig over, we decided to set out on the town. On the way out of Star Eyes, the pianist introduced me to the owner, Mr. Masakuni Iwaki. Just before he did so, Donny said, "Do you know the jargon, the lingo? In any establishment for eating and drinking, especially a club like this, the owner is called the master. And the master of this place is from Ise, where—I understand—you will be going next."

"That's right."

I shook hands with, and bowed to, Master Masakuni Iwaki from Ise, who turned out to be very much the inobtrusively hip, cordial owner of a jazz club. I bowed and thanked him for his hospitality that night.

When we walked into the Jazz Aster *kissaten,* I felt I'd been squeezed into a box. Five stools stood before a counter, two of them occupied, one by a man who was resting his head on the counter or had passed out. The man next to him was talking in a fully animated manner to the proprietor, whom I was introduced to: Master Tsuneo Hashimoto. He stood directly in front of a rack of LPs encased in transparent plastic covers, the room's light—reflected on them— producing the effect of some sort of flickering, glistening halo surrounding his head.

When Donny and I sat down on two vacant stools, the man with his head on the counter sprang to attention, as if awoken by a loud temple bell, and Donny, joining the discussion we'd interrupted, impressed me with his Japanese, a language he handled with the same smooth touch he'd exhibited on piano. Master Hashimoto leaned below the counter and produced a box of memorabilia that he was obviously quite proud of, and I would learn why. I was shown pictures of himself as a young man, dressed in a kimono, entertaining Thelonious and Nelly Monk. He pointed to a corner of the *kissaten,* where a Count Basie band jacket stood on a rack, a gift from—Count Basie. He showed me a drawing done just for him, a highly idealized portrait of Stan Getz.

"Yeah, a hundred years ago," the man who'd been comatose when we walked in said when Master Hashimoto showed us another photo of himself as a very young jazz fan.

I looked around the cramped room and tried to imagine the heyday of this *kissaten,* eager Japanese jazz fans scribbling notes or jotting down hasty transcriptions of solos by Monk or Getz, or Count Basie's own pinched display of piano artistry.

Thanking Master Hashimoto profusely, watching him tuck away his box of treasures, Donny and I set out for Swing, a no less interesting but more spacious place, a club featuring live jazz. There, an amateur combo, a trio made up of young musicians (the drummer a medical doctor), was—unfortunately—packing it up for the night. The club's owner, guitarist Sunao Wada, was—also unfortunately—not there. I was introduced to his wife, a gracious woman whom I would see represented (it seemed) by one of Wada's incredible pieces of sculpture made completely from tinfoil, a female figure, a "madonna" nursing a baby, that Donny told me to check out in the men's room. The figure was as sumptuously healthy and full as the sculptor Maillol's *Pomona,* whose hands extend fruit as a gift. But the wildest piece in the club was a sculpted dragon, several feet long, occupying one corner above the bar: a dragon with cow's ears, a carp's whiskers, a *shika's* (deer's) antlers, and a human penis of proud proportion—all made from tinfoil Sunao Wada had collected for years from chewing-gum wrappers and other sources. I was introduced to two Japanese women, one of whom—tall, willowy, dressed in black, carrying a fake book—turned out to be a vocalist who'd sung with the trio that night. I managed to say, in Japanese, that I was sorry I'd missed her. Donny talked with the doctor/drummer about some problem he was having with his elbow, we drank, and I realized it was nearly 3:00 in the morning, dark night of the soul time, especially if you have a train to catch early in the morning. Donny—who'd turned out to be one of the most important sources of information I'd encountered in Japan and a hell of a lot of fun to boot—drove me back to my hotel.

26

R AND R: YOKOYAMA–JIMA, THE ISE SHRINE, AND THE WEDDING ROCKS

THE RYOKAN ISHIYAMA IS SITUATED on the small island of Yokoyama-jima in Ago Bay. I had picked a *ryokan* as far from any "urban" activity as I could get: what I thought would prove to be an ideal spot in which to rest and reflect on whatever I'd learned so far about jazz in Japan.

In Isuzugawa Station, I saw a sign that read "Welcome to the Spiritual City, Ise," but I went on to Kashikojima, saving the two shrines at Ise Jingu for another day. When, after a two-minute ferryboat ride, I entered my room on the island, sliding open a pair of shōji doors, I let the splendid view of Ago Bay evolve before my eyes. The customary *yukata* (summer kimono) sat crisply folded on an inviting futon. But sleep was the last thing on my mind. I drank my fill of the view, put on the *yukata,* and went in search of an *ofuro,* or Japanese bath. I located a huge steaming tub that was obviously intended for use by more than one person (I could have swum laps in it!) but that I had—at 3:00 in the afternoon—all to myself. I slowly eased my travel-weary body into the smoldering water, got settled into a mode of somatic ecstasy, and remained there for what seemed like hours (but was probably about forty-five minutes). I'd reached a wondrous *no-mind* state, beyond mere comfort, and I didn't care who came in. No one did, and, baked to insensibility, I finally got out, gently carrying IT—*sunyata* (perfect emptiness) or "great death" (surmounting both death and life)—back to my room. It was the lightest heavy load I've ever had to carry. I gazed at the silhouette of the mountains that surround the Ise Shrine far in the distance. Fishermen maneuvered what looked like punts among buoys they'd set out to mark their nets, a sort of abacus spread over the waters at strategic points, nets they now drew up at the close of day. I sat there, drinking green tea, realizing that—for perhaps the first time in my life— I could think of nothing *more* I wanted than what I had before me, right *there*. Taoists and Zen Buddhists call this state *sono-mama* (suchness), but at the moment I didn't care what it was called and only tried to find a name for it later, when I discovered that the kanji for "meditation" is the source of the Japanese character for "Zen": the left radical meaning both "religion" and "happiness," the right "alone." In the future, when I thought of the very best jazz I'd heard in Japan and searched for a way to describe it, I would think of *that* sacred moment on Yokoyama-jima in Ago Bay.

Later, I began to go over my list of questions prompted by Akira Tana's thesis on jazz in Japan, the questions I'd set out to answer on this journey. I came to the conclusion that the answer to nearly all of them was *hai*. Tana had written about the artistic benefits of a culture with long-standing traditions, the respect for artists it fosters, admiration for skill in *any* craft, and of "as wide a dissemination of the art form as possible"—all of which, throughout my travels, I had seen ample evidence of when it came to jazz.

While Akira had cited, and praised as an advantage, the stable social and economic background of Japanese musicians, free from open conflict or cutthroat competition among themselves (the sort that could prompt such sharp division or even animosity in the States), he *did* have reservations about Japanese jazz artists being in a position to understand the full import, the political significance, of the music's history. However, I still felt as I had before: that jazz—in its position now as a truly *international* language and not a platform or agenda espousing extramusical elements—had, in the hands and minds of the Japanese, acquired the *sono-mama* (suchness) of being what it was: music. Had the Japanese themselves finally acquired, as Akira hoped they would, "meaningful expression of their own, as opposed to a mere imitation of American jazz"? Had the "time of idolatry of American performers of the music" truly come to an end? Had Japanese artists, surmounting the "major hurdle of creating what [was] felt to be an honest expression of *Japanese* jazz," finally acquired *authenticity?* Again, based on what I'd heard, my answer was an unqualified *hai*. I did not feel I was a mere advocate, inflating the importance of the music above and beyond what it *was*—

the merit jazz in and from Japan had earned on its own. Many of these artists, I now believed, were aware of how exceptional their cultural background is, how their "Japanese character" might best be expressed with "uniqueness and validity" in the future—whether through tango (as Makoto Ozone preferred) or Masahiko Satoh's use of traditional elements. The options were out there, whereas twenty years ago—when Tana had written his thesis—there had been, I felt, a tendency to avoid or feel threatened or even embarrassed by them. I felt that what Akira Tana held out as "hope" for the future twenty years ago had come to pass.

While the bubble economy had come and, if not gone, was on the wane, and "abundant employment opportunities" (a "more positive environment than that of America," as Tana had seen it) had become a debatable issue (some musicians and producers I'd talked to found the current situation "difficult"), I still couldn't help but be impressed—attending performances in clubs that offered jazz *every* night of the week—by what seemed a healthy state of the art. While the audience for jazz in Japan remained much as Akira Tana had classified it (students, recent college grads, upper- and middle-class *sarariman*, artists in other fields aware of the merits of the music), a new category had been added, as Donny Schwekediek had so joyously pointed out: housewives! Jazz in Japan was no longer just a symbol of nonconformity (although some of that was still going on) but was appreciated now, I felt, in strictly musical terms. While a plethora of Berklee or North Texas State–style institutions—a flourishing curriculum, set programs—had not sprung up in twenty years time, I could not agree with Tana that "jazz education in Japan had failed," for I had found a fully functional system that, in terms of Japanese traditions, made even more sense: the hands-on study that Donny had found so rewarding—working with a *sensei,* that modern variation of the *iemoto* system that had existed in Japan for centuries. All in all, the Japanese jazz scene struck me as quite healthy, and I could always think of, and find, jazz in and from Japan within a larger—more meaningful or substantial—context of Japanese life or cultural tradition. The art form did not seem as isolated, dangerously "special," as estranged from mainstream or "ordinary" living as it does in the United States.

This summary running through my mind, I noticed the sun disappearing behind the mountains, the sky streaked now with bright pastel beneath dark clouds. The water became a mix of tranquilizing purple and midnight blue. Lines spotted with buoys that fishermen had left standing resembled a flock of birds settled in strict rows upon the water. The sky turned a quick scarlet now, a florid flash, then shut off like a light, leaving me glancing into serene darkness, my ears assailed by the water's stillness and the absence of light. I closed the shōji doors, knowing that in the morning I would travel north again to visit the most revered shrine in Japan.

I went to both the Inner Shrine and the Outer Shrine at Ise Jingu. The Inner Shrine could be said to represent mainstream music, the Outer Shrine free or avant-garde jazz, although the analogy doesn't pan out completely because—like so much else in Japan—*both* shrines are as traditional as Japanese sacred tradition can be. The Inner Shrine, called Naiku, is dedicated to Amaterasu, the Sun Goddess; the Outer Shrine, called Toyoukedaijingu (or Geku for short), is dedicated to Toyouke-Omikami, goddess of grain and agriculture. The architecture is beautiful: the buildings made of unpainted *hinoki* (cypress) wood, as simple as Shaker furniture in design, a sort of highly refined twelve-bar blues (to add even another style to the jazz analogy). I discovered, overlooking a green pond, a pavilion enclosed by a bright red knee-high fence, and I could only think, "Wow, what a great *bandstand!*" The thought wasn't as sacrilegious as it sounds, because (as I would learn later) court dances *were* performed there once, to ancient music.

On my return trip to Ryokan Ishiyama, I got off the train at the town of Futamiagaura, where the Meoto-Iwa (Wedding Rocks) are located—a popular spot for Japanese lovers. Two large rocks set in the sea, united by a sagging rope, are named for Izanagi and Izanami, the "Adam and Eve" (also said to be brother and sister) of Japan. The wind swirled, the air was cold, but none of that seemed to annoy or distract the many young lovers there to insure good fortune for their future lives together. Shivering, I thought of songs I knew with the word "love" in the title: tunes such as "Love Me or Leave Me," "You Don't Know What Love Is," "Easy to Love," "I Can't Give You Anything But Love," "Like Someone in Love," "Love Is Here to Stay," "When I Fall in Love," "You Call It Madness (But I Call It Love)," "Beautiful Love," "I've Never Been in Love Before," and on and on. I blessed the lovers that surrounded me, pronounced a quick prayer for Betty and myself, for our longevity; then walked back along the sea to the train station, alone.

27

Osaka Again: Takeo Nishida, Tadao Kitano, Noriko Nakayama, and the Arrow Jazz Orchestra

I HAD JUST TWO DAYS LEFT to spend in Japan, and following my retreat on Yokoyama-jima island, they would prove suitably packed with jazz. I took a room in a place called the Sunrise Inn, in Kaizuka (south of Osaka) because it afforded easy access to Kansai Airport but would also allow me to get back to Namba Station in Osaka in about half an hour. My new residence, while not affording the absolute *shizukana shima* (tranquil island) atmosphere of Ryokan Ishiyama, was advertised as "a century-old inn," and my room was suitably small and austere. In the morning, before heading for Osaka, I could drink tea from a dark salmon and pale brown cup, its handle so large it looked the victim of some sort of taffy pull. That cup made me think of much of the music I'd heard: raw, lovely (in the sense of *sabi*: rustic, simple, fleeting), both sad (*mono no aware*) and joyous, but refined (*shibui*). I wanted to steal that cup, to take it home with me as an *omiyage,* but I didn't.

Back in the States, Sumiko Inoue (of the IDEA organization) had given me the name of Takeo Nishida, manager of the Arrow Jazz Orchestra (a very successful professional big band), owner of a musical production company named Sound Knew, and head of a jazz school in Osaka. When I phoned him, he said he would send someone to meet me at Namba Station who would then escort me to a hall where the Arrow Jazz Orchestra would be rehearsing that day. At Namba, I was making an unsuccessful phone call when I heard my name ("Biru Mai-nor-san?"), and looking up, I saw an attractive woman with wide bright eyes, somewhat tall (by Japanese standards) and stately in a chic (but not at all trendy) sort of way. This was my escort, Noriko Nakayama.

We hopped a subway to what appeared to be, once we arrived, a large cultural complex. The grounds were impressive, even in the rain, which had suddenly arrived in force. One of several buildings housed the Arrow Jazz Orchestra. Along a wall outside the rehearsal room stood a line of abandoned shoes: a complete big band's worth. Inside, the group's leader, pianist Tadao Kitano, still wore shoes (pulling rank?), but everybody else—the complete trumpet, trombone, sax, and rhythm sections—wore slippers. The band was playing "Sweet Georgia Brown" when we walked in. Takeo Nishida greeted us, offered us two chairs against a wall, and then rushed back to his managerial chores.

The next tune was "Green Dolphin Street," but it got off to a bad start—which Nishida let the group know in no uncertain terms. The drummer bowed in apology, and Kitano, at the piano, reset the tempo. Once into the tune again, the drummer made amends, fully, for whatever delay or consternation he'd caused—even providing a shrewd, resourceful break that put him back in Nishida's good graces. You could tell the group was made up of pros, not just because of tight, driving section work but also well-conceived solos that were a delight to listen to (I would learn later that the *best* soloists were not even present at rehearsal that day). The Arrow Jazz Orchestra also seemed to be having a hell of a good time, joking between numbers, clowning or looking suitably "cool" or indifferent, or both. Nishida offered considerable input, shouting "Dame, dame!" (Wrong, wrong!) after another small blunder or musical indiscretion, then "Onegai shimasu" (Please, in the sense of, "Let's try it again!"). He was a short but imposing, cocky, persuasive man with energy to spare. He was fastidious and demanding, a perfectionist, a man with a mission, intent on getting things *right*.

"They will only have this one rehearsal before their upcoming concert," Noriko whispered to me, "but because they play together so frequently, that is all they will need." She did add that the band was seeing some of the charts for the first time. When the group took a break, I was introduced to the lead trumpet player, Nobuo Miyaoka, and trombonist Koichi Nakai, who has his own group named Hozhg. I also talked briefly with band leader/pianist Tadao Kitano, who started the Arrow Jazz Orchestra in 1958, when he was just twenty-four years old. Did *he* select the tunes the band played, or did Mr. Nishida? He said he was the "regular band leader" and also the pianist and arranger. I asked if the arrangement of "Sweet Georgia Brown" was his.

"No, no, no. *Are wa* [as for that tune] Count Basie, but the arrangements are usually my own. We give a concert every other month. We also play for hotel dinner parties and to accompany vocalists. We often do that, along with our regular concerts. The band members work very steadily because we also have jobs [musical gigs] other than just the regular concert. Tunes such as 'Sweet Georgia Brown' and 'Green Dolphin Street' are a part of our regular repertoire. We play them a lot. But we have two thousands tunes in our repertoire now."

"Hontō wa!" (Wow!) I said, and the others—musicians who had gathered around us to hear what Tadao Kitano had to say about the band—laughed.

"We will play fourteen to fifteen tunes at the concert," Kitano continued. "We will be working with a singer named Mary Nakamoto, and she'll sing 'Teach Me Tonight,' 'Lover Come Back to Me,' 'Misty,' and— . . . I'm not sure about *all* of the songs, because I am meeting with her tonight."

He showed me a list. About four tunes would be done with the vocalist; the rest were instrumentals. I asked the musicians gathered how they got started playing with the band, and Mr. Kitano went first.

"I opened a nightclub, the Club Arrow. I started it myself. I had an orchestra, right from the start. When they came to Japan, we accompanied Oscar Peterson, Sammy Davis Jr., Dizzy Gillespie. Also Bill Berry. *Min'na de* [We played *together*]."

I asked if there were Japanese instrumentalists who'd sat in or performed with the band.

"Sleepy Matsumoto. Makoto Ozone, the pianist. He played with my band for three years," Tadao Kitano said. "He was a student of mine. *Kodomo da!* [He was a child!] *Jūgo* to *jūhachi* [Age fifteen to eighteen]. Before he went to the United States and Berklee College of Music."

I mentioned the amateur big bands that had come to the Monterey Jazz Festival, including Osaka's fine Global Jazz Orchestra. Kitano was familiar with them, and I said that the popularity of big band music in Japan—especially at a time when such bands were having such a tough go of it in the States—intrigued me.

"There are just a *few* professional big bands or orchestras here," Mr. Kitano said. "Mostly they are amateur or university student bands."

"But the Arrow Jazz Orchestra is a professional big band, and playing *regularly,* so your music must be appreciated. You have a following. Is it difficult to keep such a band afloat?"

"We have a great manager," Tadao Kitano said. The other members of the band laughed and nodded their heads.

At that moment, the "great manager" himself, Takeo Nishida, called out that it was time to resume the rehearsal. Reassembled, the Arrow Jazz Orchestra launched into "Time Check," a classic swing riff tune, and once again the band's section work was impressive. Nobuo Miyaoka provided appropriate Maynard Ferguson screeches; the drummer—whose name I failed to learn—goaded the group on persuasively; and the entire sax section offered a tight unison solo, à la Super Sax. "My Romance" was taken at a slow pace, an alto sax solo highlighting the bridge, and Tadao Kitano provided a piano interlude that possibly went on a tad too long. Someone's beeper went off, band members chortled, but Kitano—absorbed in his interlude—did not seem at all amused.

When the rehearsal came to a close, the band members whipped out their date books or pocket computers while Takeo Nishida ran down upcoming events. Noriko and I retrieved our shoes as a group of classical musicians arrived for *their* rehearsal in the room. Outside, rain descended in droves. With the largely worthless assistance of a pretty but fragile Japanese umbrella, we ran to Takeo Nishida's car. Safely inside, I hummed a few bars of "Isn't It a Lovely Day to Be Caught in the Rain?"—whereas what I really wanted to do was shake myself like a dog. When Nishida arrived, we drove to his Sound Knew office. He chattered all the way about his many projects (my recorder tucked away, unfortunately, out of reach just then). While he certainly wasn't shy on ego, unlike other Japanese, I could understand why, given the many "hats" he wore. He said that he'd learned much of what he knows about jazz and arranging while practicing on a neighbor's piano and that this neighbor, the owner of a print shop, was now one of the orchestra's major sponsors.

When we arrived at his office, Takeo Nishida returned to citing his many responsibilities: manager, producer, promoter, arranger. How did he handle them all?

"Komedi" (Comedy), he responded. Noriko was translating, and we all laughed. The phone rang, and he snatched it up.

"I wear many hats," Takeo Nishida continued after the call. "My goal is to promote jazz, to bring jazz—through the Arrow Jazz Orchestra—to as many Japanese people as possible. But I am only human. However, I have my dream. And to make that dream happen, I *must* act as promoter, producer, presenter, manager, arranger—as well as being a *comedian*." He laughed. "Let's say there are five people in Japan who truly love jazz, who are genuine jazz fans. But I don't want to aim for just five people. That's no good. *Motto, motto, motto!* [More, more, more!] I want the other 95 percent of the people to understand jazz!"

I asked just how one went about making that happen.

"First I have to let people know that jazz is *fun,* that it is fun music. Let's say the trumpet plays a short theme, a familiar theme that has been around for a long time." By way of example, Nishida hummed the opening bars of "When the Saints Go Marching In." "Many members of the audience know this theme only. But then comes the improvisation, the ad lib part. The audience *wakarimasen* [doesn't understand]. They don't even understand what the ad lib or improvisation is based on, where it comes from. So I have a program called 'What Is Jazz?' It is separate from our regular concerts. I am presenting this, which is a program all of its own, at various schools: regular high schools and junior high schools. It is a project intended for students."

I mentioned the highly successful Monterey Jazz Festival clinicians program, in which jazz musicians go to schools and teach performance skills alongside the history of the art, so that students will get a sense of where the music came from as well as "hands-on" instruction in how to play. Noriko used the phrase *rutsu o benkyō shite* (study the roots).

"I've already done that," Nishida responded. "I have two programs: 'Music around the World' and 'The History of Jazz.' We reach five hundred to a thousand students at one time, an entire school. We take the entire big band, and the presentation includes our own *ongaku* [music]. I am the emcee or master of ceremonies. We start out by playing a simple American folk song, 'My Old Kentucky Home,' in the 'classical' style. Then I discuss the difference between this style and a jazz interpretation. There are two people on stage, along with the band. Myself and a young woman." (Of course! The inevitable *bijin.*) "We establish a dialogue, and I ask her, 'What is the difference between the two styles?' She says, 'There is no conductor for jazz as something *written.*' Then the drummer starts in with the classic jazz /~~/~~/ rhythm on the ride cymbal. I ask if this rhythm is something merely added—or is it *jazz* itself? 'No no no no no,' she responds. 'Jazz *can* be played from a written arrangement, just like classical music, but the melody comes out so *flat,* so in jazz we change that melody.' A combo from the band—piano, bass, drums, sax, flute—plays that melody, but not legato. We play it staggered, with starts and stops, rubato, with unexpected sustained or whole notes. Yet throughout this the piano player maintains the same obbligato or 'classical' configuration—to show how the strictly jazz interpretation is evolving. We play 'Take the "A" Train,' and the bassist provides walking bass, and the pianist begins to play . . ." Here Nishida, impressively, *played* the piano part by singing it.

"Blue notes," I said.

"Blue notes! To create tension. Tension in the voicings. After this, we play a piece of traditional classical music, but we use jazz harmony." Takeo Nishida began to sing something by Mozart, adding jazz harmony as best he could. "Do you know this?"

"Mozart's Sonata no. 6," I said, feeling like a smart-ass but obviously having a good day.

"Yes!" We all laughed. "And next I explain the difference between the use of harmony in jazz and in classical music. *Soshite mō ichido* [consequently, once again] we return to 'My Old Kentucky Home,' and we put it all together. The drummer sets the jazz rhythm on his ride cymbal, the walking bass comes in, the piano plays jazz harmonies, and the vocalist says, '*This* is jazz.' And we even add some 'lacing' or fill from Mozart!"

When I asked Nishida if he conceived and designed the program, he first said yes, then changed his mind and said, "Then again, *no,* because jazz, the music itself, is more important than anything I did with it. The music itself has the most important message. *Someday* I will know how to teach the most important thing [Nishida used the Japanese word *ichiban*], which is improvisation. I ask the piano player to ad lib or improvise on 'Old Kentucky Home.' After the piano player has done so, I ask a sax player to play the same thing, but he says, 'I *can't!*' To ad lib or improvise is *in* the moment—and that's what I try to get across to the students. It *can't* be done exactly the same way twice—even by the pianist himself! So we start with the theme again. Then we introduce a soloist or improviser and return to the theme so they can see, or hear, and understand just what happened. But the girl says, 'Fine, but there's still one element that is missing.' I ask, 'What is that?' And she says"— here he clapped his hands together, suddenly, joyously, loudly— "'Hand clapping!' Unfortunately, in Japan, traditionally, hand clapping comes on the first beat."

I asked if he could get a Japanese audience to think in and switch to two and four.

"*Sō, sō, sō* [Yes, in their way]. The drummer emphasizes that beat, and we practice that rhythm with everyone."

Throughout this demonstration, Takeo Nishida had displayed near missionary zeal, a zest or enthusiasm I felt had to carry over to his audiences, no matter what age. He clearly loves—no, *adores*—jazz music. Now, in one final fit of enthusiasm, he began to imitate a full band version of "When the Saints Go Marching In," realized that wasn't the tune he wanted, said "gomen nasai" (please excuse my mistake), and adroitly switched back to "My Old Kentucky Home." "After we finish, one-two-out, I say, *'Ja, sore wa jazu desu!'* [This then is jazz!]"

"And do you bring in the history of the music? The evolution of styles—such as swing, bop, hard bop, modal, free jazz? Is that a part of the program in the schools?"

"Not in Japanese schools, no. Most of the music teachers on the junior high and high school level do not *play* jazz. Some might be agreeable to presenting the history of jazz, but others would not. But I have to really promote the program as it is. I have to sell it myself. The older players, such as Kitano, used to look down on people who do not understand jazz, but my generation feels that we must educate people. I understood that it was something I *must* do. It was my duty to teach people who did not understand. I don't want Japanese people to think that jazz is *muzukashii* [difficult] to understand. I want to explain it to them, so they can see the various elements simply, clearly. I want to make the music accessible. So, *nagara* [at the same time], I am a *comedian*." He laughed.

We discussed the issue I'd brought up with Tadeo Kitano: how to keep a big band afloat or active today.

"There are, in Japan, about the same number of jazz fans as there are for classical music," Nishida responded. "In Sapporo, in Hokaido, there is a Philharmonic Orchestra. This is true in Sendai in Honshu also. Each city or prefecture sponsors the classical orchestras, supports them, but for the same number of fans, there are thirty professional classical orchestras as opposed to two or three for jazz. I realized that if you divided *all* those fans into two, and the jazz band was well managed, it could not only survive but make a profit! And I've proved that people who think it's financially difficult or impossible to support a big band are *wrong*. It can be done. Our regular concerts maintain a high performance level, but ordinarily when audience and musicians came together, I've had to make concessions. I must compromise."

I'd noticed that, in this band, a very democratic policy seemed to be in effect. *Many* different musicians took solos, so there appeared to be considerable depth. Did he ever run into problems letting so many people solo?

"Our motto is *'Junana no kosae ga hikaru bando!'* [In this band, seventeen characters shining!] Our members are the same; they're *all* good, so it's not necessary to designate a lead trumpeter as superior and just give him the solo part. We give it to any or all of the members of the trumpet section. Each player is complete in himself."

Noriko asked a question, in Japanese, on her own: "So you don't want members of the band to follow a leader?"

"No, no, no, no. I'm not saying that. It's so hard for me to explain my philosophy on this matter: that each member of the band is the same. I would need someone who is a wiser translator than you."

In the painful moment of silence that followed this exchange I realized that Takeo Nishida's democratic stance, his generous attitude toward the instrumentalists in the band (all men), did not extend to all genders. Noriko's feelings had been hurt, obviously. She stopped translating. Nishida launched into a prolonged set speech that, while interesting (my daughter-in-law Yoko would assist me in the translation later, when I returned to the States), I could not now help but regard with mixed feelings.

"My philosophy can be compared to the thinking in Japanese culture itself. Do you know about the Three Arrows?" He addressed this question to Noriko, who did not respond. "In Japanese society, we think that, in a contest, if three arrows should break, that's okay. But if all three do not break, that's very important. The Japanese people believe in this philosophy: if one person can't do it, that's not so good. But if three people can't do it, or if three people *can,* that's good. This is a very strong attitude, the attitude of *consensus* in Japanese society. But it is not the best attitude. I think the Arrow Jazz Orchestra could be called a more adult orchestra. We are independent. Each one of us is completed as a musician. Sometimes organizations—sponsors such as Yamaha, perhaps—want to provide instruments to musicians because they feel *their* product sounds better than others. I don't agree with that policy because I want each character to shine in the orchestra, not the instruments.

When you hear a solo, you should recognize it as *that person's* solo, not Yamaha's, or whatever vendor's. Each person should shine. But in Japanese society, people do not let *you* improve on your own, just by yourself. They say a thing must be done by everyone together, not just you alone."

Noriko had stopped smoldering, somewhat, and interjected, in Japanese: "You say all that, yes, you say you want each person to shine, but eventually you want a solid overall good big band rhythm . . ."

"No, this is a very sensitive issue. Japanese always want to 'pull a line,' oversimplify, but this situation is not so simple. In classical music, the rhythm is up to the composer, but in jazz, each player can make his own arrangement, he can shape the rhythm the way he wants. Each player can recompose, but you also hear the entire group, the whole band making music. If they can *get together,* it will be the whole group making music but you can still see and hear each individual . . ."

"Mr. Nishida wants to say," Noriko said, "that in the United States, the individual *comes first;* there is much respect for the individual's skill and the individual dominates. That is because they were born in the U.S. and that's part of their environment. But in Japan, we *kill* the individual personality in order to make the group better. The group comes first. But Mr. Nishida would like to change this situation. He believes that the *individual* is the real thing that characterizes jazz."

Once again, I paraphrased Tiger Okoshi's major league baseball players analogy, and my own feelings about jazz having become an international language, and asked Takeo Nishida if *he* felt Japanese jazz musicians were playing on a level with Americans. And once more, this final question provided a glimpse into a side of Japanese "sociology" I had not bargained for, for once again Mr. Nishida said that his opinion would be hard to translate so perhaps later . . .

"No, no, don't say that," Noriko snapped back (much to her credit, as I would realize later). "We don't know that Bill-san will have a translator later, so you must explain to *me* fully, now. There is no point for me to be here if you don't, and I will *leave* if you will not explain to me and let me translate!"

"*Ano* . . . [Well then . . .]," Takeo Nishida said, "I do not feel it's a matter of playing on a certain *level*. It's a matter of expressing your feelings, even at a *lower* level." Then he added, as an aside to her (which Yoko translated later), their contest of wills persistent but no longer unpleasant (one-sided), "If you were not here today, I would have tried to tell him this in my very limited English: that *jazz* is like this too—trying to bring out what you feel, no matter how difficult that is. *That* is the more important thing, the most important thing."

"Kokoro ni" (In and from the mind/heart), I said, understanding his intent.

"Yes, *kokoro* is most important," Noriko said.

Takeo Nishida smiled and laughed, slowly. We were one big happy band, or *dantai* (group), again.

"No more questions," I said. "Dōmo arigatō."

After the interview, Nishida gave me a generous packet of information: fliers and brochures, plus a recent CD release by the Arrow Jazz Orchestra called *Boplicity*. One brochure featured a striking photo of the seventeen-piece orchestra (*junana no kosae ga hikaru bando:* seventeen characters shining) at work beneath red and green spotlights; a bio of Tadao Kitano; photos of each member of the band; and a postscript written by Eiji Kitamura, who had been featured on occasion with the orchestra—as he seems to have been with just about every jazz aggregate in Japan. The packet also contained an article in English that cited the demise of the Count Basie and Woody Herman bands, praising the resilience and longevity of the Arrow Jazz Orchestra, which, "for nearly 40 years now . . . has beat the odds, carrying the banner of big band jazz . . . cruising into its fifth decade with its creative powers undiminished."

Takeo Nishida is a driving force behind what I realized was not just a viable, many-faceted musical and educational institution, but something of an empire. Before meeting Noriko that morning, I had scouted out the St. James Jazz Club in Osaka, a nightspot owned by the wife of pianist Takehisa Tanaka, whose recording *When I Was at Aso-Mountain,* subtitled *Elvin Jones Introduces Takehisa Tanaka,* I liked. The two musicians enjoy, apparently, a friendship that dates back several years. I hoped to go to the club that evening, but sitting in Nishida's Sound Knew office, I had no idea exactly where we were in Osaka. Nishida said we were about fifty minutes away from Namba Station. He offered to drive me all the way back to my hotel in Kaizuka (Osaka sprawls endlessly, like L.A.) but said he would first like to swing by his jazz school—which was fine with me, for I was curious to see it.

The Arrow Jazz Orchestra Music School, started in 1988, can boast of 240 students, but it's no commodious Berklee College of Music.

Everything—including all of those students, it seemed—was crammed into small quarters reached by a miniscule elevator; yet in spite of cramped space, you could sense the excitement in the scant air, the curiosity and vitality of what appeared to be college-age students clustered in front of a jazz video or avidly perusing books or scores that sat on tables in a single room. Arrow Jazz Orchestra members serve as instructors and give lessons in rooms that seemed no bigger than phone booths. The combined sound of various musical pursuits was distracting but exciting, the entire scene charged with animation, its own fine tempo or pulse. I was glad I'd seen it, for it reinforced my impression of the active involvement of young people in jazz life in Japan and certainly contradicted (or altered with time) Akira Tana's opinion that jazz education in Japan had "failed."

Takeo Nishida dropped me off at a train station, and Noriko, who'd been dozing in the car while he talked nonstop (in Japanese, little of which I caught because he spoke so excitedly, so rapidly), walked me up to the ticket window. We parted against a backdrop Edward Hopper would have loved: beneath a dim light beside tracks that stretched away in two directions.

28

RETURN TO THE OVER SEAS CLUB AND HISAYUKI TERAI

A s the train from Kaizuka to Namba Station sped through the residential and industrial sprawl that stretches from Kansai Airport to Osaka, I sat back and made a mental list of what I was going to miss most about Japan. The music was at the top of the list, of course. Yet I also thought of the fringe benefits that had provided a context for it, among which stood the *shizuka* (tranquil or calm) potential of the various *ryokans* I'd stayed in. Perhaps at home I could construct my own little *hōjō* (ten-foot hut) and stock it with lots of Japanese jazz CDs.

I thought of Japanese *teineisa* (politeness or civility): what Junichiro Tanazaki, in *The Makioka Sisters,* calls "scrupulous attention to the proprieties." That's a lost art in America, it seems—if, aside from folks like Henry James and Edith Wharton, anyone ever valued it much at all. Yet I also realized that, as something of a culturally conditioned "free spirit," I would more than likely find the enforced, obligatory, integral systems of Japan (including civility or politeness) intolerable—an imposition imposed on a daily basis. However, as a tourist surrounded by such customs, a mere observer in Japan, I could (safely, at a distance) take delight in the survival of such small courtesies—the "kindness of strangers."

I would miss those *himitsu no basho* (private or secret places): retreats you can repair to when the benefits of civilization—the riotous pace of cities—crowd in upon you. But they are not the distant shelters or havens we crave in the States ("wilderness"). I would miss the abundance of temples and shrines *within* the heart of every city I visited in

Japan—not our stone churches (built on feudal models, fortresses to withstand time and invaders) but fully accessible garden spots that celebrate natural cycles of impermanence—sacramental buildings *at one* with plants and grass and trees rather than deliberately divorced from that "pagan" presence.

I'd miss *sono-mama* (suchness, or making do with what you have) as applied to the problem of available *space* in Japan, a nation in which, at first feeling like the proverbial bull in the china shop, I'd eventually learned to restrain my potential for destruction, to accommodate myself to small clubs, small rooms, tiny elevators, and streets no wider than sidewalks. No longer intimidated by minimalism, I'd managed to wean myself of the American craving for spaciousness. I could actually accept the *sono-mama* of where, and when, and what I was.

And I would miss *junsui* or *mujaki* (innocence; a naïve, ingenuous quality). Some of the last examples of remarkable English I'd been collecting were discovered on T-shirts: a kid in Nagoya whose T-shirt read "Masturbation well made you go blind"; a young woman whose bright yellow T-shirt read "Gets over . . . fancied"; and a final item that rose and fell upon another girl's chest: the single word "Romeoville." I had discovered a highly active jazz scene in Japan, and I'm sure the less attractive business or "professional" aspects attendant on any art form are present there, somewhere, but I hadn't found much evidence of them, and my most lasting impression was of a very refreshing *junsui*, a nearly naïve innocence, connected with the music: a joyous, not yet jaded or shopworn attitude.

When I landed once more in the States, the first T-shirt I would see—at the San Francisco airport—showed the silhouette of a large man pointing a gun at the head of a small woman, their genders identified by trousers and a dress. A single word, "BITCH," was inscribed at the top. In spite of eagerly adopted Western hype and hustle and haste, the incessant hard sell of Americanism, I never saw anything like that in Japan.

I spent my last night in Japan at the Over Seas Club, owned and operated by its excellent house pianist, Hisayuki Terai, and his wife, Tamae—the couple I'd met and talked to briefly on the afternoon we'd first driven around Osaka with Mr. Matsumoto and his daughter, Emi. I'd promised Hisayuki and Tamae that I would return for a night of music before I left Japan—and here I was, albeit soaking wet, drenched by a sudden rainstorm I'd gotten caught in.

"Do you take requests?" I asked Hisayuki-san when I walked through the door.

He arched his brows, watching the moisture descend from my clothes and accumulate at the edge of my shoes.

"'Singing in the Rain'?" I asked, and Hisayuki laughed as his wife rushed off to find towels, and hot sake, for the chilled, wet gaijin.

Tamae is a woman of many accomplishments. Having learned English from American jazz musicians rather than textbooks, she was one of the best, most thorough, most accurate translators I found in Japan. So what ensued was a family affair, and I shall present it that way.

> *Me:* "Tell me why you started the Over Seas Club."
> *Tamae:* "He needed a place to play." [*She laughed.*]
> *Me:* "Has it been difficult, keeping the club alive, keeping it going?"
> *Hisayuki:* "It's probably about the same as it would be in your town in the States. Very hard. I am working very hard here, from morning until late at night."

Thinking of a potential audience, I mentioned the gap between generations of jazz fans in the States but said how impressed I'd been, the previous day, with the Arrow Jazz Orchestra Music School and the number of *young* jazz fans I'd seen at the Mt. Fuji Jazz Festival in Yokohama.

> *Tamae:* "It's a slow thing, yeah. The young people *do* like music. Older people tend to stick or listen to music they already know, standards like 'Autumn Leaves' or 'I Remember Clifford,' tunes like that. But the young people are very open-minded."
> *Me:* "I thought it interesting that, at Yokohama, the largest crowds had turned out for Jackie McLean and Junko Onishi, not just 'Ponta' Murakami and his quasi-rock group. They were there for good solid *jazz*."
> *Tamae:* "Yeah, they really appreciate it. And they are open to bop, beyond the standard tunes."
> *Me:* "Is this a good time in Japan for jazz?"
> *Tamae:* "No, no. It's very hard now. Probably the hardest time." [*She laughed.*]

Hisayuki: "I am afraid that things are getting worse. As a player, I had to start out by 'copying' or transcribing the music. That was the best way, the only way, for me. But it's no good to just play a transcription of what's on the record albums. The most important thing for young musicians is to see and hear musicians playing jazz *live*. To see how they count the time, how they *breathe*. If a young musician can see this he can understand what's happening, what's going on. But the great American masters are dying off, one after another, these days. The chances for young musicians to hear them are getting less and less, I'm afraid. Young musicians have a hard time now, especially in Japan."

Tamae: "And the music schools in Japan are very bad. The educational system is very bad. There are a lot of schools available to young musicians but they are so . . . old."

Hisayuki: "In Japan, the teachers are the second-class players. The teachers are people who can't *play* music."

Tamae: "They are people who have gone to, like, Berklee and just graduated. They have a degree and come back to Japan and become teachers. But they are *terrible* when they play!"

Hisayuki: "And so I tend to discriminate against Berklee graduates."

Tamae: "The jazz scene is very different now. That's Hisayuki's view."

Me: "How about finding sidemen, *good* sidemen, people to work with you: is that difficult? Good bassists, good drummers . . ."

Hisayuki [in English]: "Yeah. The bass player I have now is the *sixth* bass player I've had. And I've had *five* drummers. They were all young."

Tamae: "They like to come here to play with *him*. For the love of it, not the money."

Hisayuki: "You have a different cause if you wish to be a real jazz musician. There is one bass player in Osaka who is a great bass player. Tommy Flanagan was amazed when he listened to him. His name is Sumi. And he's working, playing in Osaka. He was once a *cook*. A chef! When he was twenty, or something like that, he went to a jazz club and he was amazed by the music, so he started playing. He has an incredible ear

259

and great dexterity. He's been playing here for sixty years now. He plays a hell of a lot of music still! New York musicians call him 'Little George.' For George Mraz."

We discussed the issue of "imitation" as it relates to jazz musicians in Japan, and that led, inevitably, to the high regard that Hisayuki has for American pianist Tommy Flanagan, the strong influence Flanagan has had on him.

Hisayuki: "At first I did not have my own style. I just *loved* Tommy Flanagan. I was Flanagan crazy. I collected all of his work, over 350 recordings by Tommy Flanagan. I learned even the shortest phrase he played as a sideman. I feel now that this was a really *silly* thing to do, but at the time, I wanted to *be* Tommy Flanagan. [*He laughed.*] I first heard him live in 1975, when Ella Fitzgerald came to Japan with Tommy. He was her accompanist. He was forty-five years old. I was twenty-three. At that first concert, Tommy's trio played for about forty minutes. And right after that, Ella came on stage and sang for one and a half hours. . . . Tommy told me to send a tape to him in New York. Before this happened I thought it was okay just to *copy* Tommy Flanagan, but once I got his request to send a tape, I tried to establish my own thing. Once, long ago, whenever I played, it was Flanagan, Flanagan, Flanagan. But after playing Flanagan, Flanagan, Flanagan, I thought, 'This is my own.' Before, one day I couldn't recognize which of us was which . . . and that day was probably the start of establishing my own style. [*Tamae laughed with appreciation, as she had throughout this account.*] Whenever I asked him, 'How did you like the tape I sent you,' Tommy always responded, 'Well, *good.*' Just 'good!' For *ten* years I kept sending him tapes. Tapes and tapes and tapes. When Tommy finally came to my house, on one of his tours of Japan, he asked me to play for him. So I started to play in our room that has a piano. Tommy listened to me. I turned to look at him. I played some more. And he said *nothing.* At one point he came over and pressed a note, my back to him still. He said, 'That finger, in your left hand, you are using it wrong.' He hadn't even been looking at me. He wasn't *watching* me. He just *heard* that. I was flabbergasted!"

Me: "Was he right?"

Tamae: "He was right!"

Hisayuki: "I played very rapidly at that time. I used four fingers of each hand. So Tommy came over and said, 'Here's what I do.' And he gave me a lesson. He showed me how he played that part, how he used *all* of his fingers. This was my first lesson: the first time, after sending him tapes for ten years, he'd *teach* me something. He had never said anything—except 'good'— until that night! But after that he would teach me at any time, any time I needed advice—on the phone, in a coffeeshop, wherever. Any time. It became very easy for him to give me advice. How to do intro, how to do endings. He taught me how to *play.*"

Tamae: "And I think Hisayuki got much better after that. As if, after that moment, he rocketed!" [*She laughed.*]

Me: "Has he heard your CD *Flanagania,* your homage to him?"

Tamae: "He said, 'It's much *different* than what I do, but it's a very nice interpretation.' And Hisayuki also has a CD called *Dalarna.* The title tune is one by Tommy that he recorded in Japan, in 1957. So Hisayuki made a CD and used 'Dalarna' as the title tune. Right after that, just a few months ago, Tommy made a recording and did 'Dalarna' again. But he hadn't recorded it or played it in any jazz club for thirty-nine years! Hisayuki is very proud, because Tommy called him and said, 'I've just recorded for a Japanese record company, and guess what tune I did?' 'Probably "Dalarna"?' 'Yes, I did!' [*We all laughed.*] We actually had Tommy here, at the Over Seas Club, in May. This May. He played *here.* And that was amazing!"

Although he does not perform, or record, outside of Japan, Hisayuki Terai's three CDs—*Flanagania, Dalarna,* and the more recent *Fragrant Times*—are available in the States through *Cadence* magazine. *Flanagania* features three original pieces by Tommy Flanagan ("Minor Mishap," which Hisayuki would play later for me; "Rachel's Rondo"; and "Mean Streets"), plus two fine tunes by Tadd Dameron: "Smooth as the

Wind" and "If You Could See Me Now." "Smooth as the Wind" is just that: showing fine accord between Hisayuki Terai and bassist Masahiro Munetake, whom I would hear later that night, a young musician who has been studying and working with the pianist for ten years. Hisayuki belongs to a tradition of what might be dubbed "aristocratic" jazz piano (Tommy Flanagan, Hank Jones, Kenny Barron, Fred Hirsch, Jessica Williams, Lynne Arriale), musicians who combine deft touch, intelligence, taste, and eloquence with firm, resolute, no-nonsense, totally dedicated purpose or drive.

I think Thelonious Monk would approve of what Hisayuki does with "Pannonica," another handsome, precise, respectful homage, replete with rare (unique) chords, tasty dynamics, a bright veneer, a fine glaze with a host of shades and hues within, mixed with appropriately abrupt or staccato effects, a class act, a rich absorption of Monk turned back into strictly Terai again. The title tune from *Dalarna* is delivered with the same respectful pride and eloquence I found on the other CD, never haughty but superbly confident, a homage not only to Tommy Flanagan but to Terai's own lifelong study, discipline, commitment.

I was curious as to how Hisayuki, isolated in a sense as he was in Osaka, had managed to get reviewed in the U.S.

> *Tamae:* "Hisayuki has a friend who's a record dealer in the States, a Japanese man who has a very small shop. We sent the CDs to him, and he sent a couple of copies to *Cadence*. After a few months, they wrote to me, saying, 'Please look at this magazine.' We were amazed. We never expected to see a review in the U.S. of Hisayuki's CDs!"

Tamae produced a copy of an August 1996 issue of *Cadence* that contained a review of Hisayuki Terai's *Dalarna*. It is a very favorable review that praises the pianist's tribute to "one of the most musical—precise, responsive, and tasteful—of jazz pianists," Tommy Flanagan, adding that "Flanagan's qualities include a certain self-effacement that says much about what Terai values." Stuart Broomer's review was one of few I'd read that seems to comprehend the unique nature of the *sensei* system on its own terms. "For all his deference, even reverence," Broomer continues, "there's nothing stiff or staid about Terai's playing. He has a developed sense of bop piano language. . . . It includes the essential amalgam of passion and rhythmic and harmonic nuance that is the hallmark of its best early players." The reviewer did raise some questions about the role of "interpreter's interpreter," saying, "Terai may sound more vital than many pianists, but whose vitality is it?" A fair question, given music that walks so worshipfully in light given off by its master, but I'd answer, "The vitality is Terai's."

We discussed the level of jazz performance in Japan, imitative or not. Hisayuki Terai's response surprised me.

> *Hisayuki:* "I really think the level of musicianship is much lower than that in the U.S. The Japanese have a handicap when it comes to being jazz musicians. It is very difficult for Japanese children to get a chance to hear jazz music in Japan. So we tend to hear the music for the first time when we are already grown up. But Tommy Flanagan grew up listening to jazz music when he was a small child. That never happens in Japan. Hopefully, from now on, the handicap will be less, because the situation is balancing out. Hearing jazz music live is not such a major thing anymore. For example, George Mraz grew up in Czechoslovakia and became a great musician—probably the greatest bass player in the world. So a Japanese musician could become number one also!"

I mentioned Akira Tana's reservation about foreign "adoption" of the music, his concern that musicians from other nations might not be as concerned about the historical or cultural significance of jazz, that they might miss out on the wider context. True?

> *Hisayuki:* "Japanese children are always watching TV. Music on TV has a great effect on these children. But TV in Japan no longer presents diverse styles of music. So there is not much exposure to jazz anymore, much less its social or historical significance."
>
> *Me:* "I'm afraid the same thing may be true in the United States, with rare exceptions."

I mentioned the writer in Boston who felt Japanese graduates of Berklee College returning to Japan might produce a unique form of

"Japanese jazz." I also mentioned Makoto Ozone's interest in tango and his indifference, now, to traditional Japanese instruments. How did Hisayuki feel?

> *Hisayuki:* "You are an American, Mr. Minor. But what do you think is going on in a Japanese musician's mind when he plays jazz? I think most Japanese first hear *melody,* not chords. After that, they recognize the rhythm. And then comes harmony, the chords. Melody first, then rhythm, then harmony. It takes time for them to recognize *all* of the elements. Japanese, traditionally, ethnically, have an ear for melody, just melody. Single tones. So it takes a lot of time to absorb everything, all of the various aspects of jazz. And after all the musical elements have been absorbed, they finally recognize the *lyrics.* They discover the lyrics, but when they sing, they don't really understand what they themselves are saying, or singing. [*He laughed.*] You must recognize the lyrics and the melody together, as *uta* [song]. Plus the rhythm and harmony. Everything! You must think, 'I really want to play it *all.*' But that really takes time. Even more time for Japanese musicians. The most important thing for me just now is the *lyrics.* It is very challenging to have the melody and the sense of the lyrics come together, emerge at the same time. Even if it's *English* with a Japanese accent! But I want to be able to make my *feelings* come across to an audience."

I confessed that the major difficulty I'd had with some of the jazz music I'd heard in Japan was with vocalists, acknowledging the difficulty of attempting to communicate intense emotion through a language, and a vocal inflection or intonational emphasis, you may not completely understand.

> *Tamae:* "They have to *study,* yes. It really does present a problem in jazz."
>
> *Hisayuki:* "But not all Japanese know karate either, or do Zen practice. So when you think about the *meaning* of a song, you are showing your very own view or feelings, as a Japanese. For me, revealing Japanese tradition comes across as playing who *I am,* expressing my own feelings, my own views, my own

relation to the music. I really love the song 'I Cover the Waterfront.' But when I play it, I want to show the Japanese way to cover the waterfront." [*Tamae laughed, in appreciation.*]

Me: "*Hontō ni!* [Wow!] What *is* the Japanese way to cover the waterfront?"

Hisayuki: "*That* would be really difficult to express in words. But there are so many *styles*. Perhaps the Japanese *umi* [sea] would be different—the experience of living by the sea."

Me: "But it's something of a traditional love song in *any* language. 'Will the one I love be coming back to me?'"

Hisayuki: "The lyrics would be the same, yes, but the interpretation of them—from a gaijin and a Japanese point of view—would be slightly different. Just to stand by the waterfront might, from a Japanese point of view, be more of a minor-key feeling. *Kanashii* [sad]. Tommy Flanagan would perhaps think that his lover will *never* come back again and accept that, so he'd better get back down to earth. But to me—playing with a young Japanese bass player as I am—I would want to give a *yume wa takara* [dream quality] to the song. I would want to present an optimistic view to young musicians, so I would not make the song quite so sad, because I expect these two lovers to get *back together!* I believe that, some day, the lovers will be united again. It's probably not all that much a Japanese/American difference, but I believe it's very important to teach this other meaning of the song to young Japanese musicians. What is this song all about? American musicians don't even have to think to understand the words, for they know the meaning easily."

Me: "Perhaps, but I'm not so sure they always do."

Hisayuki: "The most important thing I got from Tommy Flanagan is the importance of *uta* [the song, the lyrics]. He always told me to listen to Billie Holiday. All the time, all the time. Billie Holiday has had a lot of influence on Tommy's music."

Tamae: "She doesn't sound like *anybody* else. And it seems as though she is telling a *story,* just to me. It's a very individual, a very *personal* message."

Me: "Will the Over Seas Club be around for another eighteen years? If I come back in eighteen years will it still be here?"

Hisayuki: "I hope so."

Tamae: "But I don't want to be over fifty." [*She laughed.*]

Me: "Hey, that's not so bad! I'm an *akachan.*" [*This is a special Japanese word that literally means "little red thing," or baby, but in this case applied to people who've just turned sixty and no longer have any worrisome cares or responsibilities.*]

Hisayuki Terai and bassist Masahiro Munetake made my last night in Japan an absolute treat. They played Tommy Flanagan's "Minor Mishap." (Hisayuki introduced me as "a journalist from America" and reassured me at break time, "You're *not* a minor mishap.") It was all there: the deft touch, the forward momentum, the fine bop lines, speed, dexterity, passion, a certain infectious gregariousness. If I make Hisayuki Terai out to be one of my most pleasant surprises or "discoveries" in Japan, a musician of exceptional merit, it's because he was. His music is some of the most *engaging* I encountered: the epitome of Japanese craftsmanship (years of discipline resulting in skill that disclosed the success of his quest), everything down to seamless interaction with his "protégé" bassist. At one point Munetake got ahead of the tempo, and the pianist flashed a glance his way and shook his head, just enough to let the younger man know who was *sensei* in this house, but with subtlety, not in a patronizing manner. Munetake's solos were handsome constructions that evolved quite naturally from his smooth rhythmic support. Another Flanagan original, "Mean Streets," turned into an uptempo romp loaded with acrobatic bop, the bassist *there*, all the way— the tune ending with the initial notes of "I Can't Get Started."

In the morning, on my last day in Japan, standing on a street corner in Osaka waiting for the light to change, I was detained by an old woman, a crone, who asked if I understood Nihongo. When I said, "Taihen heta desu" (I speak poorly), she proceeded to bless me, right there in broad daylight, others waiting at the light—which seemed to be spending an inordinate amount of time *not* changing—amused by this scene, I'm sure. The crone blessed my *migi no te* (right hand), then my *hidari no te* (left hand), and probably would have done my entire body had the light not—blessedly—then changed.

After my plane took off from Kansai Airport, I ordered the first glass of wine (California chardonnay, of course) I'd had in one and a half months (fine wine is easy to find in Japan, but I'd gone "native" in my eating and drinking habits). When Betty left Japan from Kansai, her plane headed out toward the ocean, then dipped back inland for her one-and-only view of Mt. Fuji, crimson-glazed in sunrise. I had no such luck. Twilight time had not yet come, but Fuji was nowhere in sight. Just "water, water everywhere," and a long sea voyage ahead of me. Basho has a haiku that goes, "A day when Fuji / Is obscured by misty rain! / That's interesting." The poem purportedly points out the folly of fixed expectations, the need to accept *what is as is,* to blur distinctions between good and bad days ("Every day is a good day"), between inspiring and bland, bitter and sweet. But I really *wanted* to see Fuji and was not in a mood to find its ongoing and now final absence *omoshiroki* (the older form of "interesting" used in the poem). As compensation, I sipped my wine and thought about the deck just outside our kitchen at home, a perfect place to sit on a "good" day, a quiet spot adorned with flowers—many of which would still be in bloom—that Betty tended, making the spot a sort of miniature Eden, very "Japanese" as far as space was concerned, a splendid place to write a book about jazz in Japan.

29

BACK HOME: KOTO MASTER MIYA MASAOKA

The koto—a thirteen-string instrument with a body made from two pieces of paulownia wood, originally intended to imitate the shape of a crouching dragon—is mentioned on fifteen different occasions in Japan's first novel (and perhaps the world's), *The Tale of Genji,* written in the eleventh century. In the epic *Tale of the Heike,* a warrior finds the emperor's lost paramour by way of the unique voice of her koto playing. How then, nineteen centuries later, did a Japanese American woman born in Washington, D.C., discover and eventually master this ancient instrument, expanding its traditional capabilities to include new music and jazz?

"My cousin played the koto," Miya Masaoka told me during an interview after I'd returned to the States and just before she performed in the northern California premier of Toshiko Akiyoshi's *Jazz Suite for Koto and Orchestra.* "She was really the koto player in the family. Her name was Midori, and she was a few years older than I. We would get pictures at Christmastime or a birthday of her in kimono playing the koto. I thought, 'How beautiful.' In the meantime, I was taking piano lessons."

Miya Masaoka is a San Francisco–based performer and composer well on her way to establishing a solid international reputation. She has appeared at the Du Maurier Jazz Festival in Vancouver; the Banlieue Blues Festival in Paris (with Steve Coleman); in Banglor, India (with virtuoso violinist L. Subramaniam); with George Lewis at the Jazz Marathon in Holland; and on an Ethnic Musical Festival tour in Japan. She has performed with Akiyoshi, Pharoah Sanders, the Cecil Taylor

Orchestra, Mark Izu, Wadada Leo Smith, James Newton, and the ROVA Saxophone Quartet. Masaoka received a bachelor of arts in music (magna cum laude) from San Francisco State University and a master of arts in composition at Mills College in Oakland. A serious student of *gagaku,* she has successfully combined traditional koto techniques with cutting-edge devices. During a residency at STEIM, in Amsterdam, Holland, she developed a midi interface and expanded the koto's sonic capabilities. Her recorded work ranges from *Innocent Eyes and Lenses: Sounds like 1996: Music by Asian American Artists* to *Monk's Japanese Folk Song* with Andrew Cyrille and Reggie Workman.

Masaoka's serious interest in the koto coincided with the death of the cousin who had inspired it, by suicide. "It was pure coincidence, or maybe it wasn't; I don't know," Miya said. "A friend of mine said there was a garage sale near his home, and they were selling a koto. I had been looking for one, so I pretty much started around that period of time, after her death, when I was in college."

Masaoka studied traditional Japanese music with two *sensei,* Seiko Shimaoka and Suenobu Togi, and then went on to develop her own approach to technique and musical vocabulary. The skill she has developed over the years attracted the attention of Toshiko Akiyoshi, who came to hear her play at a Madison Square Garden concert in 1996. "I invited her, but I couldn't believe she came. She had to sit through so many others, hours and hours. I played about a ten-minute improvised solo, and I played in this large symphony: a piece that Subramanian had written. Toshiko sent me a really nice postcard saying how much she liked the music, a very very nice gesture."

The Akiyoshi/Masaoka performance I attended in October also saw its composer's "remarkable life and career" honored by way of Toshiko Akiyoshi Day in San Francisco. "It was a great experience," Masaoka said, "because the band members are really top-notch musicians. It was challenging for me because they are so precise in their rhythmic interpretation. The feeling was very positive because the piece was interesting for them, and stimulating."

Jazz Suite for Koto and Orchestra is made up of three instrumental movements, each quite different from the others. Masaoka said that, for the first section, Toshiko wrote out a scale that was "pretty much her own." Each movement had its own koto tuning. The first, in the composer's words, contrasted the serenity of "beautiful temples" with the everyday world that surrounds them, people "going about their business"—both states, or moods, existing side-by-side. Lew Tabackin's flute and four short big band flaring notes were offset by what Masaoka has described as "traditional Japanese technique and feeling on the koto"—albeit offset by smooth disciplined swing; chirping high-register koto played off against basso resonance and bent blue notes.

The second movement, introduced by Akiyoshi as having a "nice and easy" Caribbean mood ("ocean, trees, daydreaming"), found Masaoka's koto setting up a rhythmic pattern ascending in pitch, laced with Tabackin's flute. The last movement was set at a frantic urban pace ("It could be Tokyo, or New York," Akiyoshi said, "but I think I'll just say 'the city'"), resembling the *kyū*, or the suddenly urgent, hurried final section in *gagaku*, Kabuki, and Noh music. Asked if the piece as a whole follows the classic *jo ha kyū* pattern (prelude / breaking away [exposition] / "rushing to the finish"), Masaoka said, "Not intentionally, but in a sense they are there, subconsciously." Masaoka's rapidly repeated single note was matched by drummer Terry Clarke's quick high-hat riff. "I like the way it sounds," Masaoka said. "It happens again later for ten bars; then I have a long solo at the end. It was Toshiko's idea, and it's a great one. She's really incredible. She's accomplished so much in her lifetime, so I was excited to be able to play with her. She's an icon."

The koto's history is laced with somewhat rigid schools or guilds, ranging from the sixteenth-century Tsukushi-goto school (founded by a priest, Kenjun) to the instrument and style called *zokuso* (vulgar koto) of the Yatsuhashi school, started when one of Kenjun's students taught a blind man (at that time forbidden) to play. Later, you *had* to be blind to be a member of some guilds! By the eighteenth century, the koto repertoire had expanded to include use in ensembles and to accompany dance and vocal lines. In the twentieth century, Michio Miyagi, who extended the number of strings on the koto to seventeen, asserted that the new *hōgaku* (native Japanese music) should sound "as well as Debussy" and that it was time to approach music "from the standpoint of the age of Bartók." Now, Miya Masaoka has increased the potential even further, making the instrument unique and demanding in the context of jazz.

When it comes to a method of instruction, Masaoka prefers an "older way." "Students want everything explained to them, yet at a certain point you realize you don't just *explain* it. You just *do it*. You do it and watch and *listen*. The tea ceremony is like that, because you don't explain to someone, 'You pick up the lid like this.' It's learning with the *body,* and your body physically, intuitively, learns things. It's an unspoken understanding of things." Some schools are "still protective," she said. "I've had students who made me swear not to tell anyone that they were my students. If word ever got back to Japan, there could be very negative repercussions." Her own break with tradition was not "dramatic," she said. "I already had a fair amount of musical independence. I've done two tours of Japan, and they view my music as being very much *both* Japanese and American, just as I am. People often ask, What's the response there? Or, Do they think it's weird what you're doing? But actually it's not that way at all. It's very natural."

Masaoka has incorporated lesser-known traditional Japanese instruments in her work, such as the *shō* (seventeen reed pipes in a cup-shaped chest), used in "Trilogy for Sho, Bassoon and Koto"; or, in "The Wanderers and the Firefly," three *hichirikis:* short double-reed woodwinds that Sei Shonagon, author of *The Pillow Book,* found distasteful, comparing their sound to "the noisy crickets of autumn."

Japan has traditions much younger than ancient *gagaku.* In 1955, a visual arts group, Gutai Bijutsu Kyōkai (the Gutai Art Association), staged an unprecedented event. Taking over a pine grove park along the industrial beachfront in Ashiya, near Osaka, they presented a thirteen-day, twenty-four-hour, open-air exhibition that included gigantic sculptures made of abandoned machinery; a rippling-in-the-wind, bubblegum-pink vinyl sheet pinned just above the ground; and a store-bought ball set on the pavement entitled *Work B.* Other groups followed: Yayoi Kusama's Obsessional Art (reflecting the ills of society and self) and the antirationalist, anti-Europanism Fluxus movement, of which Yoko Ono was a part. Masaoka interviewed Ono for the *San Francisco Bay Guardian,* and the two discussed everything from the "animalistic side of the human voice" (as "deep-rooted memory, human history"), to politically inspired performance art, to *wakon yōsai* ("Japanese spirit/Western technique"), to the texture and smell of John Lennon's skin. Masaoka has composed a number of performance pieces herself: the "Bee Project"—a composition scored for violin, percussion, bowed koto, and three thousand live bees—and "What Is the Difference Between Stripping and Playing the Violin?"—a piece performed at the United Nations Plaza in San Francisco, for orchestra, boom box, and live strippers.

Miya Masaoka's latest adaption of traditional koto is Koto-Monster, a device that entails attaching wires to the performer and a microcomputer. Masaoka told writer Evantheia Schibsted that, playing Koto-Monster, she draws on the rich technologies and cultures of three millennia: "To me it's a way of having technology be more of an extension of the human body and mind, more humanizing." Masaoka described the process to me: "I wear rings that capture gestures, my motions, so in a certain way I almost capture the *jo ha kyu,* because that's also a motion as well. There are sensors off of each ring, and the receivers can, with an accuracy of one-third of a millimeter, detect the position of my hand. It's not random because you learn where the sounds are, and you can create pieces based on where they are in space. It's really exciting."

Miya Masaoka is a musical artist who can move effortlessly from "Kōjō no Tsuki" (Moon Over the Desolate Castle) to "Monk's Mood" and "'Round Midnight" (all on her *Monk's Japanese Folk Song* CD). On *Compositions/Improvisations,* the range of "statement" goes from delicate *yūgen* (the Japanese aesthetic concept that implying emotion is preferable, even more powerful, than explicitly stating it), to haunting minimalism, to stark percussion (the koto producing the "bombs" a drummer might provide), to the solemn brooding reflection of "Topaz" (about the relocation center where her mother was imprisoned for four years), to a handsome blues-inflected reading of Duke Ellington's "Come Sunday" and a stunning duet with flutist James Newton.

Kami no nori koto means "oracles of the gods" in Japanese. From *The Tale of Genji* to Godzilla, from crouching dragon to Koto-Monster: has the instrument retained its divine properties? "I did concerts with Ainu musicians, the indigenous people of Japan," Miya Masaoka says, "and they have a koto called *tonkori.* It actually has a little ball, a wooden ball, in it that you can shake. They say this is the soul of the instrument. We're not allowed to throw *gakaku* instruments away, even after they break. I have a closet full of these instruments, because they are *sacred.* It has to do with the Shintō belief that air, sky, rocks, rivers are spirits, embodying spirits. The koto is a *tree.* Really it is a *log.* It's just a hollow log with strings across it. When you pluck a string, it's releasing the sound of the tree, of the instrument. Even the Koto-Monster. It's part animal, part person, part computer. So it contains *all* things."

30

SADAO WATANABE, AKI TAKASE, AND KAZUMI WATANABE

I WOULD LIKE TO ALTER JUST one word in something Erich Heller has said of poetry: "In speaking about [music] we always mean more than [music], just as [music] always means more than itself." I have referred, frequently, to the persistence of music alongside everything else in Japan, but the reverse is also true: the compatibility of arts such as poetry and calligraphy with ceremonial music—and jazz. Robert H. Brower and Earl Miner have written about the "particularly fine adjustment of tone" they find in court poetry, "an instinct especially well suited to exploring states of feeling, mind and being." It should have come as no surprise to me, then, reading some of my favorite Japanese poems—*hyaku-nin-isshiu* (single verses by a hundred people)—with my daughter-in-law Yoko, when, knowing them by heart, she also began to *sing* them. Donald Keene has commented on the fact that, when the printing of books was introduced by Prince Shotoku as early as 770, it did not "take" until 1600, because of the Japanese aesthetic preference for "inconvenient and expensive manuscripts" that combined calligraphy and illustration, "so integral a part of literary works that a bare printed edition would have seemed as incomplete as a theatrical work without music." And it should have come as no surprise to me when, thinking of three fine jazz artists I had not been fortunate enough to interview, I found myself comparing them to their literary counterparts.

One such musician, Sadao Watanabe, an inveterate world traveler who was "out of town" while I was in Japan, is a seminal figure in Japanese jazz, regarded by many as its *otōsan* (father). He is the man who brought the Berklee "system" back to his native country after he attended that college in the States as the second Japanese jazz artist to do so (following in the wake of Toshiko Akiyoshi). He reminded me of the popular Japanese novelist Yukio Mishima.

Watanabe, a man who appears to have *no* political ambitions (Mishima commited seppuku—ritual suicide—after an attempted coup by his "revolutionary army," a handful of supporters who shared his ultranationalist dream of restoring Japan's military might, failed), is alive and well at age sixty-seven and flourishing as an artist who works in several musical genres. What the two have in common is the ability to mix work of considerable artistic merit with overt commercialism. Both became familiar household icons in Japan by way of mass media. Yukio Mishima appeared on TV, advertised commercial products, and established a record of being "continually at the center of sensational news," even holding an exhibition of nude photos of himself. Sadao Watanabe, too, established a reputation early as a highly respected bop alto saxophonist and then went on to produce an endless string of very popular, strictly commercial recordings that led some critics to compare him to Chuck Mangione, others, less favorably, to Kenny G. Watanabe's smiling, ruddy face has appeared on TV commercials hawking everything from Coca-Cola, Wrangler jeans, and Bravo Cologne to formal wear, coffee, and even a construction firm. Watanabe possesses a highly polished, pure alto tone and an apparently inexhaustible gift for melody— which places him squarely in the Japanese musical tradition. That tone is as unthreatening apparently as the man himself, who once told writer Diana Patrick, "If I get excited, I don't play well. I hate shouting and am looking to communicate something light and gentle." In this he differs from Yukio Mishima.

Sadao Watanabe was born in Utsunomiya, a city ninety miles north of Tokyo. He grew up hearing traditional and classical Japanese music. His father, an electrician, played and taught *biwa* (a four-string Japanese lute with high frets). At the age of fourteen, he'd never heard jazz, but "the day after the war was over," as he told writer Andrew Taylor, American Service Radio changed all that. The young Sadao ran home from school each day to listen to "Jazz Hour" on the radio. Watching Bing Crosby simulate playing the clarinet in *Birth of the Blues,* Watanabe persuaded his father to buy him one, and from that point on there was no turning back. At three cents a lesson, an old man in his neighborhood taught him basic fingering, and Watanabe "took the rest of his early musical education upon himself." Not too successfully at first, it seems, for once he started playing with local jazz bands, patrons asked the leader to "please let the clarinet boy be fired."

Later, he switched to saxophone and became proficient enough to join Toshiko Akiyoshi's Cozy Quartet in 1957. On her recommendation, Watanabe scraped together enough money for a plane ticket and attended Berklee College of Music in Boston. Gary McFarland hired Watanabe to play tenor sax and flute (it was, at the time, very rare to find a jazz musician who could play flute) in his "soft samba" band, music that at first Watanabe found dull but that—once he heard Brazilian music played by Brazilian musicians—became a key part of his musical development. Since that time, Watanabe's honors—and albums—have grown legion. By 1989, readers of *Swing Journal* had voted him Best Alto Saxophonist every year since 1959, and he had established a popular weekly radio program called "My Dear Life" (the title of one of his original tunes). In 1985, he produced Bravas Club '85, a twenty-three-day jazz festival in Tokyo (an annual event underwritten by its namesake's cosmetic company). A travel addict, Watanabe has visited, recorded in, and returned to Japan with the music of Africa, Brazil, and India—his appreciation extending from the high-life music of King Sunny Ade to the tribal music of the Masai ("They have very original music, and even the way they talk is very musical").

Whatever his reputation as opportunist, Sadao Watanabe has never fully parted company with his hard-won jazz chops. His work can be divided into three categories: Charlie Parker–influenced bop, fusion, and strictly pop or commercial recordings. On two CDs that epitomize the first mode, *Bird of Paradise* and *Parker's Mood,* he shows why he is highly regarded as a jazz artist. *Bird of Paradise* is subtitled *Sadao Watanabe with the Great Jazz Trio,* a not-so-modest matchup until you discover that the great jazz trio is made up of Hank Jones, Ron Carter, and Tony Williams. All four shine brightly. Watanabe's tone seems infinitely adjustable, for in this tough company it carries an edge of asperity, Williams's bass drum "bombs" and overriding ride cymbal (drummer as playground bully!) leaving just enough room for the saxophonist to float within: fast, agile, accurate, inventive. "Donna Lee" is taken at breakneck speed, the altoist on top of the task at every turn, phrase feeding on phrase.

Parker's Mood features James Williams on piano, whose comping is more *architectural,* perhaps, than that of Jones (the master of taste, touch, and drive), his solos more constructed, but that inspires the same mode in Watanabe, to good effect. The tunes are classics: J. J. Johnson's "Lament," "Billie's Bounce," "I Thought about You" (Watanabe providing love-letter calligraphy with his own elegant touch), and a gorgeous "Everything Happens to Me," on which Watanabe truly "sings," his tone both tender and brash.

Sadao Watanabe's early jazz legacy is well documented on *A History of King Jazz Recordings,* from 1957 through 1962, and with a range of Japanese musicians from Toshiko, tenor saxophonist Akira Miyazawa, pianist Masao Yagi, drummer Takeshi "Sticks" Inomata, and Hidehiko "Sleepy" Matsumoto, to fine fellow altoist Akitoshi Igarashi and guitarist Shungo Sawada. His fusion legacy is also well documented (*Rendezous* finds him in the good company of Steve Gadd, Marcus Miller, and Eric Gale, with Roberta Flack providing vocals on two songs), and Watanabe's agreeable, cheerful (at times saccharine) tone— however much you might be tempted to fault it—is truly often a thing of beauty on recordings like this. There's more of the same pleasing groove on a 1989 Elektra "best of" recording, *Selected,* and also a taste of the wide range Watanabe is capable of within the same genre. But perhaps the most rewarding venture in this vein (for me—I have not attempted to sort fusion from pop here, because I'm not sure I can) is a live concert held at Budōkan in Tokyo, July 1980. (Watanabe was the first jazz musician to headline at this ten-thousand-seat government-owned arena.) "Up Country" finds the Tokyo Philharmonic Orchestra declaring at the start, by way of violins on top, that this is a serious undertaking, and Watanabe receives a full round of applause just by walking on stage. The whole *package* of this production is seductive and impressive, I'll confess, making you wish you'd been there!

One of my all-time favorite CDs is a Sadao Watanabe recording I play again and again. It's one that might come under the classification of pop/jazz (bossa nova), with some folk thrown in for good measure. Although it's smooth as hell, I wouldn't relegate it to (or negate it as) "smooth jazz"; it's just *admirable. Made in Coracao* features Watanabe with guitarist/singer/composer Toquinho, from Brazil. From the first full-measure alto sax note on "Saudades de Elis" to the last on "Inquieto Amor," ten tunes float one into the other, free of friction, and with variety so subtle as to make up—for me—a suite. "Saudades" is unalloyed, unblighted by anything but sheer joy. I don't know Portuguese, unfortunately, so I just let the gentle, reflective mood of each tune, the perfect balance of Toquinho's consonants and vowels, massage my brain and take me wherever I wish to go. "Saudades de Elis" makes me want to dance and go on living forever; "Made in Coracao" is frisky, a female chorus chirping away (as economically as Brazilian beachwear), abandon under control; "Samba De Volta" is a joyous jam session.

I was not able to interview the highly respected, unique, and inventive pianist Aki Takase in Japan, not because I neglected, out of shyness or hesitation, to make such a move but because of simple geography. Takase lives in Germany, where she co-leads the Berlin Contemporary Orchestra with her husband, fellow pianist and composer Alexander von Schlippenbach. Born in Osaka, Takase—like so many Japanese musical artists—began to study classical piano early: at age three in her case (taking lessons from her mother). She played bass in her school orchestra and continued her piano studies at Toho Gakuen University in Tokyo, then moved on to jazz when a friend steered her toward John Coltrane because he was "like Beethoven." By the time she was twenty-five, she was leading her own groups. Appreciation for Coltrane, Charles Mingus, Ornette Coleman, and Albert Ayler led her in the direction of innovation and free improvisation. Duke Ellington and Cecil Taylor also served as sources of inspiration, compelling her to compose. She told *JazzTimes* writer Deni Kasrel, "In composition I can make it very clear, what I'm thinking about . . . with improvisation the ideas are there but it's easy to forget, because the notes will disappear."

Aki Takase is an excellent improviser as well as composer (she also lists Ravel, Debussy, Satie and Bartók among her influences), and her modesty belies the occasionally fierce dynamics and full-color spectrum of her performances (she studied with Yosuke Yamashita). She has also declared, "Most Japanese people, they are small. They don't have a lot of energy as a physical condition. Not like Americans who have big muscles and long fingers. For us it's not like this. Our energy is inside. We keep inner energy and we bring it up only sometimes." In recordings, Takase's energy is both internal and external, and she "attacks" a piano with the same savage and *ugokanai* (motionless) mastery that a samurai employs to best an overly proud opponent. Playing solo piano, she was the high spot at the Nuremberg East-West Festival in 1982. And again, reading one of my favorite Japanese writers, the inventively brilliant Kobo Abe, and listening to recordings by Aki Takase, I found a meaningful parallel.

Literary critic Shuichi Kato has said of Abe, "He describes fantastic scenes in an almost allegorical way, with an eeriness that is reminiscent of Kafka"—a description that could just as well apply to Takase's work, although she might object to the "eeriness" tag. If so, we could change that word to *yūrei no* (ghostly quality), for her pieces, like Abe's writing, catch one off guard and often contain unanticipated and *mezurashii* (unusual or uncommon) happenings. In a story by Abe called "Intruders," for example, from the collection *Beyond the Curve,* an obnoxious family moves into the apartment of a man named "X," uninvited, and hold him prisoner within his own lodgings. A vision of alienation and a sense of powerlessness in confrontation characterize Abe's writing.

The music of Aki Takase is nowhere as dark or fatalistic as all this sounds (Abe's excess, like Kafka's, frequently provides a *comic* effect), and Yosuke Yamashita has commented on the "unique positiveness that can be felt" in Takase. Both artists are brilliant stylists who draw on many sources (the *All Music Guide to Jazz* lists "Piano, Koto/Post-Bop, Free Jazz" under Takase's name, saying that she is "one of the most versatile figures in contemporary jazz"); both are "modernists" who make subtle use of traditional Japanese elements, masters of surprise or sudden dissonance, individualists with a surreal or offbeat (uninhibited) imagination, genuine *hatsumeisha* (inventors or originators) with an ability to move into (and out of) realms of abstraction—or allegory—others might not be willing to explore.

On her 1990 solo recording for Enja, *Shima Shoka,* Aki Takase's originality is readily apparent and consistent. "Meraviglioso," dedicated to Horst Weber, reveals her compositional skills (seven pieces on the recording are her own) and a sort of bluesy, Bud Powellish, even Tatumesque stateliness, confidence, and clarity. Her classical training provides her with a left hand (walking bass on this tune) that works just as hard as her right, but with apparent ease. Carla Bley's "Ida Lupino" provides a brooding mood, broken time, and diverse rhythmic effects. "A.V.S." (another original, her husband's initials) discloses bop chops, and "Shima Shoka" reminds one of Satie, the slowly emerging theme disclosing Takase's own fine quirks. Duke Ellington's "Rocking in Rhythm" offers a humorous, slightly perverse, highly condensed history of jazz from ragtime to right now. Takase's own "Timebends" seems caught in a gravitational field and shaped like a probability wave. "Hanabi" (which means "fireworks" in Japanese) is appropriately named.

Aki Takase teamed up with David Murray on a CD called *Blue*

Monk. It's a richly rewarding recording that puts her on a par with the great saxophonist. Takase knows the jazz past well, has mastered it (on a blindfold test given her by Horst Weber for *Jazz Podium,* she correctly identified each pianist—Bud Powell, Tommy Flanagan, Hampton Hawes, Sonny Clark, Cecil Taylor—except Elmo Hope), and she knows Monk and does him full justice. She and Murray lend a sassy strut (she with wicked, witty stride) to the title tune, and disassemble and reassemble (fine left- and right-hand counterpoint on Takase's part) on "Ask Me Now." Murray's "Ballad for the Blackman" soars, a longer (eleven minutes, twenty-nine seconds) piece whose core motif is converted into a stratospheric quest: the entire CD a first-class collaboration.

Takase teamed up with German tenor saxophonist Gunther Klatt on a salute to Duke Ellington (*Art of the Duo: Gunther Klatt and Aki Takase Play Ballads of Duke Ellington*), and in the CD's liner notes, Takase says, "When I play ballads, it's as if I am hearing solos from deep inside—stories filled with a mysterious dark eroticism. A ballad is something I want to take to bed with me. Embrace and caress and wake up to." The results live up to her words. On a CD called *Close Up of Japan,* Takase—featured with the Toki String Quartet and Nobuyoshi Ino on bass—brings her compositional and arranging skills to the fore (all of the arrangements are hers). Two violins, a viola, and cello jump to the "chase" in "Presto V.H.," a surreal, cacophonous affair. (Who's chasing who? Kobo Abe would love it! He has a story called "Beguiled" in which pursuer and pursued trade places at the close.) Astor Piazolla's "Winter in Buenos Aires" is ironically "polished" chamber music with a touch of tango toxicity mixed in, and Darius Milhaud's "Scaramouche" seems to combine gypsy Hot Club of France violin work with nineteenth-century cotillions and Gaelic step-dancing. Yet my favorite pieces on this CD are two originals by Takase: "Wagakokoro no Renaissance" (Renaissance of My Heart) and the title piece, "Close Up of Japan," the latter full of tough irony, the alienation that Kobo Abe seemed to love.

Kazumi Watanabe is another prominent musical artist I was not able to locate while in Japan. He reminds me of Haruki Murakami, whom *Time* magazine, in its inimitable manner, calls "the hip voice of a disenfranchised generation." Kuzumi Watanabe, born in 1953, has for the past fifteen years, according to the *All Music Guide to Jazz,* "been one of the top guitarists in fusion, a rock-oriented player whose furious power does not mask a certain imagination." A *New Yorker* profile noted "the almost complete absence of references to Japanese culture" in Murakami's early work; Watanabe, in an interview for *Guitar Player* magazine, said that, aside from occasional use of a pentatonic scale, whatever he incorporates from Japanese culture "just appears naturally" but that his eyes "always look toward the West." Murakami's early best-selling book was entitled *Norwegian Wood*. The main character in one novel has an affair with a former schoolmate who has tracked him down by dedicating a Beach Boys song to him on the radio. The sources of Kazumi's musical style are just as Western: Jimi Hendrix, George Benson, Ray Parker Jr., Jeff Beck, John McLaughlin, Lee Ritenour, Wes Montgomery, Larry Coryell, Bach (Kazumi Watanabe still performs acoustic classical concerts), and Villa-Lobos's preludes—which he finds "great." He finds traditional Japanese music "pretty square," telling *Guitar Player*'s Jim Ferguson, "It's composed, so there's no room for improvisation. It's not written down, so everything must be learned by memory. It's a way of life for the teachers"—although he does concede that music played on *shamisen* "is more free and gets close to improvisation."

The *New Yorker* profile piece spends considerable time unveiling a new Murakami, a writer who has returned to his roots after a yearlong teaching stint at Princeton, where—teaching it—he took a serious interest in Japanese fiction and history for the first time. He wrote his powerful, uncompromising novel *The Wind-Up Bird Chronicle* in order to "face our history, and that means the history of the war." Pausing on a beach with his interviewer, he called attention to the sound of crickets chirping in the bushes and asked, "Are Westerners sensitive to the sound of insects?" Although Kazumi Watanabe does not seem to have recently undergone such an intense revelation or conversion, he does feel there are now "very good players on both sides of the Pacific. Japanese musicians have become great over the years." His fan base *is* Japanese. He told *JazzTimes* writer Bob Riedinger: "(1) Japanese audiences are very polite, very attentive, more reserved. They clap. Hooting is kept to a minimum. ('I encourage them to boogie when I perform'), (2) Japanese audiences 'like to see faces. Americans want their music straight through the ears,' and (3) 'Japanese audiences know me well.'" His trips to the States are, for a performer of international stature, infrequent, and throughout his albums tunes with (uncompromised by translation) Japanese titles proliferate: "To Chi Ka," "Sayonara," "Fu-Ren," "Tsuru-Kane Hinatango," "Kiken-ga-ippai," "Kyosei Seppun," "Yatokesa," and "Kaimon."

Born in Tokyo, Kazumi Watanabe was a Venture and Vanilla

Fudge fan as a kid and studied guitar at Tokyo's Yamaha Music School (Sadao Watanabe—no relation—was one of the creators of the curriculum, bringing the Berklee method back to Japan). Kazumi Watanabe studied with guitarist Masayuki Takayanagi for two and a half years, practicing ten to twelve hours a day. He recorded while still in his teens and founded his first group as a leader, Kylyn, in 1979. In 1983, he founded Mobo Band (*mobo* translates roughly as "modern, trendy boy"). By 1988, when interviewed by *JazzTimes,* he had been touring his native land for twelve years and had been named Guitarist of the Year by *Swing Journal* for nine.

Like Haruki Murakami again, Watanabe is fascinated with and makes full use of technology in his work. In Murakami's case, the results are fictional characters whose primary sources of communication are the Internet, MTV clips, the Walkman (perhaps they're listening to Kazumi Watanabe!), and telephone sex. In Watanabe's case the technology is guitar synthesizers. He bought his first in 1978, feeling like a "modern scientist," an experience he illustrated for *JazzTimes,* "in typically playful Kazumi fashion," by twisting imaginary knobs and making "blip-bloop-blip" sound effects. "I started out playing a synthesizer. Now I'm playing *music.*" The result is the widest possible range of musical textures and multilayered harmonies. Watanabe replicates a tenor saxophone by triggering a sampler through his Korg M-3 MIDI converter attached to his Paul Reid Smith guitar. Bassist Bunny Brunel says, "I think Kazumi is the most versatile player I've ever worked with." Fellow guitarist Larry Coryell goes even further: "Kazumi Watanabe is one of the very best guitarists in the world, and I'm *not* exaggerating."

One of the first of Watanabe's many recordings I heard was called *Mobo Club.* There I rediscovered an old friend. The guitarist, commenting on the fact that one difficulty he had in Japan was "finding a good drummer for his style of music," felt he'd finally done so with Shuichi "Ponta" Murakami, a musician whom he felt "has a very good jazz concept." The album also features a young alto saxophonist I'd heard good things about, Akira Sakata. *Mobo Club* instantly transports one to a universe reached through the miracle of electricity alone. The first tune, "Fu-Ren," Ponta-propelled, pulses hard, and Kazumi Watanabe, in whom technique and technology fully coincide, supplies some stunning gymnastics. "Kiken-ga-Ippai" is up-tempo, lively, metallic: ominous "movie" music mixed with tones that suggest the workings of one's digestive tract. "Sat-Chan" finds Watanabe playing legato lines offset by chordal accents, the piece closing with cries of "Sat-chan! Sat-chan! Sat-chan!" (*chan* is a suffix, a diminutive used mostly for children but not always). On *Mobo II,* the ambitious (fourteen-minute-long) "All Beets Are Coming" proves nearly as intriguing as its title, Watanabe impressive throughout an extended solo, pulling out all the stops, cascading, frenetic at the end.

On *Mobo Splash,* Michael Brecker joins alto saxophonists Kazutoki Umezu and David Sanborn (Watanable works with an impressive range of top artists) for more of the same. "Sometimes We Say Monk" shows Watanabe's fully playful, craggy, calliope-sounding, carnival (perhaps "circus") side; "Crisis III" is suitably deranged or distraught; and my favorite piece, "Busiest Night," takes you where the action is, ending as if some dance club became frozen in a sudden raid. On *The Spice of Life Too,* "Small Wonder" shows Watanabe's blues chops: another side of this multifaceted performer, soaring with joyous abandon. On an early recording (*To Chi Ka* [1980]), a tune with an intriguing title Haruki Murakami might appreciate, "Manhattan Flu," just plain *smokes*!

Kazumi Watanabe is truly "hip" within what physicists might call a host of "fields," his range and adaptability amazing. Before success with his novels allowed Haruki Murakami to give it up in 1981, he and his wife Yoko ran a jazz bar called Peter Cat: a "windowless underground space," coffee served by day, alcohol at night. Murakami played jazz records (Kazumi Watanabe's *To Chi Ka* perhaps?), fixed drinks, washed dishes, and read American novels. Both artists then began to speak on their own in a manner that was without precedence.

FREE IMPROVISERS

I N THE SUMMER OF 1995, a year before Betty and I went to Japan, we saw an amazing exhibit called "Scream Against the Sky" at the San Francisco Museum of Modern Art. It featured room after room of Japanese Zen'ei bijutsu (avant-garde art) produced after 1945. The title came from a 1961 statement by Yoko Ono, who was affiliated with the Fluxus group—her *Voice Piece for Soprano:*

> Scream.
> (1) against the wind,
> (2) against the wall
> (3) against the sky

In the introduction to the book that accompanied this exhibit, Alexandra Munroe writes, "Characterized by extremist action and a metaphysical mind, the special aesthetic of Japanese avant-garde culture could suggest the persistent presence of Japan's 'old gods' in a post-atomic age." Like so much else in Japan, even "avant-garde art" looked *back* nearly as far as it looked *forward.* Artists once considered outcasts because of their "perverse unorthodoxy" are now being "reclaimed as national treasures and the avant-garde culture that traditionally received little support among the Japanese establishment has come to be esteemed."

Thus the show, which contained extraordinary pieces, such as Atsuko Tanaka's *Electric Dress.* This article can actually be worn (although it must heat up rapidly—and extend the risk of electrocution?): a Christmas tree–shaped cloak that consists of painted—bright, industrial, primary red, yellow, green, blue—bulbs that blink and flash like lights in a *pachinko* parlor. Then there's Kazuo Yaki's *Circle:* a piece of ceramic sculpture shaped like a doughnut, two portions of which expose a mass of writhing, squiggling, intestine-shaped "worms." Other pieces that drew our attention were Shomei Tomatsu's shocking photos of bomb victims with their Kelosidal facial scars; Yayoi Kusama's *Accumulation #1,* a chair constructed of stuffed cloth protuberances (phalluses); Tomio Miki's fascinating, and frightening, series called *The Ear* (aluminum sculpture pieces—some twice human size—that replicate the ear and its vestibular system); Yoko Ono's *Smoke Painting,* a clump of *moji* (characters or written symbols) the viewer is encouraged to burn because the work can only be completed when it's *gone.*

One of the major movements or "schools" extolled at the exhibition was the pioneering Gutai group, founded by Jiro Yoshihara. The now legendary 1955 exhibit of the Gutai Bijutsu Kyōkai (Gutai Art Association) (see chap. 29) embodied Yoshihara's admonition to "create what has never existed before," art-making regarded as an act of total freedom, free of all strictures from the past, "a willful rite of destruction" that embraced previously unheard of methods and materials, such as painting with remote-control toys, with explosives or even bare feet. Gutai performance art preceded American and European "happenings" by several years and is said to have influenced them.

Several groups—Kyūshū-ha, Neo-Dada Organizers, Zero-Dimension, Time School, and Hi Red Center—had political aspirations. These movements were linked to violent opposition to the U.S.-Japan Security Treaty in the 1960s (as much a time of upheaval in Japan as it was in the States). Failing to forestall the treaty, the groups turned to passionate anarchism, advocating "junk art": *objets* made up of urban debris, food, and dead animals. Catalyst Taro Okamoto called upon young artists to "destroy everything with monstrous energy," thus "reconstituting" the Japanese art world. In 1963, Natsuyuki Nakanishi, of Hi Red Center, exhibited *himself* with clipped metal clothespins dangling from his eyelids, hair, and mouth. Tatsumi Hijikata, the originator of *Ankoku Butoh* (Dance of Utter Darkness), performed *Forbidden Colors*—based on the novel by Yukio Mishima—as an act of social "cultural subversion." Tokyo Fluxus artist Shigeko Kubota attached a paintbrush, dripping with red, between her legs and, "squatting like a primitive woman giving birth," executed her *Vagina Painting,* a proto-feminist performance.

By 1960, postserial and aleatory music, as well as *musique concrete,* were established at the forefront of avant-garde musical research in Japan. In 1961, a group of composition and ethnomusicology students at Tokyo University of the Fine Arts and Music founded the group Ongaku (which simply means "music"). Their aim was "to destroy composition and technique in reaction against the bankruptcy of European music." They created sound from customarily unplayable parts of instruments, such as Yasunao Tone's "Geodessy for Piano," in which, while standing on a ladder above an open piano, he dropped a tennis ball, a wine cork, a metal ring, and a felt hat sequentially onto the strings.

Among current free jazz improvisers, a direct descendent of such movements seems to be Sapporo's Ryoji Hojito, who employs the piano as a musical instrument but also as an "object," a composite of "things." Hojito places Styrofoam bits, empty beer and soft drink cans, and plastic pipes on the piano's interior strings and then rubs them with a pipe in each hand, appearing to be a carpenter or gardener at work with a saw. The *sight* of Styrofoam bits leaping like popcorn high above the strings is part of the effect. Hojito also conveys deep feeling for lyricism by way of the pentatonic Japanese scale, the latter, according to one critic, "obvious to a point where it would appear to be *obsessive*."

Similarity of approach and theory to that of the visual arts movements seems more than coincidental. Drummer Shoji Hano has worked with trumpeter Toshinori Kondo since 1975, when the latter introduced him to the martial art of Shintaido. In 1988–89, Hano played solo and with dancers in a bimonthly concert series he organized called Shintaido Performance and Drums. In 1992, he launched a group called Kamadoma-Poly Breath Percussion Orchestra. It was made up of traditional Japanese instruments such as *shime-daiko* drums and *nohkan* (a Japanese flute). Hano, whose initial musical influence was the Ringo Starr of *Abbey Road,* graduated to the "more interesting and challenging rhythms" of Max Roach and Art Blakey. Attending a Kyoto University drumming clinic conducted by Elvin Jones, he listened to Japanese drummers imitating bebop and thought, "It was not *their* style; I felt that they should be trying to get their own spirit into their music." Consequently, Hano gave up bop, and music in general, becoming a sushi chef ("I am very good at cutting fish," he said). He then took up music again when he met Toshinori Kondo, and Shintaido. He has transferred the concepts of the latter ("Throw away everything your mind and body have learned . . . return to nothingness, like a newborn baby; *then* affirm your own existence") to drumming.

Writing of Hano's "mentor" Toshinori Kondo's collaborations with Dutch cellist Tristan Honsinger (in a group called This, That and the Other), Kevin Whitehead comments on the "mood swings" of the music, "rocketing from plaintive melody to chaos, from dense ensemble textures to naked voice, from accessible tunes to inscrutable theater songs where Tristan carries on like a street crazy. It reflects the composer's [Honsinger's] ambivalence about nice music . . . he feels compelled to despoil his tender moments." Don't expect trumpet sounds you are accustomed to hearing from Kondo, the staples of the trade—Freddie Hubbard's or Roy Hargrove's open flare, the *wa wa* of Cootie Williams or Bubber Miley, the subtle Harmon mute of Miles—although you can, if you listen closely, find snatches of each. Mostly what you get is *sonance* that drastically extends the trumpet's territorial reign, transforming the instrument into all that it is *not* rather than what it *has* been. What you get is the object itself—a horn in all its metallic immediacy or, ironically, its primitive proximity to the human voice.

Toshinori Kondo, who took up the trumpet at age twelve and played in his school's marching band, has said he was attracted to this instrument "because it's loud. Trumpet has two sides. One is the battlefield: for killing. The other is for loving. I like that contradiction." He listened to Louis Armstrong, Miles, Clifford Brown, Lee Morgan, and tried to imitate their recordings but couldn't. "As a Japanese boy, bebop was more difficult for me to relate to. It was more the language of black Americans to me, but free jazz had no nationality, no race, no borders. . . . I thought that some day I should make my own music, and that's what I've been researching since then. . . . Improvised music is a stream [of blood]. From the time you get up in the morning until you go to bed at night is like improvised music. You have to be conscious of the stream of energy. If you have too much ego, you lose the way."

Another Japanese musical artist who made a severe break with tradition, in this case on a Japanese instrument (*tsugaru-shamisen*), is Michihiro Satoh. His mother played *tsugaru-shamisen,* and at the age of thirteen Satoh enrolled in a *shamisen* school. However, the teacher expelled him because older students, jealous of how quickly Satoh picked up the requisite skills, threatened to leave. He enrolled at Tokai University's School of Marine Science and Technology (in hope of becoming a ship captain!) but heard, in 1977, a concert by *tsugaru-shamisen* master Chisato Yamada. Satoh moved to Aomori in northern Japan to study with Yamada and eventually returned to Tokyo as a *tsug-*

aru-shamisen teacher. He won the national contest on this instrument in 1982 and 1983. In 1985, Satoh started "Tsugaru-Shamisen NOW," a concert series that allowed him to perform with such "out" jazz artists as saxophonists Kazutoki Umezu and John Zorn.

In his liner notes to a Satoh CD called *Rodan*, Art Lange states that it's "infinitely easier to relate with words what this music is *not*," rather than attempting "to communicate what it is." The music, Lange says, "is not a fusion (East/West/oriental/occidental/jazz/ethnic/Third Stream/ improvisational, or any other) of familiar idioms. It is not an attempt to recreate in mood or detail music from an exotic culture. It is not a watered-down blend of Japanese and American 'folk' musics. It is not music of the past, or of the future." It is, Lange claims, "music of the moment—the moment of its creation"; music that is both "confusing" and "captivating," steadfastly avoiding "consistency" yet reveling in "synchronicity." The music is "built upon the trust between like-minded collaborators . . . celebrating a collision of sound and attitudes." I have quoted these notes at some length because, it seems to me, they constitute an astute analysis of not just the music of Michihiro Satoh and *Rodan* but Japanese free improvisation (at its best) in general.

Another significant Japanese free improviser is Tokyo-born Tetsu Saitoh, who didn't start playing bass, self-taught, until he was twenty-two. He eventually studied with Nobuyoshi Ino (who appears on Aki Takase's *Close Up of Japan* CD) and then performed at an art gallery and live music club called Gaya with alto saxophonist Kazutoki Umezu and pianist Katsuyuki Itakura (more about both in a moment). When Gaya closed its doors in 1984, Satoh joined percussionist Masahiko Togashi's group and then moved on to that of guitarist Masayuki Takayanagi—impressive credentials, but Tetsu Saitoh was looking for his own *sound*, his own world of music, and found it in the tango (his first album, a solo flight, is called *Tokyo Tango* [1986], followed by *Tetsu Plays Piazzolla* [1990]), and in the theater group TAO, serving as musical director for all its productions. Cultivating collaborations with traditional instrumentalists in Japan, Saitoh formed an eleven-piece orchestra that included such instruments as seventeen-string koto, *tsugaru-shamisen*, *shō*, *hichiriki*, and *biwa*. In 1995, the four-woman group KOTO-VORTEX commissioned a piece called "Stone Out," which is performed on a CD of that name.

This recording offers traditional flavor fleshed out by contemporary effects; it is both meditative and agitating, playful and pulsating, harplike koto currents mixed with baroque counterpoint. Saitoh is an agile and fully adaptive bassist. The individual sections have names like "A Kite"; "Notice-Grief," (containing pianist Kyoko Kuroda's delicate interlude and fine interaction with Saitoh); "Consolation" (silence built around distinct tones, giving way to *taiko*-flavored jazz drumming and cacophony that's not so consoling); "Send-off" (with its *shō*-flavored "harmonica" tones); and "Just Accept," which presents a sort of piano-led baroque bebop (Kyoko Kuroda an impressive pianist) that includes tap-dance rhythms and gets pretty wild, discordant. Can you actually *squeeze* sounds out of a bass, the way you would out of a trumpet? Tetsu Saitoh can!

Saitoh has said that members of his groups are "relaxed in dealing with free improvisation because we are of the generation that doesn't expect a great deal from it," doesn't believe that "free improvisation actually gave you the greatest freedom." He admits that he had a "complex about playing a Western instrument" and that people said the more chaotic his playing was, "the more Japanese it sounded." This led him to "adapt traditional Japanese instruments" to his music, because traditional Japanese instrumentalists "understand me better than jazz musicians do."

What these musical artists have in common is a successful adaptation of a unique Japanese aesthetic (one thinks, again, of Toru Takemitsu), but an aesthetic adopted for their own purposes or effects. Other musicians do the same—such as pianists Katsuyuki Itakura, Takashi Kako, and Yuko Fujiyama; saxophonist Kazutoki Umezu (one of the most flexible or *versatile* among free improvisers); drummer Takashi Kazanaki; trombonist Masahiko Kono; and koto artist Kazue Sawai—but lean more in a "Western" direction. Katsuyuki Itakura's *Excuse Me, Mr. Satie* (made with a partner of equal wit and merriment—like Satie!—saxophonist/clarinetist Keshavan Maslak) is one of my favorite recordings. They perform actual pieces by Satie— "Gnossienne" (1, 2, and 3), "Le Piege de Medusa" (1–7)—offset by their own work, or what Maslak calls "our own compositional 'excuses'"—pieces with names like "Excuse Ant," "Funny Flag," "Same Thing with Palm Trees," and "Excuse Me for Being Boring." Erik Satie once said of a piece of his own, "I have put into it everything I knew about boredom," and Maslak adds, "I have added all the absurd non-jazz elements that I passionately could think of at the moment." Itakura's credo is "to want to play with Humor and Wit for any category of freedom music."

Pianist Yuko Fujiyama appears with trombonist Masahiko Kono and percussionist Mauro Orselli and vocalist Ellen Christi on *Reconstruction of Sound*. Christi's chanting includes isolated phrases—repeated—such as "Hello girlfriend," "Up against the wall, motherfucker," "I seen junkies curled up on the sidewalk with needles in their arms there isn't much I haven't seen," "Trust what? Trust whom?"—and simulated, largely sexual utterances interlaced with Kono's soft, graciously tearful, droning, brooding trombone—a sort of latter-day Charlie Green beside Bessie Smith. Kono admits that, in Japan, he felt he had to quash "unfitted feelings," but when he first came to New York in 1980, he felt a freedom he attributed to "jet lag." He learned much from Jimmy Knepper ("I felt both a strange tension and a certain relaxation, as if I were soaking in a hot spring") and George Lewis ("Walk, stop, run, wait, and chase"). Masahiko Kono says now, "I've learned to let my stiffness towards ideas about identity and musical style melt away little by little."

When Yuko Fujiyama finally appears on this CD, she does so with both spare reflection and somewhat directionless chordal clots and clusters. Her final piece, "Concepts," on prepared piano, is prankish, Satie-playful, and I was left wanting to hear more of her. Which I got a chance to do on her own CD called *Tag*. Robert Rusch, editor of *Cadence* magazine, produced this work and comments, rightly, on Yuko Fujiyama's "clarity of attack," her "use of space," and her "lyrical energy edge." Fujiyama studied classical music until the age of nineteen, when she gave it up and "went to school to learn jazz." Enamored of Monk and Bud Powell, her conversion to free improvisation occurred in New York in 1990, when she first heard a tape of Cecil Taylor while apartment hunting in the East Village. She was "knocked over." Fujiyama is joined by cellist Tomas Ulrich and virtuoso violinist Mark Feldman on *Tag*. "A Southern Island" displays delicate, almost "frail" impressionism, the *feel* of chamber music, but the trio doesn't stay in that mode, or mood, for long. However, overall, the tunes tend to assume the same texture, a predictability one doesn't ordinarily associate with music that purports to be "free."

I should mention another fine female free improviser, koto artist Kazue Sawai. Indeed, she is the *source* for other works; she is Brett Larner's and Shoko Hikage's (both on a CD called *Indistancing*) *sensei*. Critic John Corbett has commented on Sawai's musical resources as "at once startlingly new and extremely ancient," and Tetsu Saitoh cites her improvisational method as "shamanistic," saying that Kazue Sawai is "at the very center of traditional Japanese music, while also being the greatest heretic."

Reed artist (alto sax, soprano sax, clarinet, bass clarinet; also composer, arranger, producer) Kazutoki Umezu is one of the more flexible, versatile, and prolific of Japanese free improvisers. At Yokohama Jazz Promunard, he produced Umezu's Room, which featured himself and five rock drummers ("showing his broader music capabilities beyond jazz"). He appeared in "DOINA," a Klezmer musical; has worked with poet Gozo Yoshimasu; was active in the New York City loft scene in 1974; and formed the seven-member group Shakushain, which takes its name from a legendary Ainu hero. Umezu formed Nazo (a band that blends middle eastern music, pop, and jazz); appeared on Russian singer Valentina Ponomareva's *Live in Japan* tour; and has worked with— among artists mentioned in this book—Yosuke Yamashita, Kazumi Watanabe, Aki Takase, Nobuyoshi Ino, Masahiko Satoh, Michihiro Satoh, and the Kodo Taiko troupe.

Kazutoki Umezu appears (along with Michihiro Satoh on *tsugaru-shamisen*) on *Butch Morris' Conduction 28, Cherry Blossom,* one of a series in which the American conductor composes (on the spot), reorchestrates, arranges, and "sculpts" both notated and nonnotated music using signs and gestures at will, initiating and altering the rhythm, melody, and harmony of a piece. In other words: conducted improvisation. *Conduction 28, Cherry Blossom* combines the sound of traditional *shamisen* and *taiko* cries (along with mock Shintō chanting) with the bright static, screeching, and grating of turntables (Yoshihide Otomo on the latter, founder of the "changeable unit" or group Ground Zero, along with Mosquito Paper and the Sampling Virus Project): a sequence of musical gestures laced together by motion that strikes me as devoid of specific action, a community of improvisation to which Umezu contributes his bass clarinet.

Kazutoki Umezu can be heard to better advantage on *Wake Up with the Birds* (duets with tenor and baritone saxophonist Carlo Actis Dato of the Italian Instabile Orchestra), which features improvisations with names like "Mad Chickens," "Malicious Ladybirds," "Afrocats," "Nice Turtles," and "Pretty Pigs." After a motorcycle-sharp startup on a tune called "Wild Shells," the two saxophonists ease into a fortunate balance of folk dance, lyrical surges, handsome tonalities, and conversation that's as congenial (on occasion) as a head-on collision.

The most "far out" improvised music I heard as an extension of the "Scream Against the Sky" avant-garde tradition was on a CD called *Experimental Tokyo*, featuring eight composers, all of whom create with computers: Akira Iijima's "data improvisation" piece, "Pin-Up You, Ice Water Cup"; Akitsugu Maebayashi's "Swelling Fade-Out," which repeats the Macintosh-recorded honey-voice of a Taiwanese singer who died in 1995 over and over again; Natsuki Emura's "24 Dots," written to celebrate his sister's twenty-fourth birthday, produced on a Monophonic Synthesizer KORG MS-20 (this piece consists of segments of twenty-four blips that offset or overlap or hasten each other's pace). Emura also composed "I Rub You" and "Classical Breaded Iron Board." I'm sure you can sense the Dadaist extremes of this music, some of which is quite interesting, and some quite boring.

"Boring" is not a word you're tempted to apply to another Japanese free improvisation genre, noise music—although the word "tedious" might fit. It's fascinating, and a bit terrifying, to hear such a "polite" people engaged in an all-out send-up of big band music, such as on *Something Difference*, the most flatulently Dadaist music I've heard from Japan. Every member of this aggregate is strictly on his or her own, the music, "noise" totally uninhibited, *very* repetitious: honk and stomp R&B on a bender, carnival run amok (call out the riot cops!). The first tune, called "Kujira" (Whale), resembles a parody of Matt Wilson doing a parody of bad drumming.

A quarterly magazine, *Jazz Hihyō* (Jazz Critique), inspired Yoshiyuki Suzuki to start a Japanese Free Improvisers Web site that shows that free improvisation is alive and well in Japan—although the music you are likely to hear in Tokyo live houses remains mainstream.

291

A BEVY OF PIANISTS

J APAN WOULD ENTER THE FULLY enlightened, liberated world of the year
2000 by way of fierce contention over the fact that a ninety-seven-
pound governor of the nation's second-largest prefecture was slated to
enter the sacred ring at the Spring Grand Sumo Tournament in Osaka.
The hullabaloo that followed serves well to point out a problem inherent
to Japanese life. It wasn't the governor's *size* that sparked the contro-
versy, of course; it was her *gender*. Fusae Ota was Japan's first female
governor, and the dignitary holding that office has awarded prizes at the
annual sumo wrestling competition since 1953. However, centuries of
custom also dictate that no woman may enter the *dohyō* (the fifteen-foot-
diameter ring of sandy clay), a custom prescribed by sumo's ancient
roots in the indigenous Shintō religion and its mandates on "defilement"
(which implicate the "pollution" associated with both women and
kegare: abnormality, misfortune, or death).

A showdown came when five-hundred-pound Akebono, sumo
wrestling's governing body's "heavyweight," stepped in and said *iie* (no
way!) to the governor's visit. Outclassed (or outweighed), Ota backed
down. She assigned a male deputy to the duty in her place but vowed to
pursue the matter again the following year. (Ota's predecessor in office
had been forced to resign when charged with sexually harassing a
twenty-one-year-old female campaign worker.) A female member of
Osaka prefecture's legislature commented, "We were all so elated over
Governor Ota's victory, but the sumo confrontation was like being
splashed with a bucket of cold water. We suddenly realized that basically nothing had changed."

Reaching back to 1995, I found a news item reporting a rise in the number of Japanese women in management positions, up 82 percent since a 1986 equal employment opportunity law had gone into effect; yet the article acknowledged that "discrimination remains," due to "male-oriented social customs." In 1997, in a case "signaling a widening acceptance of women's rights," a working woman who divorced her husband because he demanded that she do all the housework was exempted from paying him the thirty-eight thousand dollars in damages for which he was suing her for leaving him. Another article even suggested that the stability of family life—for which Japan is often celebrated—is based on a tradition of "loveless marriages." One seventy-two-year-old survivor of a forty-year marriage claimed her husband had never so much as told her that he *liked* her, had never shown affection in *any* way, never complimented her on a meal, never said "thank you" for anything or given her a present. This news article concluded that this couple has a "marriage that is as durable as it is unhappy," one couple's tribute to the sanctity of the Japanese family. (The divorce rate in Japan, at a record high, is still less than half of that of the U.S., and only 1.1 percent of births in Japan are to unwed mothers—whereas the figure in the United States is 30.1 percent, and rapidly rising.)

In contrast to some of these reports, the world of jazz in Japan looked relatively egalitarian. Between my first visit in 1996 and my second in 1998, a host—or bevy—of excellent female jazz pianists (to mention just one instrument) appeared on the scene, not merely challenging but rendering obsolete any notions that existed about second-class citizenship in music. I have already mentioned Junko Onishi and Aki Takase. When I returned home in 1996, I made another fortunate musical acquaintance (although, I am sorry to say, I did not have an opportunity to interview her): pianist/composer Satoko Fujii. Fujii divides her time between New York City and Japan and, in a 1996 release of duets with Paul Bley called *Something about Water,* made an impressive debut. She has since gone on to become a major figure in the jazz world. Young and highly innovative, Satoko Fujii combines jazz, contemporary classical music, and traditional Japanese folk music, creating a highly original genre, one with her own individual stamp all over it.

Before my second trip to Japan in 1998, she would release three more CDs I was fortunate to acquire: *Indication* (solo piano), *Looking Out the Window* (with Mark Dresser on bass and Jim Black on drums), and an orchestral suite entitled *South Wind.* Each release disclosed another side of the amazing Satoko Fujii, a pianist who first began to play at age four, received classical training until she was twenty, and then stepped into jazz. Her reasons for doing so, as she explained in *Speak Magazine,* had not really involved a steady evolution so much as a return to an instinct frequently prompted when she was a child. "When I was very little," she said, "right after I began taking piano lessons, I enjoyed improvising. But after 16 years of classical training, I had big trouble trying to improvise. I was very shocked when I found that I couldn't play anything without music paper. I was just like well trained dogs that can do only the things that they are told."

Her means of coping with this situation was twofold: she by-passed a conservatory system she found absurd (faculties that regarded all forms of music other than classical as "silly—even if they haven't heard them"; a highly partisan entrance and audition system), and she returned, in order to get her "chops" back, to making music as people had in a more "primitive age." She started a band in which members "sang and clapped hands," meeting once a week in a park or in dance studios in Tokyo. "I really wanted to know what is music for humans? And why do we play music? I had big fun doing that, but I couldn't find my answer." Sotoko Fujii now feels music is "a kind of language that can approach our soul directly, without going through our brain." As far as communication goes, it is better than any other language because it's "how we can express love."

And she does all of the above in her own work. *Something about Water,* the CD of duets with Paul Bley, affords absolute delight. The title tune begins with "tinkling" that suggests both the risk of shards of broken glass and the soothing, dancing effect of water reflecting sunlight. In spite of her youth and Bley's advantage of masterful age, there's no follow-the-leader here. The pianists are peers, and it is frequently impossible to tell just *who* is responsible for *what,* so closely do their respective spirits merge. I can sense the influence of Toru Takemitsu on Satoko Fujii, for a piece such as "Stream" undertakes any and all dangerous undercurrents but, at the close, maintains a pace that just— beautifully—*evaporates.* "The Surface of It" seems composed of small, separate motes of sunlight, Debussy in slow motion, mixed with a very definite Japanese sensibility—our old friend *yūgen* again: suggestion in place of statement.

Satoko Fujii's solo piano venture, *Indication,* is equally rewarding. It contains a traditional Japanese piece, "Itsuki no Kumoriuta" (Lullaby of

Itsuki), performed in a very untraditional manner. The folk theme's spare nature is emphasized, its lulling rhythm, but a sort of blues feeling creeps in, and fine dynamics. "Vague" has a fun sort of prowling, inquisitive, feline nature to it. Satoko Fujii's deft touch appears in a peppy, playful, yet charged "210," a contrapuntal tune that makes use of the entire keyboard. "Tsuki no Sabaku" (Desert Moon) is delicate, almost barren; it moves at a portentous pace yet is loaded with transformations. In "Haru yo Koi," a graceful, impressionistic beginning turns to full-chord gospel sound. Satoko Fujii's *range* of effects (small stories to tell, like Yasunari Kawabata's "palm-of-the-hand" tales) and genres is amazing.

Looking Out the Window is a trio CD and features, again, all original compositions. The title tune is a bit of a shocker, frantic at the start, as if you were standing at a window, transfixed by some spectacle you'd rather not witness. The moods shift constantly, drenched in impermanence. "Let's Get Out of Here" turns out *not* to be what you'd think, but supplies a steady, fetching groove and melodic figures you can actually *hum*: a sort of Caribbean lark the body automatically sways to, succumbs to—witty, bold, just a tad dissonant.

One other genre the pianist/composer seems completely at home in, and provides well for, is "full orchestra." *South Wind* presents the Satoko Fujii Orchestra, an ensemble that includes her husband, Natsuki Tamura, on trumpet and uncustomary instrumentation such as a "soprano hunting horn" and something called "guitar violence." A suite called *The Seasons* is made up, appropriately, of four parts: "Indication (Spring)," "Silence (Summer)," "This Is about You (Fall)," and "Freeze (Winter)." The full piece opens with gentle Debussy-like dignity, a softhearted tenor sax solo, slow set rhythm (an orchestral approach reminiscent of Abdullah Ibrahim), trombones that buzz and sag, but the plaintive tone grows wild, converting to free counterpoint; and by the time we reach "Freeze (Winter)" the entire orchestra has erupted in bewitching harmonies.

Stuart Broomer has written, "The emergence of Satoko Fujii has been as rapid as her music is surprising," and asserts that, rich as her early work is, the depth and clarity of her musical conception "could hardly prepare a listener for the experience of *South Wind*." Fujii attended the New England Conservatory and has been identified with teachers there (George Russell, Jimmy Giuffre, Paul Bley, Joe Manieri), but the talents that emerge on this Leo Lab CD—right down to assembling a splendid group of young musicians whom she asked "to play whatever they wanted" even within the written parts—are strictly her own. The result, according to Broomer, is an ensemble that "teems and boils with raw creative energy." I completely agree.

The approach reminds me of a short story by Yasunari Kawabata called "Her Husband Didn't," in which a middle-aged married woman and a young man, both taking a Western-style painting class and riding back to North Kamakura, "collaborate," snatching a sketchbook from one another, this exchange occurring over and over again, "as though they were laying the hands of their hearts one on top of the other." About the title piece, "South Wind," Stuart Broomer writes, "Parts establish erratic relationships to one another and the piece becomes a dialogue between the fresh and the stale, the just heard and the as yet unheard . . . all shoving into a present time which has grown indistinct." The writer calls "the sheer beauty and welling intensity of 'South Wind'" the "summit of this recording." The piece is based on a pentatonic scale from Okinawa and hangs in tonal space that Fujii says is "exotic . . . even to me." The simple, childlike pentatonic theme of "South Wind" is repeated again and again, with mounting volume until, drums unleashed, it explodes into cacophony and the process begins again. Satoko Fujii is not just a pianist/composer/arranger. She is a natural *force* to be reckoned with!

Misako Kano was born and raised in Yamaguchi, Japan (near Hiroshima); started piano lessons at age five; and came to the States and attended Kent State University in 1985–86, where she studied both jazz and classical piano. She returned to Japan and received a bachelor's of music in classical piano performance and a music education degree from Shimane University. Back in the States again, she enrolled at Manhattan School of Music and received a master's degree in jazz piano performance. She became house pianist at the Cotton Club in New York, performed at the Texaco Jazz Festival, and now lives in Japan.

Kano studied and worked often with alto saxophonist Thomas Chapin, who appears on her *Breakthrew* CD (and who died of leukemia in 1998). He is also featured on *Watch Out*. What's amazing about these two outings is, recorded just three months apart, Misako Kano appears as a somewhat self-effacing, perhaps even reluctant leader on the first, and as one fully formed and very much in charge on the second. *Breakthrew* presents a mix of standards ("Never Let Me Go," "Spring Is Here," Cole Porter's "I Love You") and several originals and discloses a predilection for opening vamps. "Mao," an original tune (the name not that of Chairman Mao but of bassist Ron McClure's cat), starts out that way, but Kano displays a slightly wry, restrained style and off-center, somewhat idiosyncratic rhythms once a tune is underway. Design seems an important element in her solos, her constructions predisposed.

Watch Out takes us to another world, one in which Kano runs *wild*. Chapin is there again, Matt Wilson on drums, and Kiyoto Fujiwara on bass. All of the tunes—aside from Monk's "Well, You Needn't" (her solo stint absolutely madcap here, delightful; you can tell they were *all* having a very good time!)—are originals. "Cat Scramble" (the pianist likes *neko*, cats)—cites Misako Kano on piano and *toys*, and that's what we get at the start in place of the customary vamp: feline antics (the piano somehow sounding like an old parlor upright), everyone agile. "Zeryama" features a Monkish hunt-and-pick piano solo (Chapin "munching" in the background), and then—watch out!—Kano is fully in control of *her* gig, and digging it. Her extended solo is rift with wit, sizzle, wild charm. The title tune, "Watch Out," is a free jazz marathon, the instrumental crosscurrents (Chapin on his own tear here) nearly exhausting just five minutes into an eleven-minute outing.

Miki Kono—on a CD called *For My Mother*—is a veteran performer who waited until the ripe old age of eight before she undertook classical piano lessons. She also developed an interest in *cansone* (traditional Italian folk music); got into jazz during her college years; and, an architecture and economics major, played with the Hokkaido University big band and jazz ensemble. Later, after studying with pianist Sadayasu Fuji, she joined groups led by Eiji Kitamura and Sleepy Matsumoto. The title tune of *For My Mother* reveals her debt to "touch" and taste masters such as Tommy Flanagan and Hank Jones, her own work full of dignity and poise. Her playing seems pleased with itself, and rightly so, without being cocky. Kono does cut loose on "Mind Control," her solo work animated, the feeling festive.

Pianist Haruko Nara may be one of the most "overqualified" Japanese musicians I've run across, especially in light of the predictable eclecticism of her *My Favorite Things* CD, one that might be subtitled *Identity Crisis*. A prodigy at age five, Nara studied with opera singer Kyuko Takagi, graduated (in cultural history, having expanded her musical influences to Stockhausen and Toru Takemitsu) from Gakushuin University in Tokyo, and then came to the States. Her parents thought she was attending a three-month language course at UCLA, which she did, expanding the experience to include New York, where she attended the Manhattan School of Music in 1980, studying composition and European classics, spending evenings at jazz clubs or the Metropolitan Opera. Great credentials, but *Favorite Things* may attempt to include a few too many of her favorite things, the music distractingly diffuse.

A delightful surprise for me was the discovery of a pianist I had not heard of: Chizuko Yoshihiro. Listening to her *Conscious Mind* CD, I found myself grinning with delight, wanting to *dance*. Yoshihiro, like the others, writes her own stuff, and destiny, and she has found—apparently—a band of like-minded, hip-hop, "gypsy" spirits to embody both. The music is rhythm-infectious, spiked with salsa, *live* sounding (not machine-made), even the inevitable whips and blips serving to spice and surprise. Richard Mazda's subtle rap chant ("Man, the master of machines? Don't make me laugh! We got ourselves a billion-dollar food blender that thinks its parents came from Milwaukee") is at one with the saltant fabric, and Chizuko Yoshihiro provides occasional playful commentary on the proceedings, tongue in cheek. It's a party atmosphere that put me in mind of the best, most joyous jazz of Kazumi Watanabe.

There's lots of fine music being made by talented female Japanese pianists.

33

SECOND TRIP TO JAPAN:
THE MONTEREY JAZZ FESTIVAL
IN NOTO, AGAIN

A T HOME IN THE STATES—aside from listening to a range of music that included fine young female pianists Satoko Fujii and Misako Kano; free improvisers; and such proven pros as Sadao Watanabe, Aki Takase, and Kazumi Watanabe—I began work on this book and put the introduction on Jazz House, the Jazz Journalists Association Web site. To my surprise and delight I received some very positive responses, one from American singer Scotty Wright in Malaysia, who was on his way to Japan for a three-month gig. He passed along information I didn't have on an "after-hours mecca" in Tokyo called Terry's, in Roppongi. He described the owner as a man with a "ready grin and a real burn for anyone devoted to jazz," but someone who, "determined to keep his club a haven for Jazz folk only . . . still doesn't advertise." "One can't find him without a musician in tow," Scotty wrote, adding, "The last Sunday of each month is Jam Night, a workshop where students and pros play, eat, talk, and play some more, usually until dawn."

I also received a letter from a man in Nebraska, Robert Schneider, who, also having seen the introduction on the Web site, wrote to ask if I could help him contact old friends with whom he had played jazz in Japan back in the early 1950s. "Although 40 years or more have passed," he wrote, "the memories of those days are still fresh." One of the musicians he'd played with was Eiji Kitamura.

"I first arrived in the Sea of Japan in 1952, in February," Robert said when I contacted him by phone. "At that particular time, Japan and its cities were still recovering from the war. There weren't too many clubs. There wasn't much of a real *scene*. But the airmen's clubs [Robert was in the Air Force at the time] had Japanese bands come in and play dance music so the airmen and soldiers could dance and socialize a bit. These bands played regular stock arrangements of tunes like 'Sentimental Journey' and 'Singing in the Rain'—just in a four-beat manner, very simple, nothing exciting. The sax players had a problem getting good reeds, so I got reeds from the States for them and they started to talk to me about the Tokyo scene."

In the spring of 1952, Robert's unit was transferred to Tachikawa Air Force Base, which was about twenty-five miles from Tokyo. "The city was recovering too, a lot of reconstruction going on, a lot of new construction too, and walking into town one day, just getting familiar with Tokyo, I saw a club that looked like a clothing store that I'd been familiar with in Philadelphia. Glass front. Brand-new. It was called the Club Monoco. I decided to return that night and see what was going on. Lo and behold, I heard a *great* Japanese band called the Six Lemons— outstanding! During the band breaks, the alto player would bring out a portable recorder and he played—I was very surprised—Dave Brubeck/Paul Desmond sides on Fantasy, the very early ones. Everybody was so impressed with Paul Desmond that they forgot about Charlie Parker. Records were arriving at the record stores, and these young Japanese fellows were grabbing them up and copying them. I mean they were playing them *note for note*. Even if there was a fluff . . . that fluff was *included!* They loved that music."

Robert told me there had been a *very* active scene going on in Tokyo. After the Six Lemons, at Club Monoco, Shoji Suzuki and Eiji Kitamura started to come in, usually for a week's engagement. "They would tell me, 'I'm going to be in Yokohama, I'm going to be at such-and-such a place in Tokyo.' If I could get away to see them I would. I met Shoji before I met Eiji. I didn't know anything about him until somebody said that a very fine clarinet player was coming in. I swore it was *Benny Goodman!* He was *so* perfect! I had a white, very hard mouthpiece that was formerly Woody Herman's. I think I *might* have given that mouthpiece to Shoji, but I'm more inclined to believe I gave it to Eiji, who'd given me a black and white mouthpiece he had that worked well for me. One evening at the Club Monaco, when the Six Lemons were swinging along, a young American soldier asked to sit in. He proved to be a driving, swinging piano player from L.A.—Hampton Hawes!"

When we began to correspond, Robert Schneider mentioned an alto saxophonist named Akitoshi Igarashi.

"Oh yeah!" Robert said now over the phone. "I met the Igarashi brothers, I believe, when they played at the Club Monaco. Akitoshi and I talked about altoists. He was a very modest fellow, but his talents were very strong, even in those days. He was just maybe eighteen or nineteen years old. His brother was a fine drummer. I used to go to Tokyo when they were starting to get some important jobs. I told them to continue with music. Don't give up. Akitoshi was *very* modest, but I thought he was one of the best players I heard, without a doubt."

Robert Schneider finally got in touch with Akitoshi Igarashi in Japan and recently wrote to me, saying, "I was able to find him by contacting a jazz fan who knew who he was. In fact, his wife interviewed Akitoshi recently for a Japanese magazine. When Makoto called and mentioned my name, Akitoshi screamed, 'I remember! I remember!' So Bill, thank you for making it all possible. . . . Akitoshi was the last person I saw in Japan from the jazz world. He was playing a club date at my disembarkation base. We said sad farewells, and now forty-six years later we will be in contact again. I'll plan a trip to Japan soon."

Akitoshi Igarashi is well represented on *A History of King Jazz Recordings*. Moved by Robert's letter, I sat down and listened to his old friend playing tunes such as "I'll Remember April," "Take the 'A' Train," "Star Eyes," "Strike Up the Band," "Almost Like Being in Love," and "Sweets." His tone is smooth, immaculate, nearly blithe—a pure, warm float reminiscent of Johnny Hodges, Johnny Bothwell (of the Boyd Raeburn band), a touch of Willie Smith perhaps, or even Frankie Trumbauer's mellow C-melody sax work. Akitoshi's solos, again like Trumbauer's, are well constructed, thought out, fundamentalist (composed of basic or classic particulars) yet alert and alive, as instinctive as his cry, after forty-six years: "I remember! I remember!"

As I made progress on this book, I realized that, after two years, just one thing was missing: the *place* itself. I grew homesick for Japan. But as I said at the start, events in any life seem fortuitous, so much so that we are taken by surprise when and if they actually shape themselves into some central story. Fortunately, on that score, a fresh surprise awaited me.

I had interviewed Joe Green, president of the Monterey Jazz Festival board of directors, in connection with my book on the fortieth anniversary of the festival. We saw each other on occasion (usually jazz occasions), and he mentioned a trip he was organizing to Japan. It would be a Rotary Club–Monterey Jazz Festival tour in order to participate in the celebration of the tenth anniversary of the Monterey Jazz Festival in Noto, close by Monterey's sister city, Nanao. I jumped at the chance and flew out of Monterey on my own. I met up with the group at Kansai Airport near Osaka, a "Japan Travel Bureau representative" gathering her flock (us!) there in the arrival lobby by way of one of those amazing acts of coordination at which the Japanese seem to excel. Next thing I knew I was seated on the Haruka 44, slated to arrive in Kyoto at seven that night, where we would stop over for a couple of days.

At Kiyomizu-dera, I set out on my own at Kiyomizu Temple, and this time—rather than standing back and taking photos of Betty and Hisayo as I had before—I climbed the ramp to the three "waterfalls" myself and partook of the cold, delicious, life-enhancing (health, wealth, and general good fortune) waters of all three. And I met with Hisayo, who helped me pick out a suitable present for my daughter-in-law Yoko's sister Kazuko (whom I also saw, meeting her and three of the kids: Akimi, Haruna, and Yohei, my adorable flash-me-the-peace-sign buddy Ayako occupied at some *juku*—cram school—elsewhere). Shopping, I ran into Joe and Marilyn Green, whom I introduced to Hisayo-san (no longer the hand-to-her-mouth, giggling high school girl Betty and I had known). Later Joe couldn't resist telling our group that he'd met "this beautiful young woman that Bill claims is a *relative!*"

As part of a tour group, I was introduced to a new Japanese subculture: one that put me in mind of jazz. Tour guides are skillful improvisers, or else—like soloists who may not be willing to admit it—they recite the same licks so frequently that they *seem* spontaneous. Our guide in Kyoto was a sprightly middle-aged woman who, greeting us that first morning, said, "*Ohayōh* [Good morning]. That sounds like state of Ohio, doesn't it? We also say *gozaimasu*, which means nothing at all but is very *polite*." The woman's name was Kimiko, and she told us that, three generations ago, Japanese women were trained to "kneel squarely" and had very brittle bones, a stunted torso, and poor circulation. Modern Japanese girls, on the other hand, are having rooms in their homes constructed in which half of the floor is raised, this portion for kneeling on tatami mats while they themselves sit on Western chairs in the lower half. (Indeed, my hotel room in Wakura Hot Springs would provide just such an arrangement.) "The younger generation," Kimiko concluded, "has more chance to stretch legs." Kimiko, a veritable font of information, also told us that a Japanese husband spends eleven minutes a day with his wife and children—this stat replacing the less charitable estimate of seven minutes I'd gathered from a newspaper report at home.

Ryosho Fujii, a Buddhist monk and jazz radio DJ, sat next to me at our first banquet in the Shirasagi Room at the Ae No Kaze Hotel in Wakura Onsen, where the Monterey Jazz Festival in Noto was about to take place again. He was a short, convivial man with a bright agreeable face. He surprised me by saying that on his radio show—broadcast on a community-service station called Zero Nanao, sponsored by the Wakura Resort Tourism Bureau and Wakura Resort Hotel Association—he had, at the time the Monterey Jazz Festival celebrated its fortieth anniversary, programmed and presented *forty* radio shows—one for each year of the event's existence.

"I use very fine book called *Monterey Jazz Festival: Forty Legendary Years* for research," he said.

I looked at him in mild disbelief for a second or two, not sure just how to break the news.

"I *wrote* that book!" I blurted out.

This revelation made us fast friends forever, a fate sealed by the generous doses of beer and sake we were being subjected to. I asked him if the three-CD set put out on the Monterey Jazz Festival by Warner Bros. Malpaso records had been available to him.

"Yes, yes, I have it. And I had some other festival recordings. John Handy . . ."

" 'Spanish Lady'?"

"Yes, yes! And I'd heard the recording of Dave Brubeck with the jet plane . . . no, no, just *airplane* then!" He imitated the sound perfectly; at the first festival, in 1958, a plane, landing, passed low over the arena while Brubeck was playing "For All We Know," and the pianist inserted a few bars of "Wild Blue Yonder" in his solo, much to the crowd's delight. "I did *more* than forty programs, because I also feature people like Poncho Sanchez. And I get Karrin Allyson and *pray*." (Both vocalist Allyson and Latin bandleader Poncho Sanchez were slated to perform at this year's Monterey Jazz Festival in Noto.)

"As far as jazz in elementary school, when I was twelve, I heard *kyoku*, a type of Japanese song Americans call 'cover number' but we call 'copy.'" He laughed. "Connie Francis, for example. And Japanese would copy her. I enjoyed them. Then when I was in late junior high, my sister was studying in Kanazawa, at the university there. She took me to a jazz concert. Toshiko Akiyoshi concert. At the time Akiyoshi's husband was Charlie Mariano. It was *jazz*. Hot stuff. This was—how you say?—*inaka* [countryside, rural area]. Not Tokyo. Tokyo had lots of jazz. Clubs and *kissaten* [coffeehouses]. Those places were very popular in those days. Usually owner wasted lots of money for audio system." He laughed again. "And lots of liquor. There were some *jazu kissa* in Kanazawa. I would go there from Nanao by train. I was too poor to buy records."

Ryosho-san went on to tell me about his four years of college in Kyoto, of the many *jazu kissa* there and the live concerts that featured American artists he was hearing for the first time. "I had a folk song band then. I played guitar. We played Japanese songs, and American—those by Kingston Trio." He laughed. "I also composed my own songs."

I asked him how all this fit with becoming a Buddhist priest. In that connection, was jazz frowned upon?

"Oh no! It was *encouraged*. The only problem was: how to *play* jazz. Learning was very difficult. The college I went to was small. It had maybe two thousand students, but it had a jazz *club* [or "society" that sponsored a band]. At the American Culture Center. So I joined. One student was very good. He was into folk music, but he also listened to jazz and he was making—how do you call it?—jazz *score* of American folk song. After I graduated I went to Wyoming. In winter. I was two weeks in Wyoming. My sister was there. Her husband had been a home stay student in our house. There were nothing but sheep in Wyoming."

Ryosho-san didn't bring home any sheep, but he did manage to pick up recordings by Roberta Flack ("Killing Me Softly"), Ron Carter, Grady Tate, and Chick Corea's fusion group, Return to Forever, which he called Beyond Forever before he corrected himself. (His "mistake" suggested a Zen *koan*, I thought. A monk asked, "What is Beyond Forever?" The master said, "If you hold on to it for too long it will make an old man of you.") "I had a problem with fusion, but I let the music decide whether this is jazz or not [pure Zen!]. I think with Miles Davis also later on."

He gave me the names of some current Japanese jazz artists he admired: pianists Yuichi Inoue and Yutaka Shiina, whom I would later discuss at some length with critic Masahisa Segawa in Tokyo. Jazz aficionado/monk Ryosho Fujii was another fortunate find for me. I saw him at this year's jam session party, where Paul Contos provided handsome flute solos backed by the High School All-Stars; and I would see him throughout the weekend's musical festivities, his eyes sparkling, his broad smile and sly dance declaring his passion for this music.

I had been instructed to meet the members of our group at 7:00, in an immense, lavishly carpeted lobby, one the size of a soccer field. There, we were ushered into two lines. I was standing behind Tim Jackson, the general manager of the Monterey Jazz Festival in Monterey, when all of a sudden the entire wall before us, a wall that stretched the length of the lobby, gave way or *rose,* disclosing a giant banquet room filled with people who had risen to their feet to applaud while the theme song from *Cinema Paradiso* thundered over a speaker system.

"What did we ever do to deserve this?" I whispered to Tim as we marched into the room.

"*We* didn't do anything, Bill," he said over his shoulder. "It's the Rotary!"

The banquet-room tables were occupied by Wakura Onsen and Nanao business leaders, plus the host families that would put up members of the California All Star Band or were hosting visiting American students now. After a ceremony that included *many* speeches, we were ushered into an adjacent room for a banquet of our own—lobster, sashimi (shrimp, red snapper, tuna), yogurt with ginger flakes, ice cream set in a pearly glass container that resembled a chambered nautilus—and as if that weren't enough, we all retired to a terrace for after-dinner drinks and the most magnificent fireworks display I have ever seen. Word passed around that Mr. Sadahiko Oda, our host (owner of the Ae No Kaze Hotel and the—if possible—even more splendid Kagaya just up the street), had spent one million yen on this display, which seemed to last for hours, filling the sky with multicolored explosions, every square inch occupied by brilliantly colored wallpaper eruptions or bursts named *chōchō* (butterfly), *ki-ku* (flower), *yanagi* (willow tree), and *bo-tan* (another flower), concluding with a giant (eleven hundred meters in diameter) gold jellyfish effusion, a sparkling Sistine Chapel ceiling that dispersed itself into a shower of gold flakes that fell into the bay or drifted off into the night. A pamphlet we were given called this display "Art in a Moment" and asserted it was "the biggest fireworks display in the world"—a claim I wouldn't dispute for a second.

305

The actual Monterey Jazz Festival in Noto (the main concert) was scheduled to start at 5:00. A Japanese fusion group called Strum kicked it off, followed by the Sunny Side Jazz Orchestra. Then Yoshie Kitanaka and the Jealous Guys at 6:00 and Karrin Allyson at 6:30. However, for some odd reason, a final feast, a special dinner, had been planned for our Rotary group in the Shirasagi Room at the hotel at 5:30. How could I be in both places, the festival's Sea World setting and the hotel, at the same time? I couldn't, so I settled for food (it would have been a worse insult to skip out of the dinner), and of course the dinner was another of those unsurpassed rituals that makes its own music: in this case several successive small dishes as delicious as the most imaginatively voiced chords, *played* or served (or arranged before one) by the agile, delicate fingers of women wearing splendid blue kimonos. I did somehow manage to tear myself away early from this last repast—and before the speeches started, thank God!

I ran down to Water World, where the festival was in full swing, and arrived in time to hear Karrin Allyson sing "You'd Be So Nice to Come Home To"—which *she* was, scatting the hell out of Cole Porter after the initial chorus. She did "O Pato" (The Duck), "Nature Boy," and—or so momentary vanity informed me—"I Cover the Waterfront," just for *me*. What I'd forgotten, of course, is that a fully accomplished vocalist makes each and *every* member of an audience feel that way, but that's okay. I recovered and realized the final tune, "It Might As Well Be Spring," was being sung for *everyone*—a capacity Japanese crowd.

After the California All-Star Band performed (with its customary alacrity), the Latin avalanche began. Poncho Sanchez and his group took over, and the crowd succumbed to salsa fever. "We were going to wear our bathrobes [*yukata*]," Poncho began, "but they didn't fit! Someone will translate for you." Kyoko Muraguchi did, and when I ran into her again, the two of us just about the only persons *not* dancing, she cried out above the contagion of conga drums, "During the summertime, *everyone* wants to hear exciting music—like Latin music, which is *very* popular in Japan just now." I told her that, when I had first attended this event in 1996, I was puzzled by her role, by the large amount of *talking* that takes place on stage at a Japanese jazz concert, the length and complexity of the introductions. She smiled her best *bijin* "personality girl" smile and said, "There are so many foreign performers and foreign guests; someone has to translate into Japanese, because the audience wants to know just what's going on, who will appear next, etc. I think this is one of the traditional things in Japan." All around us, the customarily sedate but attentive crowd had gone ballistic. I saw my friend Alex Hulanicki, a former journalist now teaching in Nanao, wildly caroming with Mr. Oda's oldest daughter, who was dressed in an elaborately refined (and expensive) salmon-colored traditional kimono.

I had arranged to meet Karrin Allyson when she signed CDs at a booth set up in the food pavilion. She was there, along with the members of her group: Laura Caviani (piano), Bob Bowman (bass), Todd Strait (drums). After the signing, I sat down with Karrin at a far, fairly quiet end of the festival (this was actually during the All-Star Band's performance, and we could hear its young Australian-import vocalist singing the blues in the distance), and we had a chance to talk.

I asked her just what sort of advice she might give to a Japanese vocalist. I mentioned having made friends with the Buddhist priest/DJ and told her that we had discussed Chika, another vocalist appearing at the festival, whom he feels works with a piano player who's not really doing her any great favors. "Whatever the problem is," Karrin said, "it's not just one Japanese singers have. It's a problem that *any* singer might have who really doesn't know what she or he is doing. And I'm not saying that I know *everything* I'm doing. What I'm saying is: I am a piano player and I know what keys I want to do songs in, and I know what tempos I want. I don't depend on anyone else but myself to count these things off. I have charts. I run the show, but it takes *rehearsal.* And it takes musicians with ears and heart. And some chops too. But the musicians I play with regularly, I feel they're just so *great.* I'm so fortunate to work with them."

I gave her a hypothetical instance. Let's say you've got a young Japanese student who wants to be a vocalist. She's about halfway there, perhaps. So how do you get this young Japanese singer to a point where she can be at ease with what she does or wants to do?

"Alcohol!" Karrin said, laughing openly.

"*Bīru!*" (Beer!) I said.

"*Bīru!* Well, how does any instrumentalist sound at ease? That they're somewhat in control? They know what they're doing! The sound is always so *volatile,* because you never know what you're going to get from the sound people. If you have a decent sound check, if you get some sleep (which isn't always possible!), and if you get something to eat, you *relax.* You feel comfortable with your musicians. And even if you're not, you have charts and you know what *you're* doing. I've been doing this five to seven nights a week for years, but I didn't discover jazz until college. Like right now we are listening to a young lady who's about sixteen [the Australian import] singing with a big band. I wouldn't have known *how* to sing 'The Way You Look Tonight' when I was sixteen. I was doing other musical things. I was a classical piano major in college. And I was doing folk music, accompanying myself. And I was in an all-girl rock 'n' roll band for awhile . . ."

We were interrupted by an adoring fan who came up and said, "Miss Karrin, nice songs," and then, appropriate to what we'd been talking about, introduced his girlfriend as "amata singa" (amateur singer)—and asked for Karrin's autograph.

"*Arigatō, arigatō,*" the latter responded "She's a singer too? All right, great!"

When the couple and their friends left, I thought of the young *amata singa* and asked Karrin if she felt it was necessary to have seen *Casablanca,* to have a full context, in order to sing "As Time Goes By."

"It doesn't hurt," she replied. "It's funny because you definitely have an advantage if you know the story. Those standards that came from shows, they're *show* tunes, but I don't know all the shows they came from. Sometimes I do, sometimes I don't. I had a student at a workshop at Stanford. She was a vocal student from Japan. She swung *so hard!* She swung harder than any of the American singers there, but she had no grasp of the language. I don't remember what song she sang, but an American audience can't get past the fact that you can't pronounce words. I know how tough this is because I'm trying to do tunes in different languages too: Portuguese and French. It's very challenging. I think Japanese singers are *brave* to try it at all. I guess it's cultural. I don't know many Americans who can sit down and play the koto well. And it might be that Japan is a more restrictive society in general, right? I don't know if they feel they're allowed to 'get out' sometimes. But the things they do well are so beautiful. The details. I don't really know much about Japanese culture, except what I see and feel about it. They are very gracious usually, and the *way* they do things: all the little bowls and plates when you're dining! And they are seemingly so *kind* . . ."

I mentioned that the biggest complaint I received from Japanese jazz musicians is that their playing is not *aggressive* enough! That's the element they associate with jazz. But—aside from World War II, when the military regime took over—it does not seem an *aggressive* society.

"No, it's completely *civilized*. Who knows? But what an interesting subject you're delving into!"

"So you dig Japan?"

"I do dig Japan. I'm very much into almost all cultures, as long as they are open a bit to what we do. I really dig other cultures, because we all have so much to learn from one another."

Throughout the Monterey Jazz Festival weekend, there was no end to the royal treatment I subsumed as a sort of barnacle attached to the fluke of the Rotary Club whale. The group was taken by bus to Nanao, Monterey's sister city, where, when we disembarked, two long rows of city hall employees stood waving American flags as we passed down their ranks. In the mayor's office, we reclined in plush chairs and received ice-cold lemonade, lengthy speeches, and the gift of a lacquer box showing *kanto matsuri:* a harvest festival where lantern-laced poles (forty to fifty lanterns per pole) are balanced on the shoulders, hips, and heads of young men.

But best of all was a final party Mr. Oda gave at the resplendent Kagaya Hotel back in Wakura Onsen. This affair was held in a lavish sushi parlor, an immense room with a stream actually dividing its tatami mat floors. I sat at a counter next to Poncho Sanchez, and the entire party, which included musicians and the feted Rotarians, of course, was treated to endless rounds of—in my case—*tsumatae sake* and *sashimi* of every persuasion. Mr. Oda and his family went from person to person, seeing that all their immediate needs were met, and he asked Poncho if he would like to "fish" for squid. When the latter replied yes, he was handed a net and led to the stream, from which he extracted a large squid that was immediately converted into a delicacy by the swiftest swordsman I've ever encountered in my life: the squid sliced into fine rows, all except its head, which—eyes bulging in shock and tentacles still squiggling—appeared to remain alive, as if asking, "What the f--- happened to me?!" I was offered this prize but declined, saying "kekkō desu" (everything's fine in the food category just now), but Poncho ate it! Live and raw—pretty much the way he likes his music! He survived, and the party lasted long into the night.

When I woke up the next day and went downstairs with my luggage to meet the others, I was handed a bill for seventy dollars. Having acclimatized myself a bit too readily to the luxury of my surroundings, I had—during my stay at the Ae No Kaze Hotel—sent my laundry out: three sweat-stained T-shirts and two cotton jerseys. They were returned sealed in tidy transparent plastic, and the cost, as I discovered now, was eighty-five hundred yen, or about seventy dollars. For that price, I could have bought Betty the handsome wooden tea caddy I'd found at the craft center we'd been taken to in Kyoto but declined because it was too *takai* (expensive). I did purchase a set of earrings with the character *fuku* on them, which means happiness, good luck, or good fortune. Checking out of the hotel, I was ready now—with luck—for a more humble existence in Tokyo.

34

MASAHISA SEGAWA

I HAD MADE A PLEDGE THAT, because I had—to my satisfaction—answered the questions raised by Akira Tana's Harvard thesis on jazz in Japan, and because I no longer felt I had anything I needed to prove, I would simply relax—on my return trip—and dig the music and all that might accompany it. Perhaps my old friends in theory, *kono-mama* and *sono-mama* (suchness), had finally come home to me as actualities, rather than something distant and unattained. Who knows?

I had also, while part of the Rotary tour, spent a fortunate amount of my time with Masahisa Segawa, one of the two "Leonard Feathers of Japan" (along with Yozo Iwanami!), a delightful gentleman who would more or less set a final seal on what I'd learned about jazz in and from his native land. Segawa and I met in the comfortable Asia Center lounge where I'd interviewed Masahiko Satoh two years before. We talked a bit about big bands in Japan, and I mentioned that the Monterey Jazz Festival features at least one amateur band from Japan each year. Segawa said, laughing, "It's because they pay their own way." We then discussed the popular Japanese film *Shall We Dance* and dance band music in general in Japan.

"I think up to 1960, dances were fun," Segawa said. "All the young people danced: jitterbug, etc. But later, when rock appeared, ballroom dancing died. Just recently what we call 'social dancing' has become very popular, but this is for people who just care about *dancing*. They don't care for the music that much. When I was young, we loved both the music and dancing, and we tried to dance to the best bands. But current dancers only care about the *steps,* so big band music is not that popular for dancing, although there are many 'social dance' activities in Japan. *Many,* as shown in that movie. But that has not been connected with the development of big band jazz. I think it has been said that in the States, Stan Kenton killed dancing. He was often criticized for this."

I smiled, knowing this was true—how in high school we would go to the state fairgrounds in Michigan to dance to Billy May or Tex Beneke, or even Woody Herman, but everyone just stood around and listened and *watched* Kenton's big band perform.

Masahisa Segawa's commentary certainly helped me focus work begun long ago and fleshed out my initial historical overview. I felt a fortunate sense of *closure* now, laced with a host of fresh names I'd have to check out. I found Segawa's method interesting and a little frightening. How easy, and natural, it seemed to pigeonhole a Japanese player in this or that "school" or "vein"—an approach Segawa had adopted, I felt, out of respect for American predecessors, but not one inclined to dismantle intimations of "imitation." I still saw the Japanese as amazing transformationalists—experts, as George Sansom claimed, at digesting and assimilating a foreign culture "not imposed from without by conquest or proximity [the Occupation forces didn't *compel* the Japanese to love jazz!] but voluntarily, even enthusiastically adopted." Masahisa Segawa himself was a case in point.

"When I was three years old I was in London with my parents," he told me. "At that time, Jerome Kern's musical *Sorry* was very popular, and the most popular theme song from *Sorry* was 'Who?'" Here Segawa began to sing the tune in a warm, pleasant, idiomatic voice: "Who stole my heart away . . . who?" "My parents liked the show and bought the record, and at home they played it every day. I was three years old, and my parents would check in my room and then go out to a music house, so I stayed at home at night and played by myself. Throughout that year, without knowing the meaning, I memorized *all of the words* to 'Who?' My mother is now ninety-six years old. She has become rather aged and is losing her short-term memory, but curiously, she remembers the words of 'Who?' She may forget everything that happened yesterday the day after yesterday's happenings, but she remembers all of the English words of 'Who?' even if she can't remember what time she had her breakfast. So I jokingly say to myself, 'I have to decide what song I want to remember until I die.'" He laughed openly.

This was one of those truly *magical* moments I will admit are rare with the Japanese— because of their reticence, a reluctance not to experience feeling deeply but to express it openly. I told Segawa that, when my father was nearly ninety and was no longer *there* in terms of memory, I was playing the piano for him one day at home. We had family song sessions around the piano often throughout our life, but—whereas my dad appreciated music and could do a smoothly wicked soft-shoe on the grate in front of the fireplace—I never heard him sing. But on this occasion when I played and he sat "mindlessly" on the couch, I suddenly heard him sing, raspingly, plaintively, the words of the song, "Long ago and far away . . ." I nearly burst into tears, wondering what depths of being, still active, had prompted this response. When I told Masahisa Segawa about this, I believe we shared a universal language of empathy, of feeling—music, if you will: something that transcends any particular "culture."

"*A sō*, that happens! That happens!" he said. "We stayed just one year in London; then we came back. In 1927, as I told you, 'My Blue Heaven' and 'Song of Araby' were issued in Japan. So I remember all of the words of 'My Blue Heaven' and 'Song of Araby' too."

We discussed wartime propaganda programming of jazz and that "very unhappy unfortunate person," Tokyo Rose ("You know she had no choice as far as cooperating with the Japanese government went"). Some of those broadcasts survived, and Segawa has them: "Japanese jazz bands of 1943 playing for U.S. troops, with English interruptions. Duke Ellington's 'Solitude'—amazing! At that time already, Japanese jazz bands *could* play Duke Ellington!" Segawa said that when the government finally issued detailed instructions prohibiting jazz from being played, they ordered that all jazz records people owned at home should be brought to record stores and turned over to the government. "I knew many record store owners; we were good friends. So I asked them to keep those jazz recordings, *not* to present them to the government, and I bought them very cheap—for almost nothing. I had a very good collection of jazz records during wartime! Citizens of good will, following government instructions, punctually presented their jazz records to those stores, so I brought all of them to my home!"

"And you still have them?"

"No, they were mostly burned. A few have remained. Most were burned in the air raids."

We closed out this talk, which had reached an unanticipated emotional peak on my part, with Segawa's appraisal of the Japanese jazz scene in general.

"When you talk about Japanese jazz, please understand that there are three generations. The middle generation—people like Yosuke Yamashita, Akira Sakata, or Kazutoki Umezu—who were mostly influenced by John Coltrane. I call them the 'Coltrane Generation.' The younger generation has mostly been influenced by Wynton Marsalis. They are very *different*."

"There is criticism in the States of the sort of 'school' or set of dogmatic principles that Marsalis has established. I call it the 'Wynton Marsalis Disease.'"

"There is criticism in Japan also. Because the younger generation has not wanted to play free jazz from the beginning. They play according to *academic* concepts, although it's all right to move a little far away from the fundamentals if the passion comes. But Yosuke Yamashita or Akira Sakata would completely disregard chord progressions, and from the beginning they wished to play 'free.' I personally call that 'Japanese comical free jazz.' It appeals to some people. The musicians disregarded the fundamental chords and took short *short* phrases from popular songs and they made people *laugh*. Or they engaged in the *long* solo play of free jazz, collectively or singly. Yamashita and Sakata are both very high *technicians*. They can play the fundamentals of course, so because of their high technique, it's all right to play completely free jazz. But some of their followers have not learned the fundamental techniques. They just imitate the strange tones of Coltrane, or maybe at-random phrasing. Those people are dead now, and only these—Yamashita and Sakata—have remained. But the younger generation wants to stick more to the mainstream. The current young generation can *play,* but they don't want to go any farther than they are; they don't want to disregard set musical principles."

I mentioned the warm reception that strictly free jazz exponents from Russia—such as Sergey Kuryokhin, Vladimir Chekasin, and Valentina Ponomareva—had received in Japan.

"Yes, there are many free jazz enthusiasts in Japan," Segawa replied. "But when I organize a concert, I like to gather my wife or friends who could enjoy Benny Goodman before, and I like to present *current* jazz to them. I think groups should play *some* melody—something understandable to the general public. But there are other people—

particularly artists or writers or journalists—who like the other extremes. At present, I am trying to promote the younger generation, because I've known them from their schoolkid days, and they are trying very hard. They go to Berklee and they are coming *back* and they are working to establish *their own* jazz in Japan. Their modern jazz is, musically, of a very high standard. At the same time, I am producing the kind of standard jazz concert that appeals to the older generation, even people who are sixty or seventy years old. They like American songs that were popular right after the war, tunes like 'Sentimental Journey' or 'Paper Moon.' These people don't know where to go to listen to the jazz they used to like. They can't go to small live houses anymore, but they are waiting for standard jazz concerts—and I am trying to do these two things."

TOKYO JAZZ SCENE, 1998

OWARD THE END OF OUR conversation at the Asia Center, Masahisa Segawa asked me if I'd had a chance to go to any live houses or clubs to listen to young musicians. I told him that two years ago I'd heard lots of live music, not only in Tokyo but in Osaka, Kyoto, and Nagoya as well, but that I would only have two nights in Tokyo, this trip, before I returned to the States.

"Have you heard of the arranger and trombone player Murata Youichi? He's *very* talented and has a good orchestra. Ten pieces. All the young men play with this group regularly, at the Pit Inn in Shinjuku. You only have two days? Wait a minute, please."

Then, with typical Japanese graciousness matched with alacrity, Masahisa Segawa called the Pit Inn and arranged our visit there, that very night. First we dined and talked more jazz together, arriving at the club in time for the first set. The place was packed with a very young and enthusiastic audience. We had to squeeze into a tight spot in the back, the older man, Mr. Segawa, proving far more nimble than his large and clumsy Western fellow writer.

The Murata Youichi Orchestra contained some excellent young musicians I'd come across before, although not *live:* trumpeters Tomonao Hara and Keiji Matsushima, bassist Koichi Osamu, Yoshiro Miyoshi—an all-star band made up of jazz restoration pros, "young lions," and the results were what you might expect. I heard jazz classics such as "Goodbye Porkpie Hat" and "Heavy Weather," along with a host of originals written for specific soloists: the idiomatic range going from funky Dixieland conventions, to "Shaw Nuff" and "Hot House" bop, to Buddhist bell percussion aligned with raw rock, jouncing Jaco Pastorius–based electric bass lines, to collective free jamming. With so many fine soloists on hand, why *not* let them all play at once? Solid architectonic effects and anarchy went hand in hand, along with *lots* of spontaneous interplay. Hara smiled broadly at some witty guitar fill, then proudly provided his own sparse intelligent phrasing. Mingus-rich with invention, the entire band played with respect for each other, for Murata's charts, and for that essential ingredient of jazz: solid *swing*.

I took some photos after, Masahisa Segawa surprised (and perhaps disappointed) that I was as interested in the patrons as I was in the musicians, whom I really didn't wish to bother after their rich set. I *was* interested in the young crowd: its eager and knowing response to the music. I thanked Mr. Segawa for having introduced me to this important group.

Next day, I found the Yamano Music Company in Ginza, a seven-story record shop that Masahisa Segawa had recommended highly. I searched its richly stocked jazz bins (one whole floor devoted to jazz) and found recordings by most of the musicians Segawa had mentioned: Junko Onishi's three-CD set; fellow pianists Yuichi Inoue, Yutaka Shiina, Takehiro Honda, Kunihiko Sugano, Kon Hideki, Tsuyoshi "Go" Yamamoto, Fumio Karashima, and Daichi Kondo; saxophonists Atsushi Ikeda and Akira Sakata; and guitarists Shungo Sawada, Haruhiko Takauchi, and Satoshi Inoue. I'd have a fat suitcase going home, but all of these purchases were well worth listening to.

I probably should have quit with such small, and large, satisfaction, because the rest of my search was fruitless. I had somehow heard about Drum Museum Taikodan in Nishi Asakusa, and, by now a loyal fan of *taiko,* I thought it would be interesting to visit it. Although I eventually found it, housed in an imposing brick building, the museum was closed on both days I went, even though a *kōban* (police box) attendant assured me on the day of my first failure that I would succeed the next day. The area was curious: a sort of contraband city, it seemed, hawking all sort of electronic goodies. It was also the only *ku* (district or section) in Tokyo where I was approached by panhandlers. I also found any number of enticing signs—Apollo Music House, Show and Bar Restaurant Rockin' 69, the Boston Club, John Bruhious and New Orleans Jazz All-Stars, Karaoke House—but nothing, at the time of afternoon I was there, was *open,* including an intriguing sequence of "addresses," 6F (Percussion City), 5F (Ethnic City), 4F (Drum City). Someday, I'll return to this section of Tokyo and find out just what the hell is going on there.

I had arranged a meeting with Masanori Doi and Ichiro Ishikawa of *Jazz Life* magazine. Masanori-san actually came to a coffeeshop on Soto-bori dōri, where I was waiting, and escorted me to his office (so I wouldn't get lost finding it). He looked quite young, as did Ichiro, who translated for him. (Actually, after a while I wasn't sure just who was translating for whom; I had a Japanese vocabulary list for topics I hoped to cover, which turned out to be a good thing.) Masahisa Segawa had told me that Masanori Doi was "a good pianist," and the two young editors (Ichiro-san plays bass) gave me a slant on an interesting and quite youthful side of jazz life in Japan.

The magazine, a rival of *Swing Journal,* has a twenty-year history and a *hakkōbusu* (circulation; one of the words I'd written down) of thirty thousand. This *dokusha* (readership) is made up mostly of students and amateur musicians. I told them that what interested me about the magazine was the large number of charts and instructional devices it contained, and Doi responded, "Yes, for amateur musicians." I said that the major jazz magazines in the States had their share of feature and profile pieces, but not all that much in the way of practical application, and I thought their magazine was far more *hokatsu-teki* (inclusive, comprehensive).

"The range of our readers is very wide," Doi said. "All of the people who love jazz read *Jazz Life* because there are only three magazines about jazz available in Japanese in Japan. There is *Swing Journal* and *Jazu Seisho.*" (The latter word means "Bible.")

"But neither of those is as good as this one," I said, pointing to the copy of *Jazz Life* they had just given me. They laughed and nodded. I mentioned having seen Yoshiaki "Miya" Miyanoue on my previous trip to Japan, and we talked about the *sensei* system, as opposed to the availability of a major jazz college such as Berklee.

"Ah, Yoshiaki Miyanoue!" Doi said. "The process here is to watch and listen to *better* musicians play. And some Japanese musicians *do* go to Berklee. Our universities teach mostly classical music. Only *one* here has a jazz program. It's called Senseku Gakku, in Tokyo."

Masanori Doi had attended the Monterey Jazz Festival in Noto, the one I'd just come from, and had done so for the past two years. He thought it "a good festival," and his favorite performer this year had been Karrin Allyson. He found her a very *cute* (he used the English word; in Japanese, the closest word, *kawaii,* implies "loveliness") vocal-ist with lots of *genki* (vitality, energy). And he liked Poncho Sanchez, *mochiron* (of course). "He had everyone up and dancing." When I asked both Doi and Ishikawa who their favorite American musicians were, they each replied, "Many." In his "top five favorites," Doi included Joshua Redman, and Ishikawa added, "He plays tenor saxophone him-self," which confused me momentarily, because I thought he was a pianist. (Maybe both! We never resolved this.) But I did discover that Doi and Ishikawa play in the same band, an octet. Doi had studied with "a Japanese professional," tenor saxophonist Katsuya Sato. When I asked if their group played in the live houses, they said, "No, no, no, not *yet!* We can't play well yet in front of an audience!"

Aside from Doi's teacher, Sato, he admires Yosuke Yamashita and Masahiko Satoh, who writes an article for their magazine each month. Ichiro Ishikawa's favorite bass player is "Jaco" (Pastorius). "That's all," he added. I mentioned having seen and heard Murata Youichi's orches-tra with Mr. Segawa, and Doi replied, "Yes, good orchestra." When I commented on the young audience, he said, "Yes, the average age of jazz fans in Japan is *san-jū sai* [thirty]. Of course it depends on the musi-cians—the age or generation of the musicians."

Masanori Doi himself is twenty-eight years of age. When I asked him if the recession had hurt jazz life in Japan, he replied, "I don't see much of a change. Jazz fans are still going out to clubs."

I was one of them. I went to the J Club and discovered much the same thing there: young performers and a young (if sparse) crowd. When I arrived, Akiko Nakajima's trio set hadn't started yet, and film clips of Ben Webster and Ahmad Jamal were being shown on TV. The club was half empty and would remain that way. (Not that well informed, I didn't attempt to reach any conclusions regarding the economy.) Nakajima's trio started out with a quite plausible interpretation of "Solar," guitarist Ryo Ogihara cooking on an up-tempo solo, the drummer, Daisuke Yosh-ioka (bald and wearing a black biretta), inventive, if—within the Japa-nese jazz tradition too—excessive at times. "Solar" was followed by "But Not for Me." Akiko Nakajima's singing was competent, aside from an unfortunate rendering of "Beatrice Fairfax listen you" that ended up sounding dangerously close to "Bea-trisu Rettuce," or something like that. But Akiko was a comfortable pianist/vocalist, compatible with her cohorts, and the music was enjoyable—exactly what you would expect to hear if you had, as I had, just dropped in at a club in the States on any given night. None of the musicians looked as if they were overburdened with having a good time (how young and *serious* they seemed!) until the second set, when they were joined by alto saxophonist Saito Okura, who pumped some warm risk-taking blood into the group.

Two young women occupied the table next to me, and we chatted, and I made friends with a young man named Hiroaki Yoshida, who worked in the PC products division of an electronics firm, spoke very good English, and once played jazz guitar but had recently traded it in for flamingo guitar lessons. Hiroaki-san assisted me in a brief "interview" with Akiko; I learned that she was now twenty-six, had started classical piano lessons at three, had switched to jazz at twenty, and that the group had been together for just a year. Guitarist Ryo Ogihara is twenty-three, has been playing jazz for ten years, and studied at an institute in Tokyo, as well as with Yoshiaki "Miya" Miyanoue.

The second set opened with a solid rocker that featured Ogihara, drums and bass out of sync for a time or drowning out Akiko's solo, showing the group's lack of experience playing together. But Akiko, singing, offered a nice version of "You've Changed," and when saxophonist Saito Okura stepped up things *did* change, for he provided an aggressive edge (that element that so many Japanese musicians said they craved but felt they lacked) that seemed contagious. The entire group played better, with more *chikara* (strength or force or power), Okura's hair, parted in the middle, keeping time as it fell across his glasses. The group closed out with another "rock-out" number, the rhythm section in sync this time, and a friend presented Akiko with a bouquet of flowers—this gift from an attractive and spunky young woman named Yoshiko Uchida, who'd mastered the art of talking to someone in front of her (me, in this case) and on a cell phone at the same time. She also corrected my Japanese and told me about a jam session that would be held the next day at a place called OJS in Aoyama. She gave me typical instructions as to how to get there: "Take Kotodori Street, walk past the Blue Note, turn a corner, etc." This evening at the J Club cost me 4,300 yen—just to give an idea of what a casual jazz night on the town costs in Tokyo.

Having failed to find (even with the help of the customary lot of good Samaritans) the OJS jam session on my last night in Japan, and with Body and Soul not yet open, I stopped off at a piano bar where a pianist offered tasty but tight (nearly reluctant) interpretations of "Stella by Starlight" and "Someone to Watch over Me." The cover charge was 800 yen; a bottle of California chardonnay sold for 3,800 yen, a shot of scotch for 1,200, so I settled for Russian vodka at 700. It wasn't an ideal way to close out my stay in Tokyo, but I did witness another side—a probably fairly routine side—of jazz life in Japan. On my way back to the Asia Center, I passed an Aoyama store with a 680,000-yen kimono in the window, a beautiful "court" silver affair with black and gold filigree. For a moment I wished I were rich enough to take it home to Betty. *Shiyo ga nai* (It can't be helped). I had the *fuku* (good fortune) earrings I'd found for her in Kyoto, and they would have to do for a man of my means. I slept well that night, even though my Asia Center digs were truly claustrophobic compared to my spoiled-rotten Rotary life in Wakura Onsen! After I'd officially checked out I still had an hour to kill before I got my ride to Narita Airport, so I went to a record store and bought pop/rock CDs by Tsuyoshi Nagabuchi, Kuwata Keisuke and the Southern All Stars, Oda Kazumasa, and Yutaka Ozaki—with tunes I'd attempted to sing on our karaoke night in Nara with *watashi no sabarashii yome* (my wonderful daughter-in-law) Yoko's family on our first trip.

Once again, leaving Japan, the window of my plane—unlike Betty's when she left in 1996 and saw it at sunset—refused to afford a glimpse of Mt. Fuji. I thought of a fine piece of writing by Osamu Dazai in which, hiking up to Mitsu Pass and a vista that was supposed to be splendid, all he got was a view so completely shrouded in thick fog that he "couldn't see a thing." An old woman retrieved a large photograph of the mountain from her teahouse close by and held it high in both hands at the spot where Fujisan (Westerners mistakenly insist on calling it "Fujiyama") was supposed to be seen: "just like this, this big and this clear." Later, Dazai would learn that Hiroshige's slopes converge at an angle of eighty-five degrees, and some of Hokusai's renditions "fairly resemble the Eiffel Tower, peaking at nearly thirty degrees," but army survey maps show an angle of one hundred twenty-four degrees. Dazai concluded that "the real Fuji is unmistakably obtuse . . . almost pathetic, as mountains go." Although he would eventually *see* it and get more than his fill of Mt. Fuji, I was glad that I hadn't staked too much on this one last glance. After all, I was taking home what mattered most to me: the music. Although the actual portion of travel was over, in many ways, my jazz journey to Japan had just begun.

At customs, a somewhat stern official asked, "What do you do for a living . . . what's your work?"

"I'm a jazz writer," I replied.

He looked at me hard and handed back my passport, smiling.

"Keep writin', man!" he said.

CODA

A T THE 1999 MONTEREY JAZZ Festival, I was fortunate to participate on a panel called "The International Language of Jazz" with Anthony Brown, drummer and leader of the Asian American Orchestra. Once the panel managed to extract itself from the relentless semantic quagmire of just what "jazz" is, there seemed to be wholesale agreement on at least one of its most distinctive properties: freedom. I mentioned Russian writer Vassily Aksyonov's teenage love of the music "for its refusal to be pinned down," defining his attachment as "a Platonic rendezvous with freedom." Anthony Brown was inspirational, drawing a hand from the audience when he spoke of this aspect and the "international language" jazz has become. He cited the range of ethnicities represented in his orchestra. Anthony's father was African American/ Choctaw; his mother is Japanese. We all danced around the question, "Is the infusion of world music the wave of the future?" Our final consensus seemed to be that jazz can only profit, be revitalized by "alien" input; that the essence of the idiom (whatever that is) will be enhanced rather than diluted or threatened; that such open dialogue (what Anthony called "conversation") is basically quite healthy.

Following this panel session (Anthony had to leave early for a sound check), and as if to bear out all that we had discussed, I attended the Asian American Orchestra's performance of the *Far East Suite*. It was remarkable, the music expanded, revitalized, enhanced—dramatically altered at times yet treated throughout with respect—by the presence of such unfamiliar "jazz" instruments as the *ney* (Persian end-blown flute), the *dizi* (Chinese transverse bamboo flute), the *suona* (double-reed horn), and the *sheng* (Chinese mouth organ), producing unfamiliar tones and colors that gave the piece a whole new life of its own. The contrast on the opening section, "Tourist Point of View," among Ellington's strong bass patterns, Paul Gonsalves's warm fuzzy sax tone (setting out on an exotic voyage, but one still grounded in American urban sophistication, uptown), and Hafez Modirzadeh's morning call to prayer was exciting.

So too was the fresh life imparted by Anthony Brown's classic Asian cymbal splashes and Qi Chao Liu's slightly ominous *dizi* flavor (as opposed to Jimmy Hamilton's chirpy clarinet) on "Bluebird of Delhi (Mynah)"; Jon Jang's unique, subtle take on "Mt. Harissa" (contrasted to Ellington's own catchy vamp and more pronounced, assertive style); and Liu's sweetly dissonant, slightly bizarre—because unaccustomed—*suona* tone on "Blue Pepper (Far East of the Blues)." This last tune offered the most extreme (and enticing) departure from the original text, Ellington's knock 'em dead shuffle swing converted to a nearly slow-motion—stretched to the point of threatening to snap like a rubber band—presentation of the theme. On the final section, "Ad Lib on Nippon," Mark Izu's bowed bass and Jon Jang's nuance-filled piano were handsomely combined. Homage was paid to Ellington stalwarts such as Paul Gonsalves ("Tourist Point of View"), Johnny Hodges ("Isfahan"), Harry Carney ("Agra"), and Lawrence Brown ("Amad"), and even to Cat Anderson's screeching trumpet. But the Asian American Jazz Orchestra wisely declined to strictly replicate or compete with them (you can't out-Hodges Johnny Hodges!). To me, this performance also proved just how fruitful musical/journalistic "collaboration" (and this juxtaposition was unintended; the orchestra's performance just happened to follow the panel) might prove to be. Anthony Brown's arrangements served as living proof of what we had previously discussed: the excitement an innovative use of "foreign" vocabulary, tones, colors, structures can bring to an established work in jazz.

Anthony Brown is a remarkable musician and person. (He received his master's degree from Rutgers University and his Ph.D. in ethnomusicology from U.C.-Berkeley. He was also curator of American music and director of the jazz oral history program at the Smithsonian Institution from 1992 to 1996.) He not only explicated the charts for the sizable audience, in accessible yet "academically responsible" terms, but he conducted the group and functioned within it—with considerable panache!—as percussionist.

Not long after this event, I found myself talking to Anthony Brown at San Francisco's Legion of Honor Tech Center, where his wife works. We started out discussing the *Far East Suite,* which he did not find "unlike what we've been doing all along in the last twenty years as a musical community."

He mentioned Tatsu Aoki, a dedicated Chicago-based performer/producer who has done much to foster unique Asian American jazz, and he mentioned bassist Mark Izu, whom Anthony considers "a pivotal figure" in the Asian American jazz movement. "Mark was a bridge between the generation of pioneers," Anthony said, and performers such as Glenn Horiuchi and Hiroshima, "among the first ones back in the mid-seventies to start to integrate Japanese instruments and Japanese sensibilities into jazz." Tatsu Aoki, coming from Tokyo, was "originally a punk rocker, going to Chicago and getting turned on by the blues and jazz there, the consummate entrepreneur. He came to San Francisco, saw what we were doing with our festival, then went back home and started his own, the Asian American Jazz Festival in Chicago. Basically he transplanted all of us to start that festival. That was in '96. It was at that festival that we decided to start what ultimately became the Asian American Orchestra."

"This stuff has been brewing," he continued. "It's the hybridization of two languages: Asian and Western. And I think the *Far East Suite* represents a kind of culmination. We've become proficient at both languages; proficient enough, fluent enough so that the blending of the two, the new language that we are expressing with the other one . . . somehow has that universal quality." (I had mentioned Masahiko Satoh's exploration of the *local*—his idea that someday "you find that you are very universal," digging far enough "into your own soil" to go to "the opposite side of the earth.") "Maybe it's the synergistic effect: $1 + 1 = 3$. And basically it was a small community here in the Bay Area. We've been dealing with each other's approaches and forming a collective that made this possible. The whole thing about the local becoming universal: well, I think *all* movements in jazz are like that. Bach was just a church organist in Leipzig."

"Look at Kansas City," I said, "or the Detroit pianists . . ."

"Right! The Detroit pianists—another good example. Look at the influence there. It's like the human condition itself. We contain all the genes. We contain *everything*. Any one of us represents the rest of us. But in this regard, there was a conscious effort to create a cross-cultural expression."

When I asked if it had been difficult, in a piece like the *Far East Suite,* to strike a balance between paying homage to Ellington and Strayhorn and innovation, Anthony Brown replied, "I think that as long as you *have* that respect, as long as you approach the music—whatever your endeavor, whatever your expressive medium—with respect and acknowledgment of your predecessors, that's a great foundation to work from. To come into the music thinking, 'Yeah, I can *do* something with this'—without the awe. I didn't approach anything without envisioning Ellington or Strayhorn looking over my shoulder."

"Did they ever say, 'Hey, Anthony, don't do that!'?"

"Well, I don't know," he replied, laughing. "There *are* two far-out sections there. One is the intro to 'Mt. Harissa,' which is strict *gagaku*. I basically just took Ellington and revoiced it as a *gagaku* piece. And then of course 'Far East of the Blues,' or 'Blue Pepper,' which I completely recast, although that one was not really that far removed from Ellington, because there are pieces by him in the sixties where he's playing *free;* he's playing *out*. You would think it's the Sun Ra orchestra! So I went for that expression. It was a respect for and appreciation of Ellington and Strayhorn for their masterful contributions, but also respect for the entire legacy of jazz, as well as Asian music. I don't think I could have approached any of that or brought anything to it without having a very high regard for every element."

I asked about choosing the instrumentation. Anthony didn't use *mokugyo* (a wooden gong with fish-mouth slit) or *hichiriki* (a double-reed *gagaku* flute).

"*Hichiriki* is kind of hard to mix. Although Takemitsu can do it! To be absolutely honest, much of the instrumentation was determined by who played what—the resources available, the players and their expertise. *Shakuhachi* would have been nice, but I had a *ney* player, so I went with that. It's entirely possible I could rework the piece and incorporate other instruments. But something like the *hichiriki* is difficult. Most Japanese people find that sound quite challenging too!" He laughed. "I scored the work out in Western notation. I am familiar with much of the cipher notation, particularly in dealing with some of the Chinese performers, but everyone was versed or fluent in Western notation, so for

326

me that was a real plus. If I'd had to score it otherwise I could have, but it would have taken a lot longer. And not everything was scored. The intro to 'Ad Lib on Nippon,' for example. That was improvised."

I mentioned that, in Anthony's liner notes for the CD *Family,* he paid homage to the influence of Mark Izu again, saying that Mark originally did not just add the sound of Asian instruments to jazz but brought concepts of how to write music influenced by Asian concepts, such as breath length and cyclical structures. I said that Toru Takemitsu, too, talks about breath length, as does Masahiko Satoh, who's been heavily influenced by Takemitsu.

"The most convincing example for me was when I heard *gagaku* music and when I saw it scored. There's a piece called 'Ichikotsu-choshi,' and the phrase as notated was spanned as a breath length, and when you listen to the way it's performed, it is not *metrical* time. There's not an underlying equidistant kind of pulse going on underneath. You hear the phrase in its entirety, followed by yet another phrase which is, again, the same length—as one would calculating breath length. I was trying to count metrically, but I knew there was another dynamic at work here. It wasn't a pulse that was deciding the length of the phrase, but the actual length of a person's *breath*. So that to me was the very first telling example where I was looking at a score to the music, but the score did not accurately reflect what was going on. They were thinking in terms of breath length, rather than equidistant pulse."

"Did charts for *Family* make use of that concept?"

"My original inspiration was hearing the recording, but there is a book by Robert Garfias called *Music of a Thousand Autumns,* and he transcribed a large sample of *gagaku* music. I used this same method of transcription. I played the recording for the guys and I told them, 'This is what I want, so pay more attention to your own breath length, and at the phrase just for the notes, but as far as the actual pacing, go by your breath.' Then, because—as in a round—one phrase was played and then another, say, a second or two beats behind, I wanted the guys to go in relation to whatever the guy ahead of them was playing and not to try to follow some sort of underlying metrical structure. Takemitsu, I'll have to say, was *very* influential on this concept. I was more involved just trying to bring a Japanese sensibility before I really got to know his music, but—I know *exactly* when it was; it was sixteen years ago!—when I heard 'A Flock Descending into a Pentangular Garden,' and it changed my life. Yes, Takemitsu is *the one.* He is the master of translating and infusing Japanese cultural sensibilities into music, particularly hybridizing American or Western music."

I quoted the thoughts of Takemitsu I had jotted down from the documentary I'd seen, especially his ideas on the "circular" experience of the Japanese garden, its "cyclical rings of karma" ("I write music by placing objects in my musical garden") and the concept of *ma,* or emptiness ("A sheet of paper is not empty until you make the first mark").

"Exactly!" Anthony responded. Then laughing, having been put on the spot to respond, he said, *"He's* so eloquent in how he expresses those concepts. For me, cyclical structure came both from being familiar with Japanese music as a listener and then as a student of it. I was an ethnomusicologist, so structurally . . . well, how are you going to follow Takemitsu? How can you be as eloquent as he was? Even though Mark Izu was my initial inspiration, I remember writing—before I returned to America in 1978—a piece called 'Winter Haiku.' I wrote the piece as an homage to my folks; in this case, more to my mom. It was one of those pieces that just came out. It was written in a very sparse style and it was pentatonic. So regardless of how conscious or unconscious I was about what was going on, that *sensibility* was coming out anyway—before I met Mark, which was two years later. And before I really started to get into Takemitsu's music. I must have heard his electronic music around that time (the piece 'Ai') more than his orchestral/symphonic music."

I told Anthony how impressed I'd been not only by the Asian American Orchestra's performance of *Far East Suite* but by his "multitasking" as arranger, percussionist, emcee or explicator of the charts, and conductor. I said I usually can only do one thing at a time, but he was doing *all* of them.

"But that's what you do as a drummer, right?" He waved his arms and legs at the same time, laughing. "It's the ability to spread it out. Although I think from early on I never wanted to be *just* a drummer. I wanted to be a *musician.* I learned to read music only because I had music in me I wanted to write down. I learned how to write music before I learned how to read other people's music. That's the only reason I learned notation—because I wanted to document what was coming out of *me.* My father was a military man, but he was a great gardener. And he was a photographer. He was always doing many different things. It's probably something that I saw in him. He was a role model. And my older brother was an athlete, a musician before me, and a good student.

Plus he was great in the *street*. He could shoot pool and gamble better than anybody. So the ability to have a variety of abilities is something that was just kind of tied in. I like *anything* I'm doing. And by the way: on the albums—that's all my art work; those are my designs, all my layouts. That's all part of it too—the entire presentation."

I asked about the Asian Improv recording *Big Bands behind Barbed Wire*.

"That was a collaboration with George Yoshida [musician and author of *Reminiscing in Swingtime*]. George wanted that ambience when he told the story of the camps, because that was so important to him. He always told us the Nisei bands in the camps would get charts [of tunes like 'Tuxedo Junction' and 'In a Sentimental Mood'], and they got one for 'Don't Fence Me in.' When they got the recording, they pointed the speakers towards the guardhouses, so it was like the spirituals: there's already an implicit message. To show that irony—the hypocrisy. 'We're Americans; we listen to American music, yet you've got us here in these camps.'"

In September 1999, Glenn Ito of *EuroJazz News* posted a notice that Los Angeles–based pianist Glenn Horiuchi was undergoing a battle with colon cancer. Glenn died on June 3, 2000, at the age of forty-five. He was a marvelous musician/composer (*Issei Spirit, Manzanar Voices, Poston Sonata, Little Tokyo Suite,* and *Kenzo's Vision* on Asian Improv Records; *Oxnard Beet* and *Calling Is It and Now* on Soul Note), a serious artist holding fellowships from the NEA and the California Arts Council, a political organizer and one of the leading, most inspirational members of the Asian American creative music movement. He was also one of my early inspirations for this project—someone I had hoped to interview in depth but was not able to.

My jazz journey to Japan was over. The music continued to find me, by whatever means. In fact I was inundated by fresh, unfamiliar names I vowed to check out as best I could. I made up a list of more than fifty new musical "acquaintances" I'd heard or read about. And Japanese artists kept turning up close to home. Betty and I attended a performance by a fine young vocalist, Sami Kaneda, whose *Songs of Seven Seas* CD was named the Top Selling Jazz Vocal Album in Japan by *Swing Journal*. I continued to collect new work by Satoko Fujii, Junko Onishi, Sachi Hayasaka, and Yoshiaki Masuo; Joh Yamada's first release in America, *Bluestone;* and fascinating CDs by Aki Takase (*Le Cahier du Bal*) and Makoto Ozone (his brilliant *Virtuosi,* interpretations of classical pieces with Gary Burton).

Again, I no longer felt I had to *prove* anything about this music; it could speak fully for itself, free of proselytizing or protest. Yet I couldn't help but be pleased to find the following statement by a jazz giant, pianist Mal Waldron, speaking of his hit in Japan, "Left Alone," and the nearly kamikaze (divine wind) effect of a Japanese audience: "Oh, the audiences are fantastic. You feel the air comin' at you and you have to lean forward. Otherwise, if you stand up straight, you go backward! Japan has the best audiences in the world because there most of the people know about jazz and they love jazz. About 90 percent of the people there know about jazz—the largest percentage of *any* country. . . . I think jazz is a mirror of the world today and it has to be spontaneous to keep that relationship. . . . We speak to each other—it's like a language—and as long as you have the same vocabulary you can speak with any other musicians . . . you talk to each other."

Throughout the six years I was engaged in this project, a host of younger jazz artists flourished on the American jazz scene: Bill Frisell, Don Byron, Dave Douglas, Joshua Redman, Irvin Mayfield, Regina Carter, Ingrid Jensen, Geri Allen, Jason Moran, Benny Green, Greg Osby, Michele Rosewoman, Diana Krall, Brad Mehldau, and many more. I listened to and collected as much of their work as I could, yet I can safely say that, throughout all the time I was mostly "confined," as it were, by the scope of my project to listening to jazz in and from Japan, plus the wealth of Asian American talent I had been exposed to, I did not feel deprived in any way—in the sense that the music I was listening to was fully rewarding and provided abundant daily musical satisfaction on its own. It was *that* good!

The best way to complete this work, to "go out," is, I feel, by attempting to describe a piece that I feel is one of the most remarkable achievements in this music. I had kept up, throughout the writing of this book, a correspondence with Masahiko Satoh, and he sent me—much to my delight—the *Buddhist Music with 1000 Shōmyō Voices* recording that, up to that time, I'd heard so much about but had not had an opportunity to listen to.

The word *shōmyō* combines two characters: *shō* (voice or chant) and *myō* (light). The music consists of pentatonic plainsong similar to Gregorian chant, but in Masahiko Satoh's hands (and mind) the form is elevated to . . . well, let's find out. This was the performance of 1,000 monks (actually only 998 showed up) that took place in a Tokyo stadium. A photo shows them dressed in orange, black, green, and white robes, unfolding what look like yellow accordion pleats or "fans" (a field of daffodils worthy of Wordsworth). In the first or *shinkon* (religion) section, the monks can be heard chanting as they file into the stadium, resonance from the expectant crowd much in evidence. The monks then respond to a single guttural cry, in chorus. This is followed by an onslaught of voices mixed with *shiosai* (the sound of waves), crashing, caroming. These are frisky, not well-behaved monks, thank God. A solitary voice takes hold (this soloist, called *daiajari,* is the most respected priest), quavering, and then a sudden, overwhelming, nearly shocking response emerges, a single note—"ahhhh"—sustained by all, penetrating plainsong, a single note multiplied by 998, basic math transformed into the intricate geometry of the universe itself.

The full performance, graced with the hollow sound of *mokugyo* (the wooden fish-mouth slit drum Anthony Brown did *not* use in *Far East Suite*) and *shakuhachi,* serves as a sort of constant yet wavering bombardment of rare particulars (microtonality) and basic or core Japanese syllables (*mee, hee, nee*) united with organ tones that emerge from Masahiko Satoh's Yamaha SY 77. All this explodes into the amazing, nearly torturous seventh section, *magaraku,* a rhythmic assault in which jazz and *shōmyō* meet as one. Saxophones snort and wail, wild, relentless! These monks won't let up. This big band (even its flutes!) won't let up. The rhythm section won't let up. At some percussive pinnacle, just when you think you can't stand anymore, it all *stops,* shifts to a blessed fade, and the solitary chanter steps in again, summing up.

Respite. But the music is hardly over. We're only at the eighth section out of sixteen (halfway home!), and what follows is as wild and superbly woven as all that preceded it, combining intermittent piano punctuation, persistent chant, and a cry of awakening that turns into a ten-minute *taiko* attack, mixing strong and weak segments, as in Japanese linked verse. Fierce tympani-like rolls are laced with gongs, cymbals, clacking sticks, accretion and relaxation, ebb and flow, all this merged with an occasional cry of strictly human propulsion—"Dai!" (meaning large, reign, lifetime—take your pick!)—and the final savage vocal romp of 998 "baaad ass" monks on a rampage, a close-out that allows author/composer/pianist/genius Masahiko Satoh to sum it all up with some absolutely *lovely* piano laced with *shiosai* (the sound of waves) again, which—synthesized—sound like waves of applause and perhaps are: eternity safely embedded in its grain of sand again.

I sat back, stunned, exhausted, massively informed, and "entertained." I felt as if I had taken in—at a single sitting—Charles Mingus's "Meditations on Integration," Ellington's *Far East Suite,* Benny Goodman's 1938 Carnegie Hall version of "Sing, Sing, Sing," the "1812 Overture," Beethoven's Ninth Symphony ("Ode to Joy," indeed!), large portions of Hector Berlioz, and—thrown in for good measure—Charles Ives's "Fourth of July," in which he tried to simulate the activity of small-town bands playing Independence Day music simultaneously all over the nation. *Arigatō gozaimahsita,* Masahiko-san. And thank you, Japan. I won't say sayonara, because hopefully (as at the end of *Casablanca,* "As Time Goes By" playing in the background) this is just the beginning of a beautiful friendship. *Ato de!* (Later!)

BIBLIOGRAPHY

E. Taylor Atkins's *Blue Nippon: Authenticating Jazz in Japan* (Durham, London: Duke University Press, 2001) appeared after I had completed work on this book, and I recommend it to all whose interest has been stimulated regarding jazz in and from Japan. The following is a selective bibliography of works I found useful for *Jazz Journeys to Japan: The Heart Within*.

Abe, Kobo. *Beyond the Curve*. Trans. Juliet Winters Carpenter. Tokyo, New York, London: Kodansha International, 1991.

———. *The Woman in the Dunes*. Trans. E. Dale Saunders. New York: Vintage International, 1991.

Aitken, Robert. *A Zen Wave: Basho's Haiku and Zen*. New York: Weatherhill, 1978.

"Akira Tana: Interview" (taken and transcribed by Alwyn and Laurie Lewis). *Cadence,* February 1996, 5, 122.

All-Japan: The Catalogue of Everything Japanese. New York: Quill, 1984.

Ardoin, John. "Earthly Laughter." In program for *Wozzeck*, San Francisco Opera (1999–2000 season), 10.

Asai, Susan Miyo. "The Jazz Connection in Asian American Music." *Coda,* July/August 1991, 4–6.

Barthes, Roland. *Empire of Signs*. New York: Hill and Wang, 1982.

Bohnaker, William. *The Hollow Doll (A Little Box of Japanese Shocks)*. New York: Ballantine Books, 1990.

Boyet, Didier. "Jazz au Japan." *Jazz Magazine* (France), January 1996, 16–19.

Brand, Jude. *Tokyo Night City*. Rutland: Charles E. Tuttle, 1993.

BIBLIOGRAPHY

Broomer, Stuart. "Satoko Fujii: East West Vision." *Coda,* July/August 2000, 6–9.

Brower, Robert H., and Earl Miner. *Japanese Court Poetry.* Stanford: Stanford University Press, 1961.

Brown, J. D. *The Sudden Disappearance of Japan: Journeys through a Hidden Land.* Santa Barbara: Capra Press, 1994.

Buruma, Ian. "Becoming Japanese." (Article on Haruki Murakami.) *New Yorker,* December 23–30, 1996, 60–71.

Chadwick, David. *Thank You and OK! An American Zen Failure in Japan.* New York: Penguin/Arkana, 1994.

Chan, Sylvia. "Miya Masaoka: Musician, Composer, Performer." *Godzilla West* (fall 1996): 4–5.

Choumei, Kamono. *Hojoki: Ten Foot Square House.* Trans. Muro Masaru. Tokyo: Hokuseido Press, 1990.

Christopher, Robert C. *The Japanese Mind.* New York: Fawcett Columbine, 1983.

Collcutt, Matrin, Marius Jansen, and Isao Kumakura. *Cultural Atlas of Japan.* New York, Oxford: Facts on File, 1988.

Culbertson, Dawn C. "Kodo: Dynamic Drummers." *Zasshi,* November/December 1995, 78–79.

Davidson, Cathy. *Thirty-six Views of Mount Fuji: On Finding Myself in Japan.* New York: Dutton, 1993.

Davis, F. Hadland. *Myths and Legends of Japan.* New York: Dover Publications, 1992.

Dazai, Osamu. *Self Portraits.* Trans. Ralph F. McCarthy. Tokyo, New York, London: Kodansha International, 1992.

De Mente, Boye Lafayette. *The Japanese Have a Word for It: The Complete Guide to Japanese Thought and Culture.* Chicago: Passport Books, 1997.

Downer, Leslie. *On the Narrow Road: Journey into a Lost Japan.* New York: Summit Books, 1989.

Elder, John. *Following the Brush: An American Encounter with Classical Japanese Culture.* Pleasantville, N.Y.: Akadine Press, 1993.

Emotion of Edo: Panoramic View of Sumidagawa River by Hokusai. Tokyo: Fukui Asahido, 1998.

Feather, Leonard. "Jazz Conquers Japan." *Ebony,* October 1964, 127–34.

Feigin, Leo, ed. *Russian Jazz: New Identity.* London: Quartet Books Limited, 1985.

Feiler, Bruce S. *Learning to Bow: Inside the Heart of Japan.* New York: Ticknor and Fields, 1991.

Ferguson, Jim. "Fusion Virtuoso: Kazumi Watanabe." *Guitar Player,* April 1986, 13–21.

Franckling, Ken. "The Artistry of Makoto Ozone." *JazzTimes,* March 1988, 18.

BIBLIOGRAPHY

Fromartz, Samuel. "Anything but Quiet: Japanese Americans Reinvent Taiko Drumming." *Natural History,* February 1998, 44–48.

Fujie, Linda. "East Asia/Japan." In *Worlds of Music: An Introduction to the Music of the World's Peoples,* ed. Jeff Todd. New York: Schirmer Books, 1992.

Gagaku. Tokyo: Kikuyou Court Culture Institute, n.d.

Gehman, Richard. "Jazz over Tokyo." *Saturday Review,* March 14, 1959, 75–76.

Gourse, Leslie. "Sumi Tonooka: Secret Piano Places." *JazzTimes,* August 1990, 7.

Griffin, D. Michael. "Japanese Jazz Clubs Blow Your Socks Off!" July 29, 1997. Available at <http://www.jazzbuff.org/9612/clubs.shtml>.

Guest, Harry. *Japan.* Lincolnwood, Ill.: Passport Books, 1995.

Hale, James. "Toshinori Kondo." *Coda,* July/August 2000, 16–17.

Harby, Bill. "The Rhythm Method." (Article on Kenny Endo.) *Island Scene* (fall 1997): 8–9.

Hardiman, Jim. "Japanese Summer Jazz Festival Grosses 75G, before Sponsors." *Variety,* September 24, 1986, 145.

Hayes, Nicole. "A Man with a Vision: Abe Weinstein—Honolulu's Mr. Jazz." *East Honolulu Newspaper,* July 1996, 1.

Hearn, Lafcadio. *Kokoro: Hints and Echoes of Japanese Inner Life.* Rutland: Charles E. Tuttle, 1972.

Heine, Steven. *The Zen Poetry of Dogen.* Boston: Tuttle Publishing, 1997.

Heinrich, Amy Vladeck. *Fragments of Rainbows: The Life and Poetry of Saito Mokichi.* New York: Columbia University Press, 1983.

Hibbett, Howard. *The Floating World in Japanese Fiction.* Rutland: Charles E. Tuttle, 1975.

Hiroshige's Fifty-Three Stages on the Tokaido Highway. Tokyo: Yohan Publications, 1992.

Inada, Lawson Fusao. *Only What We Could Carry: The Japanese American Internment Experience.* Berkeley: Heyday Books, 2000.

"In Japan, It's Summer of the U.S. Jazz Festival." *New York Times,* August 25, 1982, 22.

"In Japan, Jazz Resurges as a National Passion." *New York Times,* January 7, 1988, 18.

Irokawa, Daikichi. *The Age of Hirohito: In Search of Modern Japan.* New York: The Free Press, 1995.

Iwanami, Yozo. *Hozan, Friesen + 1.* Liner notes. Next Wave: Nippon Phonogram, 1980.

Iyer, Pico. "Tales of the Living Dead." (Article on Haruki Murakami.) *Time,* November 3, 1997, 112.

"Japanese Free Improvisors." Ed. Yoshiyuki Suzuki. Available at <http://www.japanimprov.com/index.html>.

Jhaver, Niranjan. "A Brighter Sun Shines in Japan?" February 1997. Available at <http://www.allaboutjazz.com>.

Kalbacher, Gene. "Sadao Watanabe: Bop/Pop Chops." *Down Beat,* January 1987, 19–21.

Kaliss, Jeff. "East West." (Article on Toshiko Akiyoshi.) *San Francisco Examiner,* October 5, 1997, 14.

Kapleau, Roshi Philip. *The Three Pillars of Zen.* New York: Anchor Books, 1989.

Kasumi. *The Way of the Urban Samurai.* Boston, Rutland, Tokyo: Charles E. Tuttle, 1992.

Kato, Yoshi. "Multi-Tasking with Mark Izu." September 21, 2000. Available at <http://www.jazzwest.com>.

Kawabata, Yasunari. *Palm-of-the-Hand Stories.* Trans. Lane Dunlop and J. Martin Holman. New York: North Point Press, 1988.

———. *Snow Country.* Trans. Edward G. Seidensticker. New York: Alfred A. Knopf, 1956.

Keene, Donald. *Anthology of Japanese Literature: From the Earliest Era to the Mid–Nineteenth Century.* New York: Grove Press, 1955.

———. *Dawn to the West: Japanese Literature in the Modern Era: Fiction.* New York: Henry Holt and Company, 1984.

———. *Dawn to the West: Japanese Literature in the Modern Era: Poetry, Drama, Criticism.* New York: Henry Holt and Company, 1984.

———. "The *Iemoto* System: No and Kyogen." In *Fenway Court.* Boston: Trustees of the Isabella Stewart Gardner Museum, 1993.

———. *Modern Japanese Literature.* New York: Grove Press, 1956.

Kerr, Alex. *Lost Japan.* Melbourne: Lonely Planet Publications, 1996.

Kishibe, Shigeo. *The Traditional Music of Japan.* Tokyo: Ongaku no Tomo Sha, 1984.

Koestler, Arthur. *The Lotus and the Robot.* New York: The Macmillan Company, 1960.

Lady Murasaki. *The Tale of Genji.* Trans. Arthur Waley. New York: The Modern Library, 1960.

Lane, Richard. *Images from the Floating World: The Japanese Print.* New York: Konecky and Konecky, 1978.

Lester, Toni. "Toshiko Akiyoshi: A Profile." *Coda,* n.d., 35.

Levi, Jonathan. "In the Realm of the Saxes: A Long, Strange Trip through the Jazz Clubs of Tokyo." *GQ,* September 1990, 422–25.

Levin, Floyd. *Classic Jazz.* Berkeley: University of California Press, 2000.

Malm, William P. *Japanese Music and Musical Instruments.* Durham, London: Duke University Press, 2001.

Mandel, Howard. "Terumasa Hino: The Japanese Brassman, Bluestruck from Birth, Goes Straightahead." *Down Beat,* August 1990, 51.

BIBLIOGRAPHY

"Masahiko Satoh: Oral History." Taken and transcribed by Kazue Yokoi. *Cadence,* August 1994, 5–8.

Masaoka, Miya. "Koto no Tankyu: Koto Explorations." *Newsletter of the Institute for Studies in American Music* 25 (spring 1996). Available at <http://thecity.sfsu.edu/~miya/kotonotankyu.html>.

———. "Unfinished Music: A Conversation with Yoko Ono." *San Francisco Bay Guardian,* August 27–September 2, 1997, 52–55.

Maure, Jeremy, and Hannah Charton. "Sukiyaki and Chips: The Japanese Sounds of Music." In *Beats of the Heart: Popular Music of the World.* New York: Pantheon Books, 1985.

Means, Andrew. "Hiroshima Profile." *Jazziz,* January 1995, 50–52.

Milkowski, Bill. "Kazumi Watanabe: Fusion Flash from the Land of the Rising Sun Makes the Most of Technology with His New Trio." *Down Beat,* May 1990, 54–55.

Minor, William. *Monterey Jazz Festival: Forty Legendary Years.* Santa Monica: Angel City Press, 1997.

———. *Unzipped Souls: A Jazz Journey through the Soviet Union.* Philadelphia: Temple University Press, 1995.

Mishima, Yukio. *The Temple of the Golden Pavilion.* Trans. Ivan Morris. New York: Vintage International, 1994.

Munroe, Alexandra. *Japanese Art after 1945: Scream Against the Sky.* New York: Henry N. Abrams, 1994.

Mura, David. *Turning Japanese: Memoirs of a Sansei.* New York: Anchor Books, 1991.

Murakami, Haruki. *Norwegian Wood.* Trans. Jay Rubin. New York: Vintage International, 2000.

———. *The Wind-Up Bird Chronicle.* Trans. Jay Rubin. New York: Alfred A. Knopf, 1997.

"Musical Mentor to a Japanese Star: Duo Takes Orient Express to Fame." (Article on Carl Jones and Chiemi Eri.) *Ebony,* August 1962, 73.

Okakura, Kakuzo. *The Book of Tea.* Tokyo, New York, London: Kodansha International, 1989.

Olsen, Darian, ed. *Japan: A Handbook.* Tokyo: The College Women's Association of Japan, 1971.

Ono, Skyo. *Shinto: The Kami Way.* Rutland: Charles E. Tuttle, 1962.

Ouellette, Dan. "East and West." *Down Beat,* August 1989, 61.

Palmer, Robert. "From Japan Comes Another Major Export: American Jazz." *New York Times,* June 30, 1985, 19.

Patrick, Diane. "Sadao Watanabe." *JazzTimes,* March 1989, 14.

Porter, William N. *A Hundred Verses from Old Japan: Being a Translation of the Hyaku-nin-isshiu.* Rutland: Charles E. Tuttle, 1979.

BIBLIOGRAPHY

Reingold, Edwin M. *Chrysanthemums and Thorns: The Untold Story of Modern Japan.* New York: St. Martin's Press, 1992.

Reischauer, Edwin O. *The Japanese.* Cambridge: The Belknap Press of Harvard University Press, 1977.

Riedinger, Bob. "Kazumi Watanabe." *JazzTimes,* November 1988, 10.

Rothstein, Joseph. "Jazz Shines with Okoshi, Akiyoshi in Island Festival: Finale." *The Honolulu Advertiser,* July 22, 1996, B4.

Rudofsky, Bernard. *The Kimono Mind: An Informed Guide to Japan and the Japanese.* Garden City: Doubleday and Company, 1965.

"Sachi Hayasaka and Stir Up." Available at <http://www.ne.jp/asahi/stir/up/profile/profile_e.html>.

Sakaiya, Taichi. *What Is Japan? Contradictions and Transformations.* New York, Tokyo, London: Kodansha International, 1993.

Sansom, George. *A History of Japan to 1334.* Stanford: Stanford University Press, 1958.

———. *A History of Japan: 1334 to 1615.* Stanford: Stanford University Press, 1961.

———. *A History of Japan: 1615 to 1867.* Stanford: Stanford University Press, 1963.

———. *A Short Cultural History.* Stanford: Stanford University Press, 1978.

Sato, Hiroaki, and Burton Watson. *From the Country of Eight Islands.* New York: Columbia University Press, 1986.

"Satoko Fujii: Interview." Taken and transcribed by Ludwig Van Trikt. *Cadence,* December 2000, 8–10.

"Satoko Fujii and Natsuki Tamura." February 29, 2000. Available at <http://www2s.biglobe.ne.jp./~Libra/>.

Seidel, Mitchell. "The Perils of Toshiko." *Down Beat,* February 1993, 30–32.

Seidensticker, Edward. *Low City, High City: Tokyo from Edo to the Earthquake.* Cambridge: Harvard University Press, 1991.

———. *Tokyo Rising: The City since the Great Earthquake.* New York: Alfred A. Knopf, 1990.

Shibayama, Zenkei. *Zen Comments on the Mumonkan.* New York: Harper and Row, 1974.

"Shinu, Shinu, Shinu." *Time,* September 12, 1960, 60.

Silverman, Ed. "Kai Akagi." *Jazziz,* January 1995, 84–85.

Smith, Bradley. *Japan: A History in Art.* Garden City: Doubleday and Company, 1964.

Smith, Patrick. *Japan: A Reinterpretation.* New York: Pantheon Books, 1997.

Statler, Oliver. *Japanese Inn.* New York: Pyramid Books, 1962.

Stewart, Jan. "All That Japanese Jazz Beats On." *Los Angeles Times,* October 5, 1988, 1–7.

———. "Beppu Bop." *Down Beat,* December 1982, 12.

Sullivan, Joseph. "Interview: Tiger Okoshi." *Zasshi,* November/December 1995, 61–67.

Suzuki, D. T. *Zen and Japanese Culture.* New York: MJF Books, 1959.

Suzuki, Shinryu. *Zen Mind, Beginner's Mind.* New York: Weatherhill, 1970.

Tana, Akira. "Jazz in Japan: Committee on the A.B. Degree in East Asian Studies." Undergraduate thesis, Harvard University, 1974.

Tanabe, George J., Jr., ed. *Religions of Japan in Practice.* Princeton: Princeton University Press, 1999.

Tanizaki, Jun'ichiro. *In Praise of Shadows.* Trans. Thomas J. Harper and Edward G. Seidensticker. Stony Creek, Conn.: Leete's Island Books, 1977.

———. *The Makioka Sisters.* Trans. Edward G. Seidensticker. New York: Everyman's Library, 1993.

Taylor, Andrew. "Life after Fifty (Albums)." (Article on Sadao Watanabe.) *Berklee Today* (spring 1991): 13–15.

Thompson, Scott H. "Terumasa Hino: Straight-ahead and Soulful." *JazzTimes,* September 1990, 25.

Toop, David. "A Style of No Style That Spurns All Constraints." *New York Times,* May 13, 2001, 19–20.

Totman, Conrad. *Tokugawa Ieyasu: Shogan.* Union City, Calif.: Heian International, 1983.

Tourneen, Saudades. "Yosuke Yamashita." Available at <http://www.ejn.it /mus/yamash.htm>.

Valery, H. Paul. *Japanese Culture.* Honolulu: University of Hawaii Press, 1984.

Ward, Phillip. *Japanese Capitals.* New York: Hippocrene Books, 1985.

Warner, Langdon. *The Enduring Art of Japan.* New York: Grove Press, 1952.

Wilson, John S. "Jazz Artists Prominent in U.S.-Japanese Trade." *New York Times,* June 5, 1985, 21.

Wurman, Richard Saul. *Tokyo Access.* Los Angeles: Access Press, 1984.

Yanagi, Sori, ed. *The Woodblock and the Artist: The Life and Work of Shiko Munakata.* Tokyo, New York, London: Kodansha International, 1991.

Yosano, Akiko. *Tangled Hair: Selected Tanka from Midaregami.* Trans. Sanford Goldstein and Seishi Shinoda. Rutland: Charles E. Tuttle, 1987.

Yoshida, George. *Reminiscing in Swingtime: Japanese Americans in Popular Music, 1925–1960.* San Francisco: National Japanese American Historical Society, 1997.

DISCOGRAPHY

This is a selected, limited discography, taken from some of the recordings I collected for the purpose of this book.

Jazz

Akagi, Kai. *The Asian American Jazz Trio*. Evidence, ECD 22108–2, 1995.
———. *Mirror Puzzle*. AudioQuest, AQ-CD 1028, 1994.
Akiyoshi, Toshiko. *Carnegie Hall Concert: Toshiko Akiyoshi Jazz Orchestra*. Columbia, CK 48805, 1992.
———. *Desert Lady-Fantasy*. Columbia, CK57856, 1994.
———. *Remembering Bud—Cleopatra's Dream*. Evidence, ECD 22034–2, 1992.
———. *Toshiko Akiyoshi at Maybeck*. Concord, CCD-4635, 1995.
———. *The Toshiko Akiyoshi–Lew Tabackin Big Band*. Novus/RCA, 3106–2-N, 1991.
Ami, Kiyoko. *Ami: Rhapsody in N.Y.* AMF/Interculture Club, ICCJ-1001, 1991.
Amano, Shoko. *Shoko Celebrates in New York City*. BRC International, BRC-JAM-9103, 1991.
———. *500 Miles High*. BRC International, BRC-JAM-9001, 1990.
Aoki, Tatsu. *Needless to Say*. Sound Aspects Records, SASCD 047, 1992.
———. *Tatsu Aoki and Sparrow: If It Wasn't for Paul*. Southport, S-SSD-0034, 1995.
Brown, Anthony. *Big Bands behind Barbed Wire: Asian American Jazz Orchestra with San Jose Taiko*. Asian Improv Records, AIR 0045, 1998.
———. *Family*. Asian Improv Records, AIR 0027, 1996.
———. *Far East Suite: Anthony Brown's Asian American Orchestra*. Asian Improv Records, AIR 0053, 1999.

Endo, Kenny. *Eternal Energy*. Asian Improv Records, AIR 0021, 1994.

Experimental Tokyo. Innocent Eyes and Lenses, IEL0005, 1997.

Fujii, Satoko. *April Shower* (with Mark Feldman). Ewe Records, EWCC 0006, 2001.

———. *Clouds* (with Natsuki Tamura). Libra Records, 102–006, 2001.

———. *Double Take*. Ewe Records, EWCD-0019/20, 2000.

———. *Indication*. Libra Records, 202–003, 1996.

———. *Kitsune-bi*. Tzadik, TZ 7220, 1999.

———. *Looking Out of the Window*. Nippon Crown, CRCJ-9139, 1997.

———. *Past Life: Satoko Fujii Sextet*. Libra Records, 206–004, 1998.

———. *Something about Water* (with Paul Bley). Libra Records, 202–002, 1996.

———. *South Wind: Satoko Fujii Orchestra*. Leo Lab, CD 037, 1997.

Fujiwara, Mikinori. *Touch Spring*. Three Blind Mice, TBM 5033, 1989.

———. *Wild Rose*. Three Blind Mice, TBM 5038, 1991.

Fujiyama, Yuko. *Reconstruction of Sound* (with Masahiko Kono and Ellen Christi). Network Records, 2007, 1996.

Goto, Yoshiko. *Day Dream*. Three Blind Mice, TBM 2540, 1991.

Hara, Tomonao. *For Musicians Only* (with Eijiro Nakagawa). Paddle Wheel/King Record Co., KICJ 274, 1996.

Hayasaka, Sachi. *2.26*. Enja, ENJA 8014–2, 1994.

Hikage, Shoko. *Indistancing* (with Brett Larner and Philip Gelb). Leo Lab, 055, 1999.

Hino, Motohiko. *Ryuhyo: Sailing Ice*. Three Blind Mice, TBM 2561, 1988.

Hino, Terumasa. *Bluestruck*. Blue Note, B4–93671, 1989.

———. *Live! Terumasa Hino Quintet*. Three Blind Mice, TBM 2517, 1988.

———. *Spark*. Somethin' Else/Blue Note, CDP 7243–8–30450–20, 1994.

———. *Triple Helix*. Enja, ENJ-8–056–2, 1994.

Hiroshima. *Go*. CBS, FE 40679, 1987.

A History of King Jazz Recordings. King, KICJ 6001–6010, 1992.

Horiuchi, Glenn. *Oxnard Beet*. Soul Note, 121228–2, 1992.

———. *Poston Sonata*. Asian Improv Records, AIR-008, 1991.

Hosokawa, Ayako. *Call Me* (with Toshiyuki Miyama and the New Herd). Three Blind Mice, TBM 5013, 1989.

Ikeda, Atsushi. *Everybody's Music*. Paddle Wheel/King Record Co., KICJ 271, 1996.

Imada, Masaru. *Alone Together* (with George Mraz). Three Blind Mice, TBM 5003, 1977.

Inomata, Takeshi. *Bluesette: Takeshi Inomata and Force*. Venus, TKCZ-79083, 1994.

Inoue, Satoshi. *Satoshi Inoue Plays Satoshi*. Paddle Wheel/King Record Co., KICJ 285, 1996.

Inoue, Yuichi. *Blue Requiem*. Paddle Wheel/King Record Co., KICJ 339, 1998.

Itakura, Katsuyuki. *Excuse Me, Mr. Satie.* Leo Records, LR 199, 1994.

Itoh, Kimiko. *Follow Me.* Columbia, CK 45214, 1989.

Izu, Mark. *Circle of Fire.* Asian Improv Records, AIR 0009, 1992.

Kaneda, Sami. *Songs of Seven Seas.* Pangea Music International, OM-1007, 1997.

Kano, Misako. *Breakthrew.* Jazz Focus Records, JFCD027, 1998.

———. *Watch Out.* Knitting Factory Records, KFR-219, 1998.

Kato, Takayuki. *Guitar Music.* Three Blind Mice, TBM 5032, 1989.

Kawaguchi, George. *Sticks 'n' Skins: Kawaguchi Big Band.* Paddle Wheel/King Record Co., CDJ 603, 1983.

Kikuchi, Masabumi. *Tethered Moon: Kikuchi, Peacock and Motion Play Kurt Weill.* Verve, JMT 697–1240592, 1995.

Kitamura, Eiji. *Delivery* (with Yoshiaki "Miya" Miyanoue). Jazz Cook Records, JCCD-0005, 2000.

———. *Dream Dancing* (with Kotaro Tsukahara). Jazz Cook Records, JCCD-0002, 1997.

———. *Live Session: Teddy and Eiji.* Century Recordings, CECC00343, 1991.

———. *Seven Stars.* Concord, CJ-217-C, 1983.

Kobayashi, Yoichi. *Yoichi Kobayashi and Good Fellas: Autumn in New York.* Jazz Bank/Minton's House, MTCJ-1007, 2001.

Kokubu, Hiroko. *Bridge.* JVC, 2067–2, 1997.

Kono, Miki. *For My Mother.* Satellites, VACV-0006, 1997.

Masaoka, Miya. *Compositions/Improvisations.* Asian Improv Records, AIR 00014, 1993.

———. *Monk's Japanese Folk Song.* Dizim Records, 4104, 1997.

Masuo, Yoshiaki. *Are You Happy Now.* Sunnyside Communications, SSC 1083D, 1999.

———. *A Subtle One.* Jazz City/Bellaphon, 660–53–030, 1991.

Matsui, Keiko. *Under Northern Lights.* MCA Records, MCAD-6274, 1989.

Matsumoto, Hidehiko "Sleepy." *"Sleepy" Matsumoto Quartet.* Three Blind Mice, TBM 2574, 1989.

Michihiro, Satoh. *Rodan.* Hat Hut Records, Hat ART CD 6015, 1989.

Mikami, Kuni. *You Are Too Beautiful.* Vega Records, ART-1001, 1999.

Miyama, Toshiyuki (and the New Herd). *Shuko Mizuno's Jazz Orchestra '75.* Three Blind Mice, TBM 1004, 1988.

———. *Sunday Thing.* Three Blind Mice, TBM 2567, 1989.

Miyanoue, Yoshiaki "Miya." *Yoshiaki!!* (with Yoshiaki Okayasu). Paddle Wheel/King Record Co., KICJ 273, 1996.

Moriyasu, Shotaro. *The Historic Mocambo Session '54.* Polydor/Rockwell, POCJ-1879/9, 1990.

Ohno, Shunzo. *Maya.* Three Blind Mice, TBM CD 5037, 1991.

Okoshi, Tiger. *Color of Soil.* JVC, JVC-2071–2, 1998.

———. *Echoes of a Note.* VICJ-166, 1993.

———. *Two Sides to Every Story*. JVC, JVC-2039–2, 1994.

Onishi, Junko. *Cruisin'* . Somethin' Else/Blue Note, CDP 7243–8–28447–2–3, 1993.

———. *Hat Trick* (with Jackie McLean). Somethin' Else/Blue Note, CDP 7243–8–38363–2–1, 1996.

———. *Piano Quintet Suite*. Somethin' Else/Blue Note, CDP 7243–8–36483–2–0, 1995.

Osaka, Masahiko. *Favorites* (with Tomanao Hara). Evidence, ECD 22134–2, 1995.

Otomo, Yoshio. *When A Man Loves A Woman: Live in "5 Days in Jazz 1974."* Three Blind Mice, TBM 2528, 1988.

Ozone, Makoto. *Face to Face* (with Gary Burton). GPR, GRD-9805, 1995.

———. *Makoto Ozone*. Columbia, BFC 39624, 1984.

———. *Virtuosi* (with Gary Burton). Concord, CCD-2105–2, 2002.

Saitoh, Tetsu. *Stone Out*. OMBA Records, OMBA-002, 1996.

Sakata, Akira. *Dance*. Enja/Nippon Crown, ENJ-1032, 1992.

Satoh, Masahiko. *Amorphism*. CBS/SONY Group, RK 44194, 1986.

———. *Buddhist Music with 1000 Shomyo Voices*. Victor, VICG-24, 1993.

———. *Masahiko Satoh Randooga*. Nippon Crown, CRCJ-9116, 1993.

———. *Penetration: Masahiko Satoh Trio in Berlin*. Express, ETJ 65021, 1971.

———. *Prelude to a Kiss* (with violinist Junko Ohtsu). BAJ Records, BJCD 0001, 1997.

Sawai, Kazue. *Temps Couche* (with Michel Doneda and Benat Achiavy). Les Disques Victo, Victo 055, 1998.

Shiina, Yutaka. *Movin' Forces*. BMG Victor, BVCJ-617, 1994.

Shionoya, Satoru "Salt." *Salt II*. BMG Victor, BVCR-725, 1995.

Something Difference. Quint Co., B1F, 1997.

Sonnet/Spanish Flower: Tee and Company. Three Blind Mice, 5004/8, 1988.

Sugano, Kunihiko. *The Days of Wine and Roses*. Venus, TKCZ-79077, 1994.

———. *Live Life*. Venus, TKCZ-79522, 1995.

Suzuki, Isao. *Blue City: Isao Suzuki + 1*. Three Blind Mice, TBM 2524, 1988.

Takase, Aki. *Blue Monk* (with David Murray). Enja, ENJA CD 7039–2, 1993.

———. *Le Cahier du Bal*. Leo Records, CD LR 319, 2001.

———. *Close Up of Japan: Toki String Quartet/Nobuyoshi Ino*. Enja, ENJA 7075–2, 1993.

———. *Shima Shoka*. Enja, ENJA CD 6062–2, 1990.

Tamura, Natsuki. *A Song for Jyaki*. Leo Lab, 039, 1998.

Tana, Akira. *Blue Motion*. Evidence, ECD 22075–2, 1994.

———. *Looking Forward*. Evidence, ECD 22114–2, 1995.

———. *Passing Thoughts*. Concord, CCD-4505, 1992.

Tanaka, Takehisa. *When I Was at Aso-Mountain: Elvin Jones Introduces Takehisa Tanaka*. Enja, ENJ-7081–2, 1993.

Terai, Hisayuki. *Dalarna*. Flanagania Records, TF-2, 1995.

———. *Flanagania*. Flanagania Records, TF-1, 1994.

———. *Fragrant Times*. Flanagania Records, TF-3, 1997.

Three Generations: The Kennedy Center Concert, Vol. 2. Paddle Wheel/King Record Co., KICJ 332, 1998.

T. Kitano and Arrow Jazz Orchestra. *Bopularity*. Sound Knew, SK-020959, 1995.

Togashi, Masahiko. *Explosions: Live at Pit Inn Shinjuku: Masahiko Togashi and J. J. Spirits*. Venus, TKCV-79093, 1995.

———. *Session in Paris, Vol. 1: Song of Soil*. Take One Records/King, TKOJ-1501, 1994.

Tonooka, Sumi. *Here Comes Kai*. Candid, CCD79516, 1992.

———. *Secret Places*. Joken Records, BK-103, 1998.

Tsukahara, Kotaro. *Right On* (with Shiho Sukoi). TSCC, TSV-CD-0039, 1996.

———. *Spring Blues: Live at La Maison de Musique*. Jazz Republic of Tokamachi Records, JROT-007, 1992.

Twin Heroes: Jazz Battle Royal. Paddle Wheel/King Record Co., KICJ 272, 1996.

Umezu, Kazutoki. *Wake Up with the Birds* (with Carlo Actis Dato). Leo Records, LR 285, 1999.

Watanabe, Kazumi. *Mobo Club*. Polydor/Gramavision, 18–8506–1, 1985.

———. *Mobo Splash*. Polydor/Gramavision, 18–8602–4, 1986.

———. *To Chi Ka*. Denon/Nippon Columbia, DC-8568, 1990.

Watanabe, Sadao. *Bird of Paradise* (with the Great Jazz Trio). JVC, JVC-6008–2, 1977.

———. *How's Everything: Sadao Watanabe Live at Budokan*. CBS, C2X 36776, 1980.

———. *Made in Coracao* (with Toquinho). Elektra/Asylum, 9–60939–2, 1990.

———. *Selected Sadao Watanabe*. Elektra/Asylum, 9–60803–1, 1989.

Yamaguchi, Takeshi. *Angel Eyes*. Paddle Wheel/King Record Co., KICJ 317, 1997.

Yamamoto, Tsuyoshi. *Falling in Love with Love*. TDK! Records, TDCN-5057E, 1993.

Yamashita, Yosuke. *Dazzling Days*. Verve/Jam Rice, 521–303–2, 1993.

———. *Kurdish Dance*. Verve/Antilles/Jam Rice, 314–511–708–2, 1992.

———. *Sakura*. Antilles, 422–849–141–2, 1990.

———. *A Tribute to Mal Waldron*. Enja, CD 3057, 1988.

Yomada, Joh. *Bluestone*. ALFA JAZZ, ALCB-3914, 1997.

Yoshihiro, Chizuko. *Conscious Mind*. Verve Forecast, 314–518–343–2, 1993.

Classical and Traditional Music

The Azuma Kabuki Musicians. Columbia, ML 4925, n.d.

Buddhist Chant: A Recorded Survey of Actual Temple Rituals. Lyrichord, LLST 7118, n.d.

Japan: Traditional Vocal and Instrumental Music. Elektra/Asylum Nonesuch Records, 72072–2, 1976.

Joruri: Music of the Great Japanese Bunraku Puppet Theater. Lyrichord, LLST 7197, n.d.

Mera, Yoshikazu. *Mother's Songs: Japanese Popular Songs.* Grammofon AB BIS, BIS-CD-906, 1997.

Satoh, Somei. *Toward the Night.* New Albion Records, NA056CD, 1993.

Takemitsu, Toru. *Music of Takemitsu.* Telarc, CD-80469, 1998.

Takemitsu: Orchestral Works. Sony, SK 63044, 1998.

Takemitsu: Quotation of a Dream. Deutsche Grammophon, 453 495–2, 1998.

INDEX